THE BUSINESS OF KILLING INDIANS

THE LAMAR SERIES IN WESTERN HISTORY

The Lamar Series in Western History includes scholarly books of general public interest that enhance the understanding of human affairs in the American West and contribute to a wider understanding of the West's significance in the political, social, and cultural life of America. Comprising works of the highest quality, the series aims to increase the range and vitality of Western American history, focusing on frontier places and people, Indian and ethnic communities, the urban West and the environment, and the art and illustrated history of the American West.

Recent Titles
George I. Sánchez: The Long Fight for Mexican American Integration, by Carlos K. Blanton
White Fox and Icy Seas in the Western Arctic: The Fur Trade, Transportation, and Change in the Early Twentieth Century, by John R. Bockstoce
Growing Up with the Country: Family, Race, and Nation after the Civil War, by Kendra Taira Field
Grounds for Dreaming: Mexican Americans, Mexican Immigrants, and the California Farmworker Movement, by Lori A. Flores
Lakota America: A New History of Indigenous Power, by Pekka Hämäläinen
The American West: A New Interpretive History, Second Edition, by Robert V. Hine, John Mack Faragher, and Jon T. Coleman
Legal Codes and Talking Trees: Indigenous Women's Sovereignty in the Sonoran and Puget Sound Borderlands, 1854–1946, by Katrina Jagodinsky
Gathering Together: The Shawnee People through Diaspora and Nationhood, 1600–1870, by Sami Lakomäki
An American Genocide: The United States and the California Indian Catastrophe, 1846–1873, by Benjamin Madley
Frontiers in the Gilded Age: Adventure, Capitalism, and Dispossession from Southern Africa to the U.S.- Mexican Borderlands, 1880–1917, by Andrew Offenburger
Home Rule: Households, Manhood, and National Expansion on the Eighteenth-Century Kentucky Frontier, by Honor Sachs
The Cherokee Diaspora: An Indigenous History of Migration, Resettlement, and Identity, by Gregory D. Smithers
First Impressions: A Reader's Journey to Iconic Places of the American Southwest, by David J. Weber and William deBuys

The Business of Killing Indians

Scalp Warfare and the Violent
Conquest of North America

WILLIAM S. KISER

Yale

UNIVERSITY PRESS

NEW HAVEN AND LONDON

Published with assistance from the John R. Bockstoce Endowment Fund.

Yale University Press books may be purchased in quantity for educational, business, or promotional use. For information, please e-mail sales.press@yale.edu (US office) or sales@yaleup.co.uk (UK office).

Set in Electra type by IDS Infotech, Ltd.
Printed in the United States of America.

Library of Congress Control Number: 2024937392
ISBN 978-0-300-27528-5 (hardcover : alk. paper)

A catalogue record for this book is available from the British Library.

This paper meets the requirements of ANSI/NISO Z39.48-1992 (Permanence of Paper).

10 9 8 7 6 5 4 3 2 1

For Ed Westermann: friend, colleague, and mentor

CONTENTS

THE BUSINESS OF KILLING INDIANS

Introduction

Three days after people around the world celebrated the dawn of a new millennium, CBC News—one of Canada's most prominent broadcasting corporations—featured a headline that read "Two Hundred Year-Old Scalp Law Still on Books in Nova Scotia."[1] Published on January 4, 2000, the subject of the article would have struck most readers as nothing more than an unfamiliar scrap of history. Many people probably glanced at the title and then skipped over the piece entirely, thinking of centuries-old Indian policy as an odd thing to worry about and moving on to read stories on hockey, the stock market, or Y2K. If asked today, Nova Scotians who perused CBC News back in 2000 would no longer be able to recall if the Halifax Mooseheads won their game, if the Canadian Securities Exchange index went up or down, or if the fear of a possible computer crisis affected their life in any meaningful way. But that short article about scalping, so seemingly irrelevant then to most subscribers, turned out to be a groundbreaking story that cast light on an issue of tremendous historical and cultural significance.

The CBC News coverage pertained to a bounty that Nova Scotia governor Charles Lawrence implemented by executive order on May 14, 1756, imploring British settlers to "annoy, distress, take and destroy the Indians inhabiting different parts of this Province" and promising a £30 reward for every Mi'kmaq prisoner and £25 for each of their scalps.[2] Issued during the French and Indian War, such a mandate would not have elicited any shock or surprise among colonial inhabitants, who had grown accustomed to scalp warfare and attendant forms of extreme violence over the preceding decades. More than two centuries later, however, the lingering legal presence of this antiquated edict became a serious cause for concern among descendants of the Mi'kmaq scalping victims—who had entered the Land of Souls in a defiled condition—and tribal leaders approached Canadian officials to request that the law be formally repealed. "We feel it's a little slur against the Mi'kmaq people," Chief Lawrence Paul explained in an interview. The ambivalent bureaucratic response to these efforts frustrated tribe members and inflamed the controversy. Speaking on behalf of the Conservative government, Minister for Aboriginal Affairs Michael Baker told journalists that it remained unclear whether colonial jurisdiction over such a matter would have belonged to the province, the nation, or the British crown. Because the scalp law went into effect before Canadian Confederation on July 1, 1867, lawyers questioned whether modern legislators even possessed the authority to rescind it. Politicians, by contrast, argued that subsequent treaties with the tribe in the eighteenth and nineteenth centuries rendered the scalping proclamation unenforceable and therefore unimportant.[3]

Shortly after CBC broke the story, Minister Baker introduced Resolution 837 in the legislative assembly "to confirm that the 1756 Proclamation is no longer of any force or effect" and to "express our sincere regret over past hostilities." This rhetorical overture rang hollow among First Nations peoples, and the fact that Baker immediately followed it with Resolution 838, congratulating the local Lions Club for a successful senior citizens event, showed just how little he cared about the issue.[4] One tribal leader spoke out against this government ambivalence. Born at the Shubenacadie Indian Reserve in 1938, Mi'kmaq elder Daniel N. Paul served as superintendent of Reserves and Trusts for the Nova Scotia District in the 1980s and subsequently became executive director of the Confederacy of Mainland Micmacs. The author of an influential book (*We Were Not the Savages*) that portrayed a First Nations perspective on North American history, Paul remembered the time he saw a framed copy of the scalping proclamation of 1756 adorning the wall in a local tavern—a veritable trophy celebrating colonial violence—and he bluntly condemned government efforts to brush aside the matter. "Partnerships and trust cannot be built by one party using condescending, paternalistic doubletalk to try to avoid being honest with the other," he wrote. Paul accused the government of using "political spin to try to weasel its way out of repealing a document that makes [a] genocidal statement," hypothesizing that the real reason behind refusals to take corrective action stemmed from a fear that any acknowledgment of wrongdoing would result in a reparations lawsuit. "Tolerating such a hideous document on the books, although dormant, is unforgivable and does not speak well for a country that claims to be civilized," the Mi'kmaq elder concluded.[5] Frustrated with the general lack of political accountability, the widespread ignorance of First Nations culture, and the demeaning marginalization of Indigenous perspectives, Mi'kmaq spokespeople would continue to press the issue for years to come.

In January 2015, Halifax residents were reminded that the scalp law controversy still simmered in the hearts and minds of Indigenous peoples. By that time, social media had transformed the way people received the daily news. Jacob Boon, a writer for the *Coast*, noticed a thread in his Facebook newsfeed that included a link to the CBC article of January 2000, and he felt moved to report on the unresolved problem. Boon noted that numerous Canadian officials had publicly condemned the proclamation of 1756, yet the legislature had still not repealed it. Brett Loney, a spokesperson for the Aboriginal Affairs department, seemed merely to reiterate the ambivalence that officials had long shown when he quipped that the scalp act "wasn't repealed, just unilaterally unenforced, a minor difference."[6] In a segment for Aboriginal Peoples Television Network (ABTN) aired in February 2018, investigative journalist and Mi'kmaq tribe member Trina Roache reported on a closely related story involving a bronze statue of Governor Edward Cornwallis, the British founder of Halifax. Cornwallis implemented two scalp bounties between 1749 and 1752—both of them similar to the Lawrence proclamation of 1756—and the city council had recently ordered the removal of the offensive effigy.[7] Prominently situated in a public park, that memorial had become the center of another First Nations controversy when a local hairdressing business published advertisements that showed four smiling women holding packets of human hair extensions while posing alongside the metallic Cornwallis.[8] In a powerful act of symbolism, a Mi'kmaq grandmother and water protector named Elizabeth Marshall took a hairy piece of moose hide and reshaped it to resemble a human scalp. She then sold it as the forelock of Edward Cornwallis in a satirical Facebook auction, using Internet streaming to reenact the colonial scalp trade.[9] Despite all of these spectacles, and even the involvement of Canada's Truth and Reconciliation Commission, the proclamation of 1756 remained on the books. In 2019—two decades after the Mi'kmaq began their push to repeal the colonial scalping edict—elder Daniel Paul sat down to write yet another op-ed calling for legislative action and wondered if the bounty law would ever fully disappear.[10] This ongoing controversy over a centuries-old proclamation, and the concomitant tension between Mi'kmaq people and Canadian officials, provide stark reminders that traumas of the past can be traumas of the present.

For nearly 250 years, from the mid-1600s through the late 1800s, state-sponsored scalp bounties and volunteer campaigning promoted a racialized and opportunistic brand of borderlands violence, resulting in the murder and mutilation of thousands of Indians throughout North America and contributing directly to processes of colonial conquest. Central governments in Amsterdam, Paris, London, Mexico City, and Washington, DC, consistently failed to provide adequate military support and financial resources for frontier defense, so administrators in regional capitals such as New York, Quebec City, New Orleans, Boston, Ciudad Chihuahua, Austin, and Sacramento embraced autonomous approaches to warfare against Indigenous enemies. Those localized techniques often entailed the monetization of killing and captive taking, alongside horrific acts of scalping, beheading, and other forms of performative violence. Although bounty hunting, trophy taking, and paramilitary campaigning were sweeping phenomena that emerged at various times in almost every part of the continent, these trends ebbed and flowed in prominence alongside imperial conflicts involving Dutch, French, English/British, Mexican, and American operatives. Such contests typically played out on the extreme peripheries of empire, where colonial combatants struggled to prevail over powerful Indigenous neighbors, and this exasperation—coupled with racist views of Indians as barbaric and savage—led to the adoption of combat techniques that included not just plundering, slaving, and killing but also dismemberment of corpses for

4

symbolic and economic purposes. Although these tactics mostly failed in their exterminatory intent, state sponsorship of indiscriminate violence took a significant demographic toll by flooding frontier zones with murderous units whose campaigns diminished Indigenous power, reduced tribal populations, and forced weakened survivors to relocate away from traditional homelands.[11] High wages for volunteer campaigning, along with cash bounties for Indian body parts as well as the ability to take captives and keep valuable plunder, promoted a profit opportunity for civilians wherein state sponsorship of killing and corporeal mutilation constituted an important component of the policies and actions that drove colonial conquest.

Historians writing on North American violence have used terms including but not limited to "extirpative warfare," "genocidal war," "Indian war," "cutting-off way of war," and Anglo-American "ways of war" as frameworks for analyzing conflict between Natives and newcomers.[12] In concept and practice, "extirpative warfare" has been used in two distinct ways. The first involves a focus on an "indigenous consciousness of genocide" that revolved around the colonial rhetoric of extirpation—or extermination—as understood by Native peoples at the time, and this approach is generally less concerned with the outcomes than with the intentions.[13] The second version uses "extirpative warfare" as one of several fighting techniques that formed the "first way of war" in the framework of North American military history, defining the term as "unlimited warfare, manifested by the destruction of enemy noncombatants and their agricultural resources."[14] So, too, has "genocidal war" been used primarily to describe the stated intentions of US government representatives in the early republic, rather than the physical outcomes of the attendant violence that Americans carried out in support of verbalized objectives to extirpate Indigenous groups.[15] The concept of Anglo-American "ways of war" revolves around the notion that "war is defined by both violence and restraint, consciously and unconsciously, materially and mentally." Moreover, historian Wayne Lee's formulation of "ways of war" involves "capacity, control, calculation, and culture" as fundamental to understanding the North American military tradition: capacity being a state's ability to raise and deploy destructive force; control involving the state's ability to sustain and influence that force; calculation pertaining to state logics of military decision-making; culture revolving around a state's societal values with respect to warfare.[16] Although this definitional framework applies to many conflicts throughout colonial North America, it relates to the events analyzed in this book insofar as indiscriminate bounty hunting and corporeal mutilation were antithetical to restraint, evolved as localized government responses when imperial or national leaders failed or refused to mobilize traditional armed forces, demonstrated a nation-state's lack of control over frontiers and borderlands, deviated dramatically from traditional military calculations or laws of war, and developed into a subculture of racialized hatred and celebratory ritual.

While integrating and building on the foregoing concepts, I use the term "scalp warfare" as a means of differentiating the functions, actors, and outcomes of the extreme violence described in this book from prior studies in the field. Scalp warfare describes a specific type of performative violence that characterized many of the frontier conflicts between settlers and Indigenous peoples in North America. Although the particulars varied slightly in each time and place, I generally define "scalp warfare" as an indiscriminate technique for conquest involving localized state sponsorship of nonprofessional fighting units whose members were driven by intense personal and often racialized hatred of an enemy, along with the possibility of material gain in the form of plunder as well as body parts redeemable for rewards and displayable for glory. As a descriptor, "scalp warfare" incorporates the economic and performative functions of this form of killing; it conveys the mutually recognized state of hostility between actors; and it highlights outcomes of the conflict that involved unrestrained mutilation of corpses and postmortem celebrations among perpetrators—characteristics that did not always apply in "extirpative warfare," "genocidal war," "Indian war," "cutting-off way of war," and Anglo-American "ways of war."

Scalp warfare often involved material gain and racialized rhetoric as motivations for what political scientist Lee Ann Fujii calls "extra-lethal violence." Defined as "physical acts committed face-to-face that transgress shared norms and beliefs about appropriate treatment of the living as well as the dead," extralethal violence entails graphic deeds such as trophy taking, rape, disfigurement, burning alive, scalping, and beheading. In performative acts of extralethal violence, how people are killed is just as important as how many people are killed.[17] Extralethal violence toward Indians was sometimes performed individually, as seen in the case of Hannah Duston in seventeenth-century Massachusetts, and sometimes collectively, as demonstrated in the activities of James Kirker's scalping crews in nineteenth-century Mexico.[18] Fujii calls these collective acts "violent display," noting that the public staging of violence for people to "see, notice, and take in" shapes the identity of entire communities because even casual observers act complicitly in such processions. Deliberate staging of bodies and body parts is the crucial component of violent display. With scalp warfare, this most often occurred when the killers decorated their belts, guns, horses, or homes with scalps, when local lawmakers hung redeemed scalps from the eaves of courthouses or churches and across public plazas, when townspeople used scalps as the celebratory centerpieces of parades and parties, and when theatrical scalp dances were organized to mock the victims.[19]

In cases that involved Euro-Americans as perpetrators, scalping was a widely visible form of extralethal violence that carried racially expressive functions. North American settlers who participated in various forms of violent display used the severed body parts of people from hated racial groups as part of a process that formed a shared sense of belonging within their communities. In the instances where primary aggressors were Indian men allied with colonial agents, the performative purpose had more to do with cultural considerations and long-standing intertribal rivalries, as well as individual material gain and glory for those who took scalps or other body parts.[20] Today, regardless of the individual or collective nature of the violence, humanitarian law defines these types of deeds as war crimes, but the international conventions that provide frameworks for the prosecution and punishment of violators had not yet occurred when Dutch settlements, French colonies, English/British commonwealths, the Republic of Texas, and Mexican as well as American states incentivized scalp warfare.[21] As a form of extralethal violence directed toward North America's Indigenous peoples, scalping remained perfectly legal and widely accepted into the late nineteenth century, and indeed many state laws encouraged bounty hunting and trophy taking.[22]

7

Scalp warfare was a fierce but widely embraced occupation that arose when local legislators encouraged their citizens, as well as some Indian allies, to assert state hegemony in the absence of adequate traditional military forces by killing enemies in exchange for cash rewards, captives, and plunder, and the concomitant public display of severed body parts as trophies created a spectacle of horror with profound communicative power.[23] This formed one component of an early North American military tradition, but it differed in important ways from the more routine operations of regular armies as well as provincial or local militias that are most commonly associated with frontier conflicts. Civilian campaigning against Indians took the form of volunteer, ranger, and bounty-hunting units that operated outside the organizational constraints of an army or militia—historian Marcus Cunliffe described such groups as "independent companies . . . of belligerent amateurs"—and their actions often involved indiscriminate and unrestrained acts of extralethal violence. Colonial policymakers devised scalp laws to augment regular armies and traditional militias rather than to bolster their ranks with additional men of the same military status. Public officials clearly and consistently distinguished between salaried enlisted troops and unsalaried independent volunteers. Some bounties explicitly excluded armies and militias from participation, while others allowed them to claim cash rewards for Indian body parts and captives but at far lower prices than the civilian operatives. In any case, these codified differentiations between militias and paramilitary operatives indicates that colonists viewed civilian operations as being outside the parameters of conventional military structures.[24]

In North America's militia-based societies, able-bodied men within a specified age range (often sixteen to sixty) typically had a legal obligation to enlist, although many of these individuals never experienced combat and instead constituted a reserve force. In contrast, the campaigns discussed in this book involved men volunteering for one-time offensives outside the confines of compulsory militia service, although there were instances—particularly in the English/British colonies and nineteenth-century California—where militia activity and scalp warfare could overlap. Furthermore, scalp warfare in French Canada and Louisiana, Mexico, and Texas often included Indian warriors who participated alongside Euro-American settlers, a multicultural and multiracial dynamic of these paramilitary groups that did not usually pertain to state militias.[25] As historian Fred Anderson notes, "Professional military ideals have not always and everywhere been determining factors, or even significant ones, in motivating the men who made up the army or fought the war in question."[26] Although this observation held true for many colonial militias—whose temporary nature, professional training, operational techniques, leadership structure, and standards of military conduct diverged widely from that of regular armies—the paramilitary units and individual actors who practiced scalp warfare fit Anderson's description to an even greater degree, and in so doing they played an important part in the processes of violent conquest that historians have attributed primarily to soldiers and militiamen. This is not to say that army officers, militia commanders, and the tens of thousands of men who enlisted in such military organizations did not influence conflicts with American Indians—indeed, they did have a profound impact on colonization and conquest across North America from the 1600s through the 1800s. Rather, the point here is to acknowledge and examine another type of operative in the form of paramilitary volunteers, rangers, and bounty hunters whose campaigns originated with local funding and sponsorship, whose treacherous ambushes rose to incredible levels of indiscriminate brutality, whose attacks claimed thousands of Indian lives in performative extralethal ways that significantly affected the ethos and spirituality of deceased victims as well as survivors, and whose personal motivations stemmed from material gain, racial hatred, and societal glory.

Through scalp warfare, regional policymakers representing North American empires and states embraced and promoted killing as a devastating form of hateful aggression.[27] The terminology that observers used to describe these government contractors varied across time and place—in New France they were called auxiliaries, in Mexico people labeled them adventurers, Texans famously named them rangers, and in California the word "volunteer" came into fashion—but the indiscriminate combat tactics and the devastating demographic outcomes were much the same regardless of the diction one chose to characterize perpetrators. Although Indians resisted scalp hunters with tremendous skill and lethal results, the deliberate targeting of women, children, and the elderly went beyond traditional European fighting strategies and indicated an intent not just to defeat and remove but to humiliate and exterminate Indigenous enemies. Administrators in imperial and national capitals repeatedly criticized and struck down local scalping programs even as paid killers continued to perpetrate massacres and acts of extralethal violence that were bound to regional rather than national projects of settlement and economic development. By incentivizing murders and massacres through lucrative bounty programs, salaries for volunteers, and the right to take plunder and captives, these governments became arbiters of racialized and retributive forms of conflict, using the motivation of material gain to compel the formation of paramilitary outfits. Driven by a deep disdain for Indians whom they struggled to defeat or remove, lawmakers instrumentalized the human instinct for profit by monetizing the unrestricted maiming, slaying, and desecrating of enemies.

In the cases of colonial New Netherland and New France, the English/ British colonies, and nineteenth-century Texas, scalp warfare was a form of frontier violence that transpired within broader processes of conquest, and its array of practitioners included both male and female settlers as well as Indigenous allies from many different tribes who operated on cultural, economic, and political motivations. The outcome of those scalp warfare campaigns can be understood within the framework of extralethal violence that served a predominantly performative function for the colonial and Indigenous societies involved. In Mexico and California, however, state-sponsored scalp warfare rose to the level of genocide because it proliferated to a far greater extent in terms of the frequency of killing and the depth of demographic devastation, and the well-organized participants acted systematically and relentlessly in their attempts to exterminate racial groups. To put it another way, the centuries-long process of colonialism in North America does not constitute a monolithic act of genocide, but it also cannot be said that genocide never occurred with respect to Native Americans. A careful consideration of scalp warfare demonstrates that specific policies and actions that occurred in specific times and places fall outside the commonly used categories of settler colonialism and ethnic cleansing, two analytical alternatives to genocide that highlight a lust for land and resources behind the subjugation and geographic removal of Native peoples.[28] This book focuses on attempts to annihilate tribes rather than assimilate individuals or relocate groups, examining instances of scalp warfare that destroyed significant percentages of particular Indigenous groups' populations while also meeting one or more of the criteria outlined in the United Nations convention on "the Crime of Genocide" that occurred in 1948.

As defined in those United Nations proceedings, genocide involves "acts committed with intent to destroy, in whole or in part, a national, ethnical, racial or religious group, as such." This can occur within five frameworks: "(a) Killing members of the group; (b) Causing serious bodily or mental harm to members of the group; (c) Deliberately inflicting on the group conditions of life calculated to bring about its physical destruction in whole or in part; (d) Imposing measures intended to prevent births within the group; (e) Forcibly transferring children of the group to another group."[29] Coined by the Polish lawyer Raphaël Lemkin in 1944, the term "genocide" originated within the context of Nazi Germany and the Holocaust, and so, too, did the postwar United Nations discussions derive primarily from German efforts to exterminate the Jewish population. The term and concept have since expanded in their political and scholarly applications, but the UN definition of genocide plays a prominent role in such determinations, and I use it throughout this book as one criterion for analysis. There is also no agreement among scholars, politicians, or activists about a statistical threshold for the occurrence of genocide. Between 1933 and 1945, Nazis killed an estimated two-thirds of the 9.5 million European Jews. In the Rwandan genocide of 1994, Hutu militants systematically murdered at least 500,000 Tutsis, representing no less than two-thirds of the Tutsi population at that time. These two paradigmatic examples of genocide share a very high population loss within a short timeline, although in both cases the precise figure is widely debated, and the same numerical uncertainty holds true for most examples of scalp warfare on the North American frontiers. Although a two-thirds figure is not necessary as an evidentiary basis for the occurrence of genocide, it nonetheless establishes that population figures are an important consideration, and therefore I have taken casualty estimates into account as another criterion for analysis throughout this book.[30]

"Savages we call them," wrote Benjamin Franklin in 1783, "because their manners differ from ours, which we think the Perfection of Civility."[31] Franklin was generations ahead of his time with such ideas, but he foretold the work of recent scholars who have rightly pointed out the racial and political motivations behind intercultural hatred, exterminatory policy, and extralethal action.[32] Historian Daniel Richter notes that "Whites and Indians had to learn to hate each other," since neither Europeans nor Indians had a basis for racial animosity before initial contact in the sixteenth and seventeenth centuries.[33] As one important aspect of North American colonialism, the horrifying brutality of scalp warfare made hatred an easy lesson to learn and an impossible lesson to forget, especially after some massacres that claimed hundreds of men, women, and children as victims. Along with issues of race and politics that undergirded policies of paid killing, state commodification of body parts points to a sinister financial impulse that also drove colonial conquests. Just as American slave catchers and slave traders made a profitable industry out of the nation's economic dependency on the chattel system, so, too, did frontier bounty hunters turn state reliance on scalp warfare with Indians into an extralethal occupation with commercial and racial underpinnings.[34] In a seminal essay, Benjamin Madley argues that "state-sponsored body-part bounties . . . are another manifestation of exterminationist intent and genocidal crimes that appear frequently in the history of the United States and its antecedents." Referring to scalping policies as "genocidal command structures," he points out that bounty hunting represented a form of institutionalized murder, and the present study adds nuance to this point by showing that scalp warfare sometimes rose to the level of genocide and sometimes did not.[35] Occurring at the intersection of race and individual economic interest, state-sponsored scalping meshed two common methods of conquest: exploitation of Indigenous labor through enslavement and destruction of physical bodies through killing.[36] The performative manner in which paid killers carried out those indiscriminate schemes points to extralethal impulses that framed local Indian policies throughout North America, regardless of whether those policies fall within the category of genocide.[37]

The decentralization aspect of scalp warfare highlights policy and action in North America as a localized rather than a nationalized practice, providing one specific way of thinking about the political conditions under which extralethal conquest (New Netherland, New France, the English/British colonies, and Texas) or genocide (Mexico and California) occurred with respect to Native American peoples. Moreover, an analysis of scalp warfare within the analytical framework of extralethal violence contributes to discussions on Native American genocide that began in the wake of the Columbus Quincentennial in 1992 while also answering Madley's more recent call for "additional detailed case studies . . . of genocide's occurrence and frequency."[38] As a form of policy directed at Indigenous peoples, bounty laws typically involved a decentralized state outsourcing institutional violence to paramilitary units. Whether it concerned English/British assemblies, French intendancies, Mexican administrations, the Republic of Texas legislature, or US state governments, regional political structures and their capacities to promote extreme violence demonstrate connections across time and place that add important layers of detail to voices that make sweeping generalizations about the occurrence or nonoccurrence of Native American genocide over the entire colonial period.

To use Madley's words, some flawed genocide arguments rely on "lumping when splitting is in order," and to that end scalp warfare provides an example of the splitting approach.[39] Within the context of colonial North America and the question of Native American genocide, the splitting approach aims to recognize and grant agency to Indigenous nations and cultures as such, by focusing on the individual experiences of particular groups as they encountered and resisted colonialism. Conversely, lumping approaches to Native American genocide tend to rest on a foundation of collective "American Indian" and "First Nations" identity that scarcely existed before the twentieth century. The lumping argument that Euro-American colonization of North America constituted one long-running genocide typically relies on an implied assumption that all Indians were racially, ethnically, or culturally the same. In reality, each Indigenous group experienced colonial violence in its own way, and those encounters sometimes fell within the framework of genocide and sometimes did not. In a special issue of *Western Historical Quarterly* in 2016 dedicated to genocide debates, Walter Hixson spoke of the splitting method when explaining that "all genocides are not the same," and he noted that some episodes and themes in North American history—to which this book adds scalp warfare—point to state logics of conquest that revolved around "race and space" as vindicating motivations.[40] Even more recently, in a *Journal of American History* essay Tai Edwards and Paul Kelton examined the role of germs and disease in precipitating massive demographic decline among Indigenous groups, framing this process within studies of genocides. They rightly stated that "violent crimes"—and this would include such extralethal acts as scalping massacres—"were in fact more traumatic because they . . . undermined social structures that biologically and culturally sustained communities."[41] This notion speaks directly to statistical thresholds for genocide—another contested aspect of the scholarly debate—and this book weighs in alongside the work of Edwards and Kelton by demonstrating that mortality rates and population percentages, though important, can also distract from the sanguinary human effects that manifested themselves in extralethal atrocities.[42] An examination of scalp warfare indicates that systematic outsourcing of state violence to private contractors, volunteers, and rangers was a particularly devastating tactic that arose from decentralization, and this understanding in turn helps to move conversations away from lumping and statistics as the sole litmus tests for the occurrence of genocide. Two considerations highlighted throughout these pages—the outsourcing of institutional violence and its extralethality—add important historical and conceptual details to understandings of the conditions under which genocides occur. In short, scalp warfare was almost always genocidal in its intent, but it was less often genocidal in its outcome. The concept and practice of scalp warfare therefore offers a specific way of thinking about the Native American genocide question within the parameters of the United Nations definitions and humanistic impacts of the violence.

During the course of Euro-American colonialism in the seventeenth and eighteenth centuries, as well as American westward expansion in the nineteenth century, Native peoples most frequently emerged as victims of scalp warfare and extralethal violence, but in some cases they also acted as participants and perpetrators. Indians often killed other Indians in concert with colonial legislators, state governors, militia officers, ranger captains, and independent bounty hunters, doing so not out of racial hatred but for a variety of reasons that included masculine honor and bravery, intertribal animosity and revenge, strategic political and economic alliances, and material gain. Colonial officials typically saw Indian counterparts—even those with whom they formed alliances—through a lens of racial inferiority, believing that they were cleverly taking advantage of their wards as part of strategies to defeat common enemies. In reality, Indigenous men who campaigned, fought, killed, and scalped were anything but the wards of settlers or the pawns of imperial governments. Somewhat paradoxically, scalp warfare enabled some Native nations, groups, and individuals to capitalize on the violent conquests occurring in their midst, as they recognized opportunities to kill traditional enemies and profit materially from something they might have done anyway for their own cultural and political reasons.[43] The pages that follow examine the complexity of alliances between Natives and newcomers that revolved around shared economic interests and diplomatic objectives during times of conflict, when pursuit of wealth and power overlapped with hatred of enemies to fuel scalp warfare.

With all of this said, it is important for readers to be aware of several things that this book does not address. Although sweeping in temporal and geographic scope to include multiple colonial powers and dozens of Indian tribes across three centuries of North American history, I do not attempt a comprehensive accounting of every documented act of killing or scalping. Nor do I analyze the separate subject of Indians who practiced corporeal mutilation for cultural or spiritual purposes, as these traditions often predated European arrival and involved, to varying degrees, many different tribes.[44] Moreover, traditional military forces in the form of enlistees receiving a national government salary campaigned against Indians in almost every theater of Euro-American settlement from the 1600s onward, but I examine those regular army and militia operations only in passing as a way to compare the motivations of state, local, and individual actors. The ensuing narrative addresses but does not attempt a thorough examination of the widespread captivity and enslavement of Indians—as many as five million of them in New Spain alone—even though this practice had clear economic and racial motivations that can be categorized alongside scalp warfare as a vicious tool of colonial conquest.[45] Last, I do not include a stand-alone chapter on the nineteenth-century United States but instead have integrated an analysis of the federal government's role into sections on the early American republic, Texas, and California. This organizational approach is not meant to imply that Americans did not perform indiscriminate acts of extralethal violence across the western frontier—the Sand Creek Massacre of 1864 comes immediately to mind, although there are many other examples.[46] Rather, such atrocities occurred sporadically across a sweeping geographic scope and a broad period of time, and in many cases no government agency or entity directly sponsored these independent actions in the ways that local leaders formally encouraged and incentivized civilian operatives who killed and mutilated Indians. My exclusion of certain examples is not intended to diminish the severity or significance of those events but rather to indicate that such instances did not fall within the same paradigm of regional government sponsorship in a decentralized state. These important considerations aside, the ensuing chapters focus on Dutch, French, English/British, Texan, Mexican, and American operatives as well as specific indigenous groups—Abenakis in French Canada and Choctaws in French Louisiana, confederated Iroquois in the northern English/British colonies, Delawares and Shawnees in Mexico, Lipan Apaches in Texas, and many others—who participated in scalp warfare as part of decentralized state programs.

Readers may wonder how many Indians were killed as a direct result of state-sponsored scalp warfare. A precise number will always be impossible to ascertain, and even a reasonable estimate remains difficult for several reasons. Like the systems of Indian slavery that proliferated across much of North America, policies of paid scalping targeted Indigenous peoples who were generally viewed as racially inferior and demographically dispensable, meaning that some of the killings were not recorded. Even those Indians whose deaths and disfigurements were documented rarely had the dignity of being named, and a sad anonymity accompanies the fate of almost all victims. Available statistics on scalping derive primarily from bounty hunters who bragged about their deeds and government employees who tallied trophy redemptions for fiscal recordkeeping. In the case of perpetrator and eyewitness testimonies, exaggerated body counts were common, because such individuals aimed to inflate their reputations and amplify the horror of their exploits. By contrast, state officials often understated the extent of killing and scalping, as some of them tried to veil the practice from disapproving kings and presidents, while others sought technical reasons to disqualify trophies from payment to minimize treasury expenditures. Yet another complicating factor in any quantitative analysis involves widespread fraud. Administrators in New France complained about Indian allies who would cut the black hair from a horse's tail and meticulously dress the strands to look human before presenting it for reward. Bounty hunters also learned to slice a single scalp into two equal parts and stretch the skin, like a tanned deer or buffalo hide, so that each one resembled a full-sized piece, thus artificially doubling the number of kills to secure additional payouts. In nineteenth-century Mexico, policymakers discovered that their contracted agents were killing innocent mestizos whose black hair was almost indistinguishable from that of Apaches, leading to the formation of committees to examine scalps before issuance of payment.[47] Even in the official records of legislatures—where stenographers recorded the number of scalps redeemed and the amount of money disbursed—it is impossible to know for sure how many of those body parts actually belonged to Indians.

In 2021, a group of Penobscot filmmakers and researchers found evidence of sixty-nine scalp proclamations in New England between 1675 and 1760, and they concluded that at least 375 Indians perished as a direct result of those laws.[48] These statistics offer a good starting point, but as the documentary's producers acknowledged, findings were limited in scope and tell only one part of a much larger story. All told, well over one hundred different scalping laws were implemented across North America, some of which included rewards for captive women and children to be sold as slaves. Future research may yield a more accurate accounting, but my conservative approximation of scalp warfare's human toll is that somewhere between ten thousand and twenty thousand indigenous men, women, and children were scalped—and thousands more killed but not scalped—between implementation of a bounty in New Netherland in 1641 and payment of the last known reward in Mexico in 1886. Wounded Indians escaped from almost every attack, and we will never know how many of the maimed later succumbed to their injuries. Many others were killed during the fighting, but surviving kin frantically carried the bodies from the field to save them from the indignity of being scalped and to enable proper ceremonies or burials at a later time. Moreover, these approximations do not account for tens of thousands of Indians abducted as part of the same state-sponsored methods of scalp warfare, and many of those captives ultimately died as a direct result of their brutal enslavement. It is also important to note that a significant proportion of these figures can be attributed to Mexico and California during a forty-year period in the mid-1800s. Scalp warfare took a particularly devastating toll in those two places, and tribes suffered population losses ranging from about 30 percent among the Southern Apaches to around 90 percent in the case of several California groups.

At first glance, these numerical estimates may seem like a metaphorical drop-in-the-bucket or fish-in-the-sea compared to the tens of millions of Indians who perished from disease, famine, enslavement, and traditional warfare during the centuries after European arrival.[49] But the true impact of scalp warfare should be assessed both alongside and beyond mortality rates and population percentages. "Violence can never be understood solely in terms of its physicality," two recent anthropologists explain, because "violence also includes assaults on the personhood, dignity, sense of worth or value of the victim."[50] In a similar vein, Macarena Gómez-Barris writes of state violence having an afterlife manifested in survivors as well as future generations, while Kidada Williams describes the ways in which family members experience "the aftershocks" of extreme violence.[51] These traumatic afterlives and aftershocks of killing are found in many Native oral histories and oral traditions revolving around scalp warfare. Important social, cultural, and psychological elements underlie all statistical figures, as people not only lost their lives but in many cases suffered a postmortem dismemberment that left an indelible spiritual imprint on the soul of the deceased and a corollary emotional impact on surviving kin and their descendants. Written records scarcely show it, but every victim had family and friends who grieved their loved one's death and desecration, and to neglect or marginalize that humanistic element is to ignore a deeper meaning of the violence. Scalp warfare also had devastating effects beyond the physical murder and mutilation of individual people, the psychological trauma inflicted on surviving acquaintances, and the cultural toll exacted on targeted groups. Because they sought material gain above all else, profiteers plundered Indian villages and captured women and children, selling thousands of them into slavery. Regardless of the total number of casualties, the campaigners that local government agents set loose on Native enemies incited fear through communicative acts of extralethal violence. Most broadly, practitioners of scalp warfare contributed in significant ways to the colonial conquest of North America, particularly in contested borderlands zones where traditional military operations against skilled Indigenous fighters often proved ineffective.

Statistical estimates aside, the ubiquity of paid killing and scalping across time and place demonstrates the interconnectivity of individual economic interest, intertribal rivalry, colonial racism, and extralethal violence as driving forces behind the breadth and severity of North America's many Indian conflicts. Whether it involved Dutch newcomers on Staten Island, English/British colonists in Massachusetts and Acadia, French settlers and their Indian allies in the Saint Lawrence River Valley and along the lower Mississippi River, American legionnaires in the deserts of northern Mexico, Rangers in the Texas Hill Country, or volunteer companies from California mining towns, the scalp warfare that spanned three centuries and multiple sovereignties relied on ruthless rogues who transformed their intense hatred of enemies into an occupation that met their own financial and cultural needs. Alongside the ongoing operations of soldiers and militiamen, these volunteers, rangers, and bounty hunters formed a key component of local government strategies for destroying Indians in peripheral regions where central power bowed to regional interests. Although they acted primarily in economic self-promotion rather than nationalistic service to a country, scalpers such as Hannah Duston, John Lovewell, John Johnson, James Kirker, John Joel Glanton, Ben Wright, Walter Jarboe, and George Wythe Baylor played prominent roles in advancing nation-building objectives at the expense of any Indians who stood in the way.

"Lifting Hair" in French Canada and Louisiana

In 1703, a man named Dubosq—one eyewitness described him in racial-ized jargon as "the son of a savage and a Frenchwoman"—fell captive to a party of ten Iroquois. At one point, the eight men and two women who held Dubosq retrieved a stash of brandy and "invited the prisoner to imitate them in their debauchery." He later claimed to have feigned drinking by tak-ing swigs of liquor from the bottle but letting the liquid dribble slowly out the corner of his mouth and down his neck and chest, thus remaining sober while the captors became intoxicated. When the drunk Indians finally fell asleep, Dubosq bound and gagged the two women and "armed himself with a strong ax, with which he . . . greeted each one [of the men], one after the other, with a great blow." Both females were forced to watch as he scalped all eight corpses before setting off for Montreal to seek a reward and bask in newfound celebrity status. Dubosq strutted straight to the governor's office, "where he entered with a majestic air, holding in one hand eight large sticks at the end of which hung eight long hairs, and in the other his two prisoners whom he made walk in front, tied like children." He received £240 worth of merchandise as payment for the scalps, that being, according to one French observer, "the rate . . . that we usually pay for each hair that our savages bring [in]."[1] Dubosq achieved immediate renown in local lore, an indication that indiscriminate attacks on Indians and state sponsorship of extralethal violence were becoming increasingly common as strategies for conquest, just decades after colonial officials enacted North America's first lucrative bounties.

The form of scalp warfare that developed across colonial New France beginning in the late 1600s typically involved local government officials and religious agents who worked in tandem to formulate strategic alliances with powerful Indigenous groups such as the Wabanaki Confederacy tribes in Canada and the Choctaws in Louisiana. Governors, intendants, and missionaries who lacked the military manpower and material resources to effectively dominate the contested lands on which they settled resorted to irregular fighting techniques that evolved from the implementation of bounties to incentivize Indian allies during combat with enemy tribes as well as rival English colonists to the east. The French brand of scalp warfare in North America almost always involved Native auxiliaries who acted as state practitioners of extralethal violence, attacking other Indigenous groups whom they viewed as longtime competitors and adversaries while simultaneously reaping the material rewards that French officials offered for their services. Although some Indians did participate in and benefit from the bounty programs that arose in contemporaneous New England, only in New France did Indigenous peoples make up the majority of scalp hunters. Paid scalping was a brutal occupation in all times and places where it occurred, yet the extent of direct Indigenous involvement sets the French mode of scalp warfare apart from the variations that developed in the English colonies, Mexico, Texas, and California. On one hand, this model evolved outside the parameters of organized army and militia units. On the other, it complicates the "lumping" arguments for Native American genocide as a monolithic colonial act spanning hundreds of years, insofar as this state outsourcing of scalp warfare in New France often entailed members of some Indigenous nations or groups targeting people of other Indigenous nations or groups through the motivations of material gain and intercultural animosity.

Dubosq was certainly not the first man to take scalps or heads in the borderlands of French Canada and New England. Many of North America's Indians, including confederated Wabanakis who allied with French agents in Canada and the Five Nations adversaries they targeted, scalped or otherwise disfigured corpses of enemies long before European settlers arrived. Although precontact tribes performed this type of extralethal violence primarily for symbolic and ritualistic purposes, such tactics would eventually inspire the body part bounties that Dutch, French, and English administrators implemented beginning in the seventeenth century.[2] In 1644, seven Algonquins led by a man named Diescaret ambushed fifteen Iroquois men in canoes as they waded ashore on a riverbank near Fort Richelieu, killing eleven of them and taking two prisoners. "The combat over," Jesuit priest Barthélemy Vimont related, "the victors went to seek the dead bodies, scalped them, and embarked on their return journey" to the French mission near Quebec City. Approaching Vimont's religious outpost, the Algonquins sang triumphantly as "the scalps of those who had been killed in the fight, attached to the ends of some sticks, fluttered in the air at the will of the wind." The French missionary Jean Baptiste Etinechkaouat praised these acts of violent display, which effectively signaled an alliance between Natives and newcomers revolving around the destruction of common enemies. Proclaiming that Diescaret "behaved valiantly," Vimont offered a word of advice to colleagues in New France, saying that "it is no little hold gained over the Savages, to hinder them from venting their fury on those who, when they hold them, treat them with fiendish cruelty." Using the racialized rhetoric that so often characterized colonial perspectives on Indians, the Jesuit priest identified a process of retributive violence and postmortem mutilation that attended many prior conflicts between tribes, implying that fellow Frenchmen would be smart to play such rivalries to their advantage during wars against imperial competitors.[3]

Years later, Jesuit missionary Jacques Bruyas described his Iroquois disciples at Saint Francis Xavier as "cruel and inclined to blood and carnage," claiming that "the passion for killing men is so great that they willingly go 300 Leagues and more to remove one scalp."[4] As the voyager René-Robert Cavelier, Sieur de La Salle, made his way through the Great Lakes and down the Mississippi River during his exploration of interior North America in 1678–82, he described calumet ceremonies during which his Potawatomi and Miami hosts danced while holding the scalps of slain Iroquois enemies.[5] These types of gruesome spectacles may have bothered some moralizing proselytizers, but as the seventeenth century progressed many colonists found inspiration in Native scalping practices when formulating their own fighting tactics and wartime policies. As the foregoing examples show, Catholic priests and missionaries became deeply involved in scalp warfare, not as practitioners of extralethal violence themselves but rather as influential colonial agents who encouraged the Indians to whom they had religious access to attack, kill, and mutilate Indigenous enemies of the French. In a reflection of the localized nature of scalp warfare, the religious element's participation occurred not inside the parameters of official church doctrine but rather at specific missions and among individual missionaries. Such sponsorship of the killing and corporeal mutilation of Indians also contradicted a sixteenth-century papal declaration affirming the humanity of the so-called New World's Indigenous peoples.[6] Local religious agents who encouraged and enabled scalp warfare defied the central church and the pope in the same way that colonial officials who implemented bounties and paid rewards bucked the orders of parliaments and kings.

Embracing a warfare technique known as *lever des chevelures*, or lifting hair, policymakers in Canada and Louisiana drew in part from their superficial knowledge of traditional Indigenous scalping practices such as those mentioned above.[7] But the bounty programs wherein Catholic priests and French officials began to dally in the macabre had policy roots in New Netherland, where Governor Willem Kieft devised and implemented one of colonial North America's earliest scalp acts. In the late 1630s, waves of Dutch newcomers arrived from Europe and populated both banks of the lower Hudson River. These settlers dislocated Raritan Indians, who in turn felt economic and political pressure from a recent decline in the fur trade, as well as the governor's attempt to levy taxes on Native peoples beginning in 1639. In response, they began striking the new Dutch settlements in a series of destructive depredations. In retaliation for these indigenous attacks—including one raid that left four colonists dead—Kieft issued a mandate on July 4, 1641, that promised ten fathoms of wampum for every Raritan head, regardless of age or sex, and twenty fathoms for specific individuals known to have participated in a recent assault on Staten Island.[8] By distributing the reward in shell beads—a traditional form of Indigenous wealth and power—rather than Dutch currency, the edict necessarily recognized Indigenous protocols in a time and place where European newcomers lacked the power to fully impose their will. Kieft's plan also revolved around strategic alliances with Native proxies who would assume the risk of fighting and perform the state's extralethal violence as proof of their victories.[9] Like the neighboring Puritans in Massachusetts—who infamously decapitated Pequots with whom they were at war in the 1630s—Dutch settlers could use severed Indian heads for purposes of violent display to dissuade further Raritan attacks while also forging a sense of communal identity around macabre mementos as symbols of their own triumphs.

This grisly new approach to Indian conflict had its detractors, including David de Vries, a prominent member of Kieft's "Twelve Men" advisory council, whose own homestead had been the target of a Raritan raid. Believing that "no profit was to be derived from a war with the savages," De Vries feared that the new policy would exacerbate rather than mitigate interethnic violence and racial hatred. He recognized that Raritans were just as likely to retaliate with even greater force as they were to cower and retreat in fear of being killed and dismembered. But his lamentation went unheeded, because Kieft and the other ten councillors remained committed to the beheading experiment as part of state policy.[10] Administrators for the West India Company eventually joined De Vries in voicing disdain for this approach to colonial conflict, calling body part bounties "unnatural, barbarous, unnecessary, unjust, and disgraceful."[11] Because these rhetorical protests came from across the Atlantic, they had no real bearing on the course of scalp warfare in the North American colonies from which the West India Company drew its profits.

However distasteful this new scalp warfare technique may have seemed to some outside observers, Kieft's policy remained in effect, and the graduated bounty scale applied to all Raritans, with higher payouts for the killing of specific tribe members deemed more dangerous than others. From the perspective of seventeenth-century Staten Islanders who found themselves physically and logistically unprepared for combat with powerful Indigenous enemies, the idea was to leverage intertribal rivalries to their own advantage to eliminate certain Indian threats to the colony while simultaneously reducing other perceived threats by embracing those tribes as Dutch allies. Local leaders incentivized warfare with material rewards—in this case

Willem Kieft. Library of Congress Prints and
Photographs Division, LC-USZ62–51448.

wampum beads—requiring the presentation of identifiable body parts as
evidence that a person from the targeted group had indeed been killed. All
of this emanated from a prevalent European belief in superiority over "savage" Indians whom they sought to manipulate in diplomatic, political, and
religious ways. But for Indigenous peoples who occupied the region, these
reverberating conflicts and alliances that led to the corporeal desecration of
deceased kin had deeper meaning. In the Algonquian and Iroquoian ethos,
the soul is contained in the crown of the head, meaning that acts such as
scalping and beheading expose the victim's soul and allow it to escape into
an unknown netherworld apart from the rest of the physical body. For the
Raritans that Kieft ordered decapitated, the mutilation of their bodies went

far beyond an extralethal act of scalp warfare and violent display. These killings had spiritual ramifications for the deceased as well as their surviving kin, who suffered the psychological trauma of knowing that their loved one would experience afterlife in soulless shame and misery.[12]

Although Kieft and his fellow Dutch settlers embraced and developed the concept of paying rewards for body parts of enemies in New York, the earliest French bounty arose in 1688, at the onset of King William's War (Nine Years' War). Although this global contest originated in Europe when King Louis XIV intervened in German politics, aspects of it also played out on the frontiers of Acadia, Hudson's Bay, Newfoundland, and the borderlands between Quebec and New York.[13] One early development in the conflict's North American theater came when the governor of Canada used financial incentives to convince the sachem Wampolack and eleven Abenaki allies to attack members of the Five Nations (Iroquois), longtime French enemies who sided with the English in Massachusetts. As they traversed the Connecticut River Valley, these Abenakis confronted a small party of Iroquois under the leadership of Magsigpen, and a tense standoff ensued. Meeting face-to-face with weapons drawn, Wampolack informed Magsigpen that the French governor had instructed him to "kill all what you cann, bring noe prisoners but their scalps, and I'le give you ten beavers for every one of them." Magsigpen defused the situation, telling his bounty-hunting counterpart that there had recently been a ceasefire between the two warring empires and any killing or scalping might renew hostilities between New England and New France. The aggressive presence of Wampolack and his Abenaki followers in the Iroquois-dominated borderlands caused considerable anxiety among English settlers nearer the Atlantic Coast, who feared that they, too, might become targets of the scalp warfare that French officials were promoting. When the band of Abenakis returned to Quebec City in September, they brought seven scalps and one female captive to redeem as a slave, but the governor and the intendant deceptively reneged on promises of payouts in beaver pelts, saying that hostilities had officially ceased and that these acts thus occurred outside of a mutually recognized state of war between the French and English colonies.[14] Like the Dutch alliance with Native proxies in midcentury New York, this claim about the total cessation of war was steeped in Eurocentrism, revolving around a colonial view that tribes acted as wards of the state and had no conflicts or animosities of their own. But the incident did threaten to undermine fragile and mutually important agreements between Indigenous groups and colonial officials in French Canada at a time when neither group possessed the military power to fully dominate the other. With participants like Wampolack and Magsigpen acting semiautonomously in pursuit of profit and revenge, bounty systems could exacerbate rather than alleviate imperial and intertribal rivalries, just as the Dutchman David de Vries had warned decades earlier. But government decision makers in Quebec City and Montreal—the two administrative epicenters of French Canada—either failed to appreciate these risks or remained unconcerned about the possible ramifications, because these colonies came to rely more heavily on scalp warfare as a technique for conquest that bred implacable hatred between enemies.

Subservient to the crown in all matters and deeply committed to imperial objectives of settlement and conquest, religious conversion of Indians, and economic control of the land and its resources, North American officials rarely defied or even criticized a king's order. An issue arose in 1692, however, that placed Intendant Jean Bochart de Champigny and Governor-General Louis de Buade, comte de Frontenac, at direct odds with their faraway monarch. As the highest-ranking French administrators in Canada, these two men frequently disagreed with each other on policy matters, but they stood on common ground with an idea to pay 20 silver écus for Five Nations captives and 10 silver écus (equivalent to £1.5 sterling at the time, or US$276 today) for each of their scalps.[15] The higher price offered for captives nodded to the potential usefulness of living rather than dead enemies, who might convey intelligence on enemy movements or provide economic value as slaves. From his palace at Versailles, Louis XIV struck down the initiative to capture and kill members of the confederated Mohawks, Onondagas, Oneidas, Cayugas, and Senecas. This royal directive had nothing to do with any humanitarian impulse—the king had no compunction about his subjects killing Indians in the name of establishing and expanding a global empire—but instead evolved from his opposition to the monetary costs of a bounty program while a more urgent war with rival England was draining the treasury. With these considerations in mind, Louis XIV ignored Frontenac's argument that scalp payouts were "the most useful expenditure we could make, being the surest means of destroying the Iroquois Indians." Rather than eliminate bounties altogether, though, the king simply wanted to reduce prices to 2 silver écus per male scalp and 1 silver écu per female scalp, effectively cutting expenses by a factor of five. That order fell on deaf ears across the Atlantic.[16]

Headquartered at Quebec City—thousands of miles away from monarchical oversight—Frontenac and Champigny shunned the king's mandate as ignorant and foolish, knowing that paltry payouts for such dangerous work were unlikely to encourage anyone to take up arms against skilled Indian fighters on a remote multinational frontier. In a joint communication, the governor and the intendant cautiously lectured their king and his minister (to whom colonial officials reported) about the importance of alliances with certain Indigenous groups as part of the larger war against British forces in North America, saying that "gratuities" for Iroquois scalps helped to solidify crucial pacts with the Wabanaki Confederacy of Eastern and Western Abenaki, Maliseet, Mi'kmaq, and Passamaquoddy tribes. In a remarkable act of defiance that underscored the significance of bounty programs to the larger imperial goal of territorial domination, Frontenac and Champigny continued their paid scalping initiative at the original pay rates, disingenuously begging the king's forgiveness and promising that "we will try to find excuses to pay the least possible."[17] This contentious interaction between the national dictates of Louis XIV and the regional preferences of French officials exemplified the tendency to pursue scalp warfare as a localized strategy for conquest that defied central authority in Europe insofar as the king previously voiced fiscal conservatism in his disapproval of paying such large rewards. As a decentralized form of state policy that revolved around the paid killing and scalping of enemies, Indian bounties indicated the relative weakness of some settler societies as well as a deeply impactful technique of extralethal violence that attended colonization.

In New France, governors acted as the king's official representatives and exercised authority over all other colonial officials as well as military

Louis de Buade, Comte de Frontenac. Bibliothèque et
Archives Nationales du Québec / 52327 / 1956129.

personnel. The governor also devised Indian policy, handled diplomatic affairs with tribes, and issued orders to direct the course of frontier conflicts
with Native enemies. The intendant, however, controlled financial matters
and held responsibility for preparing budgets, compensating troops, and
paying for defensive measures. This division of power separated policy formulation from money management, thus preventing the two most influential colonial administrators from fraudulently enriching themselves without
mutual complicity.[18] When it came to running the colonial government,
Frontenac and Champigny found themselves at odds over many things—
including ecclesiastical affairs involving Jesuit priests and Catholic
missions—and personal quarrels were not uncommon.[19] At one point, Frontenac even told the minister in France that he tolerated Jesuits only because
"I can have no other interest than the good of the colony, the trade of the
kingdom, and the peace of the King's subjects," thus reassuring superiors

across the Atlantic of his loyalty to the crown while reiterating an open disdain for the religious order's authority.[20] But the governor and the intendant remained in lockstep when it came to the local bounty program, which required a combination of Frontenac's official Indian policy and Champigny's approval of payouts from the treasury in order to properly function. Scalp warfare was an administrative imperative that could only advance with the approbation of both men, especially insofar as they each openly defied the king in these initiatives. Although the law that Frontenac and Champigny instituted in the 1690s attracted considerable attention and certainly induced some men to hunt bounties, the death toll attributable to these measures remains unknown. In fact, only a small number of scalps were redeemed as a direct result of the program, again pointing to a divergence between genocidal rhetoric and genocidal outcomes. The larger significance of the new scalp act involved experimentation with an irregular form of warfare, localized state sponsorship of that technique for conquest, incorporation of Indian allies as perpetrators, and intense hatred of Indigenous enemies that motivated extralethal tactics.

The fact that this bounty-hunting initiative produced so few scalps yet became so central to local policy indicates that French figureheads such as Frontenac and Champigny saw the value of nontraditional partnerships in borderlands zones where settlers and missionaries lacked total control over powerful Indigenous tribes and confederacies.[21] Historian Richard White has described this dynamic of Franco-Indian relations as "the middle ground," a scenario that developed when no single group was strong enough to dominate another, and all sides therefore cooperated and coexisted in strategic ways to achieve at least some of their respective interests.[22] In addition to economic affairs such as the fur trade, this middle ground phenomenon manifested itself in the ways that French governors, commanders, and missionaries courted Native proxies by promising material rewards in exchange for the scalps of those who resisted royal dominion over crucial interior beachheads in the Saint Lawrence River Valley and Great Lakes regions. In the northeast borderlands that included the contested frontiers of Canada, Acadia, New Hampshire, and Massachusetts, these diplomatic efforts most often involved Abenaki peoples. By the 1690s, French Canadian officials recognized deep tensions between the Abenakis and the English, and they capitalized on the existence of a shared enemy, tribal dependency on the fur trade, and religious bonds established through missionaries to lay the foundations for diplomacy with the powerful Indigenous nation.[23] That this middle ground existed alongside scalp warfare's strategic alliances of Natives and newcomers demonstrates the willingness of French officials and priests to declare an exterminatory intent toward some tribes while simultaneously working with others to pursue shared interests in defeating common enemies.

The Eastern and Western Abenakis that French leaders courted as practitioners of scalp warfare called the place spanning New England and Acadia Ndakinna, meaning "our land." Estimated to number at least ten thousand people at the time of European contact, the Western Abenakis included seven subgroups—Sokokis, Ossipees, Cowasucks, Missisquois, Pennacooks, Winnipesaukees, and Pigwackets—while the Eastern Abenakis consisted of three bands—Kennebecs, Androscoggins, and Penobscots. Officials in Canada referred to all Abenaki-speaking groups as the "great Nations of New England," a title suggesting some degree of respect for the tribe's power and influence. King Philip's War (1675–78) had a devastating impact because it transformed Ndakinna into a combat zone and pushed many of the tribal divisions toward French outposts to the north and west. Driven to the fringes of their traditional homelands, not only did Abenakis share in French hostility toward the English and the Iroquois, but many also settled and assimilated at missions along the Saint Lawrence River. This proximity to colonial settlements made them some of Canada's foremost allies in every major imperial conflict between 1688 and 1763 and gave Catholic proselytizers considerable influence over the tribe's participation in scalp warfare.[24]

Reeling from adverse effects of the Iroquois-English alliance—which included two massive Five Nations attacks near Montreal Island, the first one, in 1689, claiming the lives of more than one hundred French Canadians and destroying fifty-six farms, and the second strike leaving twenty-four colonists dead and much of the Montreal settlement in ruins—Frontenac and Champigny expanded the scalp warfare strategy to include a *petite guerre* (little war) approach that transformed experimental bounties into an official state policy of extralethal violence.[25] The petite guerre tradition of frontier fighting in North America involved indiscriminate guerrilla tactics and incorporated Indian auxiliaries into the military equation, with the objective of intimidating enemy populations and destroying their ability to subsist.[26] Throughout New France, petite guerre coalesced with scalp bounties at the points of financial gain and personal hatred of foes to produce strategic diplomatic and military alliances between Natives and newcomers.[27] One key analytical takeaway from the French approach to scalp warfare is that the practices of extralethal violence and violent display were not limited to settlers, as Indigenous actors frequently participated in bounty programs and perpetrated acts of corporeal mutilation in order to punish tribal enemies and secure material benefits from government agents. Indians who scalped other Indians lacked the underlying racial motivations that attended other forms of colonial violence, but these men still acted with opportunistic impulses because they expected various forms of compensation for their deeds, and they may not have performed such horrific acts for the benefit of French governors and Jesuit priests had it not been for promises of rewards and plunder.

There were at least two reasons that Frontenac and Champigny—and many French administrators after them—agreed on the petite guerre strategy of paying bounty hunters as paramilitary auxiliaries. The first involved a general view of Indians as racially inferior and a more specific perception of non-Christianized Indians as "savage"—and thus fit for scalping.[28] The second reason emanated from continuous pressure applied from Versailles to achieve battlefield victory over the English and their Iroquois allies at minimal financial expense. Within the context of King William's War, Frontenac repeatedly complained that he lacked adequate military manpower and requested more troops from the minister in France. Those requisitions yielded little immediate support, and the governor instead pursued unconventional options including scalp bounties to recruit more independent volunteers as fighters. In 1691, Canada had 1,313 regular troops, but this number decreased to 1,120 the following year, forcing colonial officials to rely more heavily on allied Indian combatants as King William's War raged on. Regardless of who did the killing, warfare was always expensive, and the conflict with England continued to drain the king's wealth and try his patience. In 1691, the French treasury allocated 99,000 livres for combat expenses in New France, and a year later the amount increased to 193,000 livres even though the number of soldiers on the payroll decreased by 15 percent. By 1693, the expenditure skyrocketed to over 750,000 livres (about US$9.5 million today), and each shipment of specie that arrived in Quebec City came with a royal remonstrance against wasteful spending. Louis XIV disapproved of bounties within a narrow view of fiscal conservatism, rejecting the arguments from Champigny and Frontenac that scalp warfare performed by Indian allies reduced state operating costs because it eliminated the need for hundreds of troop salaries and the equipment to sustain professional soldiers during long campaigns.[29] That local officials continuously reverted to scalp warfare despite increasing royal commitments to traditional military operations speaks to the ongoing inadequacy of soldiers and militiamen in fighting powerful Indigenous groups on the extreme peripheries of European empire.

Frontenac and Champigny committed themselves to scalp warfare as a strategy for frontier combat during King William's War, even at the risk of angering their king and losing their jobs. At the same time, Joseph Robineau de Villebon, the French governor of Acadia, was supplied with ample presents to distribute among Abenaki subgroups in the Port Royal region, both as a gesture of good faith and to ensure their continued opposition to the so-called Bostonnais (English settlers in Massachusetts).[30] Writing from Europe, the French minister condoned the distribution of material rewards in exchange for the killing of Native foes when he instructed Villebon to ensure that all Abenakis "will be animated by no other desire than that of making profit out of the enemy."[31] The priest of the Society of Foreign Missions stationed on the Penobscot River, Father Louis-Pierre Thury, was equally complicit in convincing Indigenous allies to fight imperial rivals across the New England and Acadian borderlands. Whenever he ceremoniously converted Indians to Catholicism, Thury also tried to indoctrinate them to believe that English colonists must be expelled from North America, an outcome that would serve both French and Abenaki interests. The priest recruited two hundred Abenaki fighters under the leadership of the sachem

Madockawando, and he accompanied these Indigenous proxies as they attacked and plundered the settlement of York in the Massachusetts Bay Colony on January 24, 1692. These Abenakis burned the town and killed some one hundred English settlers, and they took an additional eighty captives to Acadia, where Villebon congratulated their success and distributed rewards for an unspecified number of scalps and slaves.[32] The operation proved the efficacy of a multidimensional strategy for scalp warfare that involved specialized pacts with "friendly" Indians, cooperation among influential religious leaders, and bounty incentives for killing and dismembering hated enemies.

Two years later, Father Thury duplicated his deadly feat by joining a French military officer, Claude-Sébastien de Villieu, to lead more than two hundred Abenakis in an ambush at Oyster River (present-day Durham, New Hampshire). The attack that occurred on July 18, 1694, aimed to disrupt an English diplomatic endeavor that could have swayed several Abenaki subgroups away from their alliance with New France, but it also resulted in the deaths of 104 settlers and the captivity of 27 more. Villieu immediately marched with a small detachment of Abenakis to Montreal, where he presented thirteen scalps to Frontenac and entertained the governor with gruesome tales of the slaughter.[33] From his outpost in Acadia, Villebon praised the aptly named Oyster River Massacre as a fortuitous development in his nation's ongoing conflict with England and her colonial subjects. "The English are in despair, for not even infants in the cradle were spared," Villebon wrote with the characteristic indifference to humanity that accompanied colonial acts of extralethal violence. He understood that the devastation wrought upon men, women, and children would help undercut pending alliances between Abenakis and New Englanders to the ultimate benefit of New France.[34] For his part in these macabre affairs, Thury received high commendation from French officials, who suggested a personal pay raise to honor the priest's extraordinary ability to enlist Indigenous allies as agents of state-sponsored murder and mutilation.[35] Here again, the possible ramifications of scalp warfare that David de Vries warned of in the 1640s came into stark relief, as some of these victims were European settlers rather than Indian enemies, and it was becoming increasingly clear that state monetization of scalps could sometimes result in retributive acts of extralethal violence against unintended targets.

Throughout King William's War, officials in Canada appreciated the importance of Indigenous cooperation and went to great lengths to strengthen those alliances, with scalp warfare being one method of doing so. In 1696, French forces laid siege to Fort William Henry at the mouth of the Penobscot River as a gesture of goodwill to the Eastern Abenakis whose homelands the British post impinged upon.[36] By promoting Indian interests in such ways, and by using bounties to incentivize active participation in the war against English colonists and their Five Nations associates, French administrators and clerics induced Abenakis to take up arms against the crown's foremost antagonists in the northeast borderlands, resulting in a dramatic diminution of Iroquois power that included the loss of nearly half of the tribe's fighting men by the time the war ended with the Treaty of Ryswick in September 1697.[37] Indian sachems such as Wampolack and Madockawando sought to capitalize on French offers of material goods in exchange for enemy scalps, leading their followers into the field to attack the English and the Iroquois alike. On at least three separate occasions— along the Connecticut River, at York, and at Oyster River—these bounty-driven campaigns claimed the lives of at least two hundred English settlers and an untold number of Iroquois, subjected hundreds more to captivity, and left smoldering ruins in their wake. The demographic devastation of such raids also carried profound symbolic power as a form of violent display, conveying a clear message of brutality and hatred that instilled deep trepidation among Five Nations peoples and English settlers who occupied the region. To be sure, scalp warfare in the petite guerre tradition did not constitute the only—or even the predominant—form of fighting during King William's War, but it did occupy an important place in the grand strategies of two imperial rivals as they competed for control over portions of North America and for the cooperation of important Indigenous allies. By the end of the seventeenth century, both the French and their English counterparts had embraced paid scalping as a combat tactic in frontier theaters of warfare, and the vicious but potentially profitable enterprise would attract more and more participants as time wore on.

King William's War ended with a veritable status quo antebellum, neither New France nor New England managing to expand their territorial boundaries or otherwise strengthen their colonial positions in meaningful ways. Perhaps the greatest yet least acknowledged impact of this war in North America involved the Iroquois and Abenaki groups who, even as allies of the two European competitors, suffered considerable losses to tribal populations. Under these circumstances, another imperial clash—Queen Anne's War—erupted just five years later. A North American offshoot of the War of the Spanish Succession in Europe, wherein Louis XIV seated his grandson on the Spanish throne as Philip V and then violated the Treaty of Ryswick by recognizing the son of James II as king of England, this European contest spilled across the Atlantic and engulfed the northeast borderlands in bloody strife for eleven years beginning in 1702. French settlers and their Wabanaki Confederacy allies clashed once more with English colonists and Five Nations combatants, with control of Acadia and Nova Scotia at stake.[38] Throughout the war, officials in New France and New England would revert to scalp warfare as a strategy for defeating one another in difficult frontier environments where guerrilla tactics and intercultural hatred bred horrific acts of extralethal violence. As both sides sought to enlist Native proxies and to encourage able-bodied settlers to grab their muskets and clinch their scalping knives, the promise of wealth in the form of cash bounties and material rewards became an increasingly prominent driving force behind cycles of retributive extralethal violence.

As officials in Quebec City and Boston—the two administrative epicenters of regional bounty laws in the early eighteenth century—implemented scalp acts with increasing fervor, they vilified one another's policies as callous and inhumane. After learning about the bounties that French Canadians were distributing to Abenaki allies, royal officials in England declared the practice "so barbarous and inhuman that it ought by any means to be prevented." They insisted that the French stop paying for scalps, but this revulsion proved hypocritical because the same English missive also threatened to reciprocate by implementing bounties of their own.[39] In 1705, Massachusetts governor Joseph Dudley complained directly to French officials about their payouts for English scalps, although he did not express opposition to similar bounties placed on the heads of his Five Nations allies, a rhetorical omission that hinted at the racial prerogatives behind colonial violence. It was permissible for the French to scalp an Iroquois, Dudley implied, but nothing short of a travesty if they or their Indian allies scalped an Englishman. Responding to these criticisms, Governor Philippe de Rigaud, marquis de Vaudreuil, excoriated his gubernatorial counterpart for a series of recent killings and massacres. Acknowledging that extreme cruelties had come to characterize Queen Anne's War in Acadia, Vaudreuil heaped blame on the English and their Iroquois auxiliaries by accusing them of assassinating prisoners "in cold blood." Regarding Dudley's objections to French scalping policies, the marquis said that his officers "only followed the example of yours" and refused further comment, insinuating that an eye-for-an-eye mentality would prevail so long as the two imperial rivals remained at war.[40] The exchange between Dudley and Vaudreuil indicated a strategy of mutual deterrence, wherein local French and English officials began to use bounties not just as a mode of scalp warfare but also in an attempt to discourage one another from enforcing those bounties at the risk of extralethal reciprocity.

British officials (the Acts of Union between the English and Scottish parliaments in 1707 created the United Kingdom, commonly called Great Britain, whereupon its citizens and colonists increasingly came to be called "British" rather than "English") tried to stem the tide of French scalping initiatives not just by implementing their own bounties—Dudley informed his overseers in London of one such scalping policy in 1709—but also through strategic diplomatic efforts aimed at sabotaging crucial partnerships between New France and the Wabanaki Confederacy.[41] One year after his terse exchange with Governor Dudley, Vaudreuil met a group of Abenakis at Quebec City and learned of a recent conference at Fort Orange in New York. During the meeting, British agents and Iroquois representatives communicated through Flemish interlocutors to convince Abenaki leaders that their French benefactors were trying to use them as dispensable tools of warfare. When these same Abenakis spoke to Vaudreuil a short time later, they insisted that "what the English told us is true" and demanded a share of the spoils. "Since the war started, far from having any profit from it,

our homes are filled with English scalps," these Abenakis claimed through
an interpreter. The frustrated Abenakis also pointed out that no payment
had been made for these extralethal services to the French crown, asking
that lead and gunpowder be distributed to tribe members in reward.[42]
Vaudreuil responded to the Abenakis with characteristic paternalism, telling his "wild children" that they should never be so gullible as to cooperate
with the wily British and promising "to help you whenever you are attacked
either here or in Acadia." The governor also objected to the claim that Indian allies had not been adequately compensated for their war efforts, insisting that the tribe's condition had improved as a result of their alliance with
New France and the material benefits derived therefrom. Vaudreuil promised to continue paying 10 silver écus for enemy captives—the same amount
that Frontenac and Champigny established a decade earlier—and to distribute gunpowder as soon as the next shipment of war matériel arrived from
Europe. But he also said that no scalp bounties would be issued to tribe
members because it "seems too inhumane to me."[43] This would have been
a major philosophical departure from his predecessors in the 1690s, none of
whom expressed any humanitarian hesitation about scalp warfare. In reality, the governor seems to have been using moral qualms as an excuse to
avoid large payouts that might attract scrutiny from Versailles, perhaps remembering Louis XIV's objections to the expenses that Frontenac and
Champigny incurred with their initial bounty program. Vaudreuil had already revealed in the letter to Governor Dudley that he had no real compunction against scalping or otherwise disfiguring dead enemies as a method
for encouraging the cooperation of Wabanaki Confederacy men as combatants in Queen Anne's War.

Vaudreuil's continuation of bounties for Iroquois prisoners, along with
the issuance of gunpowder and other supplies to Abenakis, helped to retain
members of the Abenakis within the French orbit of allies. If British com-
plaints were any indication, French officials continued to offer payouts for
scalps, and this had a pronounced impact on frontier combat regardless of
whether officials actually upheld their promises of compensation. In 1708,
George Vaughan traveled from New Hampshire to London to address
the prestigious Council of Trade and Plantations, a committee of eight

crown-appointed British noblemen who advised on economic affairs in the colonies.[44] Part of a prominent merchant family and a Harvard graduate who also served as colonel in a colonial militia unit, Vaughan was a wise choice for colonial representation in the mother country.[45] Throughout New England, he told the eight councilmen, small villages lay exposed to "destruction and murder" at the hands of Indians in alliance with New France. "They strip of ye scalp of ye head and carry them to ye French at Canada where they receive a reward of £5 for every scalp so brought in," Vaughan explained with some exaggeration, as the 20 écu bounty to which he referred actually equated to about £3 per scalp. He also failed to mention that his own British colonies offered even higher prices for the body parts of French-allied Abenaki foes. His main point was not so much to underscore the barbarity of scalp warfare in North America but rather to explain that ongoing conflict with Native and French adversaries had a detrimental impact on economic production because it stymied the settlement and development of frontier lands. New Englanders "are exposed as a pray to ye wild men of ye forests, who are every year lessning our numbers," he concluded, using the colonial rhetoric of Indian savagery for dramatic effect.[46]

However appalled they might have been when informed about French policies of scalp warfare in North America, the Council of Trade and Plantations had no tangible ability to mitigate such threats to British settlements, and its voice in the matter was nothing more than a toothless rhetorical overture. Just three months after Vaughan's lecture in London, a group of Massachusetts Bay assemblymen addressed a lengthy missive directly to Queen Anne, imploring the crown to take action against French and Indian bounty hunters who plied the New England countryside. Since the beginning of King William's War in 1688, the petitioners wrote, New France and her Indigenous allies had routinely committed "bloody villanies [and] divers barbarous murthers" under the pretext of wartime strategy. "Like beasts of prey," the Massachusetts legislators continued, "[they] seek their living by rapine and spoil . . . and they are animated and encouraged to such barbaritys by the French setting the heads of your Majesty's subjects at a price upon bringing in their scalps." Although the assemblymen characteristically neglected to mention their own nearly identical scalp laws, they correctly explained that officials at Quebec City and Montreal offered a wide range of incentives to practitioners of extralethal violence, including clothing, guns, ammunition, and hunting supplies. In an obvious reference to men such as Father Thury, they also pinpointed the direct role of religious figures in French scalping initiatives when telling the queen that "priests and emissaries among [the Indians] steady them in their interests and bigoteries." With these points in mind, the colonists begged Queen Anne to give her blessing for the use of similar tactics, requesting permission to enlist Cayuga, Mohawk, Oneida, Onondaga, and Seneca members of the Iroquois Confederacy as scalp hunters to augment the colonists already eligible to participate in New England's bounty programs. They felt confident that these skilled Five Nations fighters "would, with the blessing of God, in short time, extirpate or reclaim [the Wabanakis], and prevent the incursions made upon us from Canada."[47] The incorporation of Indigenous proxies altered the racial dynamics of scalp warfare in terms of who participated in the killing, but it also aimed to capitalize on preexisting intertribal rivalries in a way that exhibited colonial racism through a common assumption that surrounding tribes were nothing more than wards of the government who could be used in place of soldiers and militiamen as combat proxies. With these wicked mindsets of retaliation animating all sides, state-sponsored killing and bounty-driven acts of violent display would remain prominent features of European rivalries in colonial North America.

Queen Anne's War ended in 1713 with France militarily defeated in Europe, whereupon the Treaty of Utrecht allowed Louis XIV to retain a Bourbon on the Spanish throne in exchange for cession of the Acadia, Hudson's Bay, and Newfoundland territories to England. These were all parts of Ndakinna that were transferred on the map without any Indigenous voice in the process, despite the direct roles of Abenakis and Iroquois in these North American manifestations of a worldwide Franco-Anglo competition. The cooling of imperial hostilities that followed this agreement brought a temporary decline in bounty hunting across the northeast borderlands—indicating once more than localized scalp warfare in colonial New France and New England was tied to larger conflicts—but neither European empire swayed from its long-term commitment to killing, enslaving, or

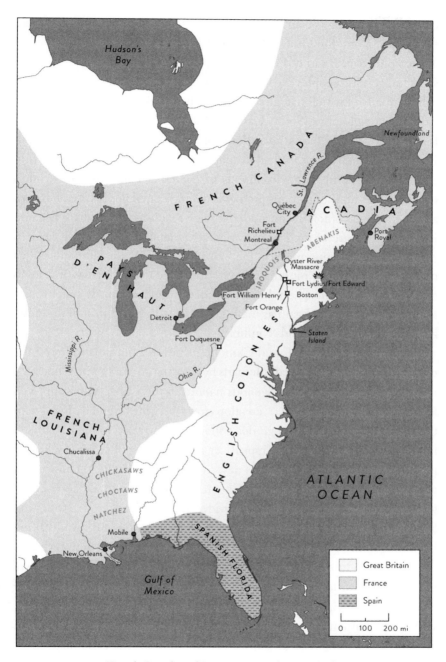

French Canada and Louisiana. Map by Erin Greb.

otherwise defeating Indians as part of the ongoing process of conquest. Farther south, along the Gulf of Mexico coastline and throughout the lower Mississippi River Basin of French Louisiana, an estimated thirty-five thousand Indigenous peoples of the Choctaw, Chickasaw, Natchez, and other tribes—many of which had already established trade relationships with the British in neighboring South Carolina—drastically outnumbered the diffuse colony's several thousand settlers, soldiers, and Black slaves. Here as in French Canada, Europeans had to adapt their political and diplomatic procedures in response to environments of contested authority where intertribal rivalries and Indigenous protocols often dictated the course of events, and the regional officials who guided foreign relations with Indians became increasingly aware of their own comparative dependency and weakness.[48] Much like their counterparts in the Saint Lawrence Valley, French settlers on this more southerly multinational frontier tried to play Native rivalries to their imperial advantage, and they repeatedly applied bounty systems and the promise of material gain as methods for initiating and sustaining strategic allies during borderlands conflicts.

French colonial officials and Catholic priests in Louisiana followed the example of their Canadian counterparts by courting alliances with Choctaws, one of the most powerful Indigenous nations in the Lower Mississippi Valley. According to the Choctaw creation story, the tribe originally fused with the Chickasaws and the two groups collectively migrated to their historical homelands east of the Mississippi River at the urging of *fabussa*, a sacred pole that guided their journey. As descendants of prehistoric Mississippian cultures, the Muskogean-speaking Choctaws whom French settlers encountered in Louisiana were politically divided into the Eastern, Western, and Sixtowns units, numbering in all about twenty-one thousand people at the beginning of the eighteenth century.[49] By that time, colonial administrators routinely tried to exploit intertribal strife for their own political and economic purposes, forging covenants with the Choctaws at the expense of neighboring Chickasaw and Natchez groups.[50] As early as the 1710s, French settlers in Louisiana were offering lucrative bounties—usually in the form of such critical supplies as guns and ammunition—to encourage some "friendly" Indians to wage war on other Indians who threatened imperial interests. Colonists representing cross and crown also continued to recognize that living captives held more diplomatic and informational value than lifeless bodies or body parts, so premiums for prisoners usually exceeded prices for scalps and gave rise to a long-lasting Indian slave trade that existed alongside the region's more prolific African chattel system. Contrarily, New Englanders tended to view Indigenous peoples not as diplomatic bargaining chips but as irredeemable heathens who stood in the way of settlement and prosperity. For these reasons, some British settlers preferred to remove or kill Indians rather than capture or convert them, although both the British and the French did regularly enslave Native peoples.[51] Based on such motivations, French officials primarily distributed bounty prizes to Indian allies, whereas British leaders preferred to pay scalp rewards to fellow colonists.[52] In the context of genocide, these differences matter because the intent was not always to exterminate a tribe. In Louisiana as in Canada, French officials implicitly discouraged indiscriminate killing of women and children when they offered higher prices for them as captives rather than corpses.

Governor Jean-Baptiste Le Moyne, Sieur de Bienville—best known for establishing New Orleans in 1718—was instrumental in the proliferation of scalping in French Louisiana.[53] In the early 1700s, according to a settler named André Pénicaut, the governor offered a bounty of 10 crowns per enemy scalp to "all the savage nations friendly to us."[54] Just twenty-six years old at the time, Bienville was a skilled diplomat who learned the language and customs of Choctaw counterparts, and he told French chancellor Louis Phélypeaux, comte de Pontchartrain, that he was doing "everything in his power to induce the Indians who are allied with the French to make war" on the colony's enemies. By offering Choctaws one gun for every scalp, he "animated them" to take up bounty hunting in 1706, resulting in the delivery of twenty-seven trophies that year alone. Louis XIV made it known once more that he did not wish to incur such expenses in Louisiana, just as he had objected to the scalping program that Frontenac and Champigny implemented a decade earlier in Canada.[55] Despite this pushback from Versailles, Bienville never forgot the usefulness of bounties as a motivator for combat, and he would revisit the strategy years after the disapproving king's death. In August 1721, during his second stint as governor, Bienville assured royal officials that the French alliance with Choctaws remained strong, and this partnership became especially important when hostilities broke out with neighboring Chickasaw and Natchez tribes.[56]

After migrating to the Lower Mississippi River during the precolonial era, Chickasaws emerged as a powerful regional group even though the tribal population of about four thousand was far smaller than that of their Choctaw relatives. The creator, Ababinili, made all Chickasaws from the soil of Earth. Signifying this deep connection to the natural environment, Ababinili consisted of four phenomena known collectively as the Four Beloved Things Above: Sun, Clouds, Clear Sky, He That Lives in the Clear Sky. These spiritual overseers dealt ultimate judgment, deciding whether a deceased person's soul would pass into "a life of joy" with deities in the sacred sky or "a life of torment" among witches in the haunted west. With homelands spanning today's Kentucky, Tennessee, Mississippi, and Alabama, the tribe embraced a "warrior tradition" that tended to cultivate conflict with neighboring groups. To replace those lost in battle, Chickasaws took captives and occasionally absorbed survivors from defeated groups.[57]

Considerably larger in population than the Chickasaws, an estimated six thousand Natchez Indians paid homage to a spiritual ruler called Great Sun, who maintained a sacred perpetual fire for the people to worship. Living in and around the Great Village of Natchez near the Lower Mississippi River, tribe members believed that they descended from a man and woman sent from the Sun to the Earth to "teach us to live better and live in peace among ourselves." They recognized and revered ancestral homelands by offering portions of their annual harvests to Great Sun, and they mourned the death of Sun chiefs through a death ritual involving the sacrifice of one hundred people during a series of strangulations and suicides.[58] Over the ensuing two decades, members of these Chickasaw and Natchez groups would bear the brunt of scalp warfare initiatives in French Louisiana.

While campaigning against Natchez peoples who had recently raided some of the settlements in his jurisdiction, Bienville circumvented central authority in France, recalling prior pushback against the scalp bounty of 1706 and realizing that royal administrators would be unlikely to support his petite guerre methods for waging war against Indians. Instead, he petitioned the local Superior Council of Louisiana for permission to implement a policy that would reward Choctaw compatriots with a musket, one pound of gunpowder, and two pounds of bullets for every scalp they redeemed, as well as 80 livres worth of merchandise for each captive they turned over to French authorities. The commissioners granted approval, declaring that "nothing can encourage better the nation of the Choctaws to carry on vigorously the war against the Chickasaws [and Natchez]."[59] By incorporating scalp warfare into the diplomatic equation, this policy of monetized murder drew on traditional Choctaw conceptualizations of wartime reciprocity and militaristic masculine honor, and it became the basis for future bounty programs in Louisiana even though the distribution of guns, ammunition, and other prizes proved exceedingly expensive.[60]

In 1729, another war with the Natchez tribe rekindled the French reliance on bounties as an incentive for fighting, as they sought Native auxiliaries to offset their own military deficiencies. Writing from New Orleans, Father Mathurin le Petit lamented recent setbacks to the fledgling plantation economy along the Lower Mississippi River. This included a massive Natchez uprising on November 28 that resulted in the deaths of 237 colonists and the captivity of dozens more, as well as another attack during which the Natchez killed two Jesuit priests "who were engaged in the conversion of the Savages." As allies of New France, five hundred Choctaws joined a smaller number of colonial troops and their African slaves in a series of retributive attacks on Natchez villages in the early months of 1730, reclaiming most of the prisoners taken during the initial uprising. Choctaw combatants also confiscated more than one hundred Black slaves from the Natchez tribe to exchange for provisions in the French colonies. Serving as missionary to the Choctaws, le Petit informed Father Louis d'Avaugour, procurator of the missions of North America, that many of these tribal allies had come to New Orleans "to receive payment for the scalps they have taken." In a subtle admission of French weakness on the Mississippi frontier, le Petit stressed that "it is necessary for us to buy very dearly their smallest services." Estimating Choctaw strength at between three thousand and four thousand fighting men, the Jesuit proselytizer understood and appreciated the tribe's hegemonic status in the Southeast. He revealed the racial and cultural prejudices that undergirded his empire's broader colonial project when complaining that the Choctaws with whom he interacted "are insolent, ferocious, disgusting, importunate, and insatiable," but le Petit also realized that Louisiana would be reliant on these formidable and savvy Indians to wage war against the Natchez tribe just as Governors Frontenac and Vaudreuil had depended on Wabanaki Confederacy allies during their conflicts with British colonists and confederated Iroquois in the northeast borderlands.[61] Much as in the policy proceedings at Quebec City during King William's War and Queen Anne's War, dependency on strategic Indigenous partnerships induced French officials at New Orleans and Mobile to implement bounties during wars against the Natchez and Chickasaw tribes, both out of military necessity and as a racialized form of warfare wherein settlers viewed Indigenous enemies as fit for scalping.

In Louisiana, much as in Canada, religious agents served a critical role as methodical middlemen between governors and chiefs, using their influence with mission Indians to solicit the services of tribal warriors as practitioners of extralethal violence. This direct involvement of priests points to the Catholic Church's prominent but unofficial role in the proliferation of scalp warfare across the frontiers of New France. Father Thury pioneered the technique at Saint Lawrence River Valley missions in the early 1700s, when he enlisted hundreds of Abenakis to pillage Iroquois and even some British villages with the promise of rewards for captives and scalps. A generation later, Father le Petit found inspiration in his predecessor's methods, working closely with Chief Paatlako to ensure Choctaw cooperation in the fight against Natchez and Chickasaw enemies on the Louisiana frontier. An unmistakable irony characterized these developments, because moralizing Catholic priests including Thury and le Petit constantly condemned Native people using the racist rhetoric of Indigenous savagery, but they simultaneously encouraged the same Indians to commit heinous acts of mass murder and corporeal mutilation by compensating them for the body parts of despised foes. "Our own people begin to be accustomed to this barbarous spectacle," le Petit conceded in a tacit admission of settlers' approbation for the scalp trade.[62]

From his base at New Orleans, Governor Bienville waged a war against the Chickasaws that mirrored le Petit's uncompromising approach to the Natchez conflict. In April 1735, Chickasaws attacked a detachment of eleven French soldiers, killing or capturing all of them, prompting an infuriated Bienville to begin planning offensive measures against the tribe. He spent the ensuing months greasing the wheels of diplomacy with Choctaw leaders to enlist their cooperation and to ensure that nearby British traders would not interfere with his efforts. Having accomplished these preliminary objectives, he organized 460 French and 100 Swiss fighters at Mobile and marched northward in March 1736, stopping along the way to recruit some 600 Choctaw auxiliaries under Chiefs Red Shoe and Alibamon Mingo. Meanwhile, Pierre d'Artaguette commanded a second army consisting of 145 soldiers and 326 Indian allies, but this contingent was routed on March 25 during an imprudent attack on the Chickasaw settlement of Ogoula Tchetoka. Seeking both revenge and spiritual closure for the families of those killed in battle, Chickasaw leaders at the nearby village of Chuckalissa built two large fires, stripped nineteen prisoners naked, and hurled them helplessly into the flames as a powerful act of violent display that occurred within Indigenous protocols.[63] Two months later, Bienville's column—which was not involved in the fighting at Ogoula Tchetoka—approached the large Chickasaw village of Choukafalya at present-day Tupelo, Mississippi. When the Chickasaws sent out five delegates for a peace parley, Choctaws accompanying Bienville treacherously killed two of them and presented their scalps to the French commander. Like d'Artaguette—who lost his own life in the fighting—Bienville and his allies suffered a major defeat in the ensuing battle and had to retreat to Mobile, where the embarrassed French commander would begin plotting a second campaign into Chickasaw homelands.[64] Whether it involved burning prisoners alive at Chuckalissa or dismembering diplomatic emissaries at Choukafalya, gruesome acts of violent display had come to characterize scalp warfare on the Louisiana frontier just as they did in the Canadian borderlands. Although Indians performed some of this violence for their own purposes—the mass burning of captives at Chuckalissa, for instance, bridged ceremonial motivation with that of revenge for prior killings and scalpings—colonial governors, church leaders, and military officers also played direct roles in the perpetration of extralethal reciprocity among Indigenous peoples because they rewarded such deeds with valuable bounties.

Having suffered significant losses during these campaigns, Choctaws repeatedly raided Chickasaw villages, driven not only by the desire to avenge deceased kin but also by the promise of material gain through plunder, captives, and bounties. In the coming months, intertribal animosity would rise to new levels of intensity. In February 1737, Bienville collected four Chickasaw scalps and one slave from a party of Choctaws that he "induced to go against this hostile nation."[65] Three months later, another French officer doled out rewards for twenty Chickasaw scalps upon delivery at Mobile, informing royal officials that local Choctaw allies "go in little bands of five, ten, twelve, twenty men . . . who will not fail to bring us back scalps."[66] In October, a force of five hundred Choctaws attacked the village at Choukafalya, razing cornfields and riding away with ten scalps. When these men returned home "proud of their success," it inspired another party to march out in pursuit of scalps, and within a few days they added six more to the tally after ambushing a Chickasaw hunting party. In a profound act of violent display intended not just for material gain but also to send an unmistakable message to their enemies, Choctaws returned to the site of the massacre at Choukafalya and disinterred two dead Chickasaws "whose scalps they had not been able to get." After slicing away the prized forelocks to redeem with French officials, they hacked the corpses into pieces and mounted them atop towering wood poles rising eerily from the silent village ruins.[67]

By the time Bienville went afield in July 1739 to seek retribution for the French defeats at Ogoula Tchetoka and Choukafalya, relentless Choctaw raiding had significantly weakened the Chickasaws. Even so, the governor encountered a series of logistical setbacks and failed to engage his enemies, resulting in a tentative peace agreement in January 1740.[68] Reporting on experiences during the Chickasaw War, Bienville, like le Petit before him, expressed a hollow sense of regret at the inhumane tactics that had come to define scalp warfare. When Choctaw associates brought him a collection of enemy scalps taken during recent campaigns, the governor admitted in the privacy of his journal that he "could not refuse them the ammunition and even the payment of hair because it was me who had them start the war."[69] According to one chief who met with British officials in South Carolina, the French constantly encouraged their Indian allies to "go Kill and Destroy, bring us plenty of Hair, plenty of Scalps."[70] Motivated by their own animosity toward neighboring tribes—the Chickasaws had killed well over one thousand Choctaws and captured hundreds more during seventeenth-century raids—as well as the allure of material gain from trading captives and redeeming scalps, Choctaws contributed in a major way to French offensives during the Natchez and Chickasaw Wars.[71] In the process of executing this brand of scalp warfare, Choctaws killed far more Indians than did the French troops under Bienville's command, a point that showcases the utility of paid scalping when effectively implemented through Indigenous alliances.

Bloody conflicts in the Lower Mississippi Valley, which saw the introduction of scalp hunting as a warfare technique in French Louisiana, entered temporary respites just as King George's War erupted in the Northeast in 1744. Bounties once again formed a strategic component of this renewed imperial rivalry—the North American theater of the War of the Austrian Succession—with both sides implementing new legal programs to incentivize civilian and Indigenous combatants. As an example of the effects, a group of Abenakis arrived in Quebec City on August 2, 1748, to collect rewards for one prisoner and a scalp taken during a skirmish near Fort Saint George in the Acadian borderlands. In another instance, an Abenaki war party traveled to Montreal to receive payment for nine scalps and six captives, and a newspaper reported that the tribe would likely carry on this warfare for the foreseeable future because "they have lost warriors and have not yet had the opportunity to take revenge to their satisfaction."[72] The reporter clearly understood the overlap between Indigenous protocols of reciprocity in warfare and the motivation of material gain as manifested in colonial bounty programs.

As part of King George's War, French administrators in Montreal distributed the equivalent of £1,867 in material rewards for 56 scalps between September 1746 and August 1747—an astonishing average of more than £33 (US$6,105 today) per scalp. They paid out another £12,686 for unquantified captives during that same period. At nearby Quebec City, officials gave the equivalent of £4,383 to their Indian allies in exchange for unspecified numbers of scalps and slaves taken during campaigns against the British and the

Iroquois. By January 1748, Governor Roland-Michel Barrin, marquis de La Galissonnière, reported that Indigenous partners had produced more than 150 scalps and 112 prisoners during their raids in New England. The payments, totaling £18,939 (US$3.4 million today), constituted 14 percent of war-related expenses for the year, demonstrating the prominence of bounty-driven scalp warfare. The fact that almost as many prisoners as scalps were presented for payment speaks once more to the labor and intelligence value that French officials saw in their Indian enemies. It also presents an important statistical detail indicating that the French version of scalp warfare, while deadly and brutal, did not rise to the level of genocide. Despite the high monetary costs, regional leaders considered scalp warfare an economical pathway to victory through the petite guerre tradition, realizing that it was still cheaper to disburse material rewards to Native allies than to pay and equip soldiers and militiamen. Following the same rationale as New Netherland governor Willem Kieft a full century earlier, French settlers understood that paid scalping shifted some of the danger associated with frontier combat onto "friendly" Indians who they viewed as dispensable objects in the grand scheme of imperial conquest.[73] Local officials would carry this philosophy into the French and Indian War (Seven Years' War), as French and British forces entered their fourth major clash of the era.

Much like King William's War, Queen Anne's War, and King George's War, the North American theater of this latest global conflict would incorporate scalp warfare as a prominent feature of frontier fighting among French, British, and Indian combatants. In the summer of 1754, a young French soldier stationed at Fort Duquesne described several expeditions—he called them "savage parties"—during which Indigenous allies attacked settlements in North Carolina, Pennsylvania, and Virginia. These campaigns produced "a lot of hair and prisoners," he wrote, recounting one instance when two hundred men returned to the fort to redeem twenty-one scalps and nine captives. The soldier provided an explicit eyewitness account of the steps involved in "raising hair," remarking that a successful bounty hunter "takes his knife and makes an incision around the hair, from the top of the forehead to the mark on the neck; then putting one foot on the victim's shoulder, whose stomach he has turned to the ground, he pulls his hair from behind forward with both hands." With a scalp thus removed from a corpse, the perpetrator "ties it to his belt and continues on his way," making sure to "scratch the skin to clean it of the blood and fibers which are attached." It was not unusual, the Frenchman explained, for a victorious warrior to return to his village with more than a dozen scalps "tied on the same stick," the weight of so many trophies being too much to carry on one's belt. With a hint of disgust, he concluded by acknowledging that both the French and the British had established "a maxim to pay for this hair, up to the amount of thirty francs value in goods," saying that such incentives contributed to the proliferation of extreme violence as tribes took to the warpath in search of scalps and captives to exchange for coveted material goods and to demonstrate masculine valor within their communities.[74]

In less excruciating detail, another French observer reported in 1754 that a group of Abenakis had campaigned in Massachusetts and returned to Montreal with thirty scalps and prisoners, expecting to be rewarded for their services, although the details of this payout were not specified.[75] On March 31, 1756, a mixed party of Abenakis and Mi'kmaqs arrived at the French outpost of Louisbourg on Nova Scotia's Cape Breton Island, bringing news of a devastating raid in New England. The Indigenous perpetrators presented a dozen forelocks to the governor at Quebec City and "were paid for their trip very handsomely," the exact amount again escaping documentation.[76] A year later, in July 1757, 150 French and Native operatives ambushed a party near Fort Lydius, a former fur-trading outpost in New York, supposedly stripping thirty-two scalps from the heads of slain enemies before riding away in triumph.[77] According to Louis Antoine de Bougainville, an aide-de-camp to General Louis-Joseph de Montcalm, marquis de Montcalm, in Canada, the number of people killed in that attack was actually just thirteen, but the Indians had cleverly split those scalps into thirty-two separate pieces before redemption. "They know how to make two or even three [scalps] out of one," Bougainville wrote in his journal, confirming another incident of profit-motivated fraud in scalp hunting.[78]

The following year, French officials learned of a brutal battle near a British outpost called Halfway's Brook, where Indian allies took eight captives and two dozen scalps. The executioners were honored for these deeds at Montreal, where Montcalm had announced rewards of 60 livres per scalp, and he issued presents to ensure that his Indigenous allies remained in a "good mood." No sooner had these rewards been distributed than another party of twenty-three Abenakis arrived with an unspecified number of scalps taken during an attack near Fort Edward in New York.[79] Jean-Baptiste d'Aleyrac, a young French officer who fought in multiple battles during the war and interacted with Abenakis in Quebec, wrote that these Indian allies "kill their prisoners and remove their hair," noting that a 30-livre scalp bounty (about US$500 today) helped to "better excite their ambition."[80] Although France would be forced to relinquish its North American empire in 1763 after losing the global contest with England, these examples illustrate the ongoing use of bounties as a wartime strategy in the colonies, where state sponsorship of scalp warfare augmented more traditional forms of fighting that involved armies and militias.

The bounties that Frontenac and Champigny introduced at Quebec City in the 1690s endured in concept and in practice for the duration of the French colonial project in North America. Although scalp warfare occurred at various times and places, it tended to ebb and flow alongside periodic outbursts in the Franco-Anglo rivalry, becoming a prominent component of the petite guerre tradition that enabled governors, intendants, and military officers to court Native allies such as the Abenakis in the Northeast and the Choctaws in the Southeast. Even during periods of relative peace between New France and New England, however, both regimes sponsored body-part bounties as a communicative form of extralethal violence designed to subjugate and humiliate tribes who stood in the way of European settlement. To varying degrees in Canada and Louisiana, eighteenth-century policymakers attempted to balance accommodationist approaches to Indian diplomacy and trade with the more aggressive imperative of territorial conquest, and in so doing they often deviated from the dictates of royal authority across the Atlantic. As a strategy of cooperation that served the political and economic interests of both the French and their Indian allies, scalp warfare exploited a human impulse for material gain to bridge the dichotomous colonial techniques of accommodation and extermination. In capitals such as Quebec City and New Orleans, royal administrators strategically incorporated Indigenous groups into the framework of colonial imperatives by offering lucrative rewards for killing and scalping, the perpetration of which was performed through acts of extralethal violence that not only served French interests in Canada and Louisiana but also fulfilled Indigenous desires for profit, revenge, and masculine honor. In one of the great paradoxes of French conquest in the Northeast and the Southeast, Abenaki warriors in the Northeast and Choctaw combatants in the Southeast acted complicitly in colonial policies that sought to subjugate other Native groups including the Iroquois, the Chickasaws, and the Natchez.

In both Canada and Louisiana, most bounty hunters were Indians who allied with local French officials for political, diplomatic, and economic reasons. This dynamic of scalp warfare across New France not only sets it apart from other examples described in this book, but also informs our understanding of the conditions under which colonial North American genocides occurred insofar as these scalping initiatives involved Indians as the primary perpetrators of state-sponsored extralethal violence against other Indians. Although this chapter is not a comprehensive accounting of every killing attributable to a French mandate, the evidence presented here suggests that at least four hundred Indians were scalped as a direct result of bounty programs across a span of approximately seven decades. This is a significant number, and the toll should be considered in body counts as well as the individual human tragedy of each life lost. Yet it still constitutes a mere fraction of the overall Indigenous casualties associated with colonization and a similarly small percentage of each tribe's eighteenth-century population. Even if the figure of four hundred deaths were multiplied by a factor of five to account for so many unknowns—those who were injured by scalpers and later succumbed to their wounds; those whose bodies were carried away by friends and family to prevent scalping; firsthand reporting errors; undocumented acts of extralethal violence; and examples omitted here—the resulting total of two thousand deaths would still be statistically low compared to the many thousands of people from these tribes who perished during the same period through disease, famine, displacement, and traditional warfare. For these reasons, it is critical to recognize the horrific demographic, psychological, and spiritual toll that New France's brand of scalp warfare wrought across portions of Native North America, but it is also useful to consider these effects within the splitting approach to genocide studies.

Scalp payouts in the form of specie, guns, and merchandise long outlived Louis XIV, indicating the extent to which outnumbered French settlers relied on strategic alliances with Indians to achieve and strengthen colonial footholds across vast swaths of interior North America.[81] Whereas French scalp bounties were predicated on motivations of material gain and hatred of enemies, officials at Quebec City and New Orleans differed from their British counterparts at places such as Boston and Portsmouth in several important ways. Although both groups viewed Indians through a similar lens of racial and religious prejudice—habitually labeling them "savages" and "barbarians"—local policy variations between these two European empires stemmed in large part from disparate legislative, diplomatic, and military procedures. As was typically the case in militia-based societies, service in the armed forces was compulsory for able-bodied men in Canada and Louisiana. But both of those geographically expansive eighteenth-century colonies had a limited number of Euro-American residents from which to recruit, so fewer civilians were available to fight Indians as independent operatives compared to more densely populated British enclaves such as New Hampshire and Massachusetts. In New France, governors instituted bounties by executive order, whereas New England legislatures conceived and codified scalp laws. In both cases, scalp warfare originated at regional rather than imperial centers of government, but the British would prove even more prolific in their promotion of civilian campaigning and Indian scalping.

TWO

Hunting Scalps in the Atlantic Coast Colonies and Early American Republic

When members of the Massachusetts general assembly approved a scalp act on September 12, 1694, they surely did not envision a thirty-nine-year-old mother being among those to collect payment. Abenakis raided the town of Haverhill on March 15, 1697, killing or capturing at least three dozen inhabitants. Among those kidnapped were Hannah Duston, her newborn baby, Martha, and Mary Neff, a nurse to the mother and child. The three captives were subsequently transferred to the custody of another group of twelve Indians, who apparently underestimated the capabilities of two women, because all of the captors went to sleep one night without posting a guard. As the unsuspecting Abenakis slumbered, Duston and Neff each grabbed a hatchet and sprang into action. With the help of a young boy named Samuel Leonardson, who had already been living in captivity for more than a year, the ladies swiftly killed ten of their lethargic kidnappers. Only two Indians escaped.[1]

It might seem that two women and a boy, alone in the wilderness and drenched in the blood of ten people whom they had hacked to death with handheld weapons, would immediately run to the nearest homestead or settlement to ensure their own safety. But that is not what happened. Thinking of the bounty program that her colony had implemented three years earlier, Duston recognized an opportunity to transform the trauma of her abduction and the death of her baby into a financial windfall. Rather than flee from the horrific scene, she turned her attention to scalping the corpses.

Duston's initial motivation for killing—to secure her freedom and avenge the murder of an infant child—quickly morphed into a profit-driven exercise of extralethal violence. The similarities between Dubosq, chronicled in the previous chapter, and Duston are striking: both taken captive by Indians, both triumphant in midnight counteroffensives with longshot odds, both civilians with an unlikely penchant for corporeal mutilation, both swayed in their actions by the thought of money.

It must have been a shocking spectacle when Duston and her two companions strode into Boston toting the scalps of ten dead Indians. With characteristically racist rhetoric, members of the general assembly lauded the three for "their service in slaying diverse of those barbarous savages" and approved disbursement of a £50 reward. As a woman, Hannah could not legally collect the funds, so her husband accepted payment. The Duston family pocketed half of the money, and the remainder was divided between Neff and Leonardson for their auxiliary roles.[2] In Boston, the influential Puritan minister Cotton Mather preached a sermon praising the three individuals for "Cutting off the Scalps of the ten wretches," crediting "God their Savior" for protecting them under such harrowing circumstances.[3] In a stark twist, the strict Puritan philosophies that demanded saintly behavior in daily life also embraced the killing and postmortem mutilation of Indians whom they viewed as heathens.[4] Indeed Duston became a veritable celebrity, her femininity and motherhood defying societal expectations when it came to fighting Indians and proving that monetary motivation and racialized hatred had no gender limits.[5] Many years later, residents of nineteenth-century New England commemorated Duston by erecting three monuments in her honor, and in so doing they tacitly memorialized scalp warfare and its colonial practitioners.[6]

Most broadly, Duston's scalping of ten Abenakis at the end of the seventeenth century popularized bounty hunting in New England. In the years following her notorious deed, Massachusetts would implement more so-called scalp acts than any other legislature, and colonies such as New Hampshire, New York, Pennsylvania, and Virginia followed suit as the eighteenth century progressed. Along with similar scalping policies enacted across France's inland North American empire, the widespread implementation of bounties along the northern Atlantic Coast and across the English/British colonies perpetuated an aggressive, profit-driven form of scalp warfare that went beyond the more fundamental objectives of conquest through regular army and militia operations. State commodification of scalps and captives, and the concomitant sanction of extralethal violence and violent display, demonstrates that interconnected economic and racial impulses drove these policies and actions. As time went on, English/British lawmakers extended bounty programs to militia units, hoping that eligibility for rewards would equate to increased enlistments, and this legal structure indicated that policymakers drew clear distinctions between independent civilian bounty hunters and the men who served more formally in local militias. With the enactment of bounties, frontier conflict took on broader racial and economic meaning as some settlers temporarily abandoned their longtime trades in favor of an occupation that entailed killing Indians, plundering their villages, and redeeming body parts for cash payouts and material goods.[7]

Despite the ubiquity of bounty laws in the English/British colonies, decades of scalp warfare produced relatively few quantifiable deaths and desecrations. Although the exterminatory rhetoric directed toward Indian tribes aligned with genocide's definitional intent to eliminate a racial or ethnic group, the actual outcome of English/British scalp warfare in terms of body counts does not meet even the lowest statistical thresholds for the occurrence of genocide. The vagueness of historical records—including periodic allusions to "hundreds of scalps" hanging in villages and "collections of scalps" adorning the walls of courthouses and other public buildings—suggests that far more Indians were scalped than the documented cash redemptions indicate. But even so, the number of persons killed as a direct result of scalp warfare in the English/British colonies could not be more than a few thousand across the entire eighteenth century, a time when tens and perhaps even hundreds of thousands of Indians in that region perished through disease, displacement, and traditional warfare. The English/British brand of scalp warfare did not rely as heavily on Indian allies as proxies, but it still took a terrible toll on Indigenous victims and their families, and this state-sponsored extralethal violence formed an important element of colonial conquest. In New England as in New France, these outcomes should be understood through a splitting approach to Native American genocide.

Puritan settlers first began scalping Indians during the Pequot War (1636–38), when dismemberment of bodies became a common practice, and they did so again forty years later during King Philip's War, but in both cases combatants acted primarily for communicative purposes and not in coordinated response to a government's financial incentives.[8] Instances of violent display characterized these two conflicts—the Puritans, for instance, mounted decapitated Indian heads atop poles as a threat to would-be attackers and to celebrate their own triumphs—and laid the groundwork for future monetization of such extralethal practices. In 1676, Benjamin Church drew on prior experiences fighting Wampanoags and Narragansetts by forming one of the first colonial volunteer companies outside the traditional structures of a state militia. Believing that citizens "must make a business of the war," Church enlisted Indigenous allies to train and guide his men as they raided and pillaged enemy Indian camps. In so doing, he helped to develop scalp warfare techniques that would later accompany bounty hunting in New England and New France.[9] When Massachusetts Bay Colony legislators formulated a preliminary scalp law in July 1689, near the beginning of King William's War, they were mimicking the French enactment of a similar bounty one year earlier, but they also may have been thinking back to vicious wars with the Pequots and Wampanoags, and some of them surely had Willem Kieft's Dutch model in mind, too. That Church's experimental volunteer company experienced some success while patrolling the New England frontier a decade earlier nudged the legislators further in the direction of scalp warfare, and the lawmakers also drew inspiration from the prior implementation of wolf carcass bounties that paid the equivalent of one month's salary for the average town laborer.[10] The direct connection between killing predatory animals and murdering enemy Indians, with profiteering as the common thread, demonstrates the racialized ways in which English/British colonists viewed their Indigenous counterparts as subhuman. Reciprocity formed another key rationalization for extralethal violence and corporeal mutilation: English/British colonists were always quick to point out that Indians scalped people, too—the classic "they started it" argument—and indeed the documentary record is replete with examples of Indigenous fighters decapitating or otherwise disfiguring enemy corpses, sometimes for their own cultural purposes and other times for colonial agents offering them material compensation.[11]

In 1694—just one year after paranoid Puritans executed nineteen accused witches at Salem—colonial leaders codified a new bounty system that incentivized scalp warfare to encourage aggression against frontier enemies. Englishmen also sought methods for subjugating or punishing Indians who allied with French forces during King William's War. In the early stages of that conflict, Abenakis joined Mohawk and Algonquin warriors and French combatants in a series of campaigns that devastated the towns of Schenectady in New York, Salmon Falls in New Hampshire, and Casco Bay in Maine. The Eastern Abenakis entered a peace agreement with English settlers in 1693 despite concerted French attempts to sabotage diplomacy, but their Western Abenaki relatives carried on the fight.[12] To retaliate against Indigenous groups who abetted French interests, the Massachusetts general assembly offered rewards to volunteer fighters "for every Indian, great or small, which they shall kill, or take and bring in prisoner." Legislators originally set the price at £50 in colonial currency for each Indian, regardless of age or sex, but an amendment the following year reduced the amount to £25 for women and children under the age of fourteen.[13] This marked an important development in the nature of bounties, because legislators began to differentiate between Indian men—whose scalps they placed at a higher price— and women or children, who would be worth less and whose lives might therefore be spared in view of their value as captives. On June 16, 1696, assemblymen approved a complementary law that offered provisions, ammunition, and wages to anybody who rode against enemy Indians. Commonly referred to as "volunteers," these civilians would still be allowed to claim the stipulated rewards as a bonus, but all trophies and captives had to be delivered to a war commission for verification before approval of payouts.[14] In New England, scalp warfare developed as a tactical strategy wherein local administrators sought to capitalize on racial hatred of Indians as well as pre-existing intertribal animosities during times of greater military necessity, usually correlating to flareups in the ongoing Anglo-Franco rivalry.

Lawmakers revised their scalp laws on a regular basis, each time addressing fluid conditions of alliance or conflict with neighboring tribes and colonial rivals. After King William's War ended in 1697, a resurgence in bounty hunting coincided with renewed imperial clashes beginning in May 1702. As Queen Anne's War erupted across the New England and Acadian borderlands, the Massachusetts assembly passed a new act on November 16, 1703, allowing £10 (US$1,993 today) for every dead Indian over ten years of age. Before any payment, each trophy had to be examined and authenticated as a "bona fide Scalp of an Indian Enemy kill'd in fight," and any person caught presenting counterfeit hair—defined as that of a "friendly" Indian, in the racialized parlance of the times—would be subject to unspecified penalties. The small £10 reward failed to motivate colonists to partake in the dangers of scalp warfare, so the legislature amended the law two weeks later by making New Hampshire residents eligible to participate, raising the scalp price to £40 (US$7,973 today), and allowing captive Indian children to be sold into slavery as another form of financial incentive. This adjusted code yielded six rewards of £40 each, one disbursed to Richard Billing and Samuel Field for an Indian they slew in a fight at Deerfield in January 1704, and five more to Captain Tyng for scalps that his party took during a winter campaign. Hoping to build on these preliminary killings, the assembly boosted the price once more, to an unprecedented £100 per scalp.[15] With such substantial profits on the line, soldiers of fortune took the field throughout 1704, but only two groups collected any money. In June the Massachusetts treasury paid Johnathan Wells and Ebenezer Wright for one scalp that they took during a campaign against Indians and their French allies at Deerfield, and in October another premium went to John Shipley and Samuel Butterfield for a man killed and scalped at Groton. In both instances, the claimants kept all plunder taken during their outings as additional compensation.[16] The tribal affiliation of these scalped Indians escaped historical records, but administrators must have believed that they were enemy Abenakis since they issued rewards. Moreover, the eight redeemed scalps surely represent only a tiny percentage of an unknown number of Indian casualties during the corresponding two-year period in which they were taken. The results of this renewed bounty system, while fulfilling a rhetorical objective of extermination on the part of local English lawmakers, did not by default equate to genocide when one considers that the Abenaki population totaled some ten thousand persons at that time.[17]

Residents of neighboring New Hampshire watched these developments with keen interest, and Governor Joseph Dudley implored his own provincial council to emulate the Massachusetts example even though it produced just eight scalps over two years. On January 20, 1704, just as Captain Tyng collected his bounties in Boston, five assemblymen in the New Hampshire capital of Portsmouth agreed to a premium of £32 per Indian without specification of tribe, age, or gender. With their colony's participation in scalp warfare officially underway, government officials immediately notified three local commanders—Captains Shadrach Walton, Winthrop Hilton, and John Gilman—of the new law so that they could begin recruiting volunteers. Although bounties were paid to Robert Thompson for one scalp and to another unnamed individual for an Indian killed on the Oyster River, the leaders of New Hampshire found themselves disappointed with the overall results and were clearly expecting much higher body counts and far more civilian participants.[18] Samuel Penhallow, an English migrant who sat on the provincial assembly at the time, admitted that the bounty program "at first seemed a great encouragement, but it did not answer what we expected." He lamented that the perceived Indian threat to New England was not eliminated or even noticeably diminished, concluding that the promise of rewards failed to produce the colonial government's desired outcome of Indian extermination.[19]

Scalp warfare was an incredibly risky undertaking, not only because it meant direct confrontation with armed Indians who could—and almost always did—defend themselves in a fight, but also because it was expensive to recruit and maintain a private army of volunteers. This explains why the Massachusetts assembly had to keep increasing bounty prices and also why so few men responded to New Hampshire's initial offering in 1704. The prevailing hatred of nonallied Indians was not by itself enough to induce most men to take up arms, nor did £10 or even £32 per trophy make it worth the effort and risk. But at a £100 rate, more people heeded the call because triumphant expeditions could reap handsome rewards. Even so, not all scalp hunters succeeded, and some suffered significant financial losses as a result of their failures. In 1704, Lewis Bane petitioned the Massachusetts assembly seeking reimbursement for the costs of provisioning his twelve-man excursion, even though he did not hand over a single scalp. Wary of discouraging other aspiring bounty hunters, the government approved his claim and wrote it off as one of the many costs of doing business with an unsavory lot of fortune seekers performing the state's work of conquest.[20] Bane and his battalion may have avoided a total financial loss, but they had nothing to show in profits for several weeks of campaigning, and such a fruitless outcome must have caused other would-be operatives to think twice before committing themselves to scalp warfare in place of their regular income-producing occupations.

This expensive new precedent for covering the various costs of failed paramilitary operations did little to dampen the enthusiasm of legislators, most of whom continued to support scalping schemes despite the rising burden on taxpayers. On December 30, 1704, Massachusetts lawmakers expanded the program by extending eligibility to enlisted soldiers and militiamen who previously could not claim cash rewards for Indian body parts. This extension owed largely to the relative lack of visible results from civilian bounty hunters and the corresponding belief among local officials that they needed to enlist more participants if scalp warfare was to achieve the desired outcome of extermination. The structural change to scalp laws also signaled a major transformation in the underlying philosophy of a bounty system because, unlike civilian volunteers, those in the militia already drew a salary from the treasury. In addition to their regular pay of 2 shillings per week, privates could now collect a reward for each scalp presented to authorities.[21] Taken collectively, state-funded reimbursement for supplies and bonus payments to soldiers and militiamen forced the assembly to tweak its graduated pay scale. Regular troops working on salary would receive £10 per scalp, while militiamen—whose paychecks were substantially less—could claim £20 per scalp. Unsalaried civilian volunteers were allowed £100 for each Indian killed, but this amount was reduced to £60 if they sought reimbursement for campaign costs.[22] This prevented bounty hunters from double-dipping to claim both the £100 premium for a scalp and remuneration for their outfitting expenses. Governor Dudley explained the program to London's Council of Trade and Plantations in 1709, telling the royal administrators that he "set the Indian rebels' heads at £100 each" as a retributive response to French bounties that offered similar payouts on Iroquois scalps.[23] The scalp laws of 1704 in Massachusetts demonstrated that local officials drew strict distinctions among soldiers, militiamen, and volunteers as three categories of militant operatives. The nature and practice of scalp warfare thus forced legislators to acknowledge and embrace an independent type of paramilitary campaigning that fell outside traditional European views of combat.

Massachusetts operated under these parameters for the duration of Queen Anne's War, but only a handful of individuals collected payouts, and none exceeded half a dozen scalps at one time. Even though existing records paint an incomplete picture of scalp warfare's demographic toll on targeted tribes, the number of Indians killed as a direct result of these earliest English bounty programs likely did not exceed a few hundred, and even then the majority of those casualties must not have actually been scalped because very few rewards were distributed. For the first two decades of its standardized bounty system, the Massachusetts assembly relied on colonists to take the field on their own initiative. That strategy changed on June 5, 1711, when a new act called for state recruitment of forty men for the explicit purpose of marching into the backcountry "to annoy the enemy there." Drawing a salary of 20 shillings per week, the new group of volunteers would be more than just another militia unit, because the mandate calling for their enlistment also encouraged them to take scalps at the rate of £10 each. The line between scalp warfare and traditional military operations was beginning to blur at the interstices of racial hatred and extralethal violence. State leaders now issued a blunt order for the formation of a salaried cohort of scalpers who were not explicitly defined as militia.[24] Despite their paychecks from the government, these operatives remained paramilitaries and thus retained a high level of autonomy that would not have applied to a state-regulated army or militia. One year after the revised scalp law of 1711, the assembly raised wages for its bounty hunters by 6 pence per diem and increased the reward sixfold, but these developments came near the end of Queen Anne's War, and as the imperial conflict cooled, so did the administrative impetus to underwrite scalp warfare.[25]

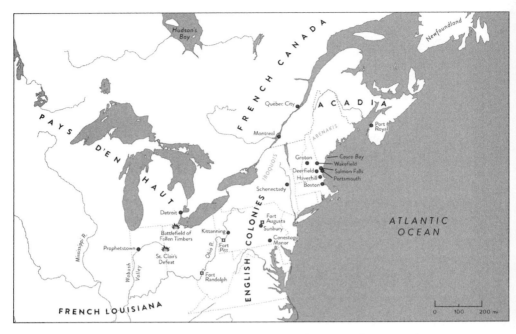

The English colonies and the Acadian borderlands. Map by Erin Greb.

The larger imperial contest between England and France had temporarily abated, but the blatant omission of the Eastern and Western Abenaki, Maliseet, Mi'kmaq, and Passamaquoddy nations from the Utrecht agreement ending Queen Anne's War in 1713, along with increasing British settlement of Ndakinna—the traditional Abenaki homelands—ensured that regional conflicts between Natives and settlers would periodically flare up.[26] Focusing their attention on Wabanaki Confederacy enemies who had fought alongside the French, New Englanders made a concerted effort to enlist the services of Cayuga, Mohawk, Oneida, Onondaga, and Seneca (Five Nations) allies in the bounty hunting scheme, especially once Governor Samuel Shulte and Lieutenant Governor William Dummer of Massachusetts commenced a new war with Indians in 1722.[27] Calling themselves Haudenosaunee, or "People of the Longhouse," these five Iroquoian-speaking tribes—whose homelands stretched southward and eastward from Great Lakes shores and bordered Ndakinna—cemented their enduring alliance sometime between 1450 and 1600, well before any involvement in contests between New England and New France. According to Iroquois oral tradition, the confederation of tribes originated when a Huron prophet named Deganawidah tried to calm the war-torn Iroquois homelands by converting an Onondaga man known as Hiawatha from a killer to a pacifist. After his personal transformation, Hiawatha preached the message of harmony and tranquility to Tadadaho, another powerful Onondaga so rage-filled that snakes protruded Medusalike from his head. Together these two reformed leaders founded a league of tribal nations to spread peace in place of violence. Numbering about ten thousand individuals at the beginning of the seventeenth century, the Iroquois Confederacy included expert diplomatists and skilled fighters who formed a powerful Indigenous bulwark against European expansion. Their size and influence forced colonial officials to forego the preferred Indian policies of conquest, and British settlers instead used bounty systems as one method of incorporating the tribes' men into scalp warfare against the despised French and their Wabanaki Confederacy allies in Canada and Acadia.[28]

At Dummer's bidding, the Massachusetts assembly formulated a treaty with the Five Nations (which became the Six Nations once they took in Tuscarora refugees) in January 1723, encouraging their participation in armed campaigns against the French and Abenakis. As the British recognized the critical role of strategic alliances and sought to mimic the French incorporation of Indian allies, the confederacy's fighters would now be eligible to collect bounty payments, provided that two or more colonial representatives spoke as witnesses on their behalf when presenting the prizes to a supervisory council. Legislators thus hoped that Iroquois practitioners of scalp warfare would "heartily Join with us in the War, Wee are Entered into" against the Wabanaki Confederacy nations and their principal leader Grey Lock.[29] Massachusetts also began to pass special scalp acts for individual parties, eschewing the deployment of traditional militias by allowing volunteers to operate by commission after negotiating their own terms with the local government. This state-sponsored contract killing became the favored option for those inclined to lead groups of fortune seekers, because it placed the financial burden of supplies and subsistence squarely on the legislature while guaranteeing a regular salary for participants, even if they did not kill a single Indian during the term of employment. For British bounty hunters, this was a smarter approach because it created a legally binding contract with the government, minimized financial risks, and ensured a base pay for everyone involved. This hybridized approach blurred the boundaries among traditional armed forces, militias, and paramilitaries, and bounties thus became a veritable bonus for success, although these special terms benefited only colonial volunteers. Iroquois allies did not enjoy the same recognition within the Massachusetts legal system and thus could not directly negotiate scalping contracts with local officials, a point that underscores the racialized marginalization that Indigenous groups faced despite their crucial roles in scalp warfare.

One expedition that took advantage of these contract killing laws involved John Lovewell, Josiah Farewell, and Jonathan Robbins. These three individuals petitioned the Massachusetts assembly in November 1724, asking that their party be paid 2 shillings, 6 pence per diem plus £100 for every scalp redeemed, and they also insisted that the government loan guns to Indian auxiliaries who would join them as guides. Having just doled out one bounty to Noah Ashley of Westfield and another to Jacob Ames of Groton, all while praising "the good service done this province," the legislators enthusiastically approved this latest request and sent the team afield with best wishes.[30] With a lucrative state contract in hand, Lovewell had little trouble recruiting and outfitting a company of thirty men to march with him. On December 19, 1724, his volunteers encountered two unsuspecting Indians who had separated from their larger clan while foraging. For Lovewell and his followers, this was an ideal scenario that played perfectly into the treachery of their ilk: two people simply could not defend themselves against thirty armed men. The bounty hunters sprang into action, killing the man and imprisoning his younger companion. They returned to Boston with the adult scalp and the boy captive, collecting a total of £150 from the lieutenant governor. Based on these quick results, Lovewell easily raised another company at the town of Dunstable, where eighty-seven new recruits flocked to his command as participants in what became known as Dummer's War. The volunteers departed for the frontier on January 29, 1725, and three weeks later they located a camp of ten Indians near present-day Wakefield, New Hampshire. "Not one escaped alive," Lovewell bragged in his campaign diary. They returned to Boston on March 9 to collect payment, which amounted to more than £1,000 in bounties plus regular wages for five weeks in the field and plunder confiscated from the campsite.[31] The expedition yielded a small fortune, but the triumph would be short-lived for Lovewell, who perished two months later while attacking an Abenaki village near Pequawket in Maine. With dozens of warriors swarming around them, the same band of cutthroats that once enjoyed overwhelming advantages when ambushing outnumbered parties of two and ten Indians now found themselves on the wrong end of the odds game. Only twelve of the forty-seven scalp hunters survived the affair, and the triumphant Abenakis mutilated Lovewell's corpse in a symbolic act of reciprocity.[32] His gruesome fate made it clear that extralethal violence could cut both ways, and Indigenous targets were perfectly capable and willing to counteract colonial aggression through equally shocking acts of violent display that reinforced mutual animosities undergirding scalp warfare. Lovewell had become New England's most prolific bounty hunter, and martyrdom at the age of thirty-three situated him alongside Hannah Duston in local lore.

Lieutenant Governor Dummer agreed to a ceasefire on July 31, 1725, and within a year two treaties had been negotiated with sachems representing the Wabanaki Confederacy.[33] British settlers thus attempted to assert greater control over the maritime Acadian frontier, where French settlers and their Indian allies still made up over 90 percent of the population, and this latest phase of violence cycled into a tenuous peace.[34] Although the Massachusetts colony never rescinded existing scalp acts—a clear indication that hatred of Indian enemies never really went away—eighteen years would pass without the codification of any new bounty laws. Once imperial rivalries cooled and Indigenous enemies either negotiated treaty terms or relocated beyond settlement zones, government leaders saw little reason to disburse large sums of money to opportunistic Indian hunters. This relatively long global peace between England and France lasted until the eruption of King George's War in 1744. With the flames of imperial rivalry fanned anew, the Massachusetts and New Hampshire assemblies reinstated scalp laws annually as part of a broader war effort against France and its Indigenous auxiliaries, who were similarly incentivized through scalp warfare.

New Hampshire took the lead in implementing bounties at the onset of King George's War, recognizing that more than six hundred Mohawk and Abenaki Indians had already allied with French officials at Montreal and Quebec City.[35] In response to Governor Benning Wentworth's inquiry about "what Premium I may promise for scalp money," the legislature issued a mandate on May 24, 1744, that allowed civilians to claim £50 per Indian scalp, while salaried soldiers would receive just £5 each. They instructed Wentworth to call up a company of volunteers "to hunt and seek the Indians where they can find them, and take or destroy them."[36] The first new act in Massachusetts came on October 25 of that year. It pledged £100 for the scalp of a male Indian over the age of twelve and £105 for a captive man, while women and children were worth £50 dead or £55 alive. Neighboring New Hampshire eventually adopted an identical pricing scheme. These revised bounties marked a significant departure from previous codes in the two New England colonies, because they expanded the reward structure to include captives and offered larger amounts for the living than the dead. Such a transition in administrative strategizing indicated that local British officials, like their counterparts in New France, had begun to see value in the unfree labor as well as the strategic intelligence that surviving Indians might be forced to provide. These bounty acts of 1744 represented the first known instance in either New France or the British colonies that a substantial payout was promised for a captive rather than a dead Indian warrior. This was an important legal and strategic development, insofar as it indicated another shift away from attempted extermination by allowing for the enslavement rather than the murder of adult male enemies. Within the parameters of King George's War, these provisions applied only to those tribes allied with the French and not to ostensibly neutral or uninvolved groups, and the colonial government notified members of the Six Nations (Iroquois) who remained on amicable terms that they must not range past a stipulated "boundary line" beyond which all Indians would be considered hostile.[37]

A year and a half later Massachusetts extended this system to militiamen, enabling them to claim £75 per male scalp and £37 pounds each for women and children. Once again, New Hampshire followed suit with similar valuations. Under these terms, Captain Eleazar Melvin secured a state contract to recruit two hundred men for six months, entitling each participant to an enlistment bonus of 25 shillings, a monthly salary of 25 shillings, and weekly allowances of 5 shillings for provisions plus incentives for redeeming Indian scalps.[38] The Massachusetts assembly broadened this initiative even further by raising another party of sixty contract killers to operate alongside more than eight hundred enlisted soldiers. This hybridized tactic meshed scalp warfare with traditional military approaches to frontier conflict in the same way that previous generations of New Englanders had done during Queen Anne's War and Dummer's War. This put intense pressure on regional tribes as colonists temporarily abandoned their normal avocations to participate in a potentially lucrative but sanguinary commerce in capturing and killing Indians.[39]

Although many people responded to the legislature's call for civilian campaigners, some New England officials grumbled that the reinvigorated scalping program "has been found ineffectual," a point that came into stark relief when French commander Rigaud de Vaudreuil led seven hundred French Canadians and Indian allies in the capture of Fort Massachusetts on August 20, 1746. This devastating counterattack showed local leaders that their use of scalp warfare was not adequately vanquishing Indigenous enemies who maintained alliances with New France, nor was it discouraging acts of reciprocal extralethal violence. Rather than lower their expectations or concede defeat, however, local officials simply raised the premium on scalps. Beginning in April 1747, unwaged volunteers in Massachusetts could collect £250 for each Indian killed west of Nova Scotia, while salaried militiamen and soldiers would receive £100 per trophy. In a striking move that underscored the ruffian nature of scalp warfare, the assembly sweetened the deal by purchasing barrels of rum for its bounty hunters.[40] One French officer, Charles de la Boische, marquis de Beauharnois, complained directly to Massachusetts governor William Shirley in July, saying that the new scalping initiative should be abolished immediately because innocent settlers would become targets of retributive measures. But this plea went unheeded in the British colonies, and both sides continued to offer bounties for the duration of King George's War.[41]

As if to spite Marquis de Beauharnois for his galling request, New Hampshire increased its scalp premium to an astronomical £400, with the caveat that claimants must possess a bounty-hunting warrant from the governor. Portsmouth's council revealed the racial hatred that undergirded state sanction of extralethal violence by refusing to make any distinction between living or dead, young or old, male or female; nor did the members bother to identify any specific tribes as "friendly" or "unfriendly."[42] Although scalp codes in these two New England colonies often mirrored each other in terms of pricing and eligibility, New Hampshire's laws reflected a stronger commitment to extermination based on the universal inclusion of all Indians as eligible targets, and it also represented a stark reversal of the laws of 1744 that incentivized the capture more than the killing of adult male Indians. Still, fortune seeking remained far more common than the achievement of fortune: by August of that year only one man in Massachusetts—John Beaman of Northfield—had redeemed a scalp for payment.[43] This dearth of results did not, however, discourage Captain Melvin from seeking another bounty arrangement "to go after the Indian enemy for four months," nor did it prevent Isaac Waldron, Jonathan Longfellow, and Sam Walton from negotiating similar agreements to raise their own paramilitary groups. Waldron contracted with the Massachusetts assembly to lead an expedition of two hundred volunteers in pursuit of Abenakis, "or any Other, that in a hostile manner shall oppose them," while Longfellow and Walton struck separate deals with the New Hampshire council "to go out after the Indians upon the Scalp Bounty."[44] The vagueness of these arrangements is noteworthy, indicating that the scalp hunters were ready and willing to kill any Indian they could find and that the legislators involved had no concern for the semantics of tribal affiliation or allied status.

New Hampshire and Massachusetts continued to promote scalping expeditions into the early years of the French and Indian War, during which their longtime Wabanaki Confederacy enemies raided villages and fought colonists with impunity.[45] Although militias constituted a primary method of enlistment during the war, New Hampshire supplemented this more traditional form of military operation by implementing another bounty law on July 5, 1755. This new edict declared Indigenous neighbors "Enemys, rebells & traiters," offered

£250 for their scalps, and called on "all His Majesty's subjects of this Province . . . to embrace all opportunitys of pursuing, captivating, killing and destroying all and every of the aforesaid Indians."[46] That same year, when the Penobscots refused to join Massachusetts paramilitary units, the colonial government declared them "rebels and enemies" and simply added them to the list of intended targets.[47] Farther south, Virginia's House of Burgesses raised three companies of volunteers and promised recruits £10 for the scalp of every Indian over age twelve. Lieutenant Governor Robert Dinwiddie admitted the barbarity of this tactic, but he tried to justify it by saying that French commanders were already issuing similar bounties and suggesting that he was merely keeping pace with the evolving dictates of scalp warfare. Enlisting four hundred allied Catawbas, Cherokees, and Tuscaroras to accompany the paramilitary operatives, Dinwiddie "order'd 'em out to . . . protect our front'rs and go a scalping agreeable to the French custom." Virginia would raise the price to £15 per scalp before discontinuing the program in 1758, when Dinwiddie's gubernatorial successor, Francis Fauquier, realized that contract killers were targeting neutral and even some "friendly" Indians and thus pushing otherwise unthreatening groups into alliances with the French in Canada.[48] From Fauquier's perspective, scalp bounties backfired on the colonies because, like the French officer Marquis de Beauharnois, he saw that his own Virginia constituents were falling victim to lethal retributive measures.

Another reason the Virginia governor shied away from paid scalping midway through the French and Indian War involved the murderous campaigning of Major Robert Rogers. After his parents died during an Abenaki raid, a vengeful Rogers became one of the most notorious British practitioners of scalp warfare tactics. He commanded a cohort of volunteers who plied the countryside for more than a year before John Campbell, 4th Earl of Loudoun, and commander-in-chief of the British North American army, ordered a moratorium on scalp payments in November 1756. Schooled in the British tradition of regular warfare, Loudoun had initially looked past his personal repugnance for scalping, but when aides informed him that "White Devil" Rogers and his men were four times more expensive than regular troops, the British commander decided that he could no longer tolerate the practice.[49] At the same time, local leaders in Massachusetts and New Hampshire also soured on their enthusiasm for scalp warfare—councilmen in Boston and Portsmouth had always complained about the system's failure to fully conquer enemy tribes—and neither entity passed another act or paid another bounty after Loudoun's mandate of 1756. Three years later, acting outside the parameters of an official government edict, Major General Jeffrey Amherst dispatched one hundred men to the Connecticut River Valley, where Abenakis "with a design of getting scalps" continued to raid settlements and camps at the encouragement of French bounty programs. On October 6, 1759, volunteers executed a devastating raid on the large Abenaki village at Saint Francis Xavier, where Rogers previously claimed to have counted six hundred scalps dangling from wooden poles, although reports do not indicate if any Abenaki scalps were taken during the attack. This British triumph, along with ongoing settler encroachment, military conflict, and state-sponsored extralethal violence, forced many Abenakis to flee the ancestral homelands of Ndakinna, and the final departure of their defeated French allies from the Saint Lawrence River Valley after the French and Indian War induced many tribe members to seek refuge farther north in Canada.[50]

Throughout these decades of scalp warfare in the borderlands of New England and New France, the general lack of quantifiable success in the form of redeemable body parts emerged as a consistent theme. This simple reality reveals one of the main intents behind ostensibly lucrative bounty laws. Settlers who sensed an opportunity for lump-sum payouts often responded in a predictable way, seeking access to what seemed to be easy money. Regional lawmakers cleverly exploited this human impulse for material gain to their advantage, creating a profit opportunity that enticed scores of their constituents into taking up arms against any and all Indians who threatened projects of settlement and development. In so doing, colonial officials achieved one of their primary objectives, shifting the burdens of frontier defense onto the civilian population in order to minimize reliance on a large standing army or militia. To be sure, policymakers remained ready, willing, and even enthusiastic when it came to paying scalp bounties, but in their overall strategy for waging war against Indians they also realized that the possibility of massive payouts was more important than the actual disbursement of them. Even though the total number of body parts redeemed under

Massachusetts and New Hampshire law did not exceed one hundred over the entire eighteenth century, the extralethal violence of scalp warfare still had a profound impact, because persistent campaigning and indiscriminate killing gradually diminished Indigenous power and forced most tribes to evacuate the region. Civilians acting at the behest of their local governments complemented militia units and regular soldiers when it came to fighting Native peoples, although these combined forces failed to defeat their enemies with the efficiency and rapidity that the assemblymen hoped for, and their impatience manifested itself in numerous revisions to the scalp codes that ratcheted the prices to stunning amounts.[51]

For many decades, scalp warfare in the New England backcountry ebbed and flowed alongside the olive branch and the sword. As a profitable enterprise, scalping Indians depended largely on the existence of imperial conflicts in which confederated Indian tribes allied with either the French or the English/British, and indeed these Native fighters participated in many state-sponsored acts of killing. In Massachusetts and New Hampshire, both of which stood at the vanguard of English/British interests in these conflicts, the bounty system peaked four times, in direct correlation with King William's War (1688–97), Queen Anne's War (1702–13), Dummer's War (1722–25), and King George's War (1744–48). During these momentous periods of conflict in the northeast borderlands, neither the English/British nor the French nor any Indian confederacy or tribe could effectively dominate the scene, forcing desperate actors to rely more heavily on treacherous forms of scalp warfare. This does not mean that disputes between colonists and Indians existed only within larger imperial confrontations, because localized incidents of extralethal violence and violent display recurred throughout the long colonial era. But scalp warfare clearly proliferated as a tactic during periodic crescendos in the Anglo-Franco rivalry. By midcentury, most Indians in New England and Acadia had either succumbed to the unrelenting pressures of conflict, disease, and settlement or relocated outside of those provinces. But scalp hunters, well accustomed to the transient nature of their trade, followed Indian adversaries to more westerly colonies such as New York and Pennsylvania, where legislators embraced the Massachusetts and New Hampshire models in the latter half of the eighteenth century.

New York's colonial council began to embrace scalp warfare during King George's War, and its first bounty act thus coincided with those of neighboring New Hampshire and Massachusetts.[52] "Whereas the Cruel & Barbarous Practice of Scalping our Inhabitants has been begun and carried on by the French & Indians in their Alliance," the general assembly resolved on February 27, 1746, "this Colony find themselves under an absolute necessity in Retaliation to Pursue the same Methods." Adopting the metaphorical eye-for-an-eye approach, Albany legislators repeatedly emphasized retaliatory intent, insisting that they sanctioned "that Inhuman Practice of Scalping" only because Native and French provocateurs had already been doing the same. New Yorkers encouraged Iroquois allies to join in a bounty war against any Indians allied with France, and payout amounts ranged from £5 colonial currency for the forelocks of juveniles to £20 for adult male prisoners. In a notable departure from previous laws in New England, this one set the minimum age for scalping at sixteen rather than twelve, omitted rewards for captive children, and placed no value on women.[53] At least two coteries of bounty hunters capitalized on this new arrangement despite its more restrictive legal structure. In April 1747, a treasurer in New York City expended £155 for "Prisoners and Scalps of the Enemy," and again in April 1748 the provincial assembly earmarked £365 for Indian scalps "taken by Parties Sent out from this Colony the last Summer for Annoyance of the Enemy." Mathematically, these rates suggest that the first redemption for £155 included seven adult male scalps at £20 each and three scalps of women or children at £5 each, while the second redemption likely entailed eighteen male scalps and one woman or child scalp to equal the £365 sum. In both instances, the exact number of redemptions went unrecorded, and legislative approval for payouts was buried within a laundry list of annual expenses—£30 to buy the lawmakers a "Gauger of Liquors," £30 to pay the waiter, and £20 for the doorman's salary—showing just how routine the scalping system had become in the everyday political affairs of colonial leaders who dealt with these Indigenous and imperial conflicts.[54]

In the mid-1750s, Pennsylvania also joined the list of colonies participating in scalp warfare, instituting the practice during the same year that Massachusetts discontinued its long-running program. This marked a tactical shift away from the cautious diplomacy with Indians that attended the first eight decades of Pennsylvania's colonial existence, a period sometimes called "the long peace."[55] Like its New England neighbors, Pennsylvania instituted bounty programs in direct correlation with three broader conflicts: the French and Indian War (1754–63), Pontiac's War (1763–66), and the American Revolution (1775–83). In response to Indian raids on Lancaster and Berks Counties in November 1755, Governor Robert Hunter Morris announced the colony's first reward of 700 Spanish pieces-of-eight or "Spanish dollars" (equivalent at the time to about £175, or US$32,000 today) for the heads of Shingas and Captain Jacobs, two Delaware chiefs implicated in the attacks. During a preliminary meeting in January 1756, a board of commissioners called on Captain Isaac Wayne (father of the famous American general "Mad" Anthony Wayne) to lead a party of fifty volunteers who would receive 40 pieces-of-eight for each Indian scalped.[56] The board met again on April 9, 1756, to discuss formal allocation of the funds in Pennsylvania's £60,000 defense budget, which included an official bounty system that the governor advertised via public proclamation.[57] Realizing that the aggressive new law might cause targeted Indians to retaliate on surrounding settlements, Morris also wrote a letter of justification to New York governor Charles Hardy, saying that "these measures seem to me right."[58] Richard Peters, an Anglican minister and member of the Pennsylvania governor's council who played a prominent role in strategic planning during the French and Indian War, also saw this bounty system as a necessary component of military operations. Peters referred to the Delaware and other enemy tribes as "horrid Ravagers on our Borders," telling Superintendent of Indian Affairs William Johnson that they "will continue to murder our Inhabitants and destroy their Plantations until the Government shall offer high Rewards for Scalps." Referring to the French and their Indian allies, another colonist told Johnson that "we should deal exactly with them as they do by us, destroy and scalp as they do," adding that, "necessity pleads an Excuse for following so inhuman an Example."[59] Formerly a British agent to the Iroquois, Johnson understood the cultural significance of corporeal mutilation, as well as the central role of financial and racial motivations for contract killing. Despite his rhetorical disavowal of bounties as an immoral warfare tactic, he sometimes used enemy scalps as communicative props to promote strategic diplomacy with Indians, and he also paid out at least £400 in rewards during King George's War for the forelocks of nearly two dozen men, women, and children.[60]

Not only would Johnson, as the leading Indian agent for the northern British colonies, have to explain the vicious scalping policy to peaceful subgroups of Delawares and Shawnees, but the high value placed specifically on the two Delaware headmen also invited deception. Not long after the bounty act went into effect, a man known as Indian Isaac tried to pass off a random scalp as that of the chief Captain Jacobs. An investigation confirmed the fraud, but this did not stop the persistent claimant from submitting affidavits and naming witnesses in a feeble yearlong attempt to secure payment.[61] A group of freelance fighters from New Jersey also concocted a sham scheme to cash in on the new law, attacking a family of five—identified only as George, Cate, and their three children—with the intent of pulling their scalps and presenting them in Philadelphia for 650 Spanish dollars. The perpetrators bungled the nocturnal ambush, allowing George and his kids to escape, but Cate was not so lucky. Their plan foiled, the assailants murdered the mother as she covered her children's getaway, then fled the scene without taking a single scalp.[62] The deliberate targeting of certain people whose hair might pass for that of an Indian belonging to a tribe designated for scalp bounty payments became an unintended consequence of British bounty laws, and this same deceitful trend would emerge a century later among scalp hunters in northern Mexico who killed innocent mestizos to falsely redeem their scalps as those of Apaches and Comanches.

By April 1756, one Pennsylvania inhabitant could only describe his colony's situation as "most deplorable," with many Quakers openly opposing the government's violent approach to Indian affairs. In an expression of disenchantment, Israel Pemberton and several fellow Quakers formed a benevolent society, laboriously dubbed the Friendly Association for Regaining and Preserving Peace with the Indians by Pacific Measures. A resident named Daniel Claus—who once served as an interpreter to the Mohawks—noted that "People were Surprized that the 6 Nations [Iroquois] . . . had not agreed upon knocking the Delawares and Shawanese in the head," but he also believed that bounty hunting would ultimately produce the desired result of tribal conquest and therefore remained an advocate for the program.[63] One of the governor's colleagues, councilman James Hamilton, concurred in this racial sentiment and felt convinced that civilian scalping parties were the cheapest way to "clear our Frontiers of . . . Savages."[64] Unlike the bounty laws in colonial Massachusetts, where neither Puritans nor their religious dissenters showed any compunction about killing and dismembering Native enemies, Pennsylvania's bounty programs laid bare a stark ideological disconnect among settler groups, as Quakers advocated a pacifist approach while most non-Quakers pushed for aggressive scalp warfare tactics that included state-sponsored killing and attendant forms of extralethal violence.[65]

On April 14, Governor Morris fulfilled Hamilton's wish when he stood in front of the Philadelphia courthouse and read a proclamation of war. He outlined Pennsylvania's new scalp bounty, informing listeners that anybody who would track and kill Delawares would receive lavish rewards. The treasury would pay 150 Spanish dollars (about US$6,860 today) for male prisoners over age twelve, 130 dollars for the hair of the same, and 50 dollars for female scalps. Mirroring French agreements with Abenakis, this edict applied to Pennsylvanians as well as Iroquois allies, who could claim these prizes on presentation of scalps as evidence of a killing.[66] William Denny, who succeeded Morris as governor that same year, continued this program with the belief that communicative forms of extralethal violence were critical to the ongoing war against New France and its Indian auxiliaries, who "are now renewing their ravages on the frontiers."[67] In their initial enthusiasm for bounty hunting, neither Morris nor Denny realized their strategy's shortcomings, and the tactical ineptitude of inexperienced volunteers only added to the futility. Pennsylvania's first attempt at paid scalping occasioned more failed campaigns and fraud attempts than actual reward payouts, but that did not prevent the colonial legislature from instituting a revised bounty act at the onset of Pontiac's War in 1763.

As the French and Indian War concluded and France relinquished claim to its North American empire through the Treaty of Paris, the Great Lakes frontier plunged immediately into another armed conflict. Displeased with the imbalance of power that resulted from the French withdrawal, numerous

Indigenous leaders, including the Odawa headman Pontiac, guided a confederation of Delaware, Huron, Kickapoo, Mascouten, Miami, Mingo, Odawa, Ojibwe, Piankashaw, Potawatomi, Seneca, Shawnee, Wea, and Wyandot combatants. Together these Indians carried out a series of destructive raids on British forts and settlements in the Ohio and Illinois borderlands, catapulting frontier inhabitants into a state of unmitigated panic and prompting Major General Jeffrey Amherst to declare a £200 reward (US$34,490 today) for Pontiac's scalp.[68] The Pennsylvania colony, which sat at the eastern fringe of the conflict, responded by raising volunteer forces and formulating aggressive new policies. Early in the war, when Samuel Murray and six companions shot and scalped three Indians along the Susquehanna River, Governor James Hamilton—who had just been embarrassingly denied when asking influential Indigenous leaders to allow a free trade agreement—approved a payout for the trophies and used the incident as guiding precedent for another bounty act. Hamilton hoped that news of this payment, coupled with his announcement of £10 rewards for every enemy scalp, would incite a "Spirit of enterprize" among constituents whose racialized acts of extralethal violence might demoralize surrounding Indians and thereby break down the diplomatic barriers to open commerce.[69]

Broadcasting these promises of profit, Murray recruited a scalping party of 120 men and rode out to attack a group of Munsee Indians who had been living peacefully in the vicinity of Fort Augusta. Largely unassociated with Pontiac's rebellion, the village posed minimal risk to the bounty hunters, and that was precisely the point. They sought a quick and easy payday close to home, not a long and arduous slog across the frontier. But Murray's volunteers proved inept from the outset, many of them panicking at the first sign of Indians and scurrying back to the safety of Fort Augusta. They bungled the retreat, splintering into small groups before getting lost in the woods. One of these wandering contingents stumbled on three unsuspecting Indians and promptly shot them, only to botch the subsequent scalping. As one of the attackers removed a pair of leggings from a corpse to keep as plunder, he was astonished to see another victim, who had been playing dead, rise to his feet and run away, "the skin of his face, the scalp being off, [flapping] down over his eyes so that he could not see." The scattered remnants of Murray's expedition eventually returned from the field after scalping four Indians, but none of those casualties had any direct connection to the organized rebellion raging to the west.[70] The incident revealed one of the major tactical limitations of scalp warfare, that militarily inexperienced civilians sometimes did not equate to effective practitioners of state-sponsored killing.

Unconcerned with tribal affiliations, one public official named Edward Shippen Sr. lauded Murray's scalpers for their accomplishments and demanded that the party receive £50 for each of the four scalps. Believing that prompt payment would encourage even more volunteers to dabble in bounty hunting, Shippen asked the provincial council to appropriate an additional £500 for future disbursement.[71] The Rev. Thomas Barton referenced these developments when observing in July 1763 that many of the colony's inhabitants supported a revised scalp act. Despite his religious background, Barton himself advocated such a policy, echoing the racialized anti-Indian ideology once disseminated in Cotton Mather's honorific paean to Hannah Duston and showing that Protestant pastors, like Catholic priests, could easily operate outside of the moral teachings of their own religions to embrace hateful acts of extralethal violence directed toward Indians they viewed as irredeemable savages.[72] "Vast numbers of Young Fellows who would not choose to enlist as Soldiers, would be prompted by Revenge, Duty, Ambition, & the Prospect of the Reward, to carry Fire & Sword into the Heart of the Indian Country," Barton opined. "This Method . . . is the only one that appears likely to put a stop to those Barbarians."[73] Barton's prediction that Pennsylvanians would independently take up arms against Indians came to fruition on December 14, 1763. On that date, more than 50 Lancaster County residents who came to be known as the Paxton Boys attacked a village of Christianized Indians at a place called Conestoga Manor, killing and scalping 6 of them. Two weeks later, the perpetrators killed 14 more at the town of Lancaster, boldly defying local authorities who purportedly tried to protect the converted Indians. Intent on continuing the killing spree, they rode toward Philadelphia to massacre 140 Indians who had taken refuge with Moravian missionaries, but several hundred militiamen and soldiers intercepted the Paxton Boys and dispersed them before any climactic attack occurred.

The unusual public opposition in this case owed in part to the extreme le-thality of the campaign, as well as the indiscriminate targeting of ostensibly Christianized Indians who might be unnecessarily driven to retaliate.[74] Al-though participants in the Paxton campaign are not known to have collected cash bounties for the Indians they killed, their treacherous tactics and ensu-ing acts of corporeal mutilation revolved around modes of scalp warfare that proliferated in Pennsylvania at that time.

In February 1764, as the Paxton Boys returned home unpunished from their brief but lethal campaign, "the distressed and bleeding frontier inhab-itants" of Pennsylvania memorialized the governor and assembly outlining their grievances against Indians. They claimed that many of the tribes who "pretend themselves Friends" actually subsisted at the public expense by ac-cepting gifts of food and supplies. Feeling that they had become "Tributar-ies of Savages," these taxpaying Pennsylvanians voiced support for the bounty system and thought that fortune seekers who equipped their own pri-vate armies ought to be judiciously compensated as an "encouragement to excite Volunteers."[75] In a separate letter to Governor John Penn, residents of Berks, Cumberland, Lancaster, Northampton, and York Counties railed that "Skulking parties of Indians . . . have with the most savage Cruelty, murdered Men, Women, and Children, without distinction." This, they be-lieved, required violent retribution. The complainants were particularly up-set about Pennsylvania's policy protecting certain friendly members of otherwise hostile tribes, saying that this approach to Indian affairs invited duplicity and was impossible to enforce. "Who ever proclaimed War with a part of a Nation, and not with the Whole?" they asked angrily. "In what Na-tion under the Sun was [this] ever the Custom?" Referring to the scalp law that Governor Morris enacted in 1756, the petitioners demanded that au-thorities institute yet another bounty program, overriding the current Indian policy with one of indiscriminate extralethal violence akin to the brand of scalp warfare the Paxton Boys had recently perpetrated.[76]

The Pennsylvania government responded to these biting critiques in a predictable fashion, resurrecting the colony's scalping program once more. Passed on July 7, 1764, the new law cast a broad net, naming the Delawares, Shawnees, and "others in Confederacy with them" as hostile enemies who had "in a most cruel, savage, and perfidious manner, killed and butchered great Numbers of the Inhabitants." Encouraging the murder and mutilation of these "rebels and traitors," the governor invited all citizens to participate in scalping campaigns but cautioned that members of the Six Nations remained on amicable terms and should not be harmed. Even though this latest initiative incentivized aggression against the Delawares and Shawnees, it still retained an element of the old Pennsylvania policy by protecting a handful of people from within those two tribes who independently entered a peace agreement with the colony. To make scalp warfare as easy as possible, the government would pay premiums for all trophies and prisoners delivered to the commander of any fort or the municipal leader of any town, meaning that men no longer had to travel long distances to a capital city to collect their money. Male prisoners over ten years old would bring 150 Spanish dollars, while women and children captives were worth 130 dollars apiece. For scalps, the government would pay 134 Spanish dollars per male and 50 dollars per female over the age of ten. Regular soldiers and their officers, already paid as salaried state employees, could also participate in scalping but only at a rate of one-half of these amounts.[77] Like previous lawmakers in Massachusetts, the drafters of this Pennsylvania bounty clearly differentiated between traditional soldiers and militiamen and the autonomous volunteer companies that went afield in search of scalps, plunder, and glory.

On July 26, 1764—just three weeks after the new bounty went into effect—Delawares raided a rural Pennsylvania schoolhouse and demonstrated that they, too, could perpetrate shocking acts of extralethal violence. These depredators killed and scalped the teacher, Enoch Brown, along with nine of the pupils, and took four captives. Two children survived, both of them scalped and left for dead. The massacre sparked fury throughout the colony, despite the unspoken fact that Pennsylvania's long-standing program of paid murder and mutilation had inspired the gruesome retributive attack. John McCullough, a teenager who had been living in captivity with Delawares since 1756, knew three of the combatants involved. "I saw the Indians when they returned home with the scalps," he explained after escaping years later, noting that "some of the old Indians were very much displeased at them for killing so many children." The killing and scalping of schoolchildren was so dastardly, McCullough claimed, that tribal elders like Chief Neep-paugh'-whese admonished the perpetrators as cowards, "the greatest affront he could offer them."[78] The incident splashed fuel on the simmering conflict between backcountry settlers and their Native neighbors and provided a stark reminder of how scalp warfare could backfire on unsuspecting colonists.

Despite the apparent drawbacks of the scalping paradigm—Indian bounties consistently yielded counterproductive results, as exemplified in the Paxton Boys' murderous campaign, in Murray's haphazard attack on peaceful Munsees, and in the Delawares' retaliatory schoolhouse raid—many Pennsylvanians remained committed to this type of extralethal violence well into the American Revolution.[79] Some, in fact, had become so accustomed to forms of violent display that they simply assumed a bounty would be paid any time they presented scalps or captives to local authorities. Late in 1777, for example, Colonel Archibald Lochrey and his Westmoreland County militia killed and scalped five Indians in an ambush near Kittanning. Lochrey sent the trophies to Thomas Wharton, president of Pennsylvania's supreme executive council, requesting a reward. He likely would have received one, too, had Wharton's unanticipated death not interceded to the colonel's detriment.[80] As the American colonists' war against England escalated, the Pennsylvania assembly solicited Lochrey's input on the prospect of yet another scalp act. The colonel opined that such a strategy "would give spirit and alacrity to our young men, and make it in their Interest to be constantly on the scout."[81] The same day that he received this advice, Joseph Reed, president of the Commonwealth of Pennsylvania, wrote to George Washington, commanding the Continental Army, informing him that lawmakers would soon enact a new bounty for Indian scalps and prisoners. "I fear we shall be forced into it whether we like it or not," Reed concluded, reassuring the general that "we shall do nothing in it without your advice."[82] The fact that British officers in the Great Lakes region were pulling some Delaware and Shawnee subgroups into the revolutionary conflict by rewarding those who attacked American settlements prompted local leaders and military officers to demand reciprocity.[83]

By September 1778, Delawares and Shawnees had taken at least 234 scalps at the behest of Henry Hamilton, the Redcoat commander at Detroit, who gained a seedy reputation as the "Hair Buyer General."[84] Thomas

Jefferson, refusing to approve the customary parole of a captured British officer, called the imprisoned Hamilton a "butcher of men women and children."[85] But a handful of American officials still expressed reluctance toward a retaliatory scalping policy, believing that it might hinder their broader interest in achieving independence. Some observers rightly worried that scalp warfare, by its indiscriminate nature, would result in haphazard attacks on the camps of neutral Indians such as Delaware chief White Eyes and Shawnee sachem Cornstalk, who might respond by forming coalitions with British commanders.[86] The bounty laws also led to the exhumation and desecration of Indian burials, one example involving militiamen from Kentucky who dug up bodies from Shawnee gravesites in the 1770s so that they could cut off the scalps and collect payment.[87] Reed equated all of this extralethal violence to a strategic rather than a moral dilemma, admitting that he felt "an Apprehension that it may be improved by our Enemies to a national Reproach." Some of his compatriots worried that the British would propagandize the racist savagery of American scalp hunting to cast the republican cause in an ignoble light. Although he felt no personal compunction about murdering and mutilating Indians, Reed understood these concerns and asked military officers including Colonel Daniel Brodhead to refrain from issuing scalp payouts until the issue could be resolved.[88]

As the American battle for independence raged on, one Indian tribe after another was pulled into the violence, and neutrality became almost impossible.[89] Colonial militia units and their auxiliaries repeatedly ambushed noncombatant Native groups, giving them an incentive to ally with the British. During a series of haphazard attacks on bands of previously impartial Ohio Indians in 1778 and 1779, soldiers killed five innocent Munsees, along with the family of a neutral Delaware headman named Captain Pipe. Meanwhile, at Fort Randolph in western Virginia, Captain Matthew Arbuckle imprisoned the Shawnee diplomatist Cornstalk, who was subsequently shot to death in the guardhouse alongside his visiting son.[90] In the case of Captain Pipe, the murder of family members pushed him into an alliance with the British, and he soon began leading retributive campaigns against American forces. In 1781, the Moravian missionary David Zeisberger met Captain Pipe at a council in Detroit, where the headman and his Delaware followers presented several scalps to British commander Arent S. DePeyster and "demanded their pay."[91] With racial perceptions of Indians as a savage enemy prevailing during America's revolutionary era, settlers and soldiers seldom bothered to differentiate between peaceful and hostile tribes or leaders, and the extreme violence that they directed toward Indigenous neighbors came to symbolize masculine valor and societal honor.[92] The case of Captain Pipe and the Delaware tribe reveals that indiscriminate attacks often backfired on perpetrators, because such acts drew otherwise neutral Indians into the war as combatants who took the scalps of white Americans for material gain and revenge.

Colonel Samuel Hunter reported on April 2, 1780, that Indians carried away more than a dozen captives during a retaliatory raid near Sunbury, Pennsylvania, and Reed acted on hardened racial perspectives when he promised that the executive council would take definitive action. The commonwealth had not yet approved a new scalp act, but he gave Colonel Brodhead permission to employ bounty hunting as a military tactic, saying that it had proved useful during the French and Indian War and might again bear fruit in the present conflict. Brodhead in turn cautioned restraint, responding that such an order "will be construed into a License to take off the Scalps of some of our friendly Delawares, and produce a general Indian War," since the tribe exercised influence "over near twenty different Nations."[93] Here, the military efficacy of employing Indian allies as agents of scalp warfare had to be weighed against the possible ramifications of in-kind retribution. Although Pennsylvania's treasury was severely depleted and could hardly afford a protracted scalp war, Reed doubled down on his favored approach. The president reassured the Rev. Joseph Montgomery that the government would do all in its power to supply frontier inhabitants with provisions and ammunition, as well as "Rewards to those who distinguish themselves." To win the war and subjugate Indians who allied with the British, Reed hoped to inspire "a Spirit of Hostility and Enterprise," and to this end he recommended special expeditions, "secretly concerted, prudently conducted, & adapted to the Nature of the Enemy."[94] Bounty hunters would be called to action once more, and all Brodhead could do was warn allied Delaware leaders to be on the lookout for treachery as they congregated at Fort Pitt.[95]

By His EXCELLENCY

Joseph Reed, Esq. *President*,

And the SUPREME EXECUTIVE COUNCIL, *of the Commonwealth of* Pennsylvania.

A PROCLAMATION.

WHEREAS the Savages in Alliance with the King of *Great-Britain*, have attacked several of the Frontier Counties, and, according to the Custom of barbarous Nations, have cruelly murdered divers of the defenceless Inhabitants of this State: AND WHEREAS it has been found, by Experience, that the most effectual Mode of making War upon and repelling the Savage Tribes has been by Parties, consisting of small Numbers of vigorous, active Volunteers, making sudden irruptions into their Country, and surprising them in their Marches: WHEREFORE, for the Encouragement of those who may be disposed to chastise the Insolence and Cruelty of those Barbarians, and revenge the Loss of their Friends and Relations, WE HAVE thought fit, and do hereby offer a Reward of THREE THOUSAND DOLLARS for every *Indian* Prisoner, or Tory acting in Arms with them, and a Reward of TWO THOUSAND AND FIVE HUNDRED DOLLARS for every *Indian* Scalp, to be paid on an Order of the President or Vice-President in Council, to be granted on Certificate signed by the Lieutenant, or any two Sub-Lieutenants of the County, in Conjunction with any two Freeholders, of the Service performed. Such Reward to be in Lieu of all other Rewards or Emoluments to be claimed from the State.

GIVEN, by Order of the Council, under the Hand of His Excellency JOSEPH REED, *Esquire, President, and the Seal of the State, at* Philadelphia, *this Twenty-second Day of April, in the Year of our Lord One Thousand Seven Hundred and Eighty.*

JOSEPH REED, PRESIDENT.

Attest. T. MATLACK, *Secretary.*

GOD Save the PEOPLE

Pennsylvania Bounty Act of 1780. *By His Excellency Joseph Reed, Esq. President, and the Supreme Executive Council, of the Commonwealth of Pennsylvania: A Proclamation* (Philadelphia: Francis Bailey, 1780), Library Company of Philadelphia, Rare Books and Other Texts, Record #000216863.

With the executive council's approbation, Reed issued a proclamation on April 22, 1780, outlining provisions for the next bounty program. The president directed his ire at "the Savages in Alliance with the King of Great-Britain," saying that an aggressive brand of scalp warfare was the only way to turn the tide of frontier raiding. He also understood that most civilians would not take up arms at their own risk and expense without some assurance of financial incentives on either the front or back end. With this in mind, the council pledged a reward of $3,000 for the capture of any Indian acting in concert with enemy tribes and $2,500 for each scalp.[96] Measured in Continental Congress dollars, or "Continentals," these amounts were much smaller than they appeared at first glance. Unlike Spanish silver dollars, this paper currency underwent severe depreciation during the Revolution. By the time printing ceased in 1780, the money was worth just one-fortieth of its original value, so the $2,500 Pennsylvania bounty amounted to about 62 Spanish dollars per scalp when adjusted for hyperinflation.[97] Captain Samuel Brady may have had this money in mind when he scalped a Wyandot man in July, two months after the bounty went into effect. One prominent Pittsburgh resident praised him as *brave, vigilant, and successfull*" as he carried the enemy's hair into Fort Pitt "in triumph." The council in Philadelphia approved a $2,500 payout to Brady in February 1781, so he received more than just the rhetorical approbation of his peers.[98] This outcome, however, represents the exception rather than the norm. Many combatants—colonists and warriors alike—may have taken scalps during their wartime operations, but only six trophies were officially redeemed for rewards before repeal of the act on March 21, 1783. Here again, the small number of scalp redemptions indicates that the prevalence of scalp warfare often did not equate to a prevalence of actual scalping. Notably, fighting between British and American forces had stopped when General Charles Cornwallis surrendered at Yorktown on October 19, 1781, and abrogation of the Pennsylvania scalp law came just months before the Treaty of Paris officially ended the American Revolution.[99]

In New York and Pennsylvania, much as in New Hampshire and Massachusetts a generation earlier, civil authorities tended to view monetized Indian scalping as a requisite component of larger imperial and racial conflicts.

Despite the frequency and enthusiasm with which Pennsylvanians reverted to scalp hunting, the assembly paid just twenty-two bounties in conjunction with its three separate laws. John Armstrong enjoyed the greatest success in these pursuits, redeeming eight scalps, but ten others also benefited: Samuel Murray scored three payouts, Daniel Cressop and Andrew Lycan each collected two premiums, and Samuel Brady, Andrew Hood, George Lynderman, William Minor, Adam Poe, Henry Shoemaker, and Alexander Wright each received one payment. Scalps were typically burned on redemption, but in the case of Adam Poe, the trophy that he delivered in 1782 found its way into the American Museum in Philadelphia, and a collection of Indian scalps also decorated the interior walls of the courthouse in Salem, Massachusetts, until the building was demolished in 1785.[100]

State-sponsored scalp warfare proliferated throughout the Revolutionary Era despite the widespread dissemination of European diplomat Emmerich de Vattel's *Law of Nations* (1758), a seminal treatise on international law that directly influenced the thinking of America's founding generation. Prominent political and military leaders, including Benjamin Franklin and George Washington, read and praised the book's ideas, which constituted notable precursors to twentieth-century human rights declarations from organizations such as the United Nations. Vattel specifically called for the protection of women, children, the elderly, and the infirm during wartime, identified noncombatants as "enemies who make no resistance," and concluded that nations at war "have no right to maltreat their persons, or use any violence against them, much less take away their lives." Though well received among republican leaders in the fledgling United States and applied to varying degrees in wars with European powers, these ideas had little practical effect on the course of frontier conflicts with Indians that many Americans viewed as savages. In fact, indiscriminate scalp warfare spited Vattel's conceptualization of "what we have a Right to do, and what we are allowed to do, to the Enemy's Person in a just war." The theoretician's assumption that "at present every nation, in the least degree civilized," was adhering to the laws of "just war" showed a glaring ignorance of North America's scalp warfare tradition and the racial hatred that drove extralethal violence during conflicts with Indigenous groups.[101]

In direct contradiction to the ideas on "civilized" warfare set forth in Vattel's *Law of Nations*, the British colonies were often communities of violence where financially and racially motivated bounty hunters targeted scores of tribes and subgroups of tribes over the course of the eighteenth century, and some of those victims—which included adult men as well as women and children—were actually living on peaceful terms with settler counterparts at the time they came under attack.[102] Colonial legislators designed bounty laws so that anyone—civilians, militiamen, soldiers, and even Indian allies—could perpetrate acts of extralethal violence as incentivized combatants, although they repeatedly drew legal distinctions between each type of participant by offering different pay rates to different people. Scalp acts sometimes hit the books in response to regionalized depredations, but most often they arose in tandem with larger imperial clashes that involved British, French, and Indigenous forces in the contested North American borderlands. The result of local bounty laws, in terms of Indian fatalities and captivities, should be understood not just in demographic and statistical terms but also as state-sponsored acts of extralethal violence occurring intermittently across many decades and in conjunction with broader political and economic ambitions on the part of settler societies. Ambivalent to the cultural and psychological effects of indiscriminate scalp warfare, governments in Boston, Portsmouth, Albany, and Philadelphia acted with exterminatory intent when they codified reward programs that encouraged the unmitigated murder and mutilation of Indian men, women, and children.[103]

The bounty laws that proliferated as a technique for conquest across much of New France and the British colonies declined in the years following the American Revolution. France had relinquished most of its North American landholdings to the British and the Spanish on losing the French and Indian War in 1763, although it briefly reacquired Louisiana in 1802 before selling it to the United States the following year. England lost control over its thirteen American colonies after surrendering at Yorktown in 1781, but the British did maintain control over Canada into the mid-nineteenth century. After the Treaty of Paris formalized its independence in 1783, the fledgling United States functioned haphazardly under the Articles of Confederation, which denied Congress the authority to raise a national army but explicitly allowed individual states to wage war against Indian tribes that posed an "imminent" threat.[104] When the Constitution was ratified in 1788, it empowered the federal government to regulate commercial relations with Indian tribes and, even more broadly, "to raise and support armies" for national defense. The Constitution's authors intended to consolidate authority over Indian affairs at the federal rather than the local level of government, but some states—including Texas and California in the mid-1800s—would act autonomously in formulating policy and combating Native peoples whom they viewed as threats to settler safety and economic development.[105]

Throughout much of the colonial era, English/British legislators monetized the killing and scalping of Indigenous enemies, creating a tempting profit opportunity that many settlers and even some allied Indians tried to take advantage of. Despite the clear racial motivations behind bounty laws, the region's state-sponsored scalp warfare never came close to achieving its exterminatory intent. Approximately one hundred different English/British scalp laws went into effect during the long colonial era, but existing evidence suggests that the collective death toll of those edicts was not more than a few hundred people, representing a small fraction of the region's overall Indigenous population, with the Iroquois and Wabanaki Confederacies each estimated to number around ten thousand persons.[106] As a form of violent display, however, these acts of scalping carried significant communicative power and also became an important part of a collective community identity that revolved around anti-Indian racism.

After Pennsylvania rescinded its bounty program in 1783, scalp warfare became less systematic and more sporadic across the expanding American republic, as the new federal government embraced a regularized structure of militia and regular army soldiers. The so-called Ohio Indian War that began in 1790 provides a case in point. As increasing numbers of American settlers moved into the Northwest Territory, Indians there formed powerful confederacies and drew supplies from nearby British forts in Canada, creating a crisis of violence for President George Washington's administration. As a longtime military commander experienced in regular warfare techniques, Washington approached Congress in 1790 to raise a large army that would fight Indians in Ohio. He originally hoped to enlist 2,500 men but received approval and funding for just 1,200, leading to the formation of militia units to augment the army regulars. Decades earlier, colonists on the far western frontiers of America formed independent volunteer groups to wage a state-sponsored but autonomous form of scalp warfare against Indians. Now, with Washington as commander-in-chief, the new United States government primarily sent soldiers and militiamen to confront Indigenous groups. On October 19 and 22, 1790, detachments from this force suffered devastating defeats at the hands of Little Turtle's Miamis and Blue Jacket's Shawnees, resulting in a combined 178 troops killed. Humiliated by these engagements, the US military doubled down on its efforts, sending nearly 2,000 soldiers back into the Ohio Country in 1791. Under the command of Major General Arthur St. Clair, this enormous army was routed on November 4, 1791, when Little Turtle and Blue Jacket led an attack in the Wabash Valley that inflicted over 900 casualties. A third US army under command of Major General "Mad" Anthony Wayne eventually defeated the Miamis and Shawnees at Fallen Timbers on August 20, 1794. But this series of campaigns demonstrated the new US government's commitment to using its regular army, reinforced with militiamen, as the preferred method of waging war against Indians on the nation's frontiers, and Wayne specifically avoided the killing of noncombatants. Although these campaigns involved extirpative warfare tactics insofar as American operatives aimed to destroy enemies they encountered by targeting Indian homes and food supplies, they did not constitute a reincarnation of scalp warfare because the campaigns primarily used regulars and militia under the leadership of trained officers rather than bounty-hunting volunteers, and there was no direct monetary incentive for Wayne's troops to commit acts of extralethal violence.[107]

The US government continued this approach across the early decades of the nineteenth century.[108] Shawnees, now under the leadership of Tecumseh and Tenskwatawa, reformed a powerful confederacy of Great Lakes Indians and challenged American hegemony once more. William Henry Harrison, the territorial governor of Indiana who served as aide-de-camp to Major General Wayne during the Fallen Timbers victory in 1794, gathered a combined force of US Army regulars and local militia to march on the confederacy's seat of power at Prophet's Town near the Tippecanoe River.

Here again, an experienced military officer led a large army of regulars and militia in an attack on a sizable Indian village, using tactics that differed considerably from the treacherous ambushes of small and vulnerable camps that scalp hunters employed in the earlier English/British colonies. Harrison's men suffered over two hundred casualties but ultimately burned much of the village and its supplies of food, marking another instance of extirpative warfare that occurred outside the parameters of scalp warfare. Two years of retaliatory attacks among Tecumseh's confederacy, allied British troops, and opposing American settlers ensued, bathing the territories of Illinois and Indiana in the blood of Natives and newcomers alike. The climactic Battle of the Thames on October 5, 1813, broke the Indigenous confederacy through destructive US Army and militia operations, and the leader Tecumseh perished in the fighting.[109]

While Harrison led troops against Tecumseh's confederacy in the Northwest, another American military commander, General Andrew Jackson, waged similar campaigns against the Creeks (Red Sticks) in the Southeast. Following the so-called Fort Mims Massacre, during which a large Creek war party killed more than two hundred American settlers and Black slaves north of Mobile in August 1813, the Tennessee legislature called out five thousand militiamen to crush the tribe into submission. Neighboring Georgia and Mississippi similarly sent their militias, and a detachment of US Army regulars also participated in the multifaceted offensive that converged on Creek homelands from three directions. Jackson rose to national prominence through these military operations—as well as his victory over British forces at the Battle of New Orleans in January 1815—conducting a campaign to destroy tribal subsistence and enable uncontested settlement of the Southeast. More than one thousand Creek Indians perished during these initial campaigns, and a second series of US attacks culminated in the decisive clash at Horseshoe Bend on March 27, 1814, when Jackson's men killed more than eight hundred Creek warriors and imprisoned another three hundred women and children, with some of the soldiers taking battlefield trophies.[110] Much like Anthony Wayne in 1794 and William Henry Harrison in 1813, in the Southeast Andrew Jackson fought a war against Indians that primarily incorporated extirpative warfare techniques of destroying sources of subsistence and targeting tribal homelands with soldiers and militia, rather than the scalp warfare technique of civilian paramilitary operatives taking the field in response to local officials promising material gain in the form of bounties, plunder, and glory.

Scalp warfare occurred only sporadically during US wars against Indians in the Northwest Territory and the Southeast, primarily in isolated instances apart from the US government's preferred method of waging war with army regulars and militiamen. In one notable example during the War of 1812, Kickapoos who allied with British agents attacked settlers on the Wood River and killed several of them, leading the Illinois territorial legislature to issue an indiscriminate proclamation promising $50 for the scalp of any Indian who arrived in the settlements with "murderous intent."[111] Characteristically, this edict was devised at the local level and without the sanction of a national government, and the bounty offer was mostly symbolic within the context of a larger conflict between the United States and Great Britain during which Indigenous groups played a role as allies on each side. But thousands of miles away from the old Northwest Territory, in the deserts of northern Mexico, a systematic and sustained system of paid Indian scalping emerged in the early nineteenth century. During the decades following Mexican independence in 1821, a ruthless coterie of fortune seekers plied the arid Chihuahuan and Sonoran Deserts in search of Apaches and Comanches, whose scalps could be redeemed for princely sums in local capitals where legislators and settlers had developed an intense hatred of their Indigenous enemies.

THREE

Bounty Massacres in the
US-Mexico Borderlands

George Frederick Ruxton was no stranger to stunning sights. Born in 1821, he served as a lancer in the Spanish Civil War and then joined a British Army regiment in Canada before embarking on a perilous journey through Africa in 1845. One year later, the globetrotting Englishman found himself in Mexico, where he meandered his way through the country's vast northern frontier. On reaching Ciudad Chihuahua in November 1846, the twenty-five-year-old explorer stumbled upon a grisly scene that eclipsed the shock of all his previous experiences. As Ruxton rode into town, he noticed a long string of macabre ornaments swinging silently in the cool autumn breeze. On one side of the plaza, directly opposite the Catholic cathedral, "were dangling the grim scalps of one hundred and seventy Apaches, who had lately been most treacherously and inhumanely butchered by the Indian hunters in the pay of the state." Ruxton learned that the governor and the priest had paraded through town several weeks earlier, serenaded by triumphant melodies as they waved those trophies atop lances and poles before placing them on permanent display for all to see. "Such is the war of extermination carried on between the Mexicans and Apaches," the astonished Briton concluded with disgust.[1]

By the time Ruxton arrived in the Chihuahua capital, the shriveled forelocks had already adorned the town plaza for four months in what constituted a prolonged act of celebratory violent display. Back on July 6, 1846, the infamous scalp hunter James Kirker—whose "exploits in Indian killing would fill a volume"—led a party of forty-four men into the town of Galeana, where Southern Apaches (Ndé) belonging to the Chokonen and Nednhi tribal subgroups encamped after negotiating peace with village leaders.[2] With the legal backing of Chihuahua's bounty law and the verbal blessing of Governor José María Irigoyen, the contract killers had nothing to fear aside from the resistance their Indian targets might pose. To diminish that risk as much as possible, Mexican townspeople provided the unsuspecting Apaches with a bottomless supply of liquor the night before Kirker's men were due to arrive, making average citizens coconspirators in scalp warfare. The ensuing bloodbath claimed the lives of somewhere between 130 and 170 Apaches, most unarmed and some intoxicated. "The infuriated Mexicans spared neither age nor sex," Ruxton wrote. "With fiendish shouts they

George F. Ruxton in the 1840s. Newberry Library,
Everett D. Graff Collection of Western Americana.

massacred their unresisting victims, glutting their long pent-up revenge. . . . The fruits of the campaign were the trophies I saw dangling in front of the cathedral."[3] Government-sponsored extralethal violence had coalesced with pervasive anti-Indian racism and personal interest in the seedy side of the borderlands economy to produce one of the era's deadliest mass killings.[4]

Southern Apaches would remember the Galeana Massacre for genera-tions to come. According to Jason Betzinez, who rode alongside Geronimo in the 1880s, Mexicans gave his kinsmen as much mescal as they could drink. With "everyone lying in a drunken stupor," Kirker and his men rode into the camp, and "in a short time most of the Indians were lying in their blood, dead or dying." While the perpetrators "fell to work with sharp knives, wrenching off the gory trophies for which they would receive gold and silver from their authorities," a handful of survivors scurried northward, rendez-voused with other Apaches, and told horrific tales of the carnage they had witnessed. Chiefs Cuchillo Negro, Cochise, and Mangas Coloradas organ-ized "a great war party" of 175 men and rode into Chihuahua intent on bloody revenge.[5] Realizing that he and his troops at San Buenaventura in northern Chihuahua would be exposed to unrelenting Apache vengeance, Lieutenant Carlos Cásares lamented that "all hope for peace is gone."[6] Sev-eral years later, during a treaty council with US officers at Ácoma Pueblo in New Mexico, Mangas Coloradas cited the scalping at Galeana as a primary motivating factor in his tribe's persistent warfare against Chihuahua and So-nora. "Some time ago my people were invited to a feast," the chief told US Indian agent John Greiner. "Aguardiente or whiskey was there; my people drank and became intoxicated, and were lying asleep, when a party of Mex-icans came in and beat out their brains with clubs."[7] The US boundary commissioner John Russell Bartlett became acquainted with Mangas Colo-radas and his followers at the Santa Rita copper mines in the early 1850s, and he came to sympathize with their circumstances. "That the Indians feel the deepest hatred toward the Mexicans is true," he told readers in the United States. "Acts of treachery of the grossest and cruelest description have been practiced by the Mexicans towards them; and, though years have passed away since these events occurred, they are not forgotten by the Apaches."[8] As exemplified in the Galeana Massacre, the form of scalp warfare that developed in nineteenth-century northern Mexico constituted a systematic state-sponsored process of genocide against Apache tribes that suffered high casualty rates over a five-decade period from the 1830s to the 1880s. It also differed from the modes of scalp warfare practiced elsewhere in the eighteenth and nineteenth centuries, in that Mexico's bounty hunters often negotiated and signed private contracts with local governments, granting a businesslike legal foundation to the enterprise. In contrast, practitioners of scalp warfare in English/British Massachusetts, French Canada and Louisiana, and American California and Texas accepted various types of compensation for their extralethal acts but did not have a high level of standing with local governments to negotiate and sign their own contracts to hunt and kill Indians.

Kirker's treacherous perpetration of *bitsa-ha dogiz*—the Apache term for scalping that translates to "his head top cut off"—claimed the lives of many people and fundamentally transformed the sense of place and landscape. Such an act forever traumatized the meaning and memory of the location and redefined each person's *'igoyá'í*—a tribal concept involving mental and social conditions of reasoning, fear, anxiety, hostility, and pride.[9] For deceased victims and their living families, not only did scalping upend the crucial sense of *'igoyá'í* that formed part of individual identity, but it also carried deep spiritual dimensions within an Apache ethos. Similar to some of the Indigenous people who succumbed to bounty hunters in colonial New Netherland, New England, and New France, as well as nineteenth-century Texas and California, Southern Apaches believed that deceased persons entered the afterlife in the same physical condition that they departed Earth, meaning that any man, woman, or child who died at the hands of Kirker's cutthroats would live on in hairless shame. "There was no greater punishment for one's enemies," said Ace Daklugie, the son of Nednhi Apache chief Juh ("He Sees Ahead"). In the Apache ethos, desecration of the dead demanded that the living seek retribution. Daklugie claimed that his ancestors began reciprocating only after "both Mexicans and White Eyes scalped some of our people."[10] Another Apache reiterated that tribe members reserved scalping for "Mexicans who did awful things against the Chiricahua," and several others also insinuated that the practice emerged in response to the cash bounties that Chihuahua and Sonora offered.[11] Elaborating on these origins, one Apache informant told an ethnographer that ancestors in the mid-1800s took scalps not only to "show how much they hated their enemy" but also "to gain 'enemies-against power.' " Whenever a fighter engaged in the act of bitsa-ha dogiz, he and his companions immediately performed a ceremony and "sang one song over it" to extract the medicine power, then discarded the severed body part before returning home. Once imbued with enemies-against power, an Apache fighter believed that he could weaken future enemies of the ethnic or racial group from which the scalp was taken. In this way, the Apaches' retaliatory version of scalp warfare developed through symbolic Indigenous-centered acts of violent display intended to embolden individual warriors in ways that would enable them to better resist the extralethal violence of Mexican and American perpetrators.[12]

Along with John Johnson, John Joel Glanton, Michael Chevallié, José María Zuloaga, Michael James Box, John Dusenberry, and others, Kirker contracted with northern Mexico's state governments to enslave, kill, and mutilate Indians in exchange for cash and plunder. As nomadic tribes with trading and raiding economies, Southern Apaches and Comanches (N~~u~~-m~~unuu~~) employed mobility and targeted violence to assert their power and self-determination, and skilled fighters from each tribe carried their share of Mexicans into captivity and killed many others.[13] This posed a major challenge to settler societies in northern Mexico. Desperate statesmen in Chihuahua, Durango, and Sonora responded with bounty laws that dramatically intensified the nature and practice of intercultural violence, encouraging transnational civilian contractors—Mexican officials referred to them rather innocuously as *aventureros* (adventurers)—to assert state hegemony by attacking *los indios bárbaros* in exchange for cash rewards on slaves and body parts as well as the right to plunder the victims' horses, cattle, firearms, ammunition, and liquor. Although northern Mexico's mixed economy revolved primarily around mining, ranching, and farming, intense conflicts with Apaches and Comanches gave rise to a secondary borderlands economy wherein the state commodified contraband, captives, and corpses as a type of scalp warfare that outsourced colonial violence to private parties.[14]

As a distinct form of genocidal policy, the bounty systems in Chihuahua, Durango, and Sonora embraced an extralethal component through cash payouts for scalps.[15] The nature of these bounty programs in the US-Mexico borderlands complicates discussions on Native American genocide by extending the analysis beyond the United States and its colonial antecedents—Dutch New Netherland, French Canada and Louisiana, and thirteen British enclaves up and down the East Coast—in order to appreciate more fully the process and implementation of genocidal policy within independent Mexico and along the international border, where the roots of extralethal violence went back more than two centuries.[16]

In 1617—more than two decades before Willem Kieft offered a wampum reward for Raritan heads in New Netherland—Nueva Vizcaya governor Gaspar de Alvear y Salazar enacted the first known bounty system in New Spain, offering four hatchets, four knives, four hoes, four machetes, and a coarse garment in exchange for each scalp of a Tepehuane Indian.[17] With the rewards being distributed in scarce metallic goods and articles of war rather than actual money, the system nodded to Native interests and aimed to entice so-called friendly Indians to wage scalp warfare on behalf of Spanish officials. But this incident stands out as an anomaly in Mexico's early colonial period, and it remains unknown just how many Indigenous peoples participated as profiteers or perished as targets. Instead, a widespread system of Indian slavery developed at mines, haciendas, and latifundios, but this practice aimed to capture rather than kill victims in order to take advantage of their forced labor in ways that would enrich the Spanish crown and its New World viceroyalties. State-sponsored forms of scalp warfare and extralethal violence do not seem to have taken hold in Mexico until the late eighteenth century, when oscillating conditions of war and peace came to define New Spain's northern frontier.[18] By the 1790s, many Southern and Mescalero Apache subgroups were drawing rations and living semisedentary lives on *establecimientos de paz* (peace establishments) that in many ways resembled the nineteenth-century Indian reservation program in the United States. Other tribal bands, however, continued to raid the settlements for captives and plunder, making it difficult for Mexican administrators to distinguish between peaceful and hostile groups. In response, frustrated presidial troops captured and killed as many Indians as they could find, generating a hateful and at times confusing cycle of retributive warfare because certain Apache bands might be at peace with Chihuahua or Sonora while other tribal subgroups took the warpath against those same provinces. Moreover, military officers and their subordinates exacerbated the demographic toll of this violence by deporting captives to toil as slaves at faraway Mexican silver mines and Cuban sugar plantations.[19]

These troops also began to cut off the ears and hands of slain Indians as evidence of body counts, marking one of the earliest examples of extralethal violence and violent display in relations between Apaches and Mexicans. In March 1792, Spanish soldiers captured 82 Apaches and transported them in a chain gang to Mexico City. Somewhere along the thousand-mile journey, they killed 12 of the men during a purported escape attempt. Before discarding the corpses along the southbound trail, the guards hacked off twelve hands and carried them in a jar to serve as proof of the slaughter. This type of murder and mutilation added a sinister dimension to the enduring conflict between Natives and newcomers on the frontiers of New Spain.[20] Three years later, a prolonged war broke out between the *fronterizos* (frontier residents) of northern Mexico and their Mescalero Apache foes. Spanish campaigners killed, captured, or deported some 750 Indians before a truce abated military operations in 1799 and prompted surviving members of the tribe to seek shelter on designated peace establishments near Mexican towns including Janos and San Buenaventura.[21]

Between 1780 and 1820—the final four decades of Spanish rule in Mexico—the imperial government doled out as much as 30,000 pesos annually to supply and feed Apaches at the establecimientos de paz, a considerable expense to purchase tenuous peace.[22] Colonizers in New Mexico, Sonora, and Chihuahua had already been grappling with the difficulties of Indian policy for generations by the time Mexico won its independence with the Treaty of Córdoba in 1821. From that point on, the central government was unable to maintain a strong army or sustain economic stability, so weak and impoverished regional legislatures acted independently to promote their own security and prosperity.[23] On the northern frontier, the foremost prerequisite to these objectives involved killing, enslaving, or otherwise subjugating

Indigenous enemies through scalp warfare, especially after the insolvent na-tion-state discontinued its long-standing Indian rationing program in 1831. Soon thereafter, Chief Juan José Compá and his Southern Apache followers deserted the establecimientos de paz at San Buenaventura and Janos, signal-ing an impending breakdown of relations between the two sides and a return to targeted mobility and violence. As depredations proliferated, civilian death tolls skyrocketed, and an estimated five thousand fronterizos perished at the hands of Indigenous raiders during the first fifteen years of Mexico's republi-can era. These Indians not only posed urgent threats to the security of Mexi-can lives and property but also fell within the prevailing racial view of "los bárbaros" as legitimate targets of extralethal violence. After 1831, the Chihua-hua and Sonora legislatures never seriously considered reinstituting establec-imientos de paz in a formal way, but officials at towns such as Janos did periodically negotiate their own terms with Apache leaders and distribute food to small bands living nearby.[24] A diplomatic intervention on its face, this localized approach to Indian affairs enabled treacherous acts of killing, as Mexican soldiers and bounty hunters occasionally attacked these unsuspect-ing Apache camps to capitalize on their vulnerability.

In 1837, legislators in northern Mexico took their first steps toward a con-crete policy of Indian extermination. That year, Chihuahuenses approved a bounty system for Apache property that included a pay scale for confiscated livestock, and armed vigilantes soon began applying for *permisos* (permits) to raid Indians. Whenever state-licensed parties recovered stolen animals from an Apache *ranchería* (encampment), the lawful owners could pay a finder's fee to have the property returned to them. Permit holders could also recruit their own team of contract killers for a legalized form of scalp war-fare that called for the collection of *piezas* (body parts) to substantiate the number of deaths during a campaign. The new laws were designed so that foreign nationals and even so-called friendly Indians from the Delaware (Lenape), Shawnee (Shaawanwaki), Tarahumara (Rarámuri), Papago (To-hono O'odham), and Pima (Akimel O'odham) nations could participate as incentivized combatants.[25] By approving such a sweeping measure, Chi-huahua officials demonstrated a firm commitment to scalp warfare as their preferred method for fighting independent Indians.

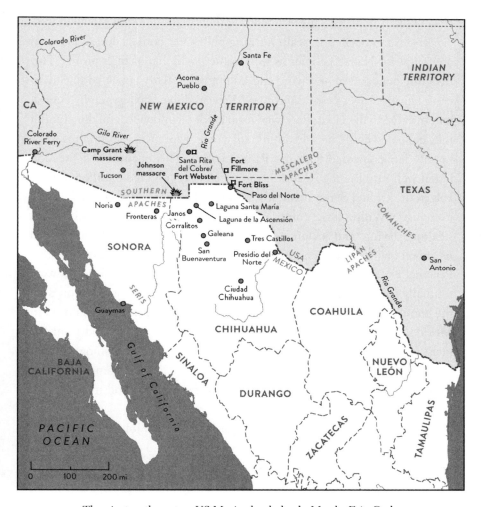

The nineteenth-century US-Mexico borderlands. Map by Erin Greb.

At a time when 85 percent of the Mexican population earned an average monthly income of just 20 pesos, these new bounties served state interests by providing alluring economic incentives for citizens to take up arms against despised enemies, because the value of plunder taken during raids equated to several months of regular wages.[26] The inclusion of Delawares, Shawnees, and other selected Indigenous groups as state contractors also indicates that officials were willing to look past their own anti-Indian racism in view of the unique tracking and fighting skills that such men provided. Foreigners also gravitated to scalp hunting below the border, due to personal contempt for Native peoples as well as the possibility of high profits. This fledgling occupation of slaving and killing particularly appealed to Americans, because silver pesos (known as Mexican dollars and generally equivalent in value to the US dollar) were legal tender worldwide, and the plunder they collected could be sold almost anywhere. Moreover, Chihuahua's first bounty law coincided with the Panic of 1837. This economic depression lasted well into the 1840s, and the adverse effects on credit and bond markets in the United States made silver and gold specie preferred mediums of exchange.[27] Within these contexts, a handful of contract killers realized that stealing, slaving, and scalping could be incredibly lucrative, and they had no moral qualms about performing the Mexican government's dirty work.[28] Personal economic gain and the enforcement of local Indian policy were mutually reinforcing, and transgressive acts of racialized violence became the common denominator linking public and private interests. In northern Mexico, extralethal violence toward Indians not only emanated from the racist predilections of colonizers but also took on broader meaning within a borderlands economy where men could pillage Indian camps, sell the women and children as slaves, kill the men for material and monetary rewards, and become public heroes in the process.

The first to take advantage of this situation was John Johnson, a native of Kentucky who immigrated to New Mexico in 1827 and eventually settled in Sonora. Recognizing profits to be made from the new bounty system, he secured a state permit and gathered seventeen men at Villa de Moctezuma on April 3, 1837. The group tracked several hundred Southern Apaches to a dry lakebed, where Johnson met with their leader, Juan José Compá. The son of an influential Chokonen Apache headman named El Compá, Juan José was born sometime in the 1780s and in 1794 was admitted to the Janos presidio school for sons of military personnel. The only Apache known to have attended this school, he learned to read and write in Spanish and acquired a unique status in northern Mexico as the disciple of an elite regional academic institution. His older brother, Juan Diego Compá, became chief of the Chokonen Apaches after their father died in 1794, and the two siblings held an influential leadership status in both Mexico and in Apachería for a period spanning four decades.[29]

In 1837, Juan José stood accused of leading a recent attack on the Sonoran town of Noria, even though he was a renowned diplomat who had lived at the San Buenaventura peace establishment until 1831 and acted as a principal signatory to three treaties with Mexican officials between 1832 and 1835. During his meeting with Compá, Johnson proposed a trade fair to swap gunpowder, food, and liquor. As the parley progressed, many participants drank to excess, and when intoxicated Apaches gathered around Johnson's wagons on the morning of April 22, the contract killers blasted them with a swivel gun concealed beneath food sacks. The ensuing massacre claimed the lives of Juan José, his brother Juan Diego, and eighteen others, including three women. Johnson and his men severed twenty scalps, and they added seven more to this tally when another group of Apaches tried unsuccessfully to avenge the perfidious murders as the perpetrators retreated toward Janos. Johnson later thanked Governor José Joaquín Calvo for affording him "the chance to render a service to the country" but expressed regret that he was unable to retrieve the forelocks of five wounded Indians who escaped.[30]

The aptly named "Johnson Massacre" quickly became the stuff of borderlands legend. Benjamin Wilson, a Tennessean who moved to New Mexico in 1833, was trapping beaver along the Gila River when the attack occurred. "The Mexican Governor of Sonora was exceedingly anxious to secure the capture and destruction of Juan Jose," Wilson wrote. "Of course it was left to Johnson to effect Juan Jose's destruction in his own way."[31] Josiah Gregg, a Santa Fe trader who heard the story secondhand, wrote that Sonorenses gave "a sort of carte blanche patent" to any men "spurred on by the love of gain."[32] Passing near the massacre site while leading the Mormon Battalion to California in 1847, Lieutenant Philip St. George Cooke paused to contemplate the "very extraordinary and treacherous" deed, and the US boundary commissioner John Russell Bartlett called Johnson "a disgrace to his nation."[33] That some Americans viewed the incident with such disgust indicates just how unpalatable indiscriminate extralethal violence could be, even in a colonizing society with widespread anti-Indian sentiments. Treachery seemed to be the primary reason for public disdain, because Johnson's perpetrators had added a deeper dimension of malice aforethought by debilitating their victims with liquor under a false flag of truce.[34]

Southern Apaches would remember Johnson's butchery with heartache and fury, and their oral traditions attest to the use of alcohol as antecedent to massacre and fuel for postkilling revelry.[35] Mangas Coloradas, who lost two wives in the incident, mentioned it during a treaty council in 1852. "While innocently engaged in trading, a cannon concealed behind the goods was fired upon my people and quite a number were killed," he informed US Indian agent John Greiner. "Since then Chihuahua has offered a reward for our scalps . . . and we have been hunted down ever since."[36] Ace Daklugie told one twentieth-century historian that Compá naively befriended Johnson and lost his life because of it. "It was not in revenge for depredations made by Apaches that these men killed, but for the money offered," he said. "A bounty was offered for Apache scalps . . . and it was collected, too." When asked if he thought Apache ancestors had been victims of genocide, Daklugie responded, "I am thoroughly familiar with its practice, it was certainly that in the case of the Apaches."[37] Narcissus Duffy Gayton, a great-great-granddaughter of Chief Victorio, described Johnson's performance of extralethal violence in vivid detail when she lamented that Compá had been "plied with liquor" before the attack. Many of her ancestors "were hacked to death with knives and sabers" in their own homelands, adversely affecting each survivor's 'igoyá'í. Gayton explained that Mangas Coloradas immediately "swore revenge" and "the ensuing slaughter lasted some fifty years."[38]

Members of the tribe subsequently embarked on five retaliatory raids across Sonora and Chihuahua, killing half a dozen Mexicans and pilfering hundreds of animals.[39] Unable to defend against this mobile onslaught with traditional military force, state leaders fell back on scalp warfare, and the Chihuahua government implemented a new bounty on July 29, 1837. Two prominent politicians, Pedro Olivares and Ángel Trías, drafted a *proyecto de guerra* (war plan) and established a special treasury account to pay for it, assessing forced loans on residents to finance the operations. Calling for the recruitment of a private army to hunt Indians, the new bounty program would pay transnational contractors 100 pesos for a "barbarian" scalp, fifty pesos for a woman's hair, and 25 pesos for each captive child.[40] This payment structure meant that all Apaches—dead or alive, young or old, male or female—could be redeemed for cash. The higher value was placed on scalps rather than prisoners, indicating the state's preference for extermination rather than removal or assimilation. Authorities in Mexico City quickly proclaimed the plan unconstitutional, and some legislators also recognized that the captivity and enslavement of Indians flew in the face of a new national ban on slavery "without any exception." Situating Mexico alongside the British Empire as a forerunner in the global abolition movement, that antislavery law went into effect on April 5, 1837—three months before Chihuahua announced the proyecto de guerra that sent scalpers and slavers into the field.[41] But federalist leaders on the northern frontier shunned their centralist counterparts in the national capital, ignored the abolition law, and moved forward with their plan for securing the lives and property of regional inhabitants through the enslavement and killing of Indigenous enemies. Josiah Gregg wrote that the "notorious Proyecto de Guerra . . . stands most conspicuous" among Mexico's schemes to fight Indians. "By this famous 'war-project' a scale of rewards was established," he told American readers, explaining that "it is rigidly complied with." Despite the Mexican government's condemnation of the war plan, Gregg watched as a man rode into Ciudad Chihuahua with a woman's scalp adorning his lance tip, "which he waved high in the air in exultation of his exploit!"[42]

Such were the ghoulish conditions of extralethal violence and violent display that attracted James Kirker. Born in 1793, Kirker emigrated from Ireland to New York City as a teenager in 1810. A decade later he found himself in Missouri, where he joined a fur-trapping expedition bound for the Rocky Mountains. By 1827 he had established his base of operations at Santa Rita del Cobre, a Spanish copper mine in the heart of Southern Apache homelands. He soon found nefarious ways to profit from these circumstances, trading guns and ammunition in exchange for horses and mules that the Apaches appropriated from Mexican haciendas. Known locally as "Don Santiago," Kirker was described as "a very hard drinking man" who trafficked contraband for more than a decade while living in friendship with his

James Kirker, notorious Apache scalp hunter in nineteenth-century Mexico, shown here in 1847. Missouri Historical Society, St. Louis.

Indian patrons.[43] Mexican officials publicly condemned him for creating a market for stolen livestock and providing the tribe with muskets, bullets, and powder to use during deadly raids. "Even though it might not be more than a kind of evil business," Governor José María Irigoyen complained in reference to Kirker's notorious gunrunning, "alien smugglers [should be] stopped."[44] A law passed in November 1834 mandated the death penalty for anybody caught trading with "rebel tribes," and one year later Mexican officials placed Kirker prominently atop their list of most-wanted criminals.[45] Chihuahua's proyecto de guerra, passed in 1837, finally upended the contraband game in Mexico's favor, but not because it led to Kirker's arrest or forced him out of the region. To the contrary, scalp warfare supplanted smuggling as the most lucrative component of the borderlands shadow economy, inducing the profiteer to betray the same Indians he once befriended.

In 1839, as Don Santiago transitioned his business interests from guns and livestock to slaves and scalps, José Agustín de Escudero examined Chihuahua's frontier woes and concluded that "war to the death with the Apaches" should become the collective battle cry.[46] On April 3, a rich mine owner named Steven Cuicier acted on Escudero's advice when he convened a meeting in the capital with the blessing of Governor Simón Elías González. Still smarting from the recent failure of a five-hundred-man military campaign, the governor was amenable to alternative strategies such as scalp warfare.[47] Remembering John Johnson's prior success, Cuicier hired Kirker to organize a party of bounty hunters, and citizens voted to form a new paramilitary organization called the Society for Making War against the Barbarians.[48] The name of this group emphasized its racist foundations, and the verbiage also appealed to potential volunteers who shared this view of Indians as subhuman. With Cuicier serving as president, the group immediately outlined "the method, expenditure, gratifications and other matters relative to the campaign which [Kirker] and some Shawnees are going to make for the Society." Cuicier's committee printed promotional pamphlets for public dissemination and implored Chihuahuenses to donate money for bounty payments, again making citizen financiers complicit in a state-sponsored system of Indian extermination. Realizing that a voluntary fundraising campaign was unlikely to produce enough capital in a cash-starved economy where most citizens lived in poverty, the city council passed mandatory taxes on the wealthy. Effective January 1, 1840, merchants, hacendados, and mining speculators would be levied at 1 percent of land values and 10 percent of cash income, placing the fiscal burden of scalp warfare on the propertied and professional classes. To direct this revenue stream into the bounty coffers, the government reduced the salaries of its employees.[49] Scalp payments would be bankrolled at the state rather than national level, a model that differed from that of Gold Rush–era California insofar as the US Congress periodically reimbursed the operating costs of so-called volunteer companies that slaughtered West Coast Indians. Chihuahua's autonomous approach effectively neutralized Mexico City's unwillingness to finance frontier army operations while simultaneously circumventing federal opposition to these genocidal measures.[50] Local interests were thus tightly bound to performative extralethal violence in a privatized brand of scalp warfare, because the national government and its more traditional military campaigning failed to provide adequate security from Indian raiding in the eyes of fronterizos.

Kirker initially left Chihuahua City with about fifty fighters and rode all the way to northern New Mexico, far beyond the jurisdiction of Cuicier's so-called Society for Making War. In September 1839, he led an attack on a band of Jicarilla Apaches camped within two miles of Ranchos de Taos. According to one witness, some of the Indians sought shelter by running into the town plaza, "but Kirker's men felt no disposition to let the savages off so easily . . . and resumed the attack within the walls of the town." Forty Indians died in the half-hour affair, and those who survived lost their livestock and property. An immediate controversy ensued, because the local government in Santa Fe refused to honor a bounty contract issued in another state, and New Mexico governor Manuel Armijo feared that Kirker's actions would undermine his recent attempts to negotiate peace with nearby tribes.[51] After this expedition, Kirker met with the War Council in Chihuahua to renegotiate his contract so that it included a daily stipend in addition to the piecework rate for scalps and captives. For the eight-month duration of the new pact, Kirker would receive 4 pesos per day, his captains 2 pesos, and the remainder of his followers 1/2 peso (twice the pay of regular army privates). The revised agreement ensured that all men would get paid regardless of success, and it essentially transformed the scalp payouts into a bonus to augment salaries. The actual bounties ranged from 50 pesos for each deceased Apache male over the age of fourteen to 25 pesos for captive boys and all women, dead or alive. If these murderous activities induced tribal leaders to seek peace, Kirker would receive a massive windfall of 28,000 pesos.[52] This new plan placed the highest value on slain men, but it differed from the law of 1837 in that state agents would now pay just as much for a female captive as for a female scalp. This seemingly minor modification had an important impact, because bounty hunters began enslaving some women rather than killing and scalping them, since the rate was identical either way. Identification of noncombatants as legitimate targets for scalping revolved around the racism that undergirded the state's codification of extralethal violence in northern Mexico. Under these parameters, bounty hunters' occasional choice to murder women and children rather than capture and sell them into slavery indicates that hatred for Indians could exceed even the strongest motivation for financial gain, because the market value of each household servant would have been greater than the 25-peso bounty that contract killers collected.

The adept Kirker had devised a lucrative scheme that compensated him for basic field operations and offered further incentives for the conquest of Indians through a tiered merit-pay system. Measuring success first in captives and corpses and second in peace treaties, the state prioritized the enslavement and killing of Indigenous enemies over their subjugation and relocation, so paramilitary operations provided the best option to achieve such objectives. But not everyone was pleased with these arrangements, demonstrating the complexity of viewpoints when it came to extralethal violence and the economic motivations that often attended its performance. Property owners did not necessarily oppose genocidal tactics against the hated Apaches and Comanches, but they grudgingly shouldered the costs of doing business with James Kirker through a state-imposed tax-the-rich scheme. Mexican army officers similarly despised their Indian enemies, but they interpreted the employment of contract killers as a blatant denunciation of their own leadership abilities that flew in the face of a professional military ethos. For their part, rank-and-file soldiers chafed at the thought of stateless rogues receiving twice the wage to perform the same dangerous work. To underscore these points, Colonel Cayetano Justíniani challenged the governor to a duel before resigning his army commission.[53]

Protests and duels notwithstanding, Kirker set out in pursuit of the Southern Apache chief Pisago Cabezón, whose recent solicitation of peace was dismissed as a ruse to discourage scalpers. Born in the 1770s, Pisago Cabezón had become a primary tribal leader by 1831, and his decisions in that capacity would influence Southern Apache relations with Mexico for more than a decade.[54] In an attack on the headman's camp at Laguna de la Ascensión on January 9, 1840, the contractors murdered fifteen people, detained nineteen more, and reclaimed seventy-three head of livestock that could be sold back to their original owners.[55] The ratio of killed to captured demonstrates the effect of the new pay scale for Apache women, as the bounty hunters now took more slaves than scalps. When Don Santiago rode into Janos to collect 1,125 pesos for the trophies and captives, he took advantage of an unexpected opportunity for additional profit. Pisago Cabezón's son, Janaso Marcelo, was at the presidio conversing with local officials, so Kirker instinctively seized him. The man was worth at least 50 pesos as a prisoner, and much more if he could be cajoled into a treaty that would trigger disbursement of the 28,000-peso reward for peace with the Apaches.[56] Although military officers like Colonel José María Elías González disparaged Kirker's brash act because it seemingly proved the effectiveness of bounty hunters, most Chihuahuenses cheered his success and implored the War Council to continue paying him. "The expedition of Kirker appears good," one local journalist applauded. "Now, perhaps, is the best time for success over the tribes, because the adversity ought to diminish their barbarity."[57] By injecting exterminationist rhetoric into his recurring column—Chihuahua's official state newspaper featured an update on Apache affairs in almost every issue—the reporter confirmed the inextricable connection between racialized extralethal violence and state Indian policy.

Four months later, when Apaches killed three Mexicans on the road between Paso del Norte and Ciudad Chihuahua, soldiers of fortune flocked once more to Kirker's ranks. He now had more than one hundred disciples, constituting a cast of characters that one eyewitness dubbed "vicious, corrupted, haughty, and undisciplined."[58] Along with a handful of convicted criminals that he plucked from prison cells, Don Santiago commanded foreign expatriates and dozens of Shawnee and Delaware legionnaires, the best known being the Shawnee leader Spy Buck. Having fled from US ethnic cleansing operations in the 1830s—including the widespread removal of tribes to Indian Territory—these Indigenous refugees became a ubiquitous component of scalp gangs in the borderlands.[59] Ancestors of these Delawares and Shawnees had been victims of British bounty hunters a century earlier, but now members of each tribe embraced scalp warfare. Much like their Euro-American comrades in the scalp trade, displaced Indigenous peoples who hunted bounties were making a living as transnational contract killers working on behalf of state governments. As relative newcomers to the violent Mexican frontier, Shawnees and Delawares did not harbor traditional enmity toward Apaches or Comanches, but they did sense an opportunity for material gain as participants in the rougher parts of the borderlands economy. Moreover, because these diasporic tribes had arrived in Chihuahua only recently, citizens and politicians did not view them through the same lens of hostility as Apaches and Comanches, and they therefore created informal alliances with Shawnees and Delawares by incorporating them into contract killing schemes.

On May 8, 1840, Kirker led his mixed battalion to a Southern Apache camp at Laguna Santa María in northern Chihuahua, where they killed six men, captured thirteen women and children, and rode away with 121 head of livestock and four barrels of whiskey.[60] Once again, the attack yielded more slaves than scalps, and Governor Francisco García Conde was so impressed with the results that he heralded Kirker as the state's greatest agent of violence.[61] By 1841, Kirker's attacks on Apache rancherías had yielded a small fortune in livestock and cash rewards. Scalp warfare was so lucrative that bounty hunters began contemplating other nefarious ways to augment their income. It did not take long for scalpers to realize that many Mexicans had black hair, usually indistinguishable from that of Apaches. When the New Orleans newspaper editor George Wilkins Kendall trekked through

Chihuahua in the winter of 1841–42 as part of the imprisoned Texan–Santa Fe Expedition, he learned that Kirker "was in the practice of bringing in counterfeit scalps." Kendall's informants were convinced that Don Santiago "did not scruple to kill any of the lower order of Mexicans he might meet with, where there was slight chance of being discovered, and pass off their top-knots for those of true Apaches."[62] Murdering unsuspecting mestizos (mixed-blood Mexicans) for their scalps was much easier and safer than campaigning in Apache country. Local authorities knew that their paramilitary operatives were killing innocent civilians to defraud the government, but they still adhered to the bounty system in recognition of its devastating effects on Apaches. In a remarkable development, officials in Chihuahua and Sonora proved willing to sacrifice their own citizens to the ruthless dictates of murder for hire if it also meant subduing and annihilating Indigenous enemies.

Despite its indiscriminate brutality, Mexico's experiment in contract killing and slaving eventually produced a tentative peace agreement, although Kirker must have been dismayed that these proceedings fell beyond the stipulations of his large bonus. Claiming that Apaches had "dismantled the frontier" and lamenting conflicts "a thousand times worse than a foreign war [and] more disastrous than civil war," Governor García Conde met with the septuagenarian Pisago Cabezón on July 4, 1842.[63] The chief's imprisoned son would be liberated in return for Apache promises to cease hostilities, repatriate Mexican captives taken during raids, and live under immobilized supervision near Janos. The treaty produced a two-year ceasefire during which depredations diminished, but relations between the longtime foes would remain volatile.

While the aging Pisago Cabezón and his followers committed themselves to cautious peace in exchange for rations and protection from Kirker's men, the younger but equally influential Mangas Coloradas shunned the treaty. Born around 1790, Mangas Coloradas rose to a leadership position in his own Chihenne local group by 1814, and a decade later his authority had expanded to include the Bedonkohe band of Southern Apaches. By the time he met with Mexican officials at Janos on March 31, 1843, Mangas Coloradas boasted nearly three decades of diplomatic and military experience as a tribal chief, and he was the only Apache man of his time to command such a wide following.[64] Standing at nearly six-and-a-half feet, Mangas Coloradas cut an imposing figure and towered over his Mexican counterparts as he told them that Apaches would refrain from further raiding. But the pact he arranged at Janos was largely a ploy to discourage scalpers, and within six months the chief was leading war parties into neighboring Sonora. Troops under José María Elías González and Antonio Narbona retaliated by killing eighty Apaches and capturing thirty more near Corralitos. Driven by soldiers and scalp hunters who repeatedly killed and mutilated his loved ones, Mangas Coloradas would soon break the agreement he made in Chihuahua in view of expanding the tribe's warpath across all of northwestern Mexico.[65]

By 1846, Apaches and Mexicans had abandoned any hope for peace, and scalp warfare proliferated once more. Kirker signed another agreement with Chihuahua officials, and on March 4, a group of fifty-four contract killers ambushed the camp of Chato and Maturán, slaying one and wounding nine others while seizing forty-four animals to resell for profit. Tribe members sought revenge two weeks later, descending on Janos in a coordinated attack that left one Mexican dead and yielded 345 head of livestock.[66] In perpetuation of this retaliatory cycle, Kirker carried out the shocking butchery chronicled at the beginning of this chapter. The Galeana Massacre came at a moment of heightened anxiety among Mexican officials. In the northernmost province of New Mexico, assemblyman Donaciano Vigil echoed longstanding racial justifications for Indian conflict when he bemoaned "the growing number of deaths the barbarians have inflicted on our countrymen." He urged fellow citizens to pursue retaliatory measures and begged the Mexican government to provide more guns and ammunition.[67] The lawmaker inspired his constituents to pursue their own acts of extralethal violence, the results of which Adolph Wislizenus spotted as he passed through Santa Fe a few weeks after Vigil's oration. The traveler found the Palace of the Governors decorated with "several strings of dried ears of Indians, killed by the hired parties that are occasionally sent out." Like the Englishman Ruxton, this German-born doctor recoiled at the sight of shriveled body parts displayed as a communicative spectacle of violent display. "In Chihuahua, they make a great exhibition with the whole scalps of Indians, [while] the refined New Mexicans show but the ears," Wislizenus wrote with disgusted sarcasm.[68] Sonoran military commander José Barrios called these types of actions "the first step" in permanently defeating Indian enemies, and he recommended a similar system of scalp warfare in his home state, "since it would be a good help against the savages." Political leaders from Chihuahua and Sonora began collaborating on a plan to augment Kirker's forces, but they temporarily shelved these ambitions midway through 1846 as the US Army invaded Mexico from multiple directions and forced a recalibration of military strategies to meet an urgent national crisis.[69]

With Mexico besieged by a powerful foreign neighbor, the attack at Galeana would be Kirker's last act as an agent of the Chihuahua government. When officials failed to pay the full amount owed for the scalps, Don Santiago turned on them as abruptly as he had on the Apaches eight years earlier.[70] He now cast his lot with American newcomers, who welcomed his services as an interpreter and guide.[71] Kirker joined Colonel Alexander Doniphan's Missouri Volunteers as they marched southward into Chihuahua on December 26, 1846. Several soldiers noted Kirker's arrival in their diaries, a testament to his wide reputation. Private Frank Edwards understood the deep hatred between Apaches and Mexicans, explaining that Kirker "was hired, at a high salary, to attempt the extermination of the tribe." He said that "the Mexicans look upon him as almost superhuman," even though some who knew the contract killer gave a value judgment when insisting that "his bravery is rather lukewarm, and that his victories have always been achieved through cunning." According to Edwards, the former Mexican agent offered to help the Americans out of spite, "having given up hunting Indians, in consequence of the government having forgotten to pay him." Another private in Doniphan's ranks, John Hughes, called Kirker a "celebrity Indian fighter" and "the TERROR of the Apaches," conjuring images of better-known figures such as Andrew Jackson and William Henry Harrison. Don Santiago's influence seems to have rubbed off on the Missourians, because when three Apaches raided their camp and stole several mules, a detachment under Lieutenant Jack Hinton overtook the culprits and scalped one of them.[72]

American military victories below the border eventually forced Mexico to cede almost half its territory—including much of the Southern Apache homelands—through the Treaty of Guadalupe Hidalgo in 1848. Article 11 of that treaty delegated responsibility for curtailing Apache and Comanche raids to the United States, which thus inherited a dilemma in Indian affairs that would give army officers and civil administrators headaches for years to come.[73] In one particularly frustrating episode, Mexican authorities complained about Ben Leaton, an American who operated a trading depot across the Rio Grande from Presidio del Norte. In 1849, Chihuahua governor Ángel Trías claimed that Leaton was "committing a thousand abuses," saying that his independent commercial relations with Apaches and Comanches enabled and encouraged their raiding below the border.[74] One year earlier, Colonel John Coffee Hays and his cohort of Texas Rangers had passed through Leaton's fort, an adobe compound with a cannon mounted on the roof and a US flag fluttering overhead. Major John Caperton, who accompanied Hays on that campaign, remembered Leaton as a "great friend to the Apaches," but also a man who "knew nothing of government or law, was a law to himself."[75] Leaton's freewheeling business pursuits—aided by his two Black slaves, Jacob and Peggy—made him a veritable reincarnation of James Kirker, who traded contraband of war to Southern Apaches at Santa Rita del Cobre in the 1830s.[76] Emilio Langberg, the Mexican inspector of military colonies at Paso del Norte, parroted Trías by accusing Leaton of trading arms and ammunition to Indians in exchange for the plunder that they robbed from Mexican towns and haciendas. Langberg invoked article 11, telling Major Jefferson Van Horne that US infantry troops at El Paso had a legal obligation to intervene in Leaton's "illicit traffic" along the border.[77] Van Horne readily conceded that Leaton "deals extensively in buying mules and horses stolen by the Indians from the Mexicans," and on at least one occasion a paramilitary outfit took refuge at Leaton's establishment during a campaign against Mescalero Apaches. To fulfill US obligations outlined in article 11, Van Horne recommended that George Deas, the department commander in Texas, establish a military post near Presidio del Norte to help combat the interrelated diplomatic crises of contraband trading and scalp hunting.[78] That the Treaty of Guadalupe Hidalgo charged the United States with responsibility for preventing raids and repat-riating captives did not, however, dissuade local Mexican figureheads from continuing and even expanding their bounty programs. As US officials such as Van Horne and Deas struggled to enforce article 11, Chihuahua became the first state to place a new scalp law on its books. On May 25, 1849, legisla-tors approved the purchase of Apache prisoners and piezas, authorizing the governor to negotiate *contratas de sangre*—blood contracts—with transna-tional practitioners of extralethal violence.

Known as Ley Quinta, or Fifth Law, this new edict declared war against "the barbarous Indians" and set the pay rate at 250 pesos for each impris-oned man, 200 pesos for every dead man's scalp, and 150 pesos for all women and children captives under fourteen years of age. These amounts equated to more than a year's wages for the average Mexican worker. To incentivize participation even more, legislators allowed contractors to keep or sell all confiscated livestock, once again wedding racialized conflict with personal economic interest. The pricing of captives at a higher rate than scalps was a notable departure from prior bounty laws, a modification that emanated from a self-described humanitarian impulse on the part of the governor. To curb fraud, local authorities would certify the identity of scalps before any payouts, but this effort to prevent the murder of innocent mestizos whose hair resembled that of Apaches or Comanches was not entirely successful.[79] Just as it had done with Kirker's bounty contract, Mexico's supreme court declared Ley Quinta unconstitutional just eight weeks after it went into ef-fect, but fronterizos disregarded this decision in a firm display of regional-ism. The Fifth Law had a broad impact, in part because it opened scalp warfare to all who wished to participate instead of limiting it to preferential deals with men such as Johnson and Kirker. To be sure, anybody who killed an Apache or Comanche in nineteenth-century Mexico would have been hailed as a hero, but before the Fifth Law that person would not have had a legal claim to money or plunder without first securing a state contract. Ley Quinta had an immediate and broad effect. In 1849 alone, Chihuahua doled out 17,896 pesos for captive and scalp bounties, and these large pay-outs attracted more opportunists to the trade.[80] When twenty-five-year-old Benjamin Butler Harris passed through Chihuahua on his way from Texas

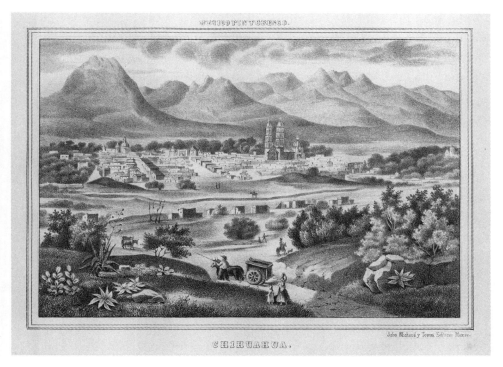

Ciudad Chihuahua, ca. 1850. Reproduced from Pierre-Frédéric Lehnert, *Album pintoresco de la República mexicana* (Mexico City: Julio Michaud y Thomas, 1850), 34.

to the California goldfields, he made note of "the tempting offer of the government reward for butchering Apache Indians," remarking that "at every place of halting we were advised that the state was offering . . . $200 for each dead warrior's head [and] $150 for each dead squaw's scalp."[81]

With aspiring slavers and scalpers taking the field under Ley Quinta, Mexican leaders labeled Kirker a traitor for helping the US Army and, in an ironic twist, placed a 10,000-peso price tag on his head. Unable to hunt Indians or chase plunder, Don Santiago followed the Gold Rush migration to California and died near San Francisco in 1852, but men from near and far eagerly took his place in borderlands scalp warfare.[82] One such individual was José María Zuloaga, a Mexican officer renowned for his indefatigable hatred of Indians and ardent opposition to any peace agreement. Although his most infamous deed occurred at Janos in 1857, when he killed several dozen Southern Apaches by poisoning their rations with strychnine, Zuloaga first cut his teeth in this gruesome pastime by collecting bounties under the Fifth Law. A onetime associate of Kirker who operated out of Corralitos, he led a civilian war party into the field in June 1849 and quickly took two Apache captives, for which he received 500 pesos in bounty money.[83]

Texans also took an interest in scalp hunting below the border, especially those with prior experience fighting Comanches. The first to seek a contract under the Fifth Law was Michael H. Chevallié, a former Texas Ranger from San Antonio. Just two days after the scalp act went into effect, he arranged with Chihuahua's *comisión de guerra* (war commission) to hunt Apaches. When Cornelius C. Cox, a veteran of the Republic of Texas Navy, passed through the northern Chihuahua town of Paso del Norte en route to West Coast goldfields in 1849, he quipped that one hundred or more men would likely abandon his overland party to join Chevallié's ranks as scalp hunters because the lucrative bounty was "great inducement to those who are fond of fighting."[84] To outfit his company, Chevallié received two advance payments, including 500 pesos from the state treasury and 2,000 pesos from Benjamin Riddell, an American consulate officer in Ciudad Chihuahua.[85] As a State Department employee, Riddell had to conduct his involvement surreptitiously—he mainly collected donations from Americans living in Mexico—because any official action could have implicated the United States in a regional style of scalp warfare that Mexico's central government disavowed. After just one week in the field, Chevallié's multinational party of nineteen Americans and five Mexicans killed nine Indians and took four children captive, earning a 1,500-peso payday in the state capital.[86] The incident sparked outrage throughout the country, not because Apaches had been scalped, but because armed Americans were allowed onto Mexican soil.[87] The fact that leaders in northern Mexico welcomed these foreign bounty hunters so soon after the United States Army invaded and defeated their nation in the US-Mexico War speaks to the desperation that legislators felt when attempting to mitigate Indian threats and shows that many fronterizos felt more vulnerable to Apaches and Comanches than to Americans. It also signified the pervasiveness of regionalist ideology in peripheral states such as Chihuahua and Sonora, where people harbored lukewarm feelings of obligation to a central government that had long neglected their safety in the face of continuous Indian raiding.

When the California Gold Rush enticed Chevallié farther west, another Texas Ranger stepped into the leadership role and proved himself a prolific operative. A contemporary described John Joel Glanton as "one of the most reckless and wicked" people in San Antonio, adding matter-of-factly that "he shot men for sport."[88] His exploits in Mexico would live up to that reputation. The consular agent Riddell again provided financing in the amount of 2,500 pesos, creating a murky connection between the US government and Mexican policies of genocide, and shortly thereafter Glanton's "splendidly mounted and armed" company returned to Ciudad Chihuahua with five scalps and three captives who faced a lifetime of servitude in Mexican households. The soldiers of fortune pocketed 1,300 pesos after a commission of five "experts" examined and authenticated the scalps. Encouraged by these results, Glanton and thirty followers captured an elderly Apache woman near Galeana, questioned her about the whereabouts of the tribe, then murdered her. She posed no physical threat to either the scalpers or the state and had no value as a slave because of her advanced age, so racism and financial interest clearly motivated the atrocity. George Evans, a forty-niner traveling to California, witnessed the woman's execution as he passed Glanton's crew on the overland trail but dared not protest, choosing instead to confide his horror to a diary. One of the contract killers, Santiago Ortíz, rode back to Ciudad Chihuahua and collected 100 pesos for the trophy.[89]

Glanton's company finally returned to the capital in August 1849, presenting nine more scalps—including that of Chief Gomez—taken during a strike on Mescalero Apaches in the mountains of Trans-Pecos Texas. Major E. B. Babbitt reported the incident to military authorities in San Antonio, saying that a group of Americans acting "in the service of the State of Chihuahua" had crossed the Rio Grande at Presidio del Norte—where Ben Leaton operated his contraband trade—and subsequently "killed and scalped a number of peaceable and friendly Indians." Settlers in Texas feared that survivors of this attack would retaliate on them "as the result of the shameful conduct of those degraded mercenaries."[90] The transborder scalp raid also threatened to upend diplomatic relations between the United States and Mexico. When Secretary of War George Crawford read Babbitt's report in November, he immediately contacted Secretary of State John M. Clayton to apprise him of the potential fallout. "So inhuman an outrage should draw on its perpetrators the severest punishment," Crawford wrote, predicting that Mexicans would blame future Indian raids on the United States because Glanton was an American. He pointed out the hypocrisy of Ley Quinta, saying that Chihuahua's scalping policy "is calculated to defeat its own object" because bounty hunters targeting Indians living within the United States would incite retaliatory raids into Mexico. The secretary of war hoped that State Department employees would intervene in Chihuahua to have Ley Quinta rescinded, telling Clayton that "the continuance of a system calculated to lead to the commission of such outrages and to endanger the tranquility of the frontiers is to be deprecated, and it is to be hoped it will be speedily abandoned."[91] But local Mexican officials did not care that the bloodletting occurred outside their jurisdiction, as a town council quickly verified the hair as that of Apaches and paid the requisite rewards. This included a 500-peso bonus given to Glanton "for good behavior in pursuit of the enemy." Breaking with tradition, Councilman Miguel Escobar ceremoniously burned the piezas rather than exhibit them on the public plaza. With Christmas approaching, Chihuahua officials dipped into the state's war fund once more, extracting 2,000 pesos to supply the next expedition.[92]

One of the men riding with Glanton was Samuel E. Chamberlain, a New Englander who fought in the US-Mexico War and subsequently deserted the army. While confined to a filthy guardhouse in Tucson, Chamberlain had a chance encounter with a cellmate who revealed himself to be one of Glanton's compatriots. Intrigued by Tom Hitchcock's adventurous tales of scalp warfare, Chamberlain escaped with him and the two men joined the bounty hunters at Fronteras. "There was in camp drying thirty-seven of those disgusting articles of trade, Apache scalps, cut with the right ear on, to prevent fraud," the shocked American newcomer recalled. "This was the band of cutthroats that I had joined and such was John Glanton, the Captain of the Scalp Hunters of Sonora." On their way to "cash the hair"—a phrase that clearly connoted profit motivations—the men murdered eight innocent mestizos and added their forelocks to the bag. They managed to collect payment for all the crowns, "the Mexican scalps passing for good Indian without question," and later that night, after restocking on whiskey, "a regular orgy was held in camp" as the men engaged in postmortem revelry. Claiming to be "thoroughly horrified with the hellish deeds of my companions," Chamberlain deserted the gang just before Yuma (Quechan) Indians killed Glanton and ten of his American cohorts during an ambush at the Colorado River ferry in April 1850.[93] Hoping to vindicate Glanton and discourage any additional Indian attacks on the overland trail to the Pacific, residents in San Diego and Los Angeles quickly raised a "volunteer company" of 142 men who rode out in pursuit of the Yumas. Near the end of a three-month campaign that they innocuously dubbed the "Gila Expedition," the civilian volunteers fought a group of Yumas along the Colorado River and killed several before returning to their homes in southern California.[94]

Lauding Chihuahua's "very good success" in these operations, Durango's Council of War adopted Ley Quinta on July 5, 1849. Beset by the raids of Comanches, Kiowas, and Lipan Apaches, the state government invoked the ubiquitous language of racism as it expressed a desire to negotiate with "national or foreign partisans who organize to fight the barbarous Indians." Two hundred pesos would be awarded for every Indian, "alive or dead of whatever sex, except for little children." Scalpers would also receive 10 percent of market value for property recovered from Indian camps and could collect additional compensation for horses and mules. The law required each "guerrilla band" to declare a leader who would act as an intermediary with the government. If a group abused its power or acted detrimentally to the public welfare, its permit would be revoked. Any time a town council received scalps, a committee of three would certify that the piezas "actually belong to savages who invade the state." Once investigators positively identified the evidence—a highly imperfect process, based on Glanton's fraudulent redemption of Mexican scalps—payments would be disbursed from the war fund.[95]

Under these profitable stipulations, fortune seekers quickly lined up for killing contracts in Durango. In August 1849, the local secretary of state met with Michael James Box, a veteran of Benjamin McCulloch's renowned Texas Ranger company. Box and his twenty-three followers "unanimously accepted" the state's offer to capture and murder Indians for cash salaries, and they campaigned for a month before locating a camp of Comanches and Kiowas. In the ensuing battle the contractors slew six Indians, including a chief wearing a Martin Van Buren peace medal. Pleased with these results, Durango officials renewed the agreement at a per diem rate of 2 reales (1/4 peso). Within weeks Box ambushed another group, killing four Comanches and taking 35 horses and mules from the victims.[96] Hoping to expand these operations, the governor contracted with yet another Texas Ranger veteran, John Dusenberry, at a rate of 5 pesos per day. He and thirty followers promptly killed five Indians and captured 503 horses and mules, most of which were sold back to their original Mexican owners for a handsome profit. The governor personally reached out to McCulloch, but the famous Texan declined a proposal to hunt Indians in favor of grander pursuits in the West Coast goldfields.[97]

Sonora became the third state to embrace Ley Quinta when it adopted its own version in February 1850, allowing 150 pesos for an Apache man's scalp and 100 pesos for every woman and child. Owners of recovered livestock could buy back the animals at 12 pesos per mule, 6 pesos per horse, and 3 pesos each for cattle. Sonora requested donations from citizens and implemented a 15 percent tax on tobacco products to finance the program, establishing a special war fund to manage the money. To limit government expenses in financing private armies, merchants were required to sell supplies "at cost" to bounty hunters, and committees would attempt to verify the tribe, age, and sex of all scalps before payouts. Sonora eventually amended the law to include Seri (Kongkaak) Indians—a seminomadic and nonagricultural tribe of several hundred persons residing along the Gulf of California coast and on Tiburon Island—mandating 150 pesos per dead male and 50 pesos for captive women. Seri children had no redeemable value with the state, but they could be sold into slavery through private transactions.[98] Sonora's offer of less money for Seris indicated not only that it was more dangerous to hunt Apaches but also that Apaches posed the most urgent threat to Mexican lives and property.[99]

Although several Mexican states adopted and promoted versions of the Fifth Law at midcentury, and Chihuahua governor José Cordero unilaterally lifted the licensing requirement, civilian scalp warfare never fully supplanted regular army campaigning.[100] Throughout the era, Mexican troops pursued and attacked Apaches, compounding the impact of scalp warfare against the tribe. Just three months after the Fifth Law went into effect, Colonel José María Elías González and two hundred soldiers killed four Apaches, including El Cochi, during an expedition in northern Mexico, and one of the guides was allowed to scalp the chief for payment at Janos.[101] Two years later, on March 5, 1851, Colonel José María Carrasco led four hundred Sonoran troops in a strike near Janos that killed twenty-one Apaches—including Chief Yrigóllen as well as Geronimo's mother, wife, and children—and forced sixty-two women and children into captivity.[102] The strategies of bounty hunting and army campaigning complemented each other, in that civilian fortune seekers ranged free from the bureaucratic and jurisdictional constraints of military officers and could therefore operate anytime and anywhere. This undermined the Apaches' ability to shelter themselves behind the asylum of one Mexican state or another, as they often attempted to do by negotiating peace agreements with some towns while continuing to raid others.[103] As early as 1840, Kirker's attack on Pisago Cabezón's camp near Janos showed Apaches that this tactic would no longer work when unrestrained civilians were involved, and the subsequent ambush at Galeana drove home that point.

At the very moment that three northern Mexican states implemented Ley Quinta, international boundary surveys restructured borderlands geopolitics. Commissioners John Russell Bartlett and Pedro García Conde drew a new line on the map from Texas to California, dividing regional sovereignty between the United States and Mexico, and several companies of US infantry and dragoons garrisoned Fort Bliss, Fort Fillmore, and Fort Webster to patrol the northern side of the border.[104] Despite this increased manpower, the transition from Mexican province to American territory hindered paramilitary and military operations alike. Officials in Santa Fe and Washington, DC, did not recognize preexisting bounty laws, and a new jurisdictional boundary sketched arbitrarily through Southern Apache homelands imposed an invisible but meaningful political construct that gave mobile Indians—who did not acknowledge the legitimacy of the border line and crisscrossed it at will—a significant advantage in their ability to raid northern Mexico and evade soldiers and scalp hunters.[105]

These new geopolitical realities frustrated Sylvester Mowry, an Arizona mine owner who worked as a US Indian agent at Tucson. Although he did not personally collect scalps, he openly condoned such extralethal tactics. "The Apaches cannot be tamed," he told the commissioner of Indian affairs in one annual report. "There is only one way to wage war against the Apaches . . . they must be surrounded, starved into coming in, supervised, or put to death." Echoing the racialized rhetoric of Mexican leaders, he recommended that the US government implement the same bounty program as Chihuahua and Sonora, claiming that Pimas and Papagos would happily hunt their sworn Apache enemies in exchange for material rewards. "If these ideas shock any weak-minded individual who thinks himself a philanthropist, I can only say I pity without respecting his mistaken sympathy," Mowry proclaimed. "A man might as well have sympathy for a rattlesnake."[106] Frederick Ober, a naturalist from Massachusetts, parroted these thoughts when he traveled through the region. Praising bounties for "lessening the number of los barbaros" by facilitating the death of Apache men and the enslavement of women and children at households and haciendas, he added that "the Mexican government has finally evolved a policy that should commend itself to our own."[107] Joseph Pratt Allyn, a native of Connecticut who received an appointment from Abraham Lincoln to serve on the Arizona Territorial Supreme Court in 1863, was surprised on his arrival in Prescott to hear "one and all believing and talking of nothing but killing Indians." Allyn said that Apaches "are shot wherever seen," concluding that "this sort of warfare is not likely to make the country very safe [but] it is the only way to deal with Indians."[108] Daniel Ellis Conner traversed Arizona in the 1860s alongside the scout and mountain man Joseph Reddeford Walker, and he wrote nonchalantly that "it was the rigid rule all over the country to shoot these savages upon sight."[109] These exterminatory sentiments represented the majority opinion among Arizonans—even territorial governor John Noble Goodwin gave a speech calling for the extermination of Indians—and occasionally this hatred morphed into action. The most infamous example involved the slaughter of 144 Aravaipa Apaches under Chief Eskiminzin during the Camp

Grant Massacre of 1871, although in that instance Anglo, Hispanic, and Papago perpetrators acted on racial and cultural motivations rather than cash incentives.[110] In another instance, the scalp of a slain Indian was nailed to the front door of the Prescott newspaper office, where it remained on display for many years.[111]

Despite the recommendations of men such as Mowry, Ober, and Goodwin and the celebratory exhibitions of Prescott residents, scalp warfare temporarily declined in prominence as the borderlands were saturated with military force during Mexico's War of the Reform from 1857 to 1860, the imperialistic "Grand Design" of Emperors Napoleon III and Maximilian I between 1861 and 1867, and the American Civil War that ended in 1865. The US government raised thousands of troops in New Mexico and Arizona to fend off a Confederate invasion, and once that threat subsided Unionists in the Southwest shifted some of their attention to fighting Southern and Mescalero Apaches. One direct result of this military buildup under General James Henry Carleton, the department commander in New Mexico, was the treacherous capture of Mangas Coloradas under a flag of truce at Piños Altos. Miners there promptly delivered the aging chief to the guardhouse at nearby Fort McLane, and within days US soldiers shot him, cut off his head, boiled away the skin in a black kettle, and shipped the skull to a phrenologist in New York.[112] Reflecting the sense of 'igoyá'í as it pertained to the chief's perfidious murder and decapitation, the Apache elder James Kaywaykla explained that most tribe members "abhor mutilation" because of its spiritual implications. "Little did the White Eyes know how they would pay when they defiled the body of our great chief!" he declared in poignant reference to retaliatory cycles of extralethal violence.[113] Five months after the murder and disfigurement of Mangas Coloradas, Southern Apaches ambushed US troops at a Rio Grande crossing north of the Mesilla Valley, killing three of them. The corpse of Lieutenant Ludam A. Bargie was later discovered lying in the brush, with his head chopped off and the heart torn out of his chest. Apaches deliberately chose the commanding officer—roughly equivalent to the status of a chief like Mangas Coloradas—for corporeal mutilation, and they desecrated his body using the same extralethal act of decapitation that American soldiers performed at Fort McLane.[114]

"The Apache is a true savage," Lieutenant Albert J. Fountain wrote several months later from his post at Fort McRae, just fifty miles north of the river crossing where Bargie perished. "He is a monster who delights in blood and torture, and woe to the unfortunate man who falls into his hands alive." Fountain went on to explain, with no discernable sense of irony, that his living quarters were decorated with "a score of scalps" belonging to various Apache bands.[115]

Meanwhile, as the French invasion subsided in Mexico and the republican government of Benito Juárez reclaimed power, Sonora governor Ignacio Pesqueíra revived Ley Quinta and his attention reverted to the omnipresent fear of Apache raiding. In September 1870, Secretary of State Hamilton Fish mentioned Sonora's most recent scalping initiative in his annual report to Congress. Twelve rewards of $300 each had been paid over the preceding four months, Fish explained, and a special state account had been seeded with $5,000 in startup funds to facilitate the disbursement of additional bounties. Calling Apaches the "Scourges of Sonora," the head of the US State Department hoped this foreign scalp law would "result in their extermination" and thereby remove a major Indigenous obstacle to American expansion in the US-Mexico borderlands.[116] Arizona lawmakers wholeheartedly endorsed Sonora's extralethal initiative, although they did not enact an official scalp bounty of their own. Meeting in Tucson in 1871—the same year as the Camp Grant Massacre—territorial legislators published a lengthy report about "outrages perpetrated by the Apache Indians," and Arizona representative Richard C. McCormick approvingly told US congressmen that Mexicans had "increased the bounty upon Apache scalps and waged a war of extermination."[117] Under this new scalping program, the Sonora government would ultimately distribute more than 36,000 pesos to Mexicans, Papagos, and other Indian auxiliaries who worked as agents of scalp warfare, but the initiative still fell far short of Fish's hope that the tribe would be forced into extinction.[118]

Impressed by these results in Sonora and frustrated with their own inability to catch Chief Victorio and his followers, Chihuahua officials also resurrected elements of Ley Quinta in the years following the failed French Intervention of 1861–67. Born around 1825, Victorio was a renowned fighter within his Chihenne band and became one of the preeminent Southern Apache leaders following the death of Cochise in 1874.[119] Victorio and his followers raided with impunity on both sides of the international line, capitalizing on the inability of American and Mexican diplomats to formulate a mutual agreement for transborder military operations. The Chihenne leader successfully evaded US troops for years using a combination of stealthy mobility, targeted violence, and strategic diplomacy. These Apaches also employed the special medicine power of Lozen, a sister of Victorio who became one of the few women to accompany raiding and war parties. According to Dan Nicholas, a Southern Apache man interviewed in the mid-twentieth century, "Power is a mysterious, intangible attribute difficult to explain, even by one possessing it."[120] Known among her tribe as the "woman warrior," Lozen had a metaphysical gift of visualizing the proximity and direction of approaching enemies long before they arrived. "No other has the Power of locating the enemy," one Apache explained. "She is sacred . . . she is respected above all living women."[121] Along with Lozen, Victorio and his Chihenne followers abandoned any hope for peace when they fled from the Warm Springs reservation near southern New Mexico's Cañada Alamosa in August 1879.[122] Victorio was already in his mid-fifties when Lieutenant Colonel Joaquín Terrazas, cousin of Governor Luis Terrazas, led Mexican soldiers and Tarahumara allies in a battle that killed the elusive headman and seventy-seven others at Tres Castillos on October 15, 1880. Lozen was notably absent at the time, and some Apaches attributed the defeat to Victorio's metaphorical blindness without her clairvoyant medicine power to warn of nearby enemies. From the consulate in Ciudad Chihuahua, US diplomat Louis H. Scott reported that Mexicans gave "the blood thirsty Apaches a lesson that they will remember," and he sent a telegram to State Department headquarters informing them of the watershed moment.[123]

In a scene of violent display that must have seemed eerily familiar to those who remembered previous bounty wars, Terrazas and his men rode triumphantly into the capital with sixty-eight captives and just as many scalps.[124] The spectacle was every bit a sequel to the one that Ruxton described in 1846. "The whole city turned out," an American newspaper correspondent observed with obvious admiration. "The bands played, and from the church and cathedral towers the bells rang out." The victors paraded through town waving "the ghastly scalps of the fallen enemy, held aloft to the gazing crowd." Mauricio Corredor, a Tarahumara man credited with slaying Victorio, carried the famed leader's flowing gray hair, for which he collected 2,000 pesos. Terrazas was promoted to colonel, and the state government regaled its newfound idols with 27,450 pesos in cash rewards along with uniforms, rifles, and commemorative mementos.[125] Dubbing Terrazas "our Chihuahuan hero," one person proclaimed with dramatic irony that "there is no stain in his story."[126] In the days that followed, the young Apache captives would be distributed among the city's wealthier households, while the adult women remained in prison to be used as ransom for Mexican abductees residing among the Southern Apaches.[127] Although Chihuahua and Sonora paid significant amounts of money to scalpers during the early years of the Porfiriato, as the period of Porfirio Díaz's presidency is called, these bounties summoned little enthusiasm among foreign expatriates, because it was predominantly Mexican citizens and Indian allies rather than American contractors who murdered and mutilated Apaches for financial gain in the 1870s and 1880s.

As the United States and Mexican governments tried to track Geronimo and his followers in 1885, commissioners in three Arizona counties independently offered settlers $250 per Indian scalp in a development that duplicated the calls for extermination and corporeal mutilation that Mexican legislators commonly broadcasted. "This reward system, while it may seem savage and brutal to the Northern and Eastern sentimentalist, is looked upon [in the Southwest] as the only means possible of ridding Arizona of the murderous Apaches," the *New York Times* reported, pointing out that settlers in that region intended "to act henceforth independent of the military authorities" as they prepared for "a real old-fashioned Indian hunt."[128] There is no evidence that organized civilian paramilitary campaigns took the field in Arizona in the fall of 1885, or that bounty hunters redeemed trophies for cash rewards as a result of these blusterous initiatives in Cochise, Pima, and Yavapai Counties, but they clearly drew from the long-standing tradition of scalping Apaches when circulating such proclamations. With Mangas Coloradas, Cochise, and Victorio all dead and the tribal population severely diminished by decades of deadly conflict, the last known incident of scalp warfare in the US-Mexico borderlands occurred on October 30, 1886, when Chihuahua authorities paid Luis Orozco 200 pesos for an Apache that he killed.[129] Not coincidentally, Geronimo—who was about sixty years old at the time and had lived through all of the events chronicled in this chapter, had surrendered along with his small band of followers to the US Army just a few weeks earlier, bringing the so-called Apache Wars to a conclusion.[130]

The precise impact of Mexico's scalp warfare is difficult to gauge in terms of lives lost and people captured, especially when considered alongside the campaigns of regular soldiers who also fought Indians throughout these years. During the bounty system's heyday—from the Johnson Massacre of 1837 to implementation of Ley Quinta in 1849—transnational contractors killed at least 374 Apaches, and Apaches slew no fewer than 689 Mexicans. These figures offer just a partial reflection of the harsh reality, because they pertain solely to Chihuahua, extend only to midcentury, and exclude the 3,351 known deaths (702 Indians and 2,649 Mexicans) that resulted from Comanche and Kiowa raiding during the same period.[131] One important takeaway from these statistics is the unintended consequences of contract killing: Mexicans suffered approximately two-thirds of the casualties, partly as a result of deadly tribal retaliation, but also because men such as Kirker and Glanton murdered innocent citizens to profit from scalps that could not be distinguished from those of Indians. Fronterizos endured the lion's share of fatalities, but this fact is misleading, too, because the populations of Chihuahua, Durango, and Sonora far exceeded those of independent Indians. Numbering only about 3,000 in the mid-nineteenth century, the Southern Apaches lost one-fifth or more of their members to scalpers, to say nothing of the hundreds of women and children subjected to slavery as a result of captive bounties. Indian agent Michael Steck, serving at the Southern Apache Agency in New Mexico, was not far from the truth when he reported in 1855 that the tribe "cannot bring into the field over half the number of warriors that they could have done 20 years ago."[132] Kirker himself provides an angle from which to assess this impact. After being banished from Mexico in 1847, he claimed responsibility for killing 487 Apaches.

This statistic seems like the exaggeration of a murderous braggart, and in fact Kirker's biographer was able to account for only 322 of those claimed kills in the documentary records.[133] But Kirker was just one of many profiteers who hunted Indians, so his personal tally—even in its embellished form—represents a fraction of the overall fatalities directly attributable to scalp warfare in northern Mexico.

What can be understood with more precision is the deep animosity that this extralethal style of violence bred. Traditional military operations, augmented by contract killing and slaving, took a tremendous toll, claiming thousands of Indian lives and relegating as many or more to a lifetime of servitude. Conflict between Indians and Mexicans existed long before public officials codified an exterminatory system of scalping and slaving, but this genocidal tactic pushed the carnage to unprecedented levels.[134] At least nine individuals—most of them Americans—led scalping crews that each included dozens of men, meaning that hundreds of contract killers plied the US-Mexico borderlands in search of plunder, captives, and scalps. Ringleaders including Johnson, Kirker, and Glanton devastated the Southern Apaches demographically as well as politically, because several of the tribe's headmen—El Cochi, Juan José Compá, Juan Diego Compá, Relles, Torres, and Yrigóllen—perished during incidents of scalp warfare.[135] "It has been a long time since then, but I still have no love for the Mexicans," Geronimo seethed in reference to the attack at Janos that claimed the lives of his own family as well as Chief Yrigóllen. "With me they were always treacherous and malicious. I am old now and shall never go on the warpath again, but if I were young, and followed the warpath, it would lead into Old Mexico."[136]

The Mexican model of scalp warfare differs from American examples because unlike the killings in mid-nineteenth-century California—where the men who killed Indians were predominantly white American citizens organized into "volunteer companies"—most of Mexico's contract killers were not permanent residents of the states for which they contracted, nor were they even Mexican citizens, hailing instead from the Republic of Texas, the United States, and itinerant Indigenous nations such as the Delaware and the Shawnee.[137] This multinational cooperation signaled a common goal of eradicating Southern Apaches and Comanches and typified a decentralized genocidal policy sponsored by local rather than federal administrators. The targets of these massacres had their homelands primarily within the newly redrawn boundaries of the United States, meaning that Mexican officials in the 1850s and thereafter aimed exterminatory policies at groups residing mostly outside their legal jurisdiction. One testament to the transnational intrigue of borderlands politics included the US consular agent in Ciudad Chihuahua who used his official diplomatic status on two occasions to collect funds and provide financing for Mexican bounty programs, making the United States government complicit in acts of genocide that occurred in a foreign country.

The ubiquity of alcohol is another noteworthy aspect of scalp warfare in northern Mexico. Firsthand accounts attest to the omnipresence of liquor, both as antecedent to killing and as fuel for postmortem revelry. Perpetrators such as Kirker and Glanton were notorious drinkers, and many of those who rode alongside them similarly imbibed to excess. There is no evidence to suggest that these men were drunk while attacking Indian camps; indeed, their heavily lopsided victories against formidable foes would have been difficult to achieve had they been anything but sober. But scalpers consumed enormous quantities of whiskey after each triumph. In addition to its celebratory consumption, alcohol also played a strategic role in many hostile engagements. Mexican villagers, and sometimes scalp hunters themselves, distributed liquor among Indians before ambushes, transforming otherwise skilled fighters into intoxicated adversaries with little ability to defend themselves. The casualty counts at Johnson's massacre in 1837 and Kirker's assault in 1846 would have been much lower—and many of the attackers would have lost their lives, too—had so many of the Apache men not been neutralized with liquor beforehand.

By transforming the racist rhetoric of Indian extermination into official policies of extralethal violence, nineteenth-century Mexican lawmakers acted with clear genocidal intent. Their laws ultimately failed to produce the desired outcome of eradicating hated groups, but in the case of Southern Apaches the known statistics indicate that approximately one-third of the tribal population succumbed to scalp warfare either as casualties or as slaves. Governments in Chihuahua, Durango, and Sonora implemented bounty laws and paid the requisite rewards using tax dollars and donations, making common citizens complicit in the violence, but most of the perpetrators were not Mexican nationals. Instead, the policies attracted a rather random assortment of transnational recruits—Tarahumara, Pima, and Papago auxiliaries, Shawnee and Delaware refugees, Texas expatriates, American opportunists, army deserters, and prison inmates—who shared a willingness to commit heinous acts of extralethal violence for material gain. Unattached to any national government, these men had no compunction about doing what others either could not legally or would not morally do: deceive, enslave, kill, and mutilate human beings for the sake of making money. Their livelihood depended on a weak decentralized state's failure to suppress Apache and Comanche mobility using traditional military force, and bounty hunters pursued their freelance trade with the same sense of legitimacy as any blacksmith, carpenter, miner, or merchant. "Business men always took receipts, and I wanted something to show our success," James Hobbs remarked in reference to his own participation in the scalping of nine Apaches. For men such as Hobbs, who rode alongside Kirker in the 1840s, killing for profit and plunder seemed like a normal part of the sordid borderlands shadow economy in which they operated.[138]

In the nineteenth-century US-Mexico borderlands, scalp and slave hunters fulfilled a central component of government strategies for conquering powerful Indigenous groups in a peripheral region where central authority bowed to regional command structures. When state officials hired murderers and financed their operations, they effectively shunned the use of professional soldiers in favor of scalp warfare that monetized the slaving, killing, and mutilating of Indian enemies that they viewed as subhuman savages. Mexico's bounties were ultimately counterproductive because they perpetuated war rather than peace and condemned thousands of citizens to violent deaths during retaliatory raids, but the ubiquity of contract killing and slaving across five decades demonstrates the interconnectivity of individual economic interest, colonial racism, and extralethal violence as driving forces behind genocidal policy and action. Bounty programs relied on the compulsions of ruthless rogues who transformed their hatred of Indians into an industry that met their own financial needs as well as the exterminatory policy objectives of the weak governments for which they worked. Although they acted primarily in self-promotion rather than patriotic service to a country, transnational contractors such as Johnson, Kirker, Glanton, Chevallié, Zuloaga, Box, and Dusenberry sold their services to state agents, and in so doing these men made a veritable business out of killing Indians in Mexico. At the same time, Rangers in neighboring Texas partook in similar campaigns of scalp warfare against Comanches and Lipan Apaches, and those profit-driven exploits formed another important component of state-sponsored extralethal violence in the North American borderlands.

FOUR

Scalping Atrocities on the Texas Frontier

In 1860, a US Census agent received an unforgettable lesson in the ubiquity of violence on the Texas frontier. At the small town of Weatherford thirty miles west of Fort Worth, the federal employee encountered two brothers named George Wythe Baylor and John Robert Baylor. When asked about professional occupation, twenty-five-year-old George proudly proclaimed himself an "Indian killer."[1] If the census taker interpreted this statement as a joke, he was sorely mistaken. In July of that same year, a Houston newspaper informed its readers that "Capt. Baylor sent down for our inspection the trophies of his late fight with the Indians," including a scalp, bows and arrows, shields, and other accoutrements of war. Along with his older sibling John, three accomplices, and "a Negro boy named Allen," George had ambushed a small band of Comanches in the Hill Country of central Texas. "All Indians who lose their scalps go to . . . their idea of hell . . . where the women [are] old, ugly, skinny squaws," he later wrote with unfiltered bigotry, "and as we were not in the missionary business we sent everyone to hell we could by scalping them." Having killed thirteen Comanches and recovered fifty-five horses during their five-day foray, the Baylors became local heroes—the Texas equivalents to Dubosq in French Canada, Hannah Duston in colonial New England, James Kirker in Mexico, and Ben Wright in California.[2]

Back at Weatherford, residents hosted "a grand ball and supper" to honor the two Baylors, whose human trophies were prominently displayed outside the town courthouse for all to gawk at. "A rope was stretched from pillar to pillar and the shields of the chiefs and the scalps all strung up above the heads of the dancers," George fondly remembered, "and so we had a regular 'scalp dance.' " The performance of this celebratory spectacle in front of the courthouse carried symbolic significance, implicitly nodding to a state legal structure that enabled and encouraged such acts of violent display. With an eye-for-an-eye mentality of vengeance, the brothers attempted to justify their dastardly deeds by sending the Houston newspaper editor a light-haired scalp that they recovered from a female captive that the Comanches had killed and dismembered. "The warrior's scalp now dangles side by side with hers," the journalist wrote of his new decorations, "mingling the jetty

Page No. _25._

SCHEDULE 1.—Free Inhabitants in _Beat_ _No 2_ in the County of _Parker_ State of _Texas_ enumerated by me, on the _22d_ day of _August_ 1860. _E J Brown_ Ass't Marshal.

Post Office _Weatherford_. 43

Dwelling-houses numbered in the order of visitation.	Families numbered in the order of visitation.	The name of every person whose usual place of abode on the first day of June, 1860, was in this family.	Age.	Sex.	Color.	Profession, Occupation, or Trade of each person, male and female, over 15 years of age.	Value of Real Estate.	Value of Personal Estate.	Place of Birth, Naming the State, Territory, or Country.	Married within the year.	Attended School within the year.	Persons over 20 y'rs of age who cannot read & write.	Whether deaf and dumb, blind, insane, idiotic, pauper, or convict.	
1	2	3	4	5	6	7	8	9	10	11	12	13	14	
178	178	D. Norton	40	M	W	Farmer	150	1000	Ohio					1
		L. Norton	34	F	W	Domestic			Ohio					2
		S. Norton	17	F	W	Domestic			Ohio					3
		M. Norton	14	M	W				Ohio					4
		G. Norton	12	F	W				Ohio					5
		S. Norton	8	F	W				Ohio					6
		L. Norton	1	M	W				Texas					7
179	179	J. Baylor	37	M	W	Lawyer	2000	14700	Kentucky		x			8
		E. Baylor	35	F	W	Domestic			Louisiana					9
		G. Baylor	25	M	W	Indian Killer		3000	Columbus Ohio					10
		J. Baylor	14	M	W				Texas					11
		W. Baylor	12	M	W				Texas					12
		B. Baylor	10	F	W				Texas					13
		H. Baylor	8	M	W				Texas					14
		S. Baylor	7	F	W				Texas					15
		... Baylor	5	M	W				Texas					16
		W. Baylor	3	M	W				Texas					17
180	180	C. Jordan	28	M	W	Lawyer	1800	3000	Virginia					18
		S. Jordan	28	F	W	Domestic		1300	Tennessee					19

US Census, 1860, showing the entry for George Wythe Baylor as an "Indian Killer" on line 10. Entry for "G. Baylor," US Census, Parker County, TX (1860), 25.

locks of the savage with the blonde curls of the Texan woman."³ The desktop inside a Houston printing office thus became an unlikely exhibit for the juxtaposition of two scalps, one belonging to a white woman, the other to an Indian man. This scene exuded profound symbolic power, demonstrating the deep racial hatred and strong desire for personal retribution that motivated extralethal violence on the nineteenth-century Texas frontier.

Unlike colonial assemblymen in New Netherland, New England, and New France or state officials in republican Mexico, the lawmakers of Texas never officially instituted a bounty program or systematized cash rewards for Indian scalps. Even without codified monetary incentives, however, extralethal violence became a component of intercultural conflict in nineteenth-century Texas. The style of scalp warfare that developed in Texas involved the Rangers as paramilitary operatives who sometimes rode alongside allied Indian scouts and auxiliaries, building on the hybridized combat tactics of New England and New France a century earlier. In Texas, however, violent display was more common as a form of celebration that entailed individualized trophy taking as well as mock scalp dances and public scalp exhibitions. These trends owed in part to a pervasive belief among Texans that Indians who killed and scalped white people must also be killed and scalped in retribution. Dozens if not hundreds of letters and petitions that Texas settlers wrote in regard to frontier defense read like a cacophony of gruesome tales about "savage" Indians butchering women and children, each note offering specific examples of murder and mutilation and insisting that in-kind retaliation was not only justified but obligatory.⁴

Beginning in the early 1820s, when American immigrants settled on *empresario* (foreigner) land grants in the Mexican state of Coahuila y Tejas, the racialized rhetoric of Indian extermination among both Tejanos and Anglo Texans became a driving force for extreme violence directed at the region's Indigenous groups. One of the earliest examples of scalping in Texas involved a settler named William B. DeWees, who arrived in 1823 as part of the first wave of migration that followed Moses Austin's colonization charter. Under the guidance of Robert Kuykendall and a group of civilian volunteers, DeWees took part in an attack on a Karankawa camp on the aptly named Skull Creek near the Colorado River that resulted in the deaths of nineteen Indians, and afterward he personally scalped one of the corpses "by a spirit of retaliation" and carried it home "as a trophy from battle."[5] Another participant, John H. Moore, attempted to justify the scalping by claiming that Karankawas "were obnoxious to whites" and said that they engaged in cannibalism.[6] The Kuykendall group's extralethal acts of postmortem revelry, driven by racial hatred and the colonial imperative of Indian conquest, would come to typify the motivation for scalping among Texas settlers who sought trophies of battlefield glory as well as plunder in the form of horses, saddles, guns, hides, liquor, and other valuables.

By the 1830s, as the Andrew Jackson administration pursued a demographically devastating policy of Indian removal in the South, American settlers and their chattel slaves were flooding into East Texas and soon outnumbered the region's Hispanic population by a ratio of at least four to one in many areas. In 1836, Texans rebelled against Mexico, issued a declaration of independence, fought Antonio López de Santa Anna's army first at the Alamo and then at San Jacinto, wrote a new constitution that explicitly protected the right to own slaves, and pursued a course of contested nationhood (the Mexican government refused to recognize Texas sovereignty) as the Republic of Texas.[7] With an estimated thirty thousand Indians living inside the claimed boundaries of Texas when Sam Houston took office as president, he recognized the importance of sound policy and promoted a strategy of coexistence and conciliation with certain tribes.[8] To that end, he told the Texas Congress in November 1836 that "the friendship and alliance of many of our border Tribes of Indians will be of the utmost importance to this government," announcing that diplomatic agents would be appointed to negotiate treaties with groups like the Caddos and Cherokees that might in turn become state allies against the hated Comanches.[9] On November 11, Houston dispatched messages to leaders of six tribes—including the Comanches—proclaiming that "it is now time to be at Peace with each other and bury the Tomahawk forever."[10] At the same time, he reiterated to Texas congressmen that "lasting peace and friendship" with Indians could "give security to our frontier," noting that the only alternative would be violence and suffering.[11]

The president's agents negotiated treaties with western Tonkawas at San Antonio in November 1837 and with eastern Tonkawas at Houston in April

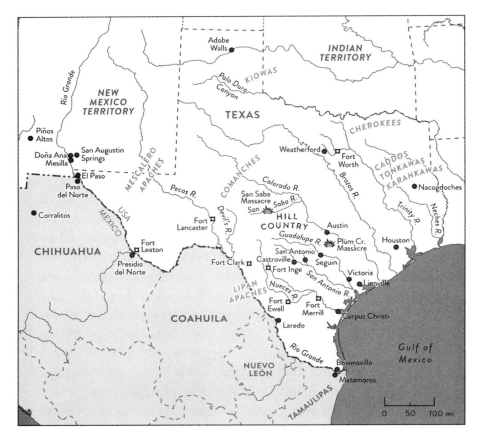

The nineteenth-century Texas borderlands. Map by Erin Greb.

1838, forging alliances wherein tribesmen would serve as scouts for Texas troops.[12] In so doing, Texas replicated one long-standing tradition of scalp warfare involving strategic partnerships with so-called friendly groups who in turn became practitioners of state-sponsored killing in a way that allowed those Indian auxiliaries to act on preexisting intertribal rivalries while benefiting from the plunder taken during successful attacks. Just a few months after the agreements with western and eastern Tonkawas, Indian agent Joseph Baker reported from his San Antonio office that tribal leaders seemed ready and eager to guide "a small force of whites" against Comanches.[13] Another critical component of Houston's peace policies came on January 8,

1838, when the Lipan Apache chief Cuelgas de Castro made his mark on the Treaty of Live Oak Point. Born in the early 1790s near the abandoned Mission San Sabá in the central Texas Hill Country, Cuelgas de Castro was the son of Chief Josef Chiquito, and this pedigree allowed a quick rise to leadership within the Sun Otter Band of Lower Lipans. Fluent in Spanish, he traveled to Mexico City as a young diplomat in 1822, meeting with leaders of the newly independent Republic of Mexico for several months before signing a treaty recognizing Mexican sovereignty in exchange for acknowledgment of Lipan land rights.[14] For Texan purposes, the Treaty of Live Oak Point formed a basis for tribal cooperation with soldiers and Rangers as they campaigned against Comanches. From the Lipan perspective, the treaty provided an opportunity to maintain independence through an alliance with the settler group that posed the most direct threat to tribal security while retaining the ability to secure resources by raiding in northern Mexico and taking plunder on campaigns into Comanchería. To Cuelgas de Castro and his followers, the arrangement made sense politically and economically because it allowed them to continue targeting their Mexican and Comanche enemies.[15]

Divided into two primary groups—the upper band of northern Coahuila and western Texas, and the lower band of southern Texas and the Rio Grande Valley—the Lipan Apache (Cuélcahen Ndé) nation numbered about a thousand persons in the 1820s and 1830s.[16] As a response to the pressures of Comanche aggression and Spanish settlement, Lipans by that time had developed what tribal historian Nancy McGown Minor calls a "shadow trade economy" that revolved around raiding and mobility in some of North America's most isolated and rugged borderlands.[17] This reliance on stealth tactics and the natural environment correlated to the Cuélcahen Ndé Creation Story, in which the Light Gray People (as Lipans call themselves) spawned from Wind, Land, Mirage, Lightning, Water, Sun, and Moon. These personified forces of nature came together in council and decided to locate themselves in "upper world," the tribal homelands that today straddle the Texas-Mexico border. Lipan leaders who met with Texas officials and American agents in the mid-nineteenth century imagined an afterlife wherein good people resided forever on a south-facing shaded grassy hillside, while bad people endured an eternity on the fiery snake-infested north side of that same hill. Much like Southern Apache groups farther west, who believed that the deceased entered a supernatural afterlife in the same physical condition as their earthly corpse, Lipan Apache ethos and identity revolved around sacred understandings of life and death in which proper ceremonial burial prevented the emergence of *bac'oc* (ghosts) that could spread disorder and sickness. Just as Lipans sought to protect themselves from being haunted by ghosts of the desecrated dead, so, too, did they practice a form of revenge scalping to subject enemies to those same otherworldly horrors. According to oral tradition, Killer-of-Enemies, a deity who lived in the sun, taught Lipan ancestors how to remove scalps during combat and ceremoniously destroy them after battle. An Indigenous form of violent display, these spiritual customs connecting mortality to anatomy motivated Cuélcahen Ndé diplomacy and warfare as two strategies in confronting Euro-American colonizers as well as rival Native groups.[18]

In the Texas capital and across the republic, settlers knew little if anything of these complex worldviews that influenced their Indigenous counterparts. Sam Houston's cautious methods for handling Indian affairs thus had many detractors, including the influential politician Thomas J. Rusk, who bluntly told the Nacogdoches empresario and legislator Robert Irion that most tribes should be exterminated rather than negotiated with.[19] Edward Burleson, chairman of the House Committee on Indian Affairs, aligned himself with Houston when stating that Texas should pursue peaceful relations with Caddos, Cherokees, Delawares, and Shawnees. But he diverged when declaring that Comanches "should be acted against offensively," recommending that two companies of mounted volunteers be raised for that purpose.[20] The president and the legislature stood largely at odds with respect to Indian policy, and that disconnect would come into stark relief during Houston's final months in office. That same year, the Texas Senate's committee on Indian affairs reported that the feared and loathed Comanches were supposedly "the natural enemies of the Mexicans whom they contemptuously denominate their stock keepers and out of which nation they procure slaves," while admitting that they otherwise knew very little about the tribe.[21]

Comanches (N**u**m**u**n**uu**) did indeed raid northern Mexico with impunity throughout the first half of the nineteenth century, but the foregoing comment from Texas authorities reflected a general lack of knowledge about the tribe's people and culture. First mentioned in Spanish documentary records in 1706, Comanches ascended in power and influence to become a dominant South Plains tribe by the end of that century. In the early 1800s, four distinctive tribal divisions emerged—the eastern Kotsotekas (Buffalo Eaters), the southern Penatekas (Honey Eaters), the central Tenewas (Those Who Stay Downstream), and the northern Yamparikas (Yap Eaters)—each with their own *paraibos*, or leaders. Comanches of all subgroups mastered the use of horses for combat and perfected marksmanship with the bow, firing steel-tipped arrows more quickly and accurately than their settler counterparts could shoot a Colt revolver.[22] They developed a powerful raiding economy that involved collective social interaction, exploitation of resources, and resistance to competition from Mexican settlers as well as neighboring Indigenous groups including the Cheyennes, Karankawas, Kiowas, Lipan Apaches, Tonkawas, and Utes. Comanche society placed high importance on honor and respect, and a person's stature within the community developed from three mutually reinforcing sources: valor in warfare; ritualistic performances of *puha* (medicine power) during raids; and redistribution of horses and other valued commodities gathered during incursions into enemy territory. Each of these pathways to status and leadership required mobilized violence performed on horseback, meaning that Comanche identity revolved largely around activities that put tribe members in direct conflict with colonial as well as other Indigenous neighbors.[23] From the Comanche viewpoint, existence and prosperity depended on acts of warfare and raiding that incorporated martial valor as a form of masculinity, puha as a form of spirituality, and gift-giving as a form of generosity.[24]

When Texas Rangers, Lipan Apaches, and Tonkawas campaigned together in Comanche homelands, plundered tribal camps, and stripped *maku?ekwisi* (scalps) from dead women and children, their actions took a devastating material and demographic toll. But they also had the less obvious effect of disrupting the Comanche ethos through acts of extralethal violence that destroyed scalped victims' puha and condemned them to an afterlife of dishonor and shame, leaving surviving kin to mourn in agony.[25] In response to such destructive acts, Comanche men formed war parties with retributive purposes that differed from raiding forays. According to the twentieth-century Comanche informant Face Wrinkling Like Getting Old, war parties required extensive preparation, and leadership responsibilities went to those who had suffered the most grievous losses. On a vengeance campaign, men might try to take enemy scalps in order to perform a Scalp Dance — "one scalp was all that was necessary" — and this revolved around ceremonial motivations rather than material gain.[26] Much like Southern Apaches, who gained enemies-against power by taking a foe's forelocks, any Comanches who engaged in acts of scalping did so in relation to spiritual understandings of medicine power within a broader context of warfare and revenge.[27]

On May 25, 1838 — just a few months after Texas senators admitted that they knew almost nothing about Comanches — Houston vetoed a congressional act "providing for the defense of the frontier," stating objections to multiple parts of the legislation. The Texas president specifically criticized the proposed law for failing to define which tribes were "hostile," realizing that the vague terminology would enable armed men to "declare any and all Indians our enemies, and attack a camp of any tribe." The result of such an edict, Houston knew, would be to encourage indiscriminate attacks on Indians living anywhere within the republic's boundaries. He also believed that this type of unrestrained warfare, prosecuted by civilians rather than military professionals, would sabotage the administration's attempts to negotiate peaceful relations through diplomacy with tribal leaders. With specific reference to Comanches, he lectured the legislators that "everything will be gained by peace, but nothing will be gained by war." Reporting shortly after the successful Lipan Apache council at Live Oak Point, a newspaper in Houston suggested a similar ambassadorial tact with Comanches. "A treaty of amity with this powerful tribe will prove almost as advantageous to Texas, as a treaty of peace with Mexico," the editor wrote in a striking international metaphor indicating that Texans viewed Comanches as an equal if not greater threat than Mexico. He implicitly referenced the unrestricted actions of independent Rangers when imploring "every good citizen" to avert hostile aggression toward the tribe in the interest of cordiality. But most policymakers in the Texas House of Representatives had a different view of Comanche relations. They promptly overrode Houston's veto by an over-whelming vote of twenty-one to two, showing the gaping disconnect be-tween the executive and legislative branches in their preferred approaches to Indian affairs generally and Comanches specifically.[28]

As the president quarreled with congressmen over Indian policy midway through 1838, the so-called Córdova Rebellion erupted in East Texas and forced Houston to rethink his conciliatory approach to the region's Indians. Vicente Córdova, a forty-year-old Tejano from Nacogdoches, led a localized uprising that included two hundred allied Kickapoo Indians who collectively rebelled against the Republic of Texas. With a mixed population of Tejano, French, and American settlers living among neighboring Delaware, Shawnee, Kickapoo, Choctaw, Chickasaw, and Cherokee tribes, Nacogdoches was a racially and culturally diverse borderlands community where residents devel-oped shared grievances against the Texas government for its approach to fron-tier affairs and Indian policy. When Houston learned of the unrest, he and Rusk organized a force of three thousand men to crush any uprising that might materialize, and he also reached out to Cherokee leaders Bowles and Big Mush—who were already angry about failed treaty negotiations—in hopes of dissuading them from joining the separatist movement. By mid-August, the immediate threat of war had abated as Córdova and his followers began to realize the futility of their scheme, but a final flurry of desperate raids along the Neches River resulted in the deaths of fifteen individuals. On October 16, Rusk's army fought the remnants of Córdova's band, killing eleven of them, and soon thereafter the ringleader learned that he would not be receiving any financial or military assistance from the Mexican govern-ment in his plight against Texas. Eventually, Córdova was ambushed along the Guadalupe River, where at least half of his remaining men perished. Three dozen of the survivors were subsequently charged with treason and ex-iled from the republic, bringing a climactic end to the short-lived rebellion.[29] Generals Hugh McLeod and Albert Sidney Johnston, both of whom partici-pated in the Texas Army's campaign, felt convinced that Kickapoos, Chero-kees, and other Indians associated with the rebellion would think twice about further resistance after seeing the heavy-handed military response.[30]

Though unsuccessful in achieving its separatist objectives, the Córdova Rebellion contributed to a growing sense of paranoia among Anglo politicians and settlers. They feared that Tejanos and Indians who disliked the new Texas government might ally with Mexican forces in a widespread counterrevolution, and this convinced many people that a permanent standing army aided by militia and volunteers would be necessary for state security. The Córdova Rebellion also had significant implications for Texas policy, because the threat of an uprising fundamentally transformed Houston's approach to Indian affairs. He pivoted from a course of diplomacy to one of hostility with most tribes, ordering Thomas H. Dyer to organize several volunteer units for an expedition in the Trinity River country of northeast Texas.[31] Captain Robert Sloan commanded one battalion that ambushed an Indian camp and, according to a participant named John P. Simpson, "the Indians were soon dispatched by the men and the scalps taken from their heads."[32] This attack represented one of the first campaigns involving a Texas paramilitary outfit known as the Rangers, their origin as an Indian fighting organization traceable in part to the anxiety emanating from the failed Córdova Rebellion. In November 1838, with Houston set to leave office, House legislators considered a bill "for the protection of the Northern and Western frontier" that called for the enlistment of a regiment of 840 mounted troops who would augment these Ranger companies. The proposal included financial incentives beyond normal soldier salaries, allowing that "all spoil captured from an Indian enemy shall be divided . . . equally among the captors, officers and men without regard to rank." The lawmakers stopped short of offering cash for scalps, but they clearly aimed at enticing men to participate in frontier combat operations by offering plunder as a reward for armed service against Indigenous enemies, and indeed the absence of a codified bounty did not dissuade some men from engaging in acts of extralethal violence.[33] These legislative tactics enjoyed broad support in Texas and became a motivating factor in the future enlistment of Rangers, whose primary duty would be to clear Indians from the republic's frontier through a tailored brand of scalp warfare that relied as heavily on racial hatred and masculine valor as it did on pecuniary ambition.

By the time Córdova's followers sat trial for treason in January 1839, a new president had taken office in the Texas capital, and the previous year's attempted uprising provided all the justification he needed to pursue an aggressive war of extermination against Cherokees, Comanches, and any other tribes that stood in the way of settler expansion. Born in 1798 in Georgia, Mirabeau Buonaparte Lamar spent the first four decades of his life in the Deep South Cotton Belt, where slave-owning planters—including members of his family—clashed with powerful Indian tribes in competition for land and resources. A well-educated man with aspirations for political office, he became owner of a local newspaper in Alabama at the age of twenty-one but suffered a series of professional defeats and personal tragedies. His wife, Tabitha, died of tuberculosis in 1830, his campaign for the US House of Representatives failed in 1832, and his older brother Lucius committed suicide in 1834. Saddened and overwhelmed, he drifted westward in 1835, arriving in Texas just eight months before the rebellion against Mexico. He befriended Stephen F. Austin and joined Sam Houston's army as a private, distinguishing himself while fighting at the Battle of San Jacinto. Within this revolutionary turmoil, Lamar's political star rose rapidly, and by September 1836 he was vice president of the new Republic of Texas.[34]

Lamar came to Texas politics with a preconceived hatred of Indians, and he repeatedly clashed with Houston on this issue until becoming president himself at just forty years of age. When Lamar delivered his first inaugural address in December 1838, he made it clear where he stood with respect to expansionism and Indian conquest. "The Texas empire will soon stretch from the Sabine to the Pacific," he declared with unfettered ambition. To achieve such lofty goals, he explained, leaders of the fledgling republic would have to implement harsh policies similar to those of the US government in the southern states from which he came. Lamar bluntly criticized Houston's diplomatic programs, claiming that "the moderation hitherto extended to the Indians on our borders has been repeatedly retorted upon us in all the atrocious cruelties that characterize their mode of warfare." In provocative language he laid bare his racial views, with direct reference to scalping as a combat tactic to be emulated. "The Indian warrior in his heartless and sanguinary vengeance recognizes no distinction of age, sex or condition, all are indiscriminate victims of his cruelties," he raved. "The wife and the infant afford as rich a trophy to the scalping knife, as the warrior who fails in the vigor of manhood." By casting Indigenous peoples as the original perpetrators of extralethal violence, he advanced his proposal for an exterminatory form of scalp warfare with the timeworn "they started it" argument that English/British and French officials repeatedly voiced in prior centuries. "If the wild cannibals of the woods will not desist from their massacres, if they will continue to war upon us with the ferocity of tigers and hyenas, it is time that we should retaliate their warfare," Lamar continued, calling for a war "which will admit of no compromise and have no termination except in their total extinction or total expulsion." To accomplish this end, the new president called for the immediate formation of a regular army as well as volunteer regiments "for active and efficient operations."[35] Lamar must have felt reassured in these statements when he received a letter just one week later, from military commander Felix Huston, declaring Indians "our most active and dangerous enemy" and claiming without specific evidence that tribe members had scalped no fewer than four hundred white settlers in the previous two years alone.[36] During the Lamar administration, extermination became an obsessive talking point among many Texans. Lawmakers in Austin transformed presidential rhetoric into state policy by passing laws that encouraged professional soldiers and civilian operatives to attack, plunder, and kill any Indians standing in the way of frontier settlement, although the legislature stopped short of enacting a scalp bounty even during Lamar's presidency. Rangers would form a crucial strategic component of this government-sponsored program to conquer Indians, although the exterminatory rhetoric did not typically equate to systematic attempts at eradicating entire tribes, and geographic relocation to either Indian Territory or Mexico became a more common outcome of the violence.[37]

Texas legislators established the Rangers as a state-sponsored paramilitary unit consisting of civilian volunteers whose activities revolved primarily around fighting Indians. Much as in a more traditional militia unit, they served periods of enlistment that rarely exceeded six months, received $1.25 per day in wages, and often had to supply their own horses and firearms. In 1845, the Republic of Texas government incurred an expense of $2,115 monthly for the payroll of John Coffee Hays's Ranger company at San Antonio, meaning that it cost more than $25,000 per year just to pay the salaries of a single unit. A litany of additional expenses such as wages for "extra-duty men" that included guides, muleteers, teamsters, and wagoners—as well as ammunition, forage, medicine, corn, flour, bacon, beef, sugar, coffee, rice, beans, and even "presents" for Indians—amounted to thousands of dollars more each month. Ranger officers also submitted pay vouchers entitling them to reimbursement for the monthly subsistence costs of "private servants"—an innocuous term for Black slaves and Mexican peons—and other miscellaneous out-of-pocket expenses. Multiple companies operated at any given time, and each group might cost more than $100,000 per year to fully provision and equip, so the state doled out immense sums for Rangers to augment regular army forces.[38]

Rangers operated mostly free from the professional and jurisdictional constraints of soldiers, and this enabled them to adopt unconventional tactics tailored to the hated Indigenous enemies they pursued. To be sure, not all Rangers partook in extralethal measures during campaigns, and many abided by the laws they swore to uphold. But the very nature of Ranger service attracted scores of ruffians who pillaged and killed Indians, becoming local heroes within a Texan culture that placed high value on martial masculinity and frontier combat experience.[39] Some of the more aggressive and violent Ranger companies supplemented their regular pay with plunder that included scalps, firearms, horses, livestock, liquor, and other contraband taken from Indian camps and villages.[40] In the remote borderlands where Rangers operated, the Texas economy resembled that of neighboring Mexico insofar as it had both legitimate and illegitimate components. It was the shady side of the Texas frontier economy that these Rangers embraced, transforming Indian conflicts into an occupation of plunder and extralethal violence. Many of the earliest Rangers practiced scalp warfare in the same vein as men who answered the call for bounty hunters in the English/British colonies and New France. In fact, several prominent Rangers left Texas in the late 1840s and signed up as paid scalpers in the northern states of independent Mexico, while others gravitated to California during the Gold Rush and led volunteer campaigns against Pacific Coast tribes.

Rangers directly complemented Lamar's policy goal of conquering Indians living within the republic's boundaries. Many enlistees shared the president's racist views of Indigenous peoples and were willing and able to act on that hatred in violent ways. One such Ranger, Robert H. Williams, parroted Lamar's inauguration speech when he claimed that Comanches and Lipan Apaches "scalped and mutilated . . . defenseless women and children" and insisted that "the wretches had things pretty much their own way" until the Texas government intervened in the late 1830s with policies of extermination. Williams proudly recalled his days as an "Indian hunter," embracing the terminology of government bounty systems and scalp warfare while emphasizing that Natives sometimes killed settlers and took their scalps, implicitly characterizing the extralethal acts that he and his companions perpetrated as justifiable retributive measures.[41]

As Lamar settled into his executive role in January 1839, the congressional committee on Indian affairs reported that "no subject is more exciting at present to the community than our Indian relations." Using the racist epithet "red man" to name all Indigenous peoples in Texas, the lawmakers openly criticized Houston's peace policies, calling for an abrupt reversal in procedure with Lamar in office. They wanted to shutter Indian agencies, fire Indian commissioners, and halt Indian diplomacy while enlisting more soldiers and Rangers to effectively swap the olive branch for the sword.[42] Through a new military act, Texas congressmen authorized the president to raise a professional force of 840 men to serve three-year terms, each with a salary of $16 per month and a $30 "enlistment bounty," along with eight companies of mounted militia for six-month durations. The Congress also approved a separate act to establish a Ranger corps that would patrol San Patricio, Goliad, and Refugio Counties, each company consisting of fifty-six individuals who would receive $25 per month. This was substantially more pay than that of soldiers, indicating the primacy that legislators placed on irregular military operations as a strategy for fighting Indians. The separate law for Rangers also indicated a clear legal distinction among professional troops, militiamen, and the independent volunteer units who carried on scalp warfare. All told, these legislative measures appropriated $1 million for frontier defense, a sum that dwarfed most other government expenditures that year.[43] With these blessings from the legislature, Lamar was free to pursue his goal of extermination, and he publicized an impassioned call for volunteers to fight what he called "the fierce and perfidious savages [who] are waging . . . an unprovoked and cruel warfare, massacring the women and children . . . the unresisting victims of the scalping knife."[44] Notably, the Mexican state of Chihuahua established and funded its paramilitary bounty hunting outfit, the so-called Society for Making War against the Barbarians, within two months of the Texas act that enlisted scores of Rangers. At least one prominent American newspaper highlighted these international parallels when informing readers of Mexico's new scalp law, noting that "Texas is [also] much interested in this private warfare against the Camanches [sic] and Apaches."[45] In this sense, the year 1839 marked a watershed moment in the history of exterminatory Indian policy and extralethal violence, because permutations of scalp warfare were codified into state military strategy across the Texas-Mexico borderlands and would remain in place for many years thereafter.

Within weeks of these legislative measures, a contingent of eighty Texans and Cuelgas de Castro's band of allied Lipan Apaches rode out under the command of John H. Moore, a veteran Indian fighter from Tennessee who had participated in Kuykendall's scalping raid against the Karankawas back in the 1820s. As longtime enemies of the Comanches, the Lipan scouts revealed that a sizable winter camp could be found on the San Saba River west of Austin. Moore was an independent operative, unattached to the Republic of Texas Army, and his recruits joined the campaign without cash salaries in hopes of executing an attack that would yield a small fortune in plunder. Cuelgas de Castro's guides located the village and Moore's men ambushed at sunrise, catching the sleeping Indians by surprise and "killing indiscriminately a number of all ages and sexes." Moore told Texas secretary of war Albert Sidney Johnston that at least one hundred Comanches perished in the bloodbath. The riverside campsite was pillaged and set ablaze as the victorious raiders rode away with everything they could carry, along with most of the tribe's prized horse herd.[46] Noah Smithwick, another native of Tennessee who had worked for many years as a blacksmith at the Austin Colony, participated in the expedition as a member of Moore's company. He recalled two instances during the massacre when Lipans attempted to scalp slain Comanches—inspired by the teachings of Killer-of-Enemies, such vengeful acts would have been calculated to subject their dead enemies to afterlives of shame and survivors to the worldly horror of bac'oc (ghosts)—but "a perfect rain of arrows" drove them away. Smithwick also acknowledged the prevalence of looting when he complained that "the Lipans got away with the lion's share of the spoils."[47] Regardless of who took scalps or claimed plunder, the rout of a sizable Comanche camp proved that scalp warfare, coupled with strategic alliances, could have a devastating impact on powerful Indigenous groups. The massacre on the San Saba River in March 1839 reinforced the utility of economically and racially motivated civilian campaigning as a method for eradicating Texas tribes, and the brutality of these tactics prompted some Comanche leaders to seek peace with the republic's government.

On March 19, 1840—one year after the deadly attack in central Texas—a group of sixty-five Penateka Comanches led by the paraibo Muguara traveled to San Antonio for an arranged council. More than half of the Indians were women and children whose presence was a strategic mechanism to dissuade overt acts of treachery or violence by their Texan hosts. The Comanches brought one captive woman, Matilda Lockhart, with them to repatriate as part of the diplomatic process. Believing that the tribe held at least thirteen more white captives—an unproven allegation that seems to have been based on Matilda's comments during the council—Texas commissioners hatched a treacherous plan to take Comanche hostages for future redemption. Inside the council chamber at San Antonio, Muguara insisted that any other captives among the Comanches must belong to other tribal bands, because Matilda was the only white woman his group had to return. General Hugh McLeod slammed the chief's statement as "a palpable lie." Colonel William G. Cooke and Lieutenant Colonel William S. Fisher quickly ordered one company of troops to enter the building and another company to surround the perimeter. With these soldiers in place, McLeod informed Muguara that he and his followers would be detained and imprisoned until the tribe delivered all other captives.

This standoff devolved rapidly into a horrific scene of violence. According to McLeod's report, one of the chiefs drew a knife from his belt, prompting a sentinel standing in the doorway to raise his loaded musket. "A rush was then made to the door" as the outnumbered Comanches attempted to escape, and desperate men grappled in hand-to-hand combat within the confines of a small room. Armed only with knives and bows, all twelve chiefs "were immediately shot" in the initial ambush, and the killing spree spilled into the city streets, where the Comanche women and children congregated. James Wilson Nichols, a teenager whose family had moved to the San Antonio area just a few years earlier, recalled that "the chiefs burs [sic] down the door and rushed out [of the room] but was shot down as fast as they come out and the fight became general and lasted about half an hour," adding nonchalantly that "the Comanches was so completely beaten and out done." Thirty-five tribe members died in the massacre, including five women and children who were shot because, according to McLeod, "it was impossible to discriminate between the sexes." Three soldiers and four townspeople also perished, victims of steel-tipped arrows "driven to the feather." When the fighting ended, twenty-nine Comanche survivors were imprisoned at the Alamo compound, and the troops confiscated "a large quantity" of buffalo robes and more than one hundred horses. The Texans selected one woman, provided a horse to ride, and instructed her to go and inform other members of the tribe that "we are willing to exchange prisoners."[48] When news of the act reached audiences in the eastern states, some people expressed outrage at such treachery, but Texans doubled down on their violent approach to Indian affairs. In Austin, newspaper editors threw their unwavering support behind the men who carried out the massacre. "All the tears of pitying philanthropists . . . who weep for the degraded savage cannot save them," one fiery column read in direct response to criticism from outside observers. "The Comanche will be exterminated from the face of the earth, or the Anglo-Saxon race will cease to exist in Texas."[49]

The butchery that Texas officers and their troops perpetrated under a flag of truce became a driving force for intensified conflict with Comanches, encouraging tribal retaliation through raiding, captive taking, and killing across the Texas frontier. Much like the Johnson Massacre of 1837 and the Galeana Massacre of 1846—both of which incorporated slaving and scalping as brutal tactics that in turn motivated intense hatred between Southern Apaches and the people of Chihuahua and Sonora—the aptly named Council House Massacre of 1840 infuriated Comanches and led to a deadly cycle of retribution. Tribal leaders wasted little time in avenging the murderous acts at San Antonio. The paraibo Potsanaquahip (Buffalo Hump)—who eventually became a prominent fixture in Comanche diplomacy and signed at least two treaties, the first in 1844 with the Republic of Texas and the last in 1865 with the United States—launched a massive raid in August 1840, striking as far south as Victoria near the Gulf Coast.[50] They attacked farms, homesteads, and settlements, driving off thousands of horses and butchering as many or more head of livestock. Panicked residents wrote to the veteran campaigner John H. Moore, telling him that "the town of Linnville has been burnt to the ground" and begging for immediate assistance.[51] John J. Linn, who lived in the path of the raid, recalled, "We were about surrounded by overwhelming numbers of these implacable enemies."[52] According to a local resident named William Watts, many terrified inhabitants fled all the way to the coast and boarded ships anchored in the bay, where horseback Comanches could not reach them.[53]

As the Comanche war party returned to tribal homelands in central Texas, they encountered a contingent of soldiers and Rangers along Plum Creek south of Austin. Nichols participated in the ensuing battle and later described an extralethal atrocity that sickened his stomach. He saw a Comanche woman shot through both legs as her horse tumbled, leaving her prostrate on the ground. Ezekiel Smith and his son, French Smith, walked up to their helpless victim and drew their sharpened bowie knives. Ezekiel grabbed the wounded woman by the hair, slit her throat from ear to ear, hacked off one of her breasts to carry home as a trophy, and sheathed the bloody blade in celebratory triumph. "That ain't a human," the father sneered as his son looked on in stupefied horror. "That's an Injun and I come to kill Injuns." Nichols commented on Ezekiel Smith's hypocrisy, explaining that the man was a devoted member of the Methodist Church who frequently led prayer meetings, yet there could hardly be "another man in America that claimed to be civilized that would act so cruel." The morning after the battle, an appointed committee divided the spoils into small piles for each man to claim, and Nichols scored a new saddle for his role in the affair.[54] At least a dozen Indians perished at Plum Creek, and Rangers reclaimed some horses and other plunder, but most of the seven hundred Comanches escaped. The campaign to avenge the Council House Massacre would rank among the largest and most successful Indian raids carried out against the Republic of Texas.[55] This series of events also laid the groundwork for an intensified, plunder-driven form of scalp warfare against the Comanches.

With the treasury depleted, President Lamar was unable to muster a sizable force of army regulars to pursue the Comanches after the Victoria raid, so the task of retribution fell to Ranger companies who would act primarily on the motivation of material gain. In September 1840, Felix Huston wrote to the Texas Congress claiming that his recent reconnaissance campaigns would contribute to the "policy pursued towards our savage Indians—utter extermination," and he asked that lawmakers pay his men for these spying services since they had secured no other form of recompense during the operation.[56] Shortly thereafter, Colonel Moore began recruiting another band of fighters from the Texas settlements, promising plunder in lieu of cash salaries. Eighteen Lipan Apaches under Cuelgas de Castro joined Moore's outfit as auxiliaries, and the company ultimately numbered 107 men, one of whom was John Robert Baylor. They struck a Comanche camp along the upper Colorado River at sunrise on October 24, 1840. Taken completely by surprise and bogged down in a blizzard, the Comanches suffered at least 140 casualties along with 35 women and children taken captive. Only two Rangers sustained wounds in the lopsided affair. With the campsite abandoned, Moore gathered over five hundred horses and distributed them among his men, along with many other valuable articles taken from the tepees before they were torched.[57] Secretary of War and Navy Branch T. Archer lauded Moore and his "Volunteer Associates" as "the champions of our liberty, the bulwarks of our safety," and residents of Austin organized a public barbecue in their honor.[58]

This sort of campaigning would continue throughout Lamar's presidency. On May 20, 1841, Captain Eli Chandler of the Robertson County Minutemen led fifty-three volunteers in an attack near the Trinity River, killing three Indians and taking twenty-three horses along with gunpowder, lead, axes, peltries, and other items valued at $3,000. The victorious Texans burned the village before riding back to the settlements.[59] One month later, Chandler's men returned to the field, killing four Indians and taking twenty-three captives at a village near the Cross Timbers on the Brazos River. These "minutemen" also confiscated sixteen horses and many other items, leaving behind an elderly woman to tell her people that captives would be held for ransom in the Texas settlements.[60] At the same time, John Coffee Hays, a twenty-four-year-old migrant from Tennessee who would become one of the most renowned Rangers of the era, was organizing his own volunteer unit at San Antonio "to drive the savages from the vicinity." He arranged with local officials to compensate men for their services in case they failed to enrich themselves with plunder. The ubiquitous youngster James Wilson Nichols immediately signed on to ride with Hays, as did another teenager from

John Coffee Hays, ca. 1850s. Library of Congress Prints and Photographs Division, LC-USZ62–83948.

Virginia named Andrew Nelson Erskine, and they both participated in deadly engagements with the Comanches in the Hill Country to the north and along the Medina River to the west. In one of these attacks, Rangers killed nine Indians and took nearly all the band's horses and saddles, but Erskine was shot and carried the unextractable lead musket ball in his right arm for the rest of his life.[61] Hays led a third campaign along the Guadalupe River north of Seguin, and his Rangers used new five-shot revolvers with devastating effect, killing twenty-three Comanches and Wacos during a massacre along Walker's Creek.[62] These forays collectively claimed the lives of at least thirty-nine Indians, and each incident enabled the campaigners to take captives and plunder the camps for valuables.

Throughout Lamar's presidential term, civilian campaigning formed a central component of the Texas government's extermination policy. The pillaging on the San Saba River, the treacherous Council House Massacre, the extralethal mutilations at Plum Creek, and the deadly campaigns of John Coffee Hays all encompassed a form of scalp warfare that relied in large part on the racial compulsions of settlers to exact a tremendous toll on Indigenous groups in Texas. Lamar left office in December 1841, his compulsive crusade to eradicate Indians through the deployment of expensive military campaigns having driven the republic deeper into debt to foreign creditors. His successor, Sam Houston, would attempt to reinstate the original policy of diplomacy, but three years of plundering and killing had made peace a veritable impossibility. Just two weeks after Houston reclaimed the executive office, he ordered Colonel L. B. Franks to determine the prospects for new treaties and informed him that "if it is practicable to make and preserve peace on our frontiers, it is my ardent desire to do so."[63] In February 1842, the president appointed Franks as the government's special agent to Lipan Apaches and Tonkawas, explaining that these two groups must remain allies of the republic and promising to reward their chiefs and fighters with "handsome presents" for services rendered in the long-standing conflict with Comanches.[64] During the previous administration, Branch Archer used his authority as secretary of war and navy to recommend three separate times that the Lipan chiefs Cuelgas de Castro and Flacco be compensated for their roles as "adroit spies," but Lamar repeatedly demurred.[65] After meeting with Lipan leaders in June 1842, Houston praised them as "valuable friends and allies" whose services as guides proved indispensable in the past and might be useful once more should Texas go to war with Mexico.[66]

Ranking among the greatest Lipan Apache leaders of his time—a Texas newspaper editor called him "one of the most shrewd and intelligent Indians we have ever seen"—Cuelgas de Castro died of illness in the summer of 1842, not long after Houston retook the presidency.[67] The following year, Texans murdered Chief Flacco's son, Flacco the Younger. About twenty years Cuelgas de Castro's junior, Flacco led the High-Beaked Moccasin band of Lower Lipans and was known among Texans as a reliable scout who wore silver arm bands to complement his tall, muscular figure. Not long before the murder of his son, journalists in Houston praised Flacco as "the bravest and most skillful leader of our Indian allies."[68] Together, Cuelgas de Castro and Flacco had negotiated agreements with Texas and ensured that their followers not only abstained from raiding the republic's settlements but also joined with soldiers and Rangers on campaigns into Comanchería. A product of Sam Houston's Treaty of Live Oak Point in 1838, the Lipan-Texas alliance endured as long as Cuelgas de Castro and Flacco held power and remained amenable to cooperation with outsiders. But with Cuelgas de Castro deceased and Flacco grieving the treacherous killing of his son, the peace quickly unraveled and Lipan Apaches expanded the scope of their raiding economy beyond northern Mexico to include South Texas and the lower Rio Grande borderlands. In response, John B. Armstrong's Ranger company attacked Chief Chiquito's band along the upper Colorado River in August 1847, and shortly thereafter Hays's unit ambushed another Lipan camp near Laredo. One Upper Lipan leader named Datíl reached out to longtime Mexican enemies three times between 1845 and 1852, attempting unsuccessfully to forge diplomatic truces that would serve the tribe's interests in its escalating conflict with Texans. These developments transformed Lipan Apaches into enemies of the state, and the same Rangers who formerly rode alongside tribe members now rode in opposition on punitive campaigns.[69] Over the ensuing decade, Lipan Apaches who once acted as state agents of extralethal violence became targets of the same indiscriminate scalp warfare tactics, as Texans began demanding that governors dispatch Ranger forces to exterminate the tribe.[70]

When he appointed Franks as a special agent for Indian affairs in 1842, Houston also hired an itinerant French "count" named Leontio de Narbonne, a "very singular . . . if not mysterious" man in his early twenties who had just arrived in Texas after a brief sojourn through neighboring New Mexico and Chihuahua.[71] As Houston's new peace commissioner, Narbonne was ordered to visit "all the Indians on our North Western frontier" and establish trading houses along the Brazos River and at other strategic points in hopes that Comanche leaders might embrace the olive branch.[72] Just as they had done in 1837 and 1838, however, Texas congressmen pushed back on Houston's diplomatic procedures, with numerous representatives condemning any type of peace policy and insisting instead on a continuation of Lamar's militarized approach to Indian affairs.[73] When Comanche leaders rebuffed his peace overtures, the president rightly ascribed their anger to the Council House Massacre—Houston called it "the unfortunate affair which occurred in Bexar"—and he told congressmen that members of the tribe "were yet crying for their kindred and that the clouds of sorrow yet rested upon their nation."[74] To this, Houston might have added that Ranger campaigning and its attendant plundering and scalping also contributed to the tribe's hostile disposition toward Texans. In his annual message, Houston attributed ongoing violence with Indians to the brutal policies of Lamar's administration, reiterating his preference for diplomacy and stressing the need to "restrain the whites from aggression" in order to secure the frontier for settlement and development.[75] When it came to Indian policy, a stark divide once again characterized the Republic of Texas government after 1842, with the executive branch advocating diplomacy and the legislative branch embracing scalp warfare through Ranger operations. These divisions remained unchanged in December 1845, when the United States annexed Texas and assumed responsibility for Indian policy in the region.[76] This shift in jurisdiction would have important legal and political implications with respect to policies of extermination, but it would not eliminate volunteer campaigning in Texas, and Rangers would continue to play a prominent role in frontier Indian conflicts for the next two decades.

On the heels of Texas statehood, more than two thousand US troops under General Zachary Taylor marched southward from their seashore campsite at

Corpus Christi to occupy the disputed Nueces Strip, and in so doing they started a war with Mexico. In June 1846, just a few weeks after Taylor's army scored victories at the Battles of Palo Alto and Resaca de la Palma, Governor James Pinckney Henderson and Lieutenant Governor Albert Clinton Horton of Texas made arrangements with US Army colonel William S. Harney that allowed the state to raise five regiments of mounted Rangers to patrol in the absence of federal troops called to fight in Mexico.[77] This agreement not only enabled Ranger operations to continue beyond the era of the independent Republic of Texas—by 1848 the number of Ranger companies stationed across Texas had already increased from five to eight—but also created a precedent for the unit's existence alongside US Army regulars.[78] Based on this mutual understanding between federal and state governments, Texas Rangers would campaign against Indians as a paramilitary unit, augmenting the services of US Dragoons and Mounted Riflemen who garrisoned forts throughout the region. While officials in Texas and Washington, DC, agreed on a strategy of hybridization between volunteer operatives and professional soldiers, they disagreed when it came to paying for expensive Ranger campaigns.

Texas legislators memorialized Congress in 1850, requesting that the federal government reimburse $53,946 associated with raising and outfitting eight mounted Ranger companies. Like their counterparts in Sacramento, lawmakers in Austin would continue to request federal funding for paramilitary operatives over the next decade.[79] The initial petition prompted a proposal in the House of Representatives to federalize the Rangers—a supportive Joshua R. Giddings of Ohio proclaimed that "volunteers were the most efficient troops in the world"—and a draft bill that never became law would have granted the president authority to raise up to 1,200 Rangers as necessity might dictate.[80] Mississippi senator Jefferson Davis later spoke in favor of federal endorsement for Ranger operations, stating that "they were necessary to restrain the Indians" even with regular troops garrisoning posts throughout Texas.[81] In February 1851, the US House of Representatives considered an appropriations bill that included a line item for $236,934 to pay "companies of Texas volunteers," but the measure led to a heated debate over Texas Indian policy, enforcement of article 11 of the Treaty of Guadalupe Hidalgo, the effectiveness of regular US troops, and the legitimacy of Ranger units as a federally financed fighting force. At one point, South Carolina representative Armistead Burt declared that "the Texan rangers for the defense of women and children were perfectly useless," and he bluntly condemned their extralethal tactics by saying that "the cutting of throats and the blowing out of brains constitute a state of hostility, and . . . I do not know any country on this continent where those amusements are indulged in with a keener relish than in that part of Texas."[82] By placing the financial burden of indiscriminate paramilitary operations on the state rather than the national treasury, US politicians shrewdly detached themselves from direct implication in the Texas style of combat and could instead point to regular army campaigning as the strategy that they officially sponsored. This congressional approach highlighted the decentralized nature of scalp warfare as a local rather than a national initiative to conquer despised Indian tribes.

In addition to misunderstandings over the fiscal responsibility for independent campaigning against Indians, government personnel diverged in their beliefs about the tactical utility of the plan. Lieutenant William H. C. Whiting of the Army Corps of Engineers inspected several Texas military posts, including newly established Fort Merrill on the south bank of the lower Nueces River, and opined that the two companies of army regulars stationed there, "acting in concert with the rangers, will afford much greater security" to nearby towns including Corpus Christi and Victoria.[83] Captain Randolph B. Marcy of the Fifth US Infantry similarly hailed "the renowned 'Texas Rangers' . . . as examples of the most efficient and successful Indian fighters that our country has produced."[84] The outspoken New Orleans journalist George Wilkins Kendall, whose participation in the ill-fated Texan–Santa Fe Expedition of 1841–42 gave him a firsthand glimpse at the vicious conflict between Comanches and settlers, echoed Whiting and Marcy when writing that the US Dragoons would be effective only if augmented by Rangers. "The Comanches are still continuing their forays upon the Texas borders," Kendall wrote, "they must be punished . . . must feel the force as displayed in the killing of their warriors." The only way to do this, Kendall believed, was to employ the extralethal tactics of Rangers.[85] One year later, military officers in San Antonio organized "a vigorous campaign against the savages," ordering that dragoon and infantry soldiers stationed below the Nueces River team with several Ranger units "until the country is cleared of those hostile Indians." In concert with this initiative, Texas governor Peter H. Bell recruited four companies of Rangers on three-month enlistments, and he eventually renewed those terms of service for six additional months.[86]

The strategic mixture of regular troops and irregular volunteers as a method for fighting formidable Indian groups had its opponents, including Texas agent Robert S. Neighbors, who met with several Comanche bands and reported to Commissioner of Indian Affairs William Medill that the only obstacle to peace was the campaigning of independent Rangers who employed indiscriminate tactics.[87] Major General George Brooks, commanding the Texas military department, likewise told Adjutant General Roger Jones that sending independent Rangers into the field would result in "a general war" because of "natural hostility to the Indians."[88] In Washington, DC, Commissioner of Indian Affairs Luke Lea advocated for a tailored Texas policy that would essentially replicate the Indian Removal Act of 1830, which coerced the yearslong relocation of Cherokees, Chickasaws, Choctaws, Creeks, and Seminoles on the Trail of Tears. Lea believed that armed forces could never fully solve the so-called Indian problem in Texas, opining that the only plausible solution would be compulsory removal of all tribes to an isolated reservation under constant government supervision. But even this reservation plan—sometimes labeled in rather haunting terms as an "alternative to extinction"—often required violent campaigning to push tribes into such conditions of subjugation.[89] The hybridized Texas model for fighting Indians with both soldiers and Rangers was also a notable departure from protocols in other parts of the American West, including neighboring New Mexico, where US military officers and territorial officials strongly discouraged and sometimes even forbade civilian operatives from taking the field against Apaches and Navajos.[90] These stark differences in strategy owed in part to a recognition of the lethal victories that Rangers achieved in campaigns against Comanches, in part to the US Army's insufficient manpower to monitor the immense Texas frontier, and in part to racial perceptions wherein government officials believed that white Rangers were more reliable and effective than Hispano volunteers.

One Ranger who operated during the postannexation era was William "Big Foot" Wallace. Born in Virginia, Wallace immigrated to Texas at the age of nineteen, and he eventually gravitated toward killing and scalping Indians. In 1848, he led thirty Rangers out of San Antonio in pursuit of Lipan Apaches who had raided his ranch near the Guadalupe River. They overtook the Indians at daybreak, intent on giving them a "bloody awakening." A thirty-minute melee ensued, the Lipans repulsing the ambush "with great desperation and obstinacy." Armed mostly with revolvers, the outnumbered Rangers eventually prevailed, and Wallace counted forty-eight corpses as he traversed the field of combat. The victorious attackers lost just two of their own men in the affair. They quickly plundered the campsite, collecting blankets and powder kegs, along with 170 horses and mules to divide among themselves before returning to San Antonio.[91] In a similar incident, Wallace and his Rangers ambushed another group of Indians, "pouring a deadly fire into them from our rifles." One of his companions, Jeff Turner—nicknamed "Indian-Hater"—scalped each of the seven slain opponents. "It was astonishing to see how quickly Jeff would take off an Indian scalp . . . one slash with his butcher-knife and a sudden jerk, and the bloody scalp was soon dangling from his belt," Wallace recalled with clear admiration. "At the same time, he never seemed to be in a hurry, but was as cool and deliberate about everything he did as a carpenter when he is working." The comparison to a carpenter indicated just how normalized scalp warfare had become in midcentury Texas. When one of the wounded Indians—Wallace repeatedly referred to them as "red rascals"—tried to mount a horse and ride away, Turner instinctively shot him "and had his scalp off before he had done kicking." With this killing completed, the Rangers nonchalantly sat down to eat a deer that they found cooking over a fire in the abandoned campsite, telling celebratory stories of masculine heroics in battle and laughing about the extralethal massacre they just perpetrated.[92]

Agent Neighbors reported in 1849 that the Lipan Apache population in the lower Rio Grande borderlands had dwindled to only about five hundred persons—most of those individuals had relocated to northern Coahuila, beyond the reach of Texas Rangers and US soldiers—demonstrating the extent to which rapid settlement and ongoing paramilitary operations such as those of "Big Foot" Wallace sapped Indigenous power.[93] In January 1851, an Austin newspaper reported that the Lipans "manifested a strong desire to be friendly . . . and will remain so, unless they are caught and murdered by some bands of outlaws."[94] By midcentury, Ranger units had been fighting and killing Indians for more than a decade, and their reputation extended far and wide. The German-born doctor Adolph Wislizenus traveled through the region and subsequently told US congressmen that "the Indians, the very scourge of the country, should be driven out or extirpated by some companies of Texas rangers."[95] When an American publisher distributed the Wislizenus report in book form just two years later, some of the Rangers were already taking concrete action to promote an exterminatory outcome on both sides of the international border. Because many of these men found motivation in material gain and racial hatred, scalp bounties that the states of Sonora, Chihuahua, and Coahuila implemented in 1849 and 1850 attracted some Rangers to Mexico. As explained in the previous chapter, local officials in Ures, Chihuahua City, and Saltillo enthusiastically enlisted veteran Texas operatives including John Joel Glanton, Michael Chevallié, Michael James Box, and John Dusenberry as civilian contractors to hunt Comanches and Southern Apaches in exchange for plunder and cash rewards. At the same time, Ranger companies continued to operate within the boundaries of Texas, and the presence of well over one thousand US Army regulars after 1849 did not deter civilians from pursuing their freelance trade as Indian fighters.[96]

Many Texans believed that the number of federal troops stationed in their state was insufficient for a region so large, and just like California lawmakers of the same era, they used claims of US government neglect as justification for supporting Ranger operations. "In default of Federal protection," Governor Francis Lubbock wrote, "the Texans protected themselves through the State rangers."[97] Melinda Rankin, a Christian missionary and schoolteacher who moved from New England to Texas in the early 1850s, similarly stated that "the name of 'Camanche' is a sound of dread alarm" and "the present military force is entirely inadequate to the emergency."[98] Texans also weighed in on Indian relations in adjacent New Mexico Territory, even though they had no legal authority there. In 1850, agent

Neighbors visited the town of Doña Ana in the Mesilla Valley north of El Paso, where he met Major Enoch Steen of the First US Dragoons. Neighbors approached the officer to discuss a nefarious land-grab scheme involving a Mexican grant on which the town was situated, but the two men also conversed about Indian raiding. Referring fancifully to this portion of New Mexico as the "West Texas frontier," Neighbors wrote to Governor Bell informing him that Mescalero and Southern Apaches "keep up a continual warfare on the settlers, and rob and murder with perfect impunity." Steen's dragoons were the only mounted troops stationed in the vicinity, and Neighbors felt that a few dozen men were woefully insufficient for the task at hand. He claimed that armed volunteers akin to the Texas Rangers would be needed in New Mexico to fight and subjugate enemy tribes through the indiscriminate tactics of scalp warfare.[99]

With exhortations like these in mind, the Texas House of Representatives recommended a policy of ethnic cleansing for their state, insisting that the US government remove all tribes and put a stop to illicit commerce in guns, alcohol, and other contraband that filtered through Native villages, government Indian agencies, and private trading posts such Ben Leaton's fort opposite Presidio del Norte. Texas congressmen claimed that such action "will do more for the protection of our frontier than the entire standing army of the U. States stationed on the line at present occupied." Politicians struck a tone of angry desperation, believing that the federal government failed to develop and enforce appropriate Indian policies, and this sense of bereavement in turn motivated local officials to embrace independent Ranger campaigning. To underscore this point, state representatives drafted a bill in August 1850 creating "a sufficient mounted volunteer force for frontier protection, whose duty it shall be to drive all the Indians from beyond the limits of the State."[100] Across the hallway in the Texas Senate, the committee on Indian affairs concluded, "We must rely for security and protection upon the stout hearts and strong arms of the youth of our State" and called for the governor to raise "an adequate number of volunteers to chastise the Indians." Senators recommended that all unappropriated state treasury funds be earmarked for civilian warfare on the frontier, claiming that US troops stationed in Texas "are utterly useless."[101]

Because state legislators supported—rhetorically as well as financially—independent operations against Indians, the Rangers would continue to play a prominent role on the militarized Texas frontier. In January 1851, Andrew Jackson Walker led eighteen Rangers in a battle with Comanches along Arroyo Gato, fifty miles northeast of Laredo. These Indians had been raiding in northern Mexico, and Walker's men sensed an opportunity to take hundreds of stolen horses from them. Several days later, Lieutenant Edward Burleson Jr. led a second Ranger attack on Comanches near the Laredo Road crossing of the Nueces River, far to the southwest of San Antonio. This fight near Fort Ewell devolved into an intense hand-to-hand melee during which two Texans died and not a single man emerged unscathed. After the surviving Comanches fled, wounded Rangers scalped and dismembered each of the four slain Indians in an extralethal act of violent display.[102] In yet another incident, Robert H. Williams participated in a scout against Comanches—he called them "devilish murderers"—west of Castroville, and his company of Rangers plundered more than two hundred horses after attacking a camp near the Rio Grande Valley. The Indians fled into Mexico, leaving Williams and his fellow operatives to feast "right royally on a fat yearling the enemy had left behind."[103] By the time the famous traveler and author Frederick Law Olmsted passed through South Texas in the early 1850s, Rangers had developed a nationwide reputation for extreme violence. He sarcastically referred to them as "so many organized tribes of civilized white Indians . . . always ready for the chase of the red-skin," going on to say that "their principal occupation has always been Indian fighting." Olmsted was no humanitarian when it came to Indigenous peoples—he universally condemned them as "malicious idiots and lunatics"—but he also felt that Texans were a bit too extreme in their views of Indians as "blood-thirsty vermin, to be exterminated without choice of means." After having met a band of Lipan Apaches on the Leona River north of Fort Inge, Olmsted suggested to his predominantly northern US readers that "some other future than extermination" would be best, although this sentiment found little support on the antebellum Texas frontier.[104]

Just one year after Olmsted's book was published in New York, a party of 102 Rangers under the command of Colonel John S. "Rip" Ford rode alongside 113 Caddo, Wichita, and Tonkawa allies in a campaign through North

Texas. The state legislature had recently appropriated $70,000 to fund this company of Rangers, although the Indian auxiliaries would not have been paid and participated in pursuit of plunder instead. This development prompted an Austin editorialist to praise lawmakers for taking "a step in the right direction." The renewal of state financing for Rangers was an urgent policy initiative, the journalist claimed, because "the United States fails to afford Texas the protection necessary to save the scalps of our citizens."[105] At daybreak on May 12, 1858, Ford's men ambushed three hundred Kotsoteka Comanches near the Canadian River in the Indian territories of far western Oklahoma. That the incident occurred outside of Texas demonstrated the loose operational protocols of independent Rangers, who sometimes ignored jurisdictional boundaries when pursuing their targets.[106] "Squads of rangers and Indians were pursuing the enemy in every direction," Ford wrote in his report. By the afternoon, men were trickling back into camp, "bringing with them horses, prisoners, and other trophies of victory." The attackers suffered just five casualties while inflicting a devastating blow on their enemies, killing seventy-six Comanches, capturing eighteen more, and taking three hundred horses as plunder at the Battle of Little Robe Creek. During a diplomatic council two months later, a delegation of Comanche leaders told Lieutenant James E. Powell of the First US Infantry that five people had been scalped and many others taken captive during this incident. Chief Pooheve Quasoo (Iron Jacket) perished in the attack, and the perpetrators hacked his famous coat of iron mail into small bits to distribute as souvenirs, sending one piece to Governor Hardin R. Runnels. Ford told Texas authorities that his campaign had proven that "the Comanches can be followed, overtaken, and beaten, provided the pursuers will be laborious, vigilant, and are willing to undergo privations."[107]

When Sam Houston replaced Runnels as governor in December 1859, he commissioned a broad investigation into Indian depredation claims dating back to 1846. After fifty-one days touring several counties in the central and southern portions of the state, agents reported nearly four hundred claims totaling more than $200,000 in livestock losses. In the minds of most Texas officials and settlers, these staggering financial setbacks justified aggressive campaigning against Indians.[108] By the time Houston received this detailed report, US Army regulars had garrisoned and patrolled much of Texas for more than a decade. But expensive depredation claims still arose regularly, and the state government correspondingly continued to pay Rangers to pursue their own style of scalp warfare against specific tribes. One Ranger, William J. "Captain Jeff" Maltby, summarized the prevailing view of Comanches when he called them "the most noted and bloodthirsty savages that ever depredated on the Texas frontier."[109] Such racialized rhetoric was one of the state's primary justifications in advocating and financing acts of extralethal violence into the Civil War years, when the temporary transition to Confederate governance allowed even greater local autonomy in military affairs.[110]

John Robert Baylor, who participated alongside his younger brother George in the scalping campaign chronicled at the beginning of this chapter, carried on an especially vicious brand of scalp warfare after the Civil War began, and in so doing he caused headaches for Rebel officials as far away as Richmond, Virginia. Born in Kentucky in 1822, Baylor migrated to Fayette County, Texas, in 1840 and immediately enlisted in Colonel John H. Moore's volunteer company to fight Comanches. A decade later, he was elected to the Texas legislature, and while living in Austin he also gained admittance to the state bar as a lawyer. In 1855, Baylor accepted an appointment as Indian agent to the same Comanche peoples he had previously fought as a paramilitary operative, and he acted in the capacity of agent for two years before trying his hand at ranching on the Clear Fork of the Brazos River.[111] These two years as an emissary notwithstanding, Baylor had established a reputation across Texas for being "well versed in Indian warfare," and a group of settlers petitioned state legislators to identify him as "a suitable person to command a regiment of Rangers."[112] In the late 1850s, Baylor rode on numerous campaigns against Comanches in North Texas, and these experiences would inspire his subsequent tactical approaches to Southern Apaches in New Mexico.[113]

When the Civil War broke out, Baylor became a lieutenant colonel and led several hundred men of the Second Regiment of Texas Mounted Rifles in an invasion of Union-held New Mexico Territory in the summer of 1861. The grandiose purpose of the campaign—and the large invasion force that would follow under General Henry Hopkins Sibley—was to vanquish US

John Robert Baylor, pictured in his Confederate officer's uniform. Arizona Historical
Society, Tucson Main Photo Collection, PC1000.

forces in the Far Southwest and extend the Confederacy's western border to
the Pacific Coast of California.[114] But Baylor often seemed more inclined to
fight Apaches than to advance the South's imperialistic objectives in the
Civil War. As he rode westward from San Antonio, Baylor began pondering
ways to kill Indians using the forces under his command. After reaching
Fort Clark in June 1861, he sent a letter to Governor Santiago Vidaurri in
Nuevo León seeking a special arrangement that would allow Confederate

soldiers to cross the international border line in pursuit of Lipan Apaches.[115] Most if not all tribe members were living in northern Mexico by that time, and they maintained independence through strategic use of what historian James David Nichols calls "play-off diplomacy" that involved continuous mobility and targeted but brief raiding forays into South and West Texas.[116] These clever stealth tactics made border security a difficult quest for Texans and Mexicans alike, and the situation particularly infuriated Baylor, who was accustomed to fighting the more militarily powerful but also more visible and confrontable Comanches. "It certainly cannot be the policy of the Mexican Government to harbor this race of miscreants, who divide their depredations between Mexico and Texas," Baylor railed, telling northeastern Mexico's most powerful caudillo that he ought to cooperate in "the destruction of a common enemy." Remembering failed southern filibuster campaigns into Latin America during the antebellum era and fearing that Confederates might threaten his own political supremacy if allowed to operate on Mexican soil, Vidaurri declined free passage across the border while instructing Baylor that he should expand his scope of warfare to include Comanches.[117] Lacking the influential governor's blessing in this proposed transnational endeavor, Baylor rode on toward New Mexico Territory without attacking any Lipan Apaches.

When Baylor's column reached southern New Mexico on July 25, 1861, the men established headquarters at the town of Mesilla and forced more than five hundred US troops from nearby Fort Fillmore into a humiliating surrender at San Augustine Springs.[118] Having thus eliminated the most immediate Union Army threat to his operations, Baylor had time to think once more about Indians, and the small bands of Southern Apaches who now began raiding Rebel picket camps up and down the Mesilla Valley fueled his anger.[119] In October, the *Mesilla Times*—a secessionist newspaper published for only a few months during the Confederate occupation—reported a recent Apache attack on the mining town of Piños Altos, claiming that Indians had "commenced a war of extermination against the whites" and insisting that soldiers and their civilian allies reciprocate accordingly.[120] On February 27, 1862, Baylor led more than two hundred graycoats on a clandestine raid into northern Mexico. Deploying his Texas troops as a mercenary force on foreign soil, Baylor ordered an attack on the ranchería of Southern Apache chief Miguel Yrigóllen outside the village of Corralitos. He took five children captive and executed four adult prisoners before hastily retreating northward across the international border. Officials throughout Mexico may have quietly celebrated the murder of hated Apache enemies, but publicly they expressed fury at the blatant violation of territorial sovereignty. Chihuahua governor Luis Terrazas chided Confederate officials for the unauthorized military invasion of his state, while journalists as far away as Vera Cruz criticized Baylor's brash operation as an insult to national honor that could not go unaddressed. Secretary of State Judah Benjamin and President Jefferson Davis conducted face-saving public relations campaigns to temper anger below the border, telling Mexican officials that the Confederate government did not have hostile intentions and condemning "such outrages as Baylor is reported to have committed."[121]

By the time Benjamin and Davis wrote conciliatory letters to their Mexican counterparts, Baylor had already acted again in his wanton pursuit of Indian extermination. This time, he enlisted the services of the "Arizona Guards," a local volunteer unit consisting of fifty-three men from the towns of Piños Altos, Doña Ana, and Mesilla. The brainchild of influential mining speculator and Indian agent Charles D. Poston, the Arizona Guards were a reincarnation of the Mesilla Guard, a civilian paramilitary unit that had operated independently for a short period in 1858 and carried out a series of deadly attacks on Mescalero Apaches living peacefully near Indian agencies at Doña Ana and Fort Thorn. Prominent lawyer and merchant Thomas J. Mastin—an avowed secessionist who abetted the Confederate occupation of southern New Mexico—mustered the Arizona Guards on July 18, 1861, for the explicit purpose of killing Apaches. When Baylor arrived at Mesilla, he promptly enrolled Mastin's men into Confederate service as a paramilitary unit akin to the Texas Rangers, recognizing their potential usefulness as Indian fighters who could operate outside the jurisdictional constraints of regular troops. Over the coming months, the Arizona Guards pursued Apaches into northern Mexico and engaged in several violent skirmishes, one of which resulted in Mastin's death. Members of the unit subsequently elected Thomas Jefferson Helm, a business partner of Mastin, to serve as their new commander.[122] Already under intense scrutiny for his illicit campaign into Chihuahua, Baylor looked to this private army, rather than to his own Texas cavalrymen, to carry out the next act of indiscriminate scalp warfare.

In a letter written on March 20, 1862—just three weeks after the inflammatory Corralitos raid—Baylor ordered Captain Helm and his Arizona Guards to perpetrate a treacherous act of exterminatory extralethal violence against the region's Indigenous groups, whom he called "cursed pests." The Texan officer instructed Helm to "use all means to persuade the Apaches or any tribe to come in for the purpose of making peace, and when you get them together kill all the grown Indians and take the children prisoners and sell them to defray the cost of killing the Indians. Buy whisky and such other goods as may be necessary for the Indians . . . and have a sufficient number of men around to allow no Indian to escape."[123] Baylor issued this order to civilian volunteers rather than Texas cavalry units, thereby repeating the trend across time and place wherein private armies perpetrated state-sponsored acts of extralethal violence and violent display. In a reflection of his status as an independent operative only loosely attached to Baylor's Confederate command, Captain Helm did not follow through with the instructions, and no attack occurred. But the idea to deceive Apaches with a diplomatic flag of truce and incapacitate them with alcohol before butchering the men and selling the women and children into slavery clearly derived from Baylor's knowledge of the exterminatory scalp-hunting tactics that men such as John Johnson, James Kirker, and John Joel Glanton used in northern Mexico during the preceding two decades.

The shocking order—which Baylor issued three days after resigning his Texas Army commission—was leaked to the press in September 1862 and quickly became public knowledge.[124] The Confederate government did not wish to alienate or provoke foreign officials in Mexico, who might in turn renounce their neutrality in the Civil War and declare support for the United States government. Mindful of this potential fallout, Secretary of War George Randolph revoked Baylor's authority to raise troops as a direct result of his "order with regard to the Indians." Fearful that Europeans might look down on such barbaric behavior toward Indians—and that such a public relations nightmare might in turn dissuade possible British recognition of the

Confederacy—Jefferson Davis condemned the instructions to Helm as "an infamous crime."[125] Just as the French king criticized localized initiatives to scalp Indians in Canada during the late 1600s, and just as Mexico's central government disavowed the bounty laws of state legislatures in the mid-1800s, so, too, did Confederate officials in Richmond publicly denounce Baylor's independent scheming to treacherously kill Indians during the Civil War. As often occurred over the long colonial history of North America, national leaders rhetorically distanced themselves from the extralethal violence of scalp warfare that proliferated at local levels of governance.

Baylor remained defiant in the face of criticism, refusing to "retract or disavow a word of the order" and referencing his personal hatred of Indians when telling the department commander that he could never change such personal convictions.[126] The acid-tongued Texan officer went a step further, attacking General Sibley—commander of the Confederate Army of New Mexico and a notorious alcoholic—for allegedly leaking the order to the newspapers. Baylor already hated Sibley and let loose on him in a published editorial, declaring with enraged sarcasm that "it is enough for him to know that there was to be a quantity of whisky used in the enterprise to shock and horrify him. . . . [He] would never resort to such means of ridding the country of these pests, but if the Indians could by any process be dissolved and converted into whisky, I have no doubt that he would drink the whole Apache nation in one week." Baylor again stood his ground, saying of the order, "I issued it, and meant precisely what I said. . . . I was at war with savages and barbarians, and my motto is to 'fight the devil with fire.' "[127] Ultimately, neither Baylor's removal from the US-Mexico borderlands nor his incendiary public statements that followed would prevent him from influencing policy matters. In a tremendous moment of irony, he was elected to the Confederate Congress in 1864 and served as a member of the committee on Indian affairs.[128]

While Baylor's brash attack in northern Mexico and exterminatory order in New Mexico occurred as a sidelight of the Confederacy's wartime mission of westward expansion, Rangers continued to campaign against Indians in Texas. The aforementioned Robert H. Williams joined an expedition of twenty-five men on an "Indian hunt"—a phrase that connoted a sense of subhuman savagery—in the remote Devil's River country of southwest

Texas in January 1864. One of the participants was Dan Westfall, a settler from the Leona River country west of San Antonio who gained a reputation as a ruthless fighter. Westfall carried a rifle with fourteen lines etched into the wooden stock, denoting his personal tally of kills and making the weapon a veritable trophy of masculine honor and the Texas Ranger campaigns to conquer Indians. This particular foray targeted Comanches who, according to Williams, "had been more troublesome than usual . . . murdering, burning ranches, and driving off stock wholesale." After a long trek that Williams called a "wild-goose chase," the Rangers rendezvoused at Fort Lancaster on the lower Pecos River. They soon located a fresh trail and tracked a band of Comanches for several days before the Indians confronted them at a riverside camp. A standoff ensued before both groups retreated from the field without fighting. Westfall was unable to add any new markings to his rifle, but Williams nonetheless expressed a sense of accomplishment in that operations like these put immense pressure on Comanches and Lipan Apaches, forcing them farther and farther from the Texas settlements while simultaneously making tribal sustenance much more difficult.[129]

By the mid-1870s, as Comanches suffered devastating defeats at Palo Duro Canyon and Adobe Walls in the Texas panhandle, Ranger activities shifted away from scalp warfare because most tribal survivors had relocated to northern Mexico or to Indian Territory. From the 1830s through the 1860s, Rangers and other paramilitary operatives in Texas killed no fewer than five hundred Indians—and likely far more than that—as part of their scalp warfare against Comanches, Lipan Apaches, and other tribes that stood in the way of settlement. While these operations had a severe impact on targeted tribes and perpetrators sometimes expressed an exterminatory intent that aligned with modern United Nations definitions of genocide, the Texas Indian conflicts as a whole reflected outcomes that revolved more around defeat and removal than destruction and eradication. The few Native peoples remaining in Texas after 1870 no longer posed a serious threat to the rapidly increasing settler population, and from that point on Texas Ranger activities shifted to include patrolling the US-Mexico border and other forms of policing that often involved racialized violence and lynching directed at the state's nonwhite populations.[130]

For the first three decades of their existence as a state-sponsored fighting force, however, Rangers spent much of their time pursuing and fighting Indigenous groups that Texans viewed as removable obstacles to settlement and development. Incentivized by the valuable plunder taken from Indian camps, inspired by the masculine glory of trophies severed from Indian bodies, and unimpeded by the tactical and legal constraints that applied to soldiers of the Republic of Texas and the United States, some independent Ranger units operated in extralethal ways intended to facilitate the conquest of hated Native enemies. Neither the Republic of Texas nor the State of Texas implemented a formalized cash bounty system for Indian scalps or captives, but the elected officials of both political entities incessantly threw around the racialized rhetoric of extermination and employed the incentive of material gain when passing laws for recruiting volunteer operatives, who in turn performed extralethal acts of violence on behalf of the state that employed them. Just as many nineteenth-century Texans were deeply committed to defeating the Indians living within their geopolitical borders, so, too, did residents of Gold Rush–era California, Oregon, and Washington adopt exterminatory policies toward the Indigenous peoples of the West Coast and Pacific Northwest. In those places, volunteer campaigning would take a devastating demographic toll on many tribes, as scalp warfare morphed into clear acts and processes of genocide.

FIVE

Volunteer Campaigning on the Pacific Coast

B en Wright was born to Quaker parents in Indiana, but any pacifism that may have been instilled through an upbringing in the Society of Friends quickly dissipated when he migrated westward during the California Gold Rush. His brutal operations against the Modoc tribe thrust him into local lore for "scalping the fallen and committing other barbarities, such as cutting off the ears, noses and fingers of the wounded before their eyes had closed in death."[1] On August 29, 1852, Wright led twenty-one civilian volunteers out of the northern California mining camp of Yreka and headed eastward to Tule Lake, where Modocs—Wright derisively referred to them as "Red Devils"—had recently killed several American settlers and attacked a Siskiyou County sheriff's posse.[2] Over the ensuing three months of relentless campaigning, the "volunteer company" perpetrated a series of extralethal attacks. They first murdered two Modoc women who were gathering roots for food, and Wright personally plunged a foot-long bowie knife into the chest of one victim. Then they charged at a party of Indians near the shores of Tule Lake, dispersing them in all directions and killing at least a dozen as they attempted to escape in canoes. After finding the decayed bodies of several white immigrants in September—all purportedly killed by Modoc fighters—Wright pressed on with added resolve, and more men flocked to his ranks. As one Yreka resident later admitted, "Hunting Indians, who had only bows and arrows, was about the best sport going in those days, and any sufficient provocation would call out a ready response

from volunteers." Frustrated with his failure to overtake and destroy the entire tribe—members of which, according to one participant, "were daily
watching our movements"—Wright resorted to the same sort of treachery
that scalp hunters used against Apaches in northern Mexico. He released
a captive Modoc woman nicknamed "Old Mary" with a message for tribal
leaders to meet him in diplomatic council at a site on the Lost River. As the
meeting progressed on November 8, Wright sprung the trap and his eighteen followers fired indiscriminately into the crowd of Indians. William T.
Kershaw, who served as first lieutenant in the company, nonchalantly called
it a "smart engagement." No fewer than 31 Modocs—and possibly as many
as 90—perished in what came to be known as the Ben Wright Massacre.[3]
The three-month campaign resulted in the deaths of 73 Modocs according
to the California legislature's official count, although historians have estimated that the toll could have been as high as 158 killed.[4]

News of the bloodletting quickly reached Yreka, where dozens of residents
had recently petitioned Governor John Bigler praising the effectiveness of independent campaigning and insisting that the state finance additional companies of local volunteers.[5] "A great crowd was collected to greet them home"
on November 29, 1852, when Wright and his crew arrived in "a grand trium-
phal march" brandishing guns, clothing, and horses decorated with "scores
of scalps." Adoring citizens hailed the men as heroes, and many people enthusiastically followed them to local saloons where "a grand scene of revelry
commenced." The perpetrators spent the next week basking in glory and
binging on whiskey, the fetid Indian scalps dangling in plain sight as unforgettable symbols of the genocidal exploits they celebrated.[6] "The whole town
seems to be wild with joy," an approving Yreka newspaper correspondent reported. "They have, by their bravery, taught the redskins that they cannot rob
and murder the white man with impunity," the journalist added, insisting
that the legislature pay the men handsomely for their deeds.[7]

Just a few days after the drunken escapade, Wright penned a short letter to
Governor Bigler asking that the "California Mounted Rangers" be compensated for "the performance of this service to the country."[8] Royal T. Sprague,
chairman of the California Senate's committee on Indian affairs, praised
Wright's crew for their actions, claiming that "the services of said companies

were demanded by the most urgent and imperative necessity" because US Army commanders stationed in the region did not respond aggressively enough to satisfy citizen appeals for protection. In a common refrain among regional officials that echoed all the way back into the seventeenth century, Sprague asserted that settlers were the true victims and that they only killed Modocs because Modocs killed them first. "The Indians commenced a most bloody, exterminating, and organized warfare upon emigrant trains of our

Ben Wright, perpetrator of scalping massacres in northern California. Oregon Historical Society, Portland, Image OrHi 1711.

fellow countrymen," he exclaimed with unintended irony. "Families were being daily most inhumanly massacred by ruthless savages." Based on this line of reasoning, he recommended that the state duly compensate Wright's volunteers for their campaign.[9] On April 23, 1853—just five months after the massacre on Lost River—California legislators created a special "war fund" and appropriated $23,000 to pay Wright and three dozen "Volunteer Rangers" who participated in the Modoc expedition.[10] In California, killing Indians could be a lucrative occupation, and Wright had successfully capitalized on the exterminatory ambitions of state leaders.

Wright did not live long enough to fully enjoy the windfall payout. He perished just three years later in a gruesome episode near the mouth of the Rogue River in southern Oregon, where he was employed as an Indian agent in the Port Orford district.[11] In February 1856, a Shoshone man named Enos and a female companion, Chetcoe Jennie, pounced on the notorious killer while he supposedly lay drunk and incapacitated in camp. Driven by intense personal hatred—the scalp hunter not only adorned the outside of his home in Yreka with Indian body parts but also whipped and publicly humiliated both Enos and Chetcoe Jennie—the two assailants hacked Wright to death with an ax, ripped open his chest, yanked out his heart, and ate it raw.[12] For Modocs and other Klamath Basin Indians, the Ben Wright Massacre carried profound meaning as a treacherous act that permanently devastated tribal families and ignited two decades of conflict with American settlers.[13] During these years, Californians and Oregonians pursued a deadly and devastating style of scalp warfare that claimed the lives of thousands of Indians and in some cases annihilated entire tribes or subgroups of tribes in systematic fashion. Along with the highly destructive form of scalp warfare practiced in northern Mexico from the 1830s through the 1880s, the California example constitutes another clear instance in which settlers and their local state sponsors perpetrated genocide against Native groups, committing acts that met numerous criteria in the United Nations definitions while also eliminating very high percentages of some tribal populations.

The Ben Wright Massacre was not the first civilian attack on Indians in the Pacific Northwest, nor would it be the last. The mid-nineteenth-century history of California, Oregon, and Washington reads like a laundry list of extralethal murders and massacres. In the spring of 1849, a northern California rancher named Sisto Beryessa led a private army of miners to a camp along the American River, where participant Antonio Coronel described "a scene of utter horror" as the men "rounded up and shot down" every Nisenan Indian they could find.[14] One month later, another group of prospectors from nearby Coloma set out to slay more Nisenans. They returned after killing at least thirty Indians, and a man named Theodore Johnson vividly recalled the spectacle of violent display as these men rode in, "every man's rifle across the pommel of his saddle, and dangling at both sides hung several reeking scalps."[15] That same year, Ramón Gil Navarro wrote in his diary that he hoped to join a volunteer company "because it would probably be more profitable than working the river [for gold] and getting next to nothing."[16] In Shasta County, Bill Fopp was mining in March 1850 when "Diggers"—a derogatory reference to Paiutes—stealthily entered his camp and stole some of the provisions. He and his partner immediately vowed revenge. "The method of punishment, often resorted to, was a very simple one," Fopp's friend explained. "About twenty or thirty miners, all armed with rifles, revolvers and bowie knives, would start out on a road into the Indian country, discover a rancheria, take it by surprise, rush upon it, and shoot, stab, and kill every buck, squaw, and papoose." Fopp apprehended an unsuspecting Indian man who had nothing to do with the camp theft and marched the captive at gunpoint to a grassy clearing. He shoved "Mr. Injun" to the ground and shot him in the back of the head, as applauding spectators "universally approved" of the execution.[17] William McCollum, a doctor from New York who traveled through the region during the Gold Rush, summarized these types of occurrences when writing that almost any miner "will leave a rich placer to wreak vengeance on one of a race that he has learned to regard as his foe."[18]

In yet another incident, Indians killed a California settler as he herded cattle, whereupon the county sheriff at Weaverville organized a volunteer company and "every man [was] required to swear that no living thing bearing Indian blood should escape them." Three days later the group attacked a Wintu camp on the Trinity River, and "all alike were slaughtered, women and children as well as men." Reportedly carrying 149 scalps, members of the party rode back to Weaverville, where townspeople reveled in a "wild scene of excitement and joy at the extermination of this tribe." Some residents even nailed the bloody trophies to their front doors as ornaments of violent display, making those who took no part in the actual murders culpable in acts of killing and corporeal mutilation.[19] In 1853, when Indians stole twenty-four head of oxen from a Shasta merchant named Tomlinson, he gathered half a dozen employees and rode out "declaring his determination to have a scalp for every ox stolen."[20] Round Valley farmer Dryden Laycock, who periodically enlisted in California's volunteer units, summarized the situation quite succinctly when he testified in 1860 that "there were so many of these expeditions that I cannot recollect the number, the result was that we would kill on an average 15 or 20 on a trip and take some prisoners which we always took to the Reserve."[21] One volunteer squad that organized at Crescent City even designed a special company flag with the unabashed slogan "EXTERMINATION" emblazoned across it.[22]

As these participants matter-of-factly explained, volunteer companies in the state of California and the territories of Oregon and Washington campaigned against Indigenous groups with devastating effect, perpetrating acts of genocidal violence that in some ways mirrored those committed in contemporaneous Mexico. Whereas Mexican agents enlisted Delawares and Shawnees as auxiliaries to face the formidable Southern Apaches and Comanches, Californians rarely sought strategic alliances with Indians because of an extreme imbalance of power between West Coast settlers and their Native counterparts. California followed the lead of Texas by avoiding the enactment of scalp bounties as a specific form of financial compensation. Even so, a prominent myth evolved in the twentieth century that resulted in many people falsely believing that scalp bounties proliferated during California's Gold Rush era, but at present there are only four known scalp bounty proposals, all occurring at the town and county levels and only one of them resulting in payouts.[23] Instead of offering scalp bounties, the California legislature paid salaries to civilian operatives who pursued, captured, enslaved, and murdered Indians. Like the Rangers in Texas, volunteers in California found economic motivation in government paychecks, land bounties, and the right to keep valuable plunder taken from Indian camps.[24] "Gold and greed," the Hupa Indian scholar and activist Jack

Norton writes, "were some of the catalytic agents that ignited the brutality, savagery, and filthiness of those early white-men."[25]

In addition to the pursuit of financial gain, volunteer fighters developed a habit of dismembering the bodies of dead Indians as an expression of racial hatred, a masculine demonstration of martial prowess, and a way to keep count of kills. Many of these scalps and severed heads ended up on public display, as local residents mimicked Ben Wright by decorating their homes with the body parts or hanging them from tent poles.[26] In their seminal works on the topic, historians Brendan Lindsay and Benjamin Madley showed that Pacific Coast and Columbia River Plateau Indians faced an onslaught of exterminatory violence beginning in the 1840s and lasting into the 1870s. Lindsay and Madley each chronicled these murderous rampages—dozens of lengthy campaigns and hundreds of individual attacks—in comprehensive detail, and the purpose here is not to repeat what they have so ably done. Rather, in the pages that follow I examine select examples of volunteer campaigns that contextualize this genocidal mode of scalp warfare within the broader frameworks of state-sponsored extralethal violence and violent display in nineteenth-century North America.[27]

For nearly three decades, civilian volunteers operated up and down the Pacific Coast with little to no restraint, indiscriminately targeting Indians with a clear intent to kill as many as possible and force any survivors into slavery at local households and haciendas or onto small reservations where they might starve to death. Volunteers operated with the blessing of local officials—governors, legislators, judges, sheriffs—who approved the formation of fighting units and enticed men to their ranks by promising valuable rewards including plunder, money, and land. As one direct result of this government-sponsored killing program, violence and warfare proliferated and Indigenous populations declined precipitously. Between the initial US Army occupation of California in 1846 and the end of the Modoc War in 1873, as Madley's exhaustive research has shown, Pacific Coast tribes killed between 920 and 1,377 settlers, while Americans in turn slew between 8,157 and 14,703 Indians. These figures reflect only direct acts of killing and do not account for the tens of thousands who died of enslavement, starvation, exposure, and illness. All told, California's Indigenous population declined from an estimated 150,000 in 1846 to just 30,000 in 1873.[28] "If genocide had existed as a term in the nineteenth century," Lindsay writes, "Euro-Americans might have used it as a way to describe their campaign to exterminate Indians."[29]

As practitioners of scalp warfare, a total of 3,414 civilians enlisted as volunteers in California between 1850 and 1861. These state agents conducted twenty-four organized campaigns, most of those lasting for months and including numerous massacres. The operations collectively inflicted a death toll of at least 1,342 Indians, many of which were scalped or otherwise mutilated as a racially driven form of postmortem celebration. A mere 19 California volunteers died over the entire eleven-year period represented in these statistics, making this one of the most one-sided conflicts in American history. The state legislature officially spent over $1.3 million equipping and compensating these paramilitary operatives, meaning that California financiers doled out an average of $968 for each Indian that volunteers killed. By comparison, US troops bore responsibility for the deaths of at least 3,741 California Indians during this same period, but the federal government covered those expenses through congressional allocations for military supplies and salaries.[30] In just five years, troop strength in California increased almost 200 percent, from a total force of 1,105 in 1854 to 2,968 in 1859, even as the US Army faced major conflicts with Mormons in Utah as well as Navajos and Apaches in New Mexico.[31] With the Far West's civilian population soaring during the antebellum decade and local inhabitants demanding federal protection from Indians, War Department officials reassigned more and more soldiers to garrison forts in the coastal states and territories.

As a prelude to this military buildup and the concurrent efforts of local officials to raise civilian armies, American migration to the Pacific Northwest had picked up pace in the mid-1840s, after fur traders and Christian missionaries established some of the earliest colonial outposts in the region. By the time Great Britain and the United States signed a treaty on June 15, 1846, agreeing to the division of disputed territory at the 49th parallel (the present international boundary between the United States and Canada), thousands of overland drifters were pouring in to farm the fertile valleys of Columbia River tributaries such as the Willamette and the Deschutes.[32] The US Census of 1850 enumerated 13,294 settlers in the newly organized Oregon

Territory, which Congress divided horizontally in 1853 to create Washington Territory, and that same census placed California's non-Indian population at 92,597 in the immediate wake of the momentous Gold Rush that began one year earlier. American merchants, miners, farmers, and stock raisers migrated to the Pacific Coast's hinterlands in astounding numbers after 1850, and Washington, Oregon, and California each grew in population by factors of four or more during the ensuing decade. By the time the nation teetered on the brink of civil war in 1860, no fewer than 484,000 white settlers lived in the three coastal enclaves, and many thousands more nonwhite people from Asia, South America, the Caribbean, and Africa toiled as coolies, peons, and slaves.[33] This boom in population imposed incredible stress on the dozens of Indian tribes who inhabited the region, placing them in direct conflict with settlers who used the same land and resources and were willing to resort to extreme violence as a means of acquiring what they coveted.

Even before California attained statehood on September 9, 1850, American settlers had begun petitioning local officials demanding permission to form volunteer units in response to Indian raids. These companies adopted organizational techniques akin to earlier militias in the English/British colonies. Although California officials enacted laws that differentiated among soldiers, militiamen, and volunteers, the words "militia," "volunteer," and "ranger" became virtually synonymous in the everyday parlance of West Coast settlers. Notably, several of California's volunteer companies gave themselves geographically themed names that included the moniker "rangers," the Eel River Rangers and Pit River Rangers being two examples. But unlike Texas, where the legislature codified and funded the "Texas Rangers" as a state-recognized organization, California's volunteer outfits did not derive their nomenclature from government officials. In fact, their tendency to dub themselves "rangers" seems to have emanated in part from knowledge of and admiration for Texas Ranger campaigns against Comanches in the 1840s, as well as the active participation and influence of former Texas Rangers who migrated to California during the Gold Rush.

In anticipation of statehood, Californians held an election and approved a constitution in November 1849, and the new legislature convened on December 15 of that year.[34] Just four weeks later, Governor Peter Burnett received a petition from seventy-three residents of Mariposa County asking that he authorize a volunteer company under the command of sheriff James Burney.[35] A slave-owning Democrat from Missouri who migrated to Oregon before making his way southward during the Gold Rush, Burnett openly advocated a war of extermination against California Indians. As governor, he signed the so-called Indian Indenture Act on April 22, 1850, that legalized the enslavement of Indigenous peoples, which in turn became a motivating factor for civilian campaigners who not only killed and scalped Indians but also captured many others to sell into servitude.[36] Burnett did not immediately muster a volunteer force to accommodate citizen demands, and he eventually resigned from the governorship, but a law enforcement official with a national reputation for violence soon took matters into his own hands.[37]

John Coffee Hays began his career as an Indian fighter in the early 1840s, when he led Texas Ranger companies on deadly operations against Comanches and Lipan Apaches, and he also campaigned below the border during the US-Mexico War. By the time he succumbed to gold fever and migrated to California in the summer of 1849, Hays was a veritable celebrity for his exploits on the international frontier. "The merits of the 'Texan Ranger' had preceded him," one West Coast newspaper reported, "and his history was perfectly familiar to the people of this state."[38] In April 1850—at the very moment that California legislators legalized Indian servitude—Hays was elected to serve as the first American sheriff of San Francisco. He enjoyed strong support from three local militias—the Happy Valley Boys, the Rincon Point Boys, and the Clark's Point Boys—who organized a Saturday afternoon political rally on Portsmouth Square and fired rockets into the air as Hays delivered a short speech to the adoring crowd. His experiences with scalp warfare in the Texas-Mexico borderlands influenced the approach that he took to Indian conflicts in northern California. Not long after taking office in San Francisco, Hays acted independently of Governor Burnett by enlisting Captain Daniel Aldrich and fifty men comprising the Aldrich Rangers to set out for "the protection of the frontier." The following year, when residents of San Diego County feared an "outbreak between the Whites and Indians," Hays promptly organized a second volunteer company and sent them south to quell any uprising that might materialize.[39]

The paramilitary tactics that Hays implemented as an elected law enforcement officer would typify California's localized approach to fighting Indians over the ensuing decade. In April 1850—the same month that Hays became sheriff—legislators provided a legal foundation for citizen armies by enacting two laws that built on the Indenture Act to create a disastrous scenario for California Indians. The first statute allowed for spontaneous formation of "volunteer or independent companies," while the second codified a more formal process for organizing militia units.[40] The approval of separate bills, one for militias and the other for volunteer companies, indicated that California lawmakers saw clear distinctions between the two types of military organizations. When John McDougal replaced Burnett as governor of California on January 9, 1851, he applied these two state laws in a way that systematized Hays's strategy, asking the state legislature to equip and pay civilian volunteers as a "surer means of more effectually punishing [Indian] aggressors." To press the issue, McDougal hyperbolically told lawmakers that the goldfields would have to be abandoned if the state did not take immediate action to suppress hostilities between miners and Indians.[41] As the governor pursued these political initiatives early in 1851, Sheriff Burney mustered nearly two hundred volunteers and organized them into the Mariposa Battalion under command of Major James D. Savage. One of the participants, Robert Eccleston, chronicled the ensuing campaign in his diary. He was relieved to hear that the California legislature passed a "war loan bill" whereby $500,000 was borrowed to finance operations and pay battalion members $5 to $15 per day depending on rank. Eccleston also noted nonchalantly that the volunteers "had a fight with some Indians & taken [sic] 10 scalps & one or two prisoners." At least seventy-three Indians perished as a result of these Mariposa Battalion operations, while each participant received on average $217 in cash payments as well as the value of plunder taken during the campaign.[42] At the same time, McDougal wrote a "special and urgent" dispatch directly to President Millard Fillmore, saying that the federal government had assigned a "totally inadequate" military force to California and claiming that his constituents would have to grapple on their own with "not less than one hundred thousand warriors, all animated by a spirit of bitter hostility." In making these exaggerated assertions, the governor hoped to convince US officials to underwrite the formation of special volunteer units—McDougal called them "hardy frontiersmen and mountaineers"—whose unrestrained field operations might "settle the whole of our difficulties" if proper financial incentives could be assured.[43]

While Sacramento lawmakers hoped in vain for a favorable response from Washington, DC—Secretary of War Charles Conrad ultimately denied McDougal's request for immediate federal intervention and bluntly criticized the governor for using such inflated rhetoric—the citizens who participated in volunteer campaigns, as well as the merchants who supplied them, began transmitting receipts directly to the state government.[44] John B. Reynolds, who served thirty-four days as a private in a volunteer battalion, sent his request for $170 ($5 per day) through power of attorney, while Manuel Thompson, who acted as a teamster on the same campaign in 1850, demanded $105 in payment. The mercantile firm of Godfrey and Teller also sought reimbursement, claiming $692 for supplies furnished to another company of volunteers.[45] To cover these and other related expenses, the state adopted an approach similar to that of Chihuahua and Sonora, where wealthy residents donated money to "war societies" that in turn paid citizens to kill Indians. In California, lawmakers called on the general population to help finance the protection they demanded by purchasing war bonds.[46] This relatively reliable method for securing financial resources and disbursing them to claimants encouraged more and more settlers to wage scalp warfare against regional tribes. Much like the people who decorated their houses with scalps, this voluntary financing made average citizens culpable in the extralethal massacres that California's Indian killers committed.

The same year that California implemented its war bond program—which paid private and institutional bondholders charitable interest rates ranging from 7 to 12 percent for their investments in killing—lawmakers also debated a new law that considered militia, volunteers, and "independent companies" as three different categories of state agents under the governor's direct authority. Frank Soulé, a coeditor for San Francisco's *Daily Alta California* who also served in the legislature and became a vocal critic of state military operations, opposed the measure and suggested with tongue in cheek that a provision be added to pay rewards of $10 per Indian scalp.

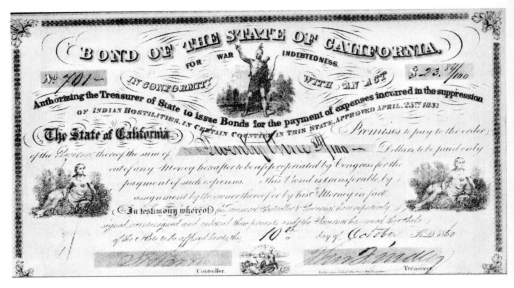

California War Bond dated October 10, 1860. California State Archives, Sacramento, California Adjutant General's Office, Military Department, Adjutant General, Indian War Papers 1850–1880, microfilm roll 3, document 954.

Soulé had immigrated across the southern route to California in 1849, passing through northern Mexico at the height of the Ley Quinta scalp-hunting initiative, and the sarcastic recommendation doubtless drew on his firsthand knowledge of and distaste for the Chihuahua and Sonora policies. The final version of the California law, passed on May 1, 1852, did not include a bounty, and lawmakers opted instead to underwrite salaries for volunteers.[47] With the support of these legislative measures, numerous campaigns took the field and culminated in the Ben Wright Massacre chronicled at the beginning of this chapter.[48] In March 1852, gold miners from Happy Camp in Siskiyou County rode to a ferry boat crossing on the Klamath River, where a large group of Indians were living, and "shot down all the men there, with several women." Emboldened by this act, they rode two miles upriver to Indian Flat and ambushed a second village, killing at least thirty people. Reporting the incident to US commissioner of Indian affairs Luke Lea, one California official condemned "this savage spirit on the part of some of the settlers" but expressed a sense of helplessness to do anything about it because the state encouraged and financed this approach.[49] It was not unusual, either in California or elsewhere in the West, for local Indian agents and other employees of the Bureau of Indian Affairs to voice their personal opposition to civilian-led forms of violence that they viewed as heavy-handed and unnecessary, but their opinions did not typically reflect official federal Indian policy. California Indian agent Oliver M. Wozencraft, who routinely condemned unprovoked and indiscriminate attacks, described one incident on King's River in July 1852 that particularly troubled him. He explained that local miners spent weeks plotting an attack at a nearby reservation during which they murdered several Indians under a headman named Pasqual, but Wozencraft's report to Governor John Bigler went unanswered. The man who led the ambush was elected county judge shortly afterward, so the US district attorney in northern California declined to investigate or pursue criminal charges because he "did not think it worthwhile to prosecute him in his own county." Like the mock scalp dances at Texas courthouses and the performative scalp parades on town plazas in Mexico, the election of a prolific scalp hunter to the local judiciary in California symbolized the state legal system's role in sanctioning scalp warfare. Wozencraft concluded that "not a week passes in which some [Indians] are not killed, or worked and starved to death" as servants and slaves.[50] Meanwhile, some local newspapers celebrated these types of "war exploits." Several editorialists made heroes of the miners and merchants who killed Indigenous peoples and plundered their camps, and such writers inspired others to participate in volunteer campaigns by printing racialized comments about "taking the hair of one of our mop-headed Indians."[51]

California superintendent of Indian affairs Edward F. Beale, who acted as a primary architect of the state's early reservation system, corroborated Wozencraft's claims by appending examples of three additional massacres to the report.[52] The first case involved a contingent of settlers who killed at least 130 Indians on the Trinity River and "carried home a bag full of scalps." The next description alluded to the Ben Wright Massacre, with Beale noting that "a party of Indian fighters . . . being determined not to come [home] without any scalps," devised a treacherous plan to exterminate an entire tribe during a sham treaty council. The third incident pertained to the killing of at least

18 Indians near Frenchtown, where the marauders afterward executed an elderly chief by hanging him in public. Not a single white man died in any of these actions, Beale pointed out, and this lopsided outcome provided "a full proof that it was a massacre of helpless and defenseless beings." As a solution to this increasingly popular tactic, Beale proposed that all Indians be placed on reservations under US military supervision. General Ethan Allen Hitchcock of the Second US Infantry supported the idea, saying that the obvious alternative would be "giving the Indians over to rapid extermination."[53] A longtime army officer, Hitchcock was known to criticize militiamen and volunteers—at one point he condemned the "swindling character" of a civilian company that formed at Humboldt and subsequently submitted a $5,000 claim to federal officials for "alleged military expenses"—and his comments on Indian extermination reflected his own professional military ethos and a concomitant aversion to paramilitary operations.[54]

Protests from federal officers such as Beale and Hitchcock notwithstanding, Californians continued to target Indians with exterminatory intent and financial motivation. In the latter months of 1853, a man named J. M. Peters organized thirty-three men into a killing squad and targeted the Tolowa village of Yontocket near the Smith River. The volunteers attacked at daybreak, killed every Indian they saw, collected any valuable items they could carry, and torched what remained of the town. White observers tallied about 150 people killed, but Tolowa oral history places the number closer to 600, making the Peters massacre one of the deadliest in California history.[55] That same year, four Napa County residents surnamed Beryessa, Briones, Mesa, and Quiera developed a veritable business out of kidnapping women and children and selling them in local communities. A whistleblower reported their actions to state officials, claiming that the four partners had enslaved at least 136 Indians of unnamed tribes in the Clear Lake region and in the process of tracking and capturing them had murdered many others "in cold blood."[56] The widely distributed *Daily Alta California* also criticized this practice and even compared it to the South's chattel slavery. "Disreputable persons . . . steal away young Indian boys and girls . . . and sell them to white folks," an editorialist explained, informing readers that slave catchers "are obliged to kill the parents" to obtain child captives.[57] Another observer,

William H. Brewer of the California State Geological Survey, put it just as bluntly when writing from Mendocino County that "kidnappers would often get the consent of the parents by shooting them."[58] Several years later, even as the Civil War was underway, the enslavement of young California Indians—who could fetch anywhere from $30 to $150 in the local marketplace—continued to occur alongside extralethal massacres that eliminated parental resistance to abduction.[59] Superintendent of Indian Affairs George Hanson corroborated the direct connection between slaving and killing, reporting to superiors in Washington, DC, that "kidnapping Indians has become quite a business of profit, and . . . is at the foundation of the so-called Indian wars."[60] Meanwhile, in neighboring Oregon Territory, legislators and their constituents adopted similar techniques for their own campaigns against Klamath Valley tribes and others that they viewed as a threat to settlement and development.

In the summer of 1854, Oregon's quartermaster general teamed with four local officials in writing a terse letter to Governor John W. Davis, who also acted as commander-in-chief of the territorial militia. The missive outlined recent Indian raids on the overland wagon roads, lambasted US troops stationed at Fort Jones and Fort Lane as "wholly inadequate," claimed that Modocs were organizing with other tribes to block the seasonal migration of Americans, and demanded the formation of temporary fighting units to deal with the apparent crisis. The petitioners pointed out that neighboring Klamath County in northern California had already dispatched volunteers for the same purpose, and suggested that Salem officials follow the example of their counterparts in Sacramento by memorializing Congress for money to "defray the expenses" of paramilitary operations.[61] Davis supported the idea in principle but lamented that the territorial treasury did not have "a single dollar" to spare for outfitting a civilian campaign or compensating its participants. For this he blamed the federal government, parroting many California lawmakers and governors by claiming that US officials three thousand miles away simply did not appreciate the urgency of the situation and failed to provide financial support for militias and volunteer companies in the absence of a sufficient regular army force. While confessing that he could not promise any pay to enlistees, the governor declared that local officials throughout the territory were free to raise their own fighting units and to compensate them in whatever way possible. Davis concluded that "our only resource is to rely upon the voluntary aid and patriotism of our fellow-citizens," and with that in mind he suggested that John E. Ross, a veteran of Ben Wright's excursion of 1852, be asked to organize a special company in southern Oregon.[62] Two weeks later, Ross issued a public call for seventy men at the town of Jacksonville, each person to serve for three months and provide his own mounts, weapons, and supplies. The new squad filled in a mere three days and immediately set out to patrol the overland trails in August 1854, just in time for the seasonal migrant rush that occurred each autumn.[63]

Captain Jesse Walker commanded the unit that Ross recruited in Jacksonville, and he led the volunteers in multiple deadly massacres over the ensuing three months. In a repetition of the Ben Wright campaign two years earlier, Walker's cohort attacked a Modoc camp on the shores of Tule Lake and burned the homes and food stores as panicked survivors fled in canoes. Numerous deadly skirmishes followed until a Modoc delegation sued for peace on September 4, promising "to be friendly and never to kill or rob another white person." The company then moved its headquarters to Goose Lake, from which point half of the men were detached to monitor the migrant road while the other half pursued a band of Paiutes on the eastern slopes of the Sierra Nevada. Walker and his followers ambushed a camp on the morning of October 6, killing at least eight Paiutes during a lengthy engagement. Five days later, they surprised another Indian village and murdered eight more. "The victory was complete," Walker bragged in his final report to Ross.[64] Afterward, Quartermaster General Charles S. Drew lauded the civilian volunteers for tracking and killing what he called "this God-accursed race," and he gave a detailed accounting of the campaign's expenses in hopes that territorial officials would find a way to compensate participants.[65]

Walker was not the only one operating in Oregon Territory during the summer and fall of 1854. When a group of Shoshones attacked a wagon train near the Hudson's Bay Company's outpost at Fort Boise in mid-August, a US infantry unit stationed at Fort Dalles marched toward the scene, but Governor George L. Curry considered this official military response insufficient and issued a call for two companies of volunteers to augment thirty-seven independent

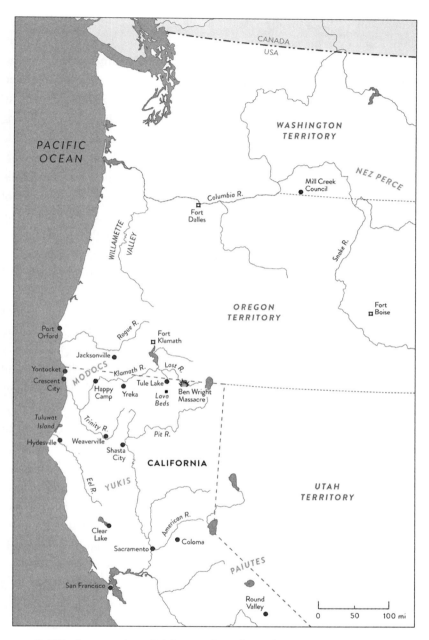

Gold Rush–era northern California and Pacific Northwest. Map by Erin Greb.

operatives who had already taken the field under command of Nathan Olney. "So long as the people of Oregon are left to protect themselves, to punish Indian depredations, and repel Indian hostilities," Curry seethed, "the expenses incident thereto ought cheerfully to be paid by Congress." He then wrote a lengthy missive to President Franklin Pierce, describing the Indian attack at Fort Boise in explicit detail. "The [immigrant] women, after suffering the most revolting treatment, were killed by torture," he claimed, "and the little children of the party burned to death." Curry complained about US Army regulars, especially foot soldiers who could not effectively pursue horseback Indians, and explained that his only recourse was to employ the services of well-mounted civilian volunteers.[66] The Oregon governor's angry letter to the president represented, in microcosm, the frustration that settlers up and down the Pacific Coast felt with respect to the US government and its strategies for responding to perceived Indian threats to farms, ranches, mining camps, and migrant trails.

While Walker and Olney led deadly campaigns in Oregon, the governor of California arranged two units—the Crescent City Coast Rangers and the Klamath Mounted Rangers—to ride out in pursuit of Tolowas. Quartermaster General William C. Kibbe equipped these volunteers with rifles and ammunition, preparing more than one hundred men to attack the Tolowa town of Etchulet on December 31, 1854. In a veritable carbon copy of the massacre at Yontocket just one year earlier, volunteers swarmed Etchulet as the sun peeked over the horizon on a crisp winter morning. Hundreds of men, women, and children were indiscriminately shot down as they ran frantically from family houses made of redwood planks. In perhaps the most statistically efficient killing spree ever perpetrated in California, only five Tolowas survived the Etchulet Massacre, and the futility of the Indian resistance can be gleaned from an account that the entire tribe possessed only three guns at the time of the attack. "The die is cast," one San Francisco editorialist wrote in a tone of disgust, "and a war of extermination commenced against the Indians."[67] With the Tolowa population of northwestern California estimated at 2,400 before the nineteenth century, the twin massacres at Yontocket and Etchulet eliminated a majority of the community within a one-year span, and a mere 200 tribe members survived into the 1870s.

"When they slaughtered at *Yontocket* and *Echulet* they didn't leave many of us," one Tolowa descendant lamented decades later, "and the only ones of us that survived are the ones that ran way back into the mountains."[68]

By the mid-1850s, most white Americans living in the Pacific Coast region had developed a complete lack of confidence in federal authorities, and local citizens as well as their territorial and state administrators overwhelmingly chose to take matters into their own hands when it came to fighting Indians. Over the ensuing four years, Oregon lawmakers passed multiple resolutions and sent three memorials to Congress seeking reimbursement for the costs of Walker's campaign, as well as additional funds to compensate other volunteers who waged an ironically termed "war of self-preservation."[69] When congressional leaders failed to respond favorably to these requests after three years, militia quartermaster Charles Drew gathered testimony from thirteen individuals who had either witnessed Indian attacks on settlers or participated in Oregon's volunteer campaigns. He presented the collection of terse reports to Congress in 1857, along with a tally of 242 American migrants reportedly killed on overland trails over the preceding twenty-three years and a thinly veiled admonition insisting that politicians appropriate money to pay the independent operatives for their services to the state.[70]

While Oregon officials such as Curry and Drew, along with numerous California figureheads, lobbied authorities in Washington, DC, for material support to underwrite volunteer operations, agents from neighboring Washington Territory took more direct action.[71] Governor Isaac Ingalls Stevens teamed with Superintendent of Indian Affairs Joel Palmer in the summer of 1855 to organize the twelve-day Mill Creek treaty council, where more than five thousand people from the Cayuse, Nez Perce, Umatilla, Walla Walla, and Yakima tribes came together to discuss terms for peace. At just thirty-five years old, Stevens already wielded significant political influence, not only serving as Washington's first federally appointed territorial governor but also presiding over the northernmost route of the Pacific Railway Surveys. These personal interests in politics and railroads coalesced in a strong motivation to either relocate regional tribes onto isolated reservations by way of treaty negotiations or else remove them from the scene entirely

Peo-Peo-Mox-Mox. Reproduced from A. J. Splawn, *Ka-mi-akin, the Last Hero of the Yakimas* (Portland, OR: Kilham Stationery and Printing, 1917), 359.

through exterminatory scalp warfare. One of his primary Indigenous counterparts during the Mill Creek council was the Walla Walla chief Peo-Peo-Mox-Mox (Yellow Bird), a renowned leader with many years of diplomatic experience. Born in 1800, Peo-Peo-Mox-Mox was twenty years older than Stevens and had already been interacting with American missionaries for two decades. In 1836, he sent his eldest son Toayahnu to be educated at a newly established Methodist mission in the Willamette Valley, but Toayahnu—renamed Elijah by the missionaries—was murdered eight years later during a trading expedition to New Helvetia in northern California. By the time he met with Stevens and Palmer in 1855, Peo-Peo-Mox-Mox had many reasons to distrust settlers, but he nonetheless sought to solidify peaceful relations as the Walla Walla and Umatilla representative by making his mark on the final treaty on June 11, 1855. In so doing, he grudgingly agreed to move his followers to a reservation in the Umatilla Valley, where they would receive $100,000 in annuities over the next twenty years. Peo-Peo-Mox-Mox himself would be awarded with a house and a personal government salary as the officially recognized chief, even though he lacked the authority to speak for all five tribes that participated in the meeting.[72]

With the Cayuses, Nez Perces, Umatillas, Walla Wallas, and Yakimas disagreeing among themselves about the outcomes of these negotiations, the Mill Creek treaty seemed destined to fail, and violence erupted within weeks of the council's adjournment. Later that summer, when Columbia Plateau Indians killed six gold miners along with the appointed Yakima agent, local officials feared that disaffected factions within the five tribes were organizing a much larger uprising to coincide with the seasonal fall migration on the overland trails. To preempt the possibility of such an occurrence, Colonel James Kelley frantically raised a company of volunteers in Oregon and set out to find Peo-Peo-Mox-Mox. Kelley's followers eventually captured the influential headman under a flag of truce. A captain surnamed Van Bergen claimed the chief's prized "war steed" as a trophy, and then the men murdered him during a purported escape attempt on December 7, 1855.[73] Two weeks later, a Puget Sound newspaper informed readers that "Old Pepe-pep-mox-mox [sic] . . . was singled out by one of the volunteers . . . and killed by a single stroke of a saber, that completely severed his head from his shoulders, which he immediately seized and rushed into camp with, and there scalped."[74] Another description of the performative killing, written many years later, explained matter-of-factly that the Oregonians "cut off his ears and pieces of the scalp were taken as souvenirs." The author of the latter account, writing under contract from the Oregon legislature to record "the heroic deeds of those brave men and noble women" who first settled the territory, dismissed the murder and mutilation of Peo-Peo-Mox-Mox as nothing more than a routine act of retribution. "It is not the office of the historian to excuse the barbarities of either race," Frances Fuller Victor wrote before going on to do just that: "It is, however, true that retaliation is an important part of the spirit of war, and that the mutilation in a comparatively slight degree of the dead body of a noted chief was hardly a sufficient reprisal, for the horrible atrocities perpetrated upon living men, women, and children by the groundless hatred of his race."[75]

The murder and mutilation of Peo-Peo-Mox-Mox near the old Whitman Mission at Frenchtown, in the southeastern extremity of Washington Territory, not only sparked the so-called Walla Walla War that lasted for the next three years but also inflicted deep spiritual wounds on the chief's surviving family and followers. Within the closely related Cayuse, Umatilla, and Walla Walla tribes of the Columbia River Plateau, beliefs and actions are governed by Tamánwit. Thomas Morning Owl characterizes Tamánwit as "our Indian law," while Armand Minthorn explains that "it's how we live, it's our lifestyle." More specifically, according to Morning Owl, "tamánwit is an ideology by which all things of the earth were placed by the Creator for a purpose," establishing an Indigenous ethos revolving around direct connections between a spirit world and the present world. Minthorn adds, "This is the law . . . that we recognize when we lose a family member," and a person's death—as well as how the death occurs—is an important part of this spiritual understanding of reality. Historian Clifford Trafzer puts it another way, explaining that "everything was connected to creation through positive and negative actions that offered a lesson or teaching of the law [of Tamánwit]."[76] Based on this Indigenous worldview, Governor Stevens and Superintendent Palmer unknowingly upended Tamánwit when they strongarmed members of the five Columbia River Plateau tribes into relinquishing traditional lands that their Creator made specifically for them to live on. This initial disruption of Tamánwit at the Mill Creek treaty council was more than enough, from the Native perspective, to bring illness and death on the people. But the subsequent murder of their chief, Peo-Peo-Mox-Mox, and the mutilation of his corpse as a celebratory act of violent display, compounded the treaty's cultural offenses and completely overturned the crucial sense of balance between life and death that tribe members understood as part of their spiritual identity.[77]

While one contingent of Oregonians sought out Peo-Peo-Mox-Mox and his Walla Walla followers, another group of volunteers formed at Jacksonville. Organized by a local man named James Lupton, the group attacked the Shasta Indian chief "Old Jake" and his band near Fort Lane on October 8, 1855, killing more than two dozen people. Although Lupton himself perished during the fighting, the so-called Lupton Massacre initiated a lengthy operation known as the Rogue River War. To avenge their leader's death, Oregon volunteers assaulted several more Shasta camps, murdering over one hundred Indians and bashing many of their brains out with clubs.[78] Over the ensuing ten months, civilians conducted several similar operations, and the company commanders clearly stated their exterminatory intent. Regular US Army troops undertook campaigns of their own, although the department commander, General John E. Wool, declared that removal to reservations was preferable to indiscriminate slaughter. Despite differences in strategic objectives, volunteer units and military battalions collectively took a heavy toll on the Indians of southwestern Oregon, reducing their population by an estimated 80 percent between 1851 and 1856. By July 1856, federal troops were marching approximately two thousand Indigenous survivors to reservations at Port Orford and Grande Ronde, bringing the Rogue River War to an end.[79]

Just three weeks after Oregon volunteers decapitated Peo-Peo-Mox-Mox in a violent upheaval of Tamánwit, and with the Rogue River War still unfinished to their north, California's Board of Examiners of War Claims had money foremost in mind. On New Year's Eve of 1855, they reported a total "war debt" of $848,549, an amount that would have been significantly higher after factoring the interest owed on hundreds of bonds that serviced that debt.[80] The terminology that state officials consistently used—they paid down "war debts" with "war bonds" issued by "war claims" committees—indicates that they thought about such finances squarely inside the framework of mutually recognized warfare between enemy combatants, and not within the context of an overwhelmingly one-sided drive to systematically exterminate a racial foe. But the executive orders of governors and the policy initiatives of legislators, as the former mustered volunteer units and the latter enacted laws to finance them, belied professions of local government helplessness in the face of any threat that Indians posed to settlers. As the antebellum decade progressed, officials in all three Pacific Coast enclaves continued to embrace and even expand the parameters of scalp warfare and extralethal violence as their preferred strategy for conquering the Indigenous peoples in their midst.

In California, one of the deadliest operations the state ever organized targeted the Round Valley region for six straight months beginning in July 1859. The campaign began in the same way as most others—with a letter to the governor demanding protection from Indians—but this time the petitioners had the backing of Serranus Hastings, former chief justice of the California Supreme Court and a wealthy ranch owner in Eden Valley. With the influential Hastings pledging to bankroll the endeavor in the absence of state financing, volunteers could feel assured of a lucrative payday. The petition to Governor John B. Weller—a former US senator who had worked feverishly to obtain congressional reimbursement of California's "war debt"—was a mere political formality, and Hastings didn't bother waiting for an answer before recruiting Walter S. Jarboe to lead a unit known as the Eel River Rangers.[81] Born in Kentucky in 1829, Jarboe was just thirty years old when he agreed to command this contingent of Indian fighters, but he had already made a name for himself through exploits in the US-Mexico War, as well as previous attacks on Indians that he perpetrated after migrating to California in the early 1850s. Between his own celebrity status and the promise of pay from Judge Hastings, Jarboe had little trouble finding enthusiastic men to fill his ranks.[82]

Jarboe's recruits operated without government approval during the months of July and August, taking a significant toll on the surrounding Yuki Indian population. Concentrating on the area between the north and south branches of their namesake Eel River, the volunteers carried out a rapid series of deadly assaults. During multiple strikes in a one-week period, they killed five Yukis and captured twenty-six more, unloading the prisoners at the nearby Nome Cult Reservation in Round Valley before hitting another ranchería and killing fifteen more. By the end of August, they had carried out three additional ambushes resulting in the murder of forty Indians and the captivity of twenty-four others.[83] Captain Edward Johnson of the Sixth US Infantry complained about these unrestrained operations, telling the department commander in San Francisco that "a war of extermination is being vigorously waged by the citizens of Round and Eden Valleys." Three Yuki mothers carrying their infant children had escaped to Johnson's post, where they revealed through an interpreter that Jarboe killed six men, four women, and four children during an attack on their camp. "I believe it to be the settled determination of many of the inhabitants to exterminate the Indians and I see no way of preventing it," Johnson concluded.[84] Less than two weeks later, Captain John Adams of the First US Dragoons submitted a similar report to headquarters. "A party of self-organized volunteers" had just ambushed a peaceful Indian village not far from his station at Fort Crook, and he felt certain that Jarboe's "murderous assaults" would continue unless either the governor or the superintendent of Indian affairs intervened.[85]

Weller did indeed intervene, but not in the way Johnson and Adams would have liked. On September 6, he hired Jarboe and his band of cutthroats as California militiamen—article 7 of the state constitution granted governors this localized form of military authority—and in so doing he conferred legal legitimacy to their operations and ensured that they would remain afield for the foreseeable future.[86] Weller's decision to form a statutorily recognized militia out of Jarboe's men typified the state's approach to regional conflicts, as California officially organized more than three hundred temporary militia units between 1851 and 1866, not counting the many unofficial volunteer companies that also operated during that same period.[87] This common course of action revealed a disingenuity behind the cacophonous demands for more federal troops and stronger military leadership in California—one prominent official derisively called the department commander, General Wool, a useless "granny"—because at the time Weller contracted with Jarboe the US War Department had more soldiers assigned to California than ever before.[88] With nearly three thousand Army regulars in the state, the federal government had clearly and forcefully responded to the requests of citizens and politicians, dedicating more manpower to the West Coast than many of the neighboring inland territories. Weller's decision to employ Jarboe under these circumstances undermined claims that volunteer operations would be discontinued if US officials committed more resources to California and Oregon.

When Weller hired Jarboe, he scolded the operative for prior indiscriminate attacks, informing him that state contractors should be careful to target only those Indians known to have stolen livestock or killed settlers.[89] These admonitions fell on deaf ears, and Jarboe's first official report to the governor's office included a laundry-list account of killings along with an announcement that seventeen new recruits had joined his ranks.[90] With this enlarged force, Jarboe quickly slaughtered twenty-five more Yukis and took twenty women and children prisoners, his company's only loss being a "valuable dog" that Indians shot during the fighting. Three days later they set upon another village near Eden Valley, killing several and taking the surviving captives to a nearby reservation.[91] When the men stumbled upon the rotting remains of a settler named John Bland, they blamed the Yukis and this became their justification for the next round of massacres. The volunteers slew eleven Indians and imprisoned thirty-three more at a camp north of Round Valley, although nineteen of these escaped while being marched to the Mendocino Reservation. Jarboe claimed that some of these captives confessed to executing Bland "by burning him at the stake," but Weller answered by reminding his captain of previous instructions to avoid indiscriminate tactics. "Your company was organized to protect the lives and property of the citizens in certain localities and not to wage a war of extermination against the Indians," the governor chided, adding that "the innocent ought not to suffer a war of extermination against a whole tribe because of the acts of a few bad Indians."[92] The same day that Weller wrote this letter, Jarboe's men killed nine Yukis and took thirty prisoners, their offense being the theft of a single cow from a Round Valley homestead.[93] These actions met with approval among some members of the local press, with one correspondent expressing a sense of awe that a group of just twenty men could perform with such incredible lethality. "It is much to be regretted that Jarboe's company is not more numerous," the editorialist mused. "He is, however, doing wonders."[94] Across northern California, a handful of newspapers enthusiastically reported Jarboe's exploits and promoted his actions as a necessary and even admirable course of action, while other periodicals condemned these killing campaigns as inhumane and unjustifiable, thus reflecting a growing division among citizens with respect to Indian policies.[95]

Weller's repeated rebukes did not deter the Eel River Rangers from their genocidal course, nor did the biting criticisms of a US Army officer who derisively nicknamed these men "minions" have any effect.[96] Undaunted by his detractors, Jarboe launched an unrelenting offensive throughout November, perpetrating four more massacres that collectively claimed the lives of over thirty Yuki men, women, and children. In a wry pushback against the governor's unwelcome protestations, Jarboe simply told him that "a lot of beef was found in their huts which established their guilt." From that point forward, the captain included blunt justifications in each report, calling attention to the discovery of purportedly stolen property—a dead horse, a butchered cow, a slaughtered pig—in the smoldering ruins of every Indian campsite that he attacked and burned. The Yukis, he raved, "are without doubt the most degraded filthy miserable stinking set of anything living that come under the head of and rank as human beings," and here he reverted to the rampant racial hatred of Indians as a secondary rationalization for the deadliness of his campaign. With tongue in cheek, Jarboe assured Weller that he would "continue to carry out your instructions and use every possible endeavor to bring them to terms with as little slaughter to them as possible."[97] When the next report reached the governor's desk two weeks later, however, it revealed that Jarboe's men had already killed thirty-seven more Indians.[98]

Based on the results of these campaigns, Mendocino County officials petitioned the governor asking that he enlarge volunteer forces so that they could expand the area of operations across a wider swath of northern California. But Weller did the exact opposite, writing a letter to Jarboe on January 3, 1860, asking that he disband the Eel River Rangers and offering "sincere thanks" to all the recruits for their services to the state.[99] Although he gave no specific reason for the sudden reversal, Weller was scheduled to vacate the governor's office just six days later, so the timing seems more than coincidental. In his last annual message to the state legislature, delivered just before the new governor's inauguration, Weller simply said that Indian raids in the vicinity of the Eel River had compelled him to take executive action, and that Jarboe's men had "succeeded . . . to a great extent."[100] Citizens of Mendocino County wasted no time in courting Weller's gubernatorial successor, John G. Downey, hoping that he would reassemble the volunteer company to provide "immediate protection against the wild Indians."[101] Jarboe also contacted Downey, summarizing his six-month expedition and enumerating twenty-three separate engagements during which he counted 283 corpses and 292 prisoners, plus an unknown number of wounded Indians who may have later perished. On the other hand, not a single volunteer died, and only four sustained wounds.[102] These statistics reveal a lot about Jarboe's scalp warfare tactics, as his men clearly selected the most defenseless targets they could find and attacked at moments of greatest vulnerability. The numbers also say something about the ineffectiveness of Indian resistance in California—in particular the Yuki tribe that these Eel River Rangers targeted—because most of these small starving groups lacked the horses, guns, and other crucial supplies that enabled other North American tribes to resist scalp warfare with greater success.

Jarboe's purpose in providing the new governor with a painstakingly detailed account of his killing spree had more to do with money than with any expectation that Downey would grant permission to resume the campaign. Weller left office without issuing funds to compensate the state-contracted volunteers, and Hastings apparently did not follow through with his initial promise of full financing, so now Jarboe wanted payment for his men. His claim included $5,364 to reimburse the cost of supplies and $5,779 to be disbursed as salaries, bringing the total request to $11,143.[103] As part of an investigation into the campaign, government interviewers deposed more than thirty residents of Round Valley to determine the accuracy of Jarboe's monetary calculations. The majority of farmers and ranchers testified that Indians had been killing their livestock for years, but at least two witnesses—a blacksmith named William Pollard and a Nome Cult Reservation employee named Lawrence Battaile—insisted that almost every account of Yuki wrongdoing had been either totally fabricated or egregiously exaggerated in order to justify deadly operations.[104] Some state politicians vocally dissented to financing such a murderous campaign. "Within the last four months, more Indians have been killed by our people than during the century of Spanish and Mexican domination," the majority report for the investigation concluded. "For an evil of this magnitude, someone is responsible, either our government, or our citizens, or both." Despite this scathing condemnation, the three dozen testimonials ultimately moved the legislature to appropriate $9,347 for the Eel River Rangers who carried out what came to be known as the Mendocino War.[105] At a time when the average miner in California's gold fields earned three dollars per day, this was a noteworthy payout, especially when considered alongside the valuable plunder that the men also took from ruined Yuki camps.[106]

In strict terms of dollar bills and dead bodies—two considerations that Sacramento lawmakers understood quite well—Jarboe's campaign was the most cost-efficient volunteer operation ever commissioned on the Pacific Coast. In 1853, the California legislature had paid Ben Wright and three dozen of his men a total of $23,000 for killing seventy-three Modocs, costing the state $315 for each dead Indian. In 1860, by comparison, Jarboe and his followers received $9,347 for killing 283 Yukis, an average of $33 per slain Indian. If the 292 prisoners are factored into the equation, then taxpayers and war bond purchasers paid just $16 for each Indigenous person killed or captured. Jarboe himself was aware of this, and he bragged to a friend in Ukiah that his men killed more Indians than any previous volunteer outfit in California.[107] When one considers the princely scalp bounties that local officials doled out across the continent over the preceding two centuries—in some cases paying the equivalent of more than one hundred dollars per murder when adjusted to the value of US currency in 1860—Jarboe's campaign stands out not just in the nineteenth-century Pacific Coast context, but also as perhaps the most economically resourceful civilian Indian campaign in North American history. Ironically, financial expediency for the state also meant diminished profitability for the contractors. Jarboe could have learned a lot from the acumen of predecessors like James Kirker, who shrewdly negotiated advance contracts with local Mexican officials that landed guaranteed salaries, windfall bounties, and performance bonuses.

The foregoing figures shine light on the motivations of public officials, settlers, and independent operatives, but they also obscure a humanistic reality for Indigenous victims. The Jarboe campaign was just one part of a much larger operation to exterminate Yukis. Between 1854 and 1864, Madley estimates that the tribal population declined from as many as 20,000 persons to only a few hundred, due to a combination of factors including disease, starvation, killing, and neglect on reservations.[108] Yukis were organized into eight subdivisions—Ta'no'm, Ukomno'm, Huititno'm, Witukomno'm, Onkolukomno'm, Sukshaltatamno'm, Lalkutno'm, and Ontitno'm—each led by its own ti'ol, or chief. Primarily hunters and gatherers, the Yuki ancestral homeland comprised the upper Eel River and Round Valley regions of northwestern California. The Creator, Taikomol (He Who Walks Alone), provided that land for them and watched over tribe members from the clouds above, unleashing lightning bolts and thunderclaps when displeased with his earthly subjects. As part of a religious ritual, deceased persons were washed in warm water, wrapped tightly in a deerskin, and buried facing east. Loved ones typically mourned for a year or more, during which time the name of the dead could not be mentioned, and they believed that all good people entered an afterlife. When Jarboe's men killed dozens of Yukis at a time and immediately drove captives away to reservations or enslavement, it prevented the performance of traditional burial ceremonies that ensured passage into an afterlife, and these dead might instead reappear in the present as ghosts.[109] Like many other North American Indigenous groups who faced forms of state-sponsored extralethal violence, murdered and mutilated Yuki Indians were deprived of a dignified afterlife and their surviving kin correspondingly suffered traumatic spiritual wounds.

As it had done for prior volunteer campaigns, the California legislature initially shouldered the costs of doing business with Walter Jarboe, but regional officials and their lobbyists in the national capital incessantly showered US congressmen with requests for federal reimbursement of these expenditures. Charles Drew, the former Oregon militia quartermaster, compiled a report for Congress in 1860 to describe the territory's conflicts with Indians over the preceding decade. Hoping to convince these politicians that federal tax dollars should be allocated to replenish Oregon's depleted treasury, he insisted that the territorial government had outsourced its militaristic response to civilian combatants only because the US Army failed to provide adequate protection to settlers and their property. Tribes of the Columbia River Plateau, he claimed, instigated the violence and acted as the primary aggressors in every major conflict, including the Rogue River War, and he openly praised Ben Wright for his attack on Modocs in northern California.[110]

Drew's efforts on behalf of Oregon—which had become a state just one year earlier, in 1859—coincided with the strenuous lobbying efforts of William Kibbe. Serving as California's adjutant general of militia, Kibbe had recently orchestrated an expedition on the Pit River that killed over 200 Indians from the Achumawi, Atsugewi, Maidu, and Yana tribes and captured 1,200 others for removal to the Mendocino Reservation.[111] At the outset, his objective was to attack "the very haunts of the savages, with a view to conquer, and if possible, rid the country forever of their presence." After the campaign, Kibbe reported that his "gallant soldiers" had "completely vanquished and subdued" all Indians they encountered, and he asked state legislators to allocate $49,468 to reimburse operational expenses plus an additional $20,000 to pay volunteer salaries.[112] In San Francisco, the *Daily Alta California* ran a lengthy article condemning Kibbe's "horrible massacre" and labeling the Pit River Rangers a "band of demons," although the editorialists still associated themselves with the prevailing line of thinking when writing in racialized terms that "the gradual extermination of the red men" seemed inevitable.[113] Shortly thereafter, in February 1860, four dozen settlers organized at the town of Hydesville to form the "Humboldt Cavalry." These volunteers proceeded to Tuluwat Island, just off the coast at Eureka, where they ambushed a large group of Eel, Mad River, and Wiyot Indians who had assembled for an annual ceremony. An estimated sixty Indians perished in the massacre, with several eyewitnesses describing the ensuing mutilation of corpses as an unimaginably brutal and revolting spectacle.[114]

As of May 19, 1860—just months after the Pit River Rangers and Humboldt Cavalry campaigns yielded "numberless scalps"—California reported an outstanding "war debt" of $702,387, and Kibbe made it his personal mission to see this amount and more earmarked for the payment of volunteers in his home state.[115] After several months courting those who held the nation's purse strings, Kibbe told Governor Downey in December 1860 that Congress would likely approve a $600,000 special funding bill, but only "if the spirit of disunion and the excitement consequent thereto does not block the wheels of Congress."[116] Just three weeks after Kibbe mailed this prophetic report,

South Carolina became the first Southern state to leave the Union, sparking a secession crisis on December 20, 1860, that led to four years of bloody fighting. But that did not prevent the fractured US Congress from allocating $400,000 — one-third less than asked for, but a substantial amount nonetheless — to pay California's volunteers for nine specific expeditions over the preceding seven years, including Kibbe's Pit River Ranger operation.[117]

When the Civil War officially began on April 12, 1861, the national conflict immediately transformed the nature of military volunteerism in Oregon and California. Despite significant localized populations of secessionists — especially in southern California — both states remained in the Union, and no less than twenty thousand residents joined the US Army. Some of these new troops remained at stations near the Pacific Coast to defend against possible Confederate attacks by land or sea, many departed for eastern battlefields, and three thousand others marched eastward from Los Angeles in 1862 to help fend off a Texan invasion of Union-held New Mexico Territory. This left plenty of soldiers to garrison camps and forts throughout California and Oregon, where post commanders could deploy them against Indians as a firm demonstration of federal power. With dramatically increased numbers — by 1862 the US military's Department of the Pacific boasted 5,900 men in uniform, about double the highest antebellum headcount — army officers led a series of lethal campaigns in California during the Civil War. Even so, West Coast settlers did not fully abandon the tradition of scalp warfare.[118] During the antebellum decade, people in Shasta City had pooled their money to pay bounties for Indian heads and scalps, and in May 1861 they did so again, paying a group of men who killed and dismembered four Wintus in neighboring Tehama County.[119] As historian Michael Magliari has demonstrated, this appears to be the only verifiable instance in which Indian scalp bounties were actually paid in Gold Rush–era California. It is notable that this occurred at the town and county levels, through independent monetary contributions from local citizens, and did not involve the state government or any codified bounty laws.[120]

In August 1862 — as Robert E. Lee's Army of Northern Virginia attempted to outflank the Union Army of the Potomac in a momentous summer campaign that culminated in a bloodbath at Antietam — an informant 2,700

miles away notified Sacramento authorities that a group of men had just returned to Arcata "covered with glory in the shape of [about 30] scalps."[121]
That same month, another independent operative named Harmon A. Good
led his followers on a two-week ride through northern California's Butte
County, where they killed and scalped eighteen Indians and captured nine
children. Innocuously nicknamed "Hi" by his friends, Good quickly distributed these captives among various white families "who wish to adopt
them."[122] This was a thinly veiled allusion to their ironic enslavement, occurring just weeks before issuance of the Preliminary Emancipation Proclamation in which Abraham Lincoln announced to the world that the abolition
of slavery had become a primary objective of the Union war effort.[123]

While the Civil War distracted some but not all attention away from civilian campaigning and the regional policies that supported such operations,
those who had participated in antebellum volunteer operations did not forget about their financial claims against the state government. Throughout
the 1860s, dozens of individual citizens submitted receipts for their own
roles in killing Indians, and officials in Sacramento committed themselves
to paying those claims either through disbursement of cash or issuance of
land bounties. The state legislature went out of its way to find veterans of
volunteer companies and ensure that they got paid, publishing advertisements in local newspapers each time new funds were appropriated for the
cause.[124] The widespread political will to compensate each and every man
who killed Indians indicated California's commitment to extermination policies in the mid-nineteenth century. In New France and the English/British
colonies, local leaders had often sought ways to reduce payments to bounty
hunters by forming authentication committees that in turn disqualified
some scalps as non-Indian counterfeits. In northern Mexico, Chihuahuans
and Sonorans monetized the murder of Apaches and Comanches, but again
state officials looked for loopholes to limit expenses, and they even annulled
James Kirker's contract in 1846 to avoid paying the outstanding balance. But
American politicians in California and Oregon never deviated from their
interest in fulfilling requests for compensation, although they did investigate some claims to prevent fraud and tried very hard to shift the financial
burden of scalp warfare onto the federal government.

The extermination program that California, Oregon, and Washington implemented throughout the mid-nineteenth century did have some vocal opponents, including white miners, US military officers, and national newspaper correspondents. Charles Pancoast, a Quaker forty-niner who adhered more closely to the religion's pacifism than did Ben Wright, expressed a sense of moral disdain when a group of fellow gold seekers attacked an Indian camp and "killed Old Men, Squaws, and Children."[125] US Navy lieutenant Joseph Revere served in California during the US-Mexico War and afterward proposed that Indians there be granted legal rights, saying, "The atrocities heretofore practiced by kidnappers [and volunteer armies] should be restrained by the remedies which the civil and criminal law extends to white persons."[126] In 1860, just a few months after Jarboe's campaign concluded, a journalist published a damning article titled "Indian Butcheries in California." The lengthy essay, first published in New York and reprinted in San Francisco, told readers about "murderous outrages . . . by men with white skins" and described several "diabolical" massacres.[127]

Perhaps the most prominent and persistent critic, however, was a nationally renowned author named J. Ross Browne. Born in Dublin, he migrated to Kentucky with his Irish family in 1833 and gravitated westward, as so many Americans did, during the California Gold Rush. Among various other jobs, he worked as a government inspector of Indian agencies, and this gave him unique insight into the corruption and violence that so often characterized relations between Natives and newcomers.[128] In 1861, he wrote a scathing account of California's treatment of Indians that appeared in the popular *Harper's Monthly Magazine*. From Browne, thousands of readers across the country learned the gruesome details of numerous Indian massacres and were told in blunt terms that California settlers "kill them in every cowardly and barbarous manner that could be devised." Browne generically referred to the state's independent operatives as "Coast Rangers," describing one massacre during which they shot every Indian in sight, "cut the throats" of lingering survivors, left sixty corpses "weltering in their blood," and rode away in search of the next victims. "What neglect, starvation, and disease have not done, has been achieved by the cooperation of the white settlers in the great work of extermination," he ominously concluded. Browne directed blame not just at the civilian perpetrators but also at federal agents. He claimed that many Bureau of Indian Affairs officials led a "very bad business," lining their own pockets through shady quid pro quos with local merchants and stock growers while simultaneously neglecting the people forced to live on California's reservations and leaving them no alternative but to steal or starve. In a vicious exterminatory cycle, Browne charged, the resulting theft of livestock prompted volunteer campaigns such as that of Walter Jarboe to take the field in deadly retaliation.[129]

Three years after Browne's revealing exposé, several hundred Colorado Volunteers perpetrated a heinous massacre of Cheyennes and Arapahoes at Sand Creek in southeastern Colorado, killing more than one hundred Indians, mutilating many of the corpses, and taking trophies that included scalps and genitalia.[130] News of the event shocked Americans across the country, including even some Californians who were accustomed to similar forms of violence in their own state.[131] Eyewitness accounts of the killing and ensuing acts of violent display near Fort Lyon were so unpalatable that Congress investigated the commanding officer, Colonel John M. Chivington, who supposedly told a public gathering that his personal policy toward Indians was to "kill and scalp all, big and little," because "nits made lice."[132] Chivington managed to avoid criminal charges, but Senator James R. Doolittle of Wisconsin subsequently oversaw a much broader inquiry into the nation's Indian affairs. The government published the extensive findings — formally titled *Condition of the Indian Tribes* but better known as the Doolittle Report — in 1867. In his introductory remarks, the Wisconsin senator wrote that "in a large majority of cases Indian wars are to be traced to the aggressions of lawless white men," an accusation that he directed at the volunteer, ranger, and militia units that plied the Texas frontier and the West Coast. While a significant part of the 532-page report covered the Sand Creek Massacre of November 1864, an entire subsection of the congressional tome pertained to events in the Pacific Northwest.[133]

Senator James W. Nesmith, who served as a militia officer during the Rogue River War before becoming superintendent of Indian affairs for Oregon and Washington, administered Doolittle's congressional investigation in those places. He and fellow co-commissioners solicited written affidavits from dozens of men personally associated with regional tribes, including settlers, politicians, soldiers, and government agents, but most of the witnesses did not even mention the exterminatory volunteer campaigns that occurred so frequently during the preceding two decades. To the contrary, some of them blatantly lied. George L. Hoffman, an agent at the Tule Farm Indian Reservation, claimed that "the Indians have always been well contented with their condition." Hoffman's false comment about happy Indians was no different than the bogus claims about happy slaves that antebellum southerners broadcasted whenever confronted about the inhumanity of their chattel system. Austin Wiley, a former superintendent of Indian affairs in California, similarly testified that peace reigned in that state "with the exception of . . . the killing of an Indian occasionally," although he conceded that "ungovernable passions of the whites" sometimes resulted in "the horrible mutilation of the bodies of their victims."[134] As these men provided testimonies to federal officials in the months following the Civil War, independent killing squads continued to operate along the West Coast. In August 1865, "Hi" Good led another campaign that claimed the lives of at least sixteen Yahi Yana Indians near Mill Creek. In another incident the following year, Californians massacred a band of Northern Paiutes, killing at least fourteen and capturing many more. And early in 1867, just as James Doolittle's final report rolled off the presses at the Government Printing Office, operatives in California killed nineteen Indians in three different attacks.[135]

Despite misleading statements from some informants, the Doolittle Report cast an overwhelmingly negative light on the previous twenty years of relationships between American settlers and the Indians they encountered in the West. Because Congress published the findings for public distribution, the investigation also lent credence to a nascent humanitarian impulse in federal Indian affairs that culminated in President Ulysses S. Grant's "Peace Policy" in 1869. The Grant administration's reform initiative sought to direct national strategies away from overt military action, instituting programs that revolved primarily around forced residency on reservations and compulsory attendance at boarding schools. This movement toward assimilation into the economic, political, cultural, and religious fabric of mainstream American society came with its own devastating effects for Indigenous peoples, many of whom starved on reservations or became sick and died at boarding schools. Although it was not necessarily the main intent, Grant's Reconstruction-era Peace Policy—along with US Army campaigning, rapidly increasing settlement across the West, and dramatically decreasing Indian populations—all coalesced in ways that discouraged the type of scalp warfare that racially and financially motivated volunteers perpetrated. In the year 1870, with the regional indigenous population reduced to just thirty thousand people, there was not a single report of a civilian-led massacre of Indians in California.[136]

In April 1873, following months of warfare between Modocs and US soldiers, federal officials met with tribal leaders at northern California's Lava Beds for a diplomatic council. A modern Modoc descendant named Cheewa James writes that "the meaning of a white flag was forever changed in the eyes of the Modocs. . . . The ghost of Ben Wright would ride again years later when at the height of the Modoc War, a peace conference was called under a white flag of truce."[137] During those talks, the headman Schonchin John said that he "remembered the treachery of Ben Wright long ago, and will trust no one." Another chief, Captain Jack, told the American agents that "my father went into the camp of Ben Wright to talk peace a great many years ago, when I was a little boy, and he and many others of the Modocs were killed, and I will put no faith in the white man's promises."[138] These painful memories of an extralethal massacre motivated violent retribution during the peace council. Modocs seized the moment to attack and kill three of the unsuspecting American representatives, including General Edward R. S. Canby, the only US military officer holding the rank of general ever to be killed in combat with Indians. The ensuing Modoc surrender in the summer of 1873 and subsequent removal of many tribe members to a small reservation in the northeast corner of Indian Territory marked a figurative end to the scalp warfare that Pacific Coast settlers so doggedly pursued over the previous three decades. To put an exclamation point on the defeat, a sham military tribunal convicted four Modoc men of murdering Canby, as well as fellow US commissioners Eleazar Thomas and Lieutenant William Sherwood, during the Lava Beds conference. On October 3, hundreds of spectators gathered at Fort Klamath to witness the hanging of Schonchin John, Captain Jack, Black Jim, and Boston Charley.[139]

The symbolism of this moment went well beyond the removal of a tribe and the execution of its leaders. When the lifeless bodies were cut down from the gallows, a US Army officer immediately removed the bags covering their heads so that he could snip strands of hair and sell the grisly keepsakes to spectators for $5 apiece. In a striking act of violent display, American officials decapitated all four Modoc men and shipped their heads inside whiskey barrels to the Army Medical Museum in Washington, DC. Eventually, a government employee packed the embalmed skulls into crates, assigned each one a catalog number, and added them to the Smithsonian Institution's eclectic assortment of artifacts. The boxes gathered dust on a shelf for nearly a century, until federal agents repatriated the human remains in 1984. This occurred several years before passage of the National Museum of the American Indian Act in 1989 and the Native American Graves Protection and Repatriation Act in 1990, each of which enacted sweeping new requirements for the handling and ownership of sacred burial artifacts.[140] In a grand ceremony at an isolated military outpost in Oregon—just as the nation's modernistic Gilded Age commenced—four Indians had been executed, their hair cut off and sold for profit, and their heads amputated for public display as mementos of conquest. It would be hard to imagine a more fitting final act in the gruesome saga of extralethal violence that defined not only the three decades of extermination campaigns directed at Pacific Coast tribes but also the three centuries of state-sponsored scalp warfare that spanned North America's long colonial process.

Conclusion

In the movie *Hostiles* (2017), Joseph Blocker—a fictional character played by the actor Christian Bale—shouts to a judgmental counterpart, "I've killed savages; I've killed plenty of 'em, 'cause that's my fucking job."[1] Hollywood usually misses the mark by a wide margin when it comes to historical accuracy, but in this dialogue the screenwriter got several things right. *Hostiles* is notable for its revisionist approach to the western film genre, with one critic praising the plot for its "conscientious attempt to reckon with the legacy of plunder and racism that flickers behind the legends."[2] With this purpose in mind, Blocker's terse but proud comment—or something very close to it—could just as easily have rolled off the tongue of any frontier scalp hunter in the seventeenth, eighteenth, or nineteenth centuries. In a mere thirteen words that include "savages," "killed," and "job," the statement captures the direct connections among racism, murder, and financial gain that undergirded scalp warfare throughout North America. Blocker slew Indians not just because he hated them but also because he got paid to do so, and he showed no remorse for his deeds or empathy for his victims. In fact, at an early juncture in the film, he was ready and eager to kill again as soon as the opportunity presented itself. Here, cinematic imagination blends with historical reality: these traits could describe John Lovewell or John Johnson or John Baylor just as accurately as they characterize the fictitious Joseph Blocker.

Outside of the movie theater, bookworms might think of the Pulitzer Prize–winning author Cormac McCarthy's *Blood Meridian; or, The Evening*

Redness in the West. Published by Random House in 1985, *Blood Meridian* has been critically acclaimed as one of the greatest western novels ever written, and the plot is loosely based on John Joel Glanton's scalping gang that slaughtered Apaches in northern Mexico during the mid-nineteenth century.[3] In producing his monumental work of fiction, McCarthy received a coveted MacArthur Genius Grant, researched the firsthand accounts of bounty hunters and government officials who paid them, moved his residence to the border town of El Paso, Texas, and even learned to speak Spanish in order to immerse himself within the US-Mexico region in which the tale was set. Although it has never been successfully adapted into a screenplay, *Blood Meridian* is notable, among other literary qualities, for its grotesque descriptions of extralethal violence and violent display, some of which correlate directly to documented historical events.[4] When the plot turns, for instance, to Glanton meeting an old Apache woman on the overland trail and killing her for the bounty money, it revolves around a true story discussed in chapter 3 of this book. "He put the pistol to her head and fired," McCarthy writes. "A fistsized hole erupted out of the far side of the woman's head in a great vomit of gore and she pitched over and lay slain in her blood without remedy. . . . Get that receipt for us. He took a skinning knife from his belt and stepped to where the old woman lay and took up her hair and twisted it about his wrist and passed the blade of the knife about her skull and ripped away the scalp."[5] The description is so detailed and so raw that one imagines McCarthy's narration to be an eyewitness account rather than the imaginative retelling of a modern writer.

As the foregoing passage suggests, readers of *Blood Meridian* are whisked away on an intense journey through a world of incredible evil. "The dead lay awash in the shallows like the victims of some disaster at sea and they were strewn along the salt foreshore in a havoc of blood and entrails," McCarthy writes in describing the semifictitious massacre of an Apache ranchería, this example being a conglomeration of factual details derived from the ambushes that John Johnson and James Kirker perpetrated in the 1830s and 1840s. "Riders were towing bodies out of the bloody waters of the lake and the froth that rode lightly on the beach was a pale pink in the rising light. They moved among the dead harvesting the long black locks with their knives and leaving their victims rawskulled and strange in their bloody cauls. . . . Men were wading about in the red waters hacking aimlessly at the dead and some lay coupled to the bludgeoned bodies of young women dead or dying on the beach. One of the Delawares passed with a collection of heads like some strange vendor bound for the market, the hair twisted about his wrist and the heads dangling and turning together."[6] Describing another extralethal massacre, McCarthy writes: "Dust stanched the wet and naked heads of the scalped who with the fringe of hair below their wounds and tonsured to the bone now lay like maimed and naked monks in the bloodslaked dust and everywhere the dying groaned and gibbered and horses lay screaming."[7] One reviewer for the *New York Times* wrote that vivid passages such as these "come at the reader like a slap in the face."[8] Another critic remarked that "unimaginable cruelty" clings to every detail in McCarthy's prose, saying that *Blood Meridian* "may be the bloodiest book since 'The Iliad.' "[9] Those who lived in the borderlands of colonial North America would sense familiar spectacles within McCarthy's depictions of killing and violent display, but modern bibliophiles might be surprised to learn that the novel's gut-wrenching sketches of scalp warfare are far more authentic than imaginary.

It is not surprising that a work of literary fiction provides perhaps the single most accurate portrayal of scalp warfare, for the depth of depravity and intensity of violence can seem at times unreal as one reads through the many historical accounts of it. The fact that Hollywood—our modern world's most prominent purveyor of fictionalized gratuitous violence in visual form—has been unable to transform McCarthy's book into a movie despite forty years having passed since *Blood Meridian*'s publication speaks volumes about just how horrific scalp warfare was. The greatest success of McCarthy's work is that it provides readers with a truly authentic account of a very dark chapter in North American history, and by doing so through a literary genre with wide public appeal it exposes large audiences to the realities of an important but underrecognized process of colonial conquest. With this in mind, the hope is that my own book will complement McCarthy's work by providing a detailed historical accounting of events across North American history—that the nonfiction *Business of Killing Indians* can be read and weighed alongside the fictitious *Blood Meridian* in a way that provides more thorough understandings and more honest reckonings with colonial violence and Native American genocide.

Whether in movies or in books, representations of Indigenous peoples and their interactions with settlers and soldiers are often hyperbolized for dramatic effect.[10] In the case of scalp warfare and its attendant extralethal violence, however, it would be hard for any screenwriter or novelist to invent a more gruesome scene than the massacres and mutilations that actually transpired—hundreds of times over again—across the frontiers of New Netherland, New France, New England, Mexico, Texas, California, and elsewhere. The incidents chronicled throughout this book—the dismemberment of ten Abenakis at the hands of the Puritan woman Hannah Duston, the burning alive of two dozen captives at the Chickasaw village of Chuckalissa, the mass killing of 150 Southern Apaches during James Kirker's alcohol-induced ambush at Galeana, the Comanche scalp hunt that George Wythe Baylor organized in North Texas, the treacherous butchery of Modocs that the ex-Quaker Ben Wright perpetrated on California's Lost River—could easily pass for sensationalized episodes from McCarthy's *Blood Meridian* or the R-rated *Hostiles*. These historical events bear stark similarities to the voyeurized violence that often occurs in imagined cinematic and literary worlds. This remarkable correlation of fact and fiction provides one reason for us to reconsider the realities and meanings of scalp warfare in the borderlands of North America.

Colonial conquest in Canada and Mexico, as well as the United States and its colonial antecedents, was a process that often entailed extralethal violence and violent display, and the foundational elements of racist rhetoric, monetized murder, and demographic destruction undergirded policies and acts of killing in every major North American empire and nation from the 1600s through the 1800s. The prevalence of monetized scalp warfare across time and place demonstrates that state sponsorship often played a key role in the nature and extent of violence in decentralized frontier zones, and the anti-Indian racism that characterized such policies indicated an exterminatory objective on the part of many lawmakers and commanders. For a variety of reasons, however, a wide chasm often separated the stated intent from the actual outcome. Because scalp hunting and plunder seeking formed

motivations for an irregular form of warfare that most often involved paramilitaries, rangers, or Native auxiliaries, such campaigns seldom yielded
the same level of physical destruction as organized army expeditions, especially in the nineteenth-century American West.[11] In some of the deadliest
encounters across New England, New France, Mexico, and Texas, skilled
Indigenous fighters acted alongside non-Indians as perpetrators, their tribal
leaders having allied with government agents in pursuit of diplomatic advantage, material gain, and revenge against traditional enemies. This com-
plicated dynamic of cross-cultural alliances blurred the boundary between
intertribal warfare and colonial violence. Furthermore, the number of Indians who fell victim to bounty hunters and rangers—either as corpses or as
captives—was likely in the tens of thousands during the long colonial era.
This constituted a small fraction of the tens of millions of Indigenous casualties and captivities across three centuries of North American conquest that
included regular army and militia campaigning as well as disease epidemics
that collectively wrought an incalculable human toll. In this sense, scalp
warfare should be viewed as one of many destructive elements of colonization, particularly notable for its commonality and brutality.

While it is important to think about these events in conceptual terms like
extralethal violence and genocide, such concepts can become a metaphorical cloak that conceals as much as it reveals, depending on whether one looks
from the top down or the bottom up. State-sponsored scalp warfare—and the
widespread murder and mutilation that resulted—offers one of the most blatant examples of extreme violence toward Indigenous peoples on the frontiers
of North America, and for that reason alone it is worth studying and concep-
tualizing these events within theoretical and statistical boundaries. But the
personalized nature and hateful intensity of scalp warfare also makes it more
than the sum of its parts. Every man, woman, and child who succumbed to a
ranger's gun or a scalper's knife underwent a dehumanizing and despiritual-
izing death with profound implications for the individual, the family, and the
community. Perhaps more so than any other victims of colonial violence,
those who died at the hands of bounty hunters and other civilian profiteers
faced an indeterminate fate in the afterlife, dispatched suddenly into an unknown spiritual world in a disgraced and disfigured form, their traumatized

loved ones left to grapple with the frightful realization that they, too, might meet a similar end. These humanistic intricacies underlie all theoretical formulations of the American Indian experience with colonial violence. The Mi'kmaq tribe's ongoing crusade to eliminate one of the last tangible vestiges of the North American scalp trade—Governor Charles Lawrence's bounty proclamation of 1756 that still lingers as law in Nova Scotia—shows that these historical traumas maintain modern relevance and that the individual human experience matters just as much as the broader analytical interpretation.

The modern implications of scalp warfare continue to be seen and felt in the news cycle, and it sometimes seems as though a broader public reckoning with this violent chapter of North American history is just around the bend. I opened this book with the story of a notorious scalp act that remains on the books in Nova Scotia, along with the clever use of social media as a form of protest against the Canadian government's refusal to remove the law. As this book goes to press in 2024, additional stories are emerging and remain unresolved. In 2018, the Halifax regional council voted twelve to four to remove a statue of Edward Cornwallis—an eighteenth-century British official who founded the town and implemented a scalp act—from a park that also bore his name. Three years later, in an unveiling ceremony that included the Mi'kmaq elder Daniel Paul, local officials renamed the public square Peace and Friendship Park, but a new controversy arose in December 2023 when town officials in Lunenburg, Nova Scotia, changed the name of Cornwallis Street to Queen Street in an act that tribe members interpreted as an insulting continuation of European traditions that failed to integrate local Indigenous culture and history.[12] In the United States, similar issues continue to arise. Just one year before the street-renaming debacle in Nova Scotia, American media outlets reported on an FBI raid in Fairfield, Maine, where an auction house specializing in Nazi and Confederate memorabilia attempted to sell a nineteenth-century Mescalero Apache scalp in violation of the Native American Graves Protection and Repatriation Act. As far as can be determined, that investigation is ongoing at the time of this writing in June 2024.[13] Clearly, the cultural legacies and political repercussions of scalp warfare will continue to emerge and give rise to difficult public conversations about memory and memorialization.

As important as it is to name the perpetrators of scalp warfare and hold them historically accountable for their actions, it is equally critical to identify the victims, remember their fates, and honor their memory. Every massacre, every murder, every mutilation had a tragic impact on the deceased and their surviving kin. When French officials at New Orleans arranged for the killing and dismemberment of Chickasaws at Choukafalya in the 1730s, it changed the meaning of fabussa that guided the tribe's spiritual and earthly journeys. When English/British assemblymen in Boston dispatched bounty hunters against Abenakis in the eighteenth century, it transformed Ndakinna into a war zone, and that violence permanently altered tribal relationships to ancestral homelands. When Mexico's scalpers ambushed a Southern Apache ranchería in 1837 and butchered Juan José Compá and nineteen others, they destroyed a tribal sense of place recognized through each survivor's 'igoyá'í. When Texans murdered Comanche chief Muguara at San Antonio's Council House in 1840, their treacherous actions stripped him of puha and condemned the headman to an eternity of dishonor. When another group of Texans killed Flacco the Younger in 1843, they unleashed bac'oc that spread illness and chaos among living Lipan Apaches. When Oregon volunteers murdered and decapitated Peo-Peo-Mox-Mox in 1855, the chief was deprived of a dignified afterlife and his Walla Walla family suffered an upheaval of Tamánwit that distorted their spiritual identity. When United States agents executed Schonchin John, Captain Jack, Black Jim, and Boston Charley in 1873, surviving Modoc onlookers saw "the ghost of Ben Wright" while an officer sold their hair as souvenirs and chopped off their heads to enhance a museum's collection. These are the types of human stories that must be told and retold as the world continues to grapple with the legacies of scalp warfare, colonial violence, and Native American genocides.

NOTES

Introduction

1. "Two Hundred Year-Old Scalp Law Still on Books in Nova Scotia," *CBC News*, January 4, 2000. www.cbc.ca/news/canada/two-hundred-year-old-scalp-law-still-on-books-in-nova-scotia-1.230906.

2. For the full text of the proclamation, see "Charles Lawrence Proclamation," May 14, 1756, in *Collections of the Nova Scotia Historical Society*, vol. 16 (Halifax, NS: Wm. MacNab and Son, 1912), 11–12.

3. "Two Hundred Year-Old Scalp Law." On the Land of Souls, see Jon Tattrie, *Daniel Paul: Mi'kmaw Elder* (Lawrencetown Beach, NS: Pottersfield Press, 2017), 29.

4. Resolution Nos. 837 and 838, Legislative Assembly of Nova Scotia, Assembly 58, Session 1, Transcripts, March 28, 2000, pp. 2707–8.

5. Daniel N. Paul, "All Doubletalk, No Action on Repealing Proclamation," *Halifax (NS) Herald*, December 8, 2000; Daniel N. Paul, *We Were Not the Savages: A Micmac Perspective on the Collision of European and Aboriginal Civilizations* (Halifax, NS: Nimbus, 1993). On Paul, see Tattrie, *Daniel Paul*, 17, 93, 121–22.

6. Jacob Boon, "It's 2015 and a Scalping Law Is Still on the Books," *Coast* (Halifax, NS), January 7, 2015, www.thecoast.ca/RealityBites/archives/2015/01/07/its-2015-and-a-scalping-law-is-still-on-the-books.

7. Trina Roache, " 'It's Not Forgotten': Mi'kmaq Bounty Never Rescinded," *APTN National News* (Winnipeg, MB), February 21, 2018, www.aptnnews.ca/national-news/not-forgotten-mikmaq-bounty-never-rescinded/. On the Cornwallis bounties, see Olive Dickason, *Louisbourg and the Indians: A Study in Imperial Race Relations, 1713–1760* (Ottawa: University of Ottawa Press, 1971), 138. On Cornwallis controversies, see Tattrie, *Daniel Paul*, 143–67.

8. Jon Tattrie, "Hair Ad Raised Ire of Mi'kmaq," *Halifax (NS) Herald*, April 25, 2010.

9. Nic Meloney, " 'The Scalp of Edward Cornwallis' to Be Sold Online by Mi'kmaq Group," *CBC News*, December 2, 2017, www.cbc.ca/news/indigenous/treaty-talks-elizabeth-marshall-auction-scalp-cornwallis-1.4425052.

10. Daniel N. Paul, "Scalp Proclamations Weren't Just Aimed at Mi'kmaw Warriors," *Chronicle Herald* (Halifax, NS), March 29, 2019.

11. James Axtell, *Natives and Newcomers: The Cultural Origins of North America* (Oxford: Oxford University Press, 2001), 272; Peter Silver, *Our Savage Neighbors: How Indian War Transformed Early America* (New York: W. W. Norton, 2008), 162; Jeffrey Ostler, *Surviving Genocide: Native Nations and the United States from the American Revolution to Bleeding Kansas* (New Haven: Yale University Press, 2019), 22. See also Thomas Peotto, "Dark Mimesis: A Cultural History of the Scalping Paradigm" (PhD diss., University of British Columbia, 2018).

12. John Grenier, *The First Way of War: American Warmaking on the Frontier* (New York: Cambridge University Press, 2005); Silver, *Our Savage Neighbors*; Wayne Lee, *Barbarians and Brothers: Anglo-American Warfare, 1500–1865* (New York: Oxford University Press, 2011); Jeffrey Ostler, " 'To Extirpate the Indians': An Indigenous Consciousness of Genocide in the Ohio Valley and Lower Great Lakes, 1750s–1810," *William and Mary Quarterly*, 3rd ser., 72:4 (2015): 587–622; Jeffrey Ostler, " 'Just and Lawful War' as Genocidal War in the (United States) Northwest Ordinance and Northwest Territory, 1787–1832," *Journal of Genocide Research* 18:1 (2016): 1–20; Wayne E. Lee, *The Cutting-Off Way: Indigenous Warfare in Eastern North America, 1500–1800* (Chapel Hill: University of North Carolina Press, 2023).

13. Ostler, " 'To Extirpate the Indians,' " 587–622; Ostler, *Surviving Genocide*.

14. Grenier, *First Way of War*, 21.

15. Ostler, " 'Just and Lawful War' as Genocidal War," 1–20.

16. Lee, *Barbarians and Brothers*, 1–11, quotations on 2, 5 (emphasis in original).

17. On extralethal violence, see Lee Ann Fujii, "The Puzzle of Extra-Lethal Violence," *Perspectives on Politics* 11:2 (2013): 410–26, quotation on 411.

18. On "collective violence," see Charles Tilly, *The Politics of Collective Violence* (Cambridge: Cambridge University Press, 2003), 3–4, 12–20. On colonial violence and Native Americans, see Ned Blackhawk, *Violence over the Land: Indians and Empires in the Early American West* (Cambridge, MA: Harvard University Press, 2006); Karl Jacoby, *Shadows at Dawn: A Borderlands Massacre and the Violence of History* (New York: Penguin, 2008); Kevin Kenny, *Peaceable Kingdom Lost: The Paxton Boys and the Destruction of William Penn's Holy Experiment* (New York: Oxford University Press, 2009); Silver, *Our Savage Neighbors*; Michael Witgen, *An Infinity of Nations: How the Native New World Shaped Early North America* (Philadelphia: University of Pennsylvania Press, 2012); Christine M. DeLucia, *Memory Lands: King Philip's War and the Place of Violence in the Northeast* (New Haven: Yale University Press, 2018); Rob Harper, *Unsettling the West: Violence and State Building in the Ohio Valley* (Philadelphia: University of Pennsylvania Press, 2018);

and Pekka Hämäläinen, *Indigenous Continent: The Epic Contest for North America* (New York: Liveright, 2022).

19. Lee Ann Fujii, *Show Time: The Logic and Power of Violent Display* (Ithaca, NY: Cornell University Press, 2021), 2–7, quotation on 2.

20. David Riches, ed., *The Anthropology of Violence* (Oxford: Basil Blackwell, 1986), 12.

21. For a seminal study, see Geoffrey Best, *Humanity in Warfare: The Modern History of the International Law of Armed Conflicts* (New York: Columbia University Press, 1980). On the origins of international law, see Jennifer Pitts, *Boundaries of the International: Law and Empire* (Cambridge, MA: Harvard University Press, 2018). On international humanitarian law, see Jean-Marie Henckaerts and Louise Doswald-Beck, eds., *Customary International Humanitarian Law*, vol. 1: *Rules* (Cambridge: Cambridge University Press, 2005), esp. 37–45 on "indiscriminate attacks" and 406–20 on "disposal of the dead." On war crimes, see Malcolm N. Shaw, *International Law*, 5th ed. (Cambridge: Cambridge University Press, 2003), 235, 1077–78.

22. On trophy taking, see Cora Bender, " 'Transgressive Objects' in America: Mimesis and Violence in the Collection of Trophies during the Nineteenth Century Indian Wars," *Civil Wars* 11 (December 2009): 502–13; and Simon Harrison, *Dark Trophies: Hunting and the Enemy Body in Modern War* (New York: Berghahn, 2012).

23. Erik R. Seeman, *Death in the New World: Cross-Cultural Encounters, 1492–1800* (Philadelphia: University of Pennsylvania Press, 2010), 269, 273–74.

24. Marcus Cunliffe, *Soldiers and Civilians: The Martial Spirit in America, 1775–1865* (Boston: Little, Brown, 1968), 215. On Indigenous peoples and scalp bounties, see Lee, *Cutting-Off Way*, 155–56, 172–73.

25. On militias, see Cunliffe, *Soldiers and Civilians*, 177–254; Lawrence Delbert Cress, *Citizens in Arms: The Army and Militia in American Society to the War of 1812* (Chapel Hill: University of North Carolina Press, 1982), 3–14; Fred Anderson, *A People's Army: Massachusetts Soldiers and Society in the Seven Years' War* (Chapel Hill: University of North Carolina Press, 1984); John Shy, *A People Numerous and Armed: Reflections on the Military Struggle for American Independence* (Ann Arbor: University of Michigan Press, 1990), 29–41; and James Kirby Martin and Mark Edward Lender, *A Respectable Army: The Military Origins of the Republic, 1763–1789* (Hoboken, NJ: Wiley Blackwell, 2015).

26. Anderson, *People's Army*, viii.

27. See Yang Su, "Mass Killings in the Cultural Revolution: A Study of Three Provinces," in Joseph Esherick, Paul Pickowicz, and Andrew George Walder, eds., *The Chinese Cultural Revolution as History* (Stanford, CA: Stanford University Press, 2006), 98.

28. On settler colonialism, see Patrick Wolfe, "Settler Colonialism and the Elimination of the Native," *Journal of Genocide Research* 8:4 (2006): 387–409; A. Dirk Moses, ed., *Genocide and Settler Society: Frontier Violence and Stolen Indigenous Children in Australian History* (New York: Berghahn Books, 2004), 3–48; James Belich,

*Replenishing the Earth: The Settler Revolution and the Rise of the Anglo-World,
1783–1939* (Oxford: Oxford University Press, 2009); and Walter L. Hixson, *American
Settler Colonialism: A History* (New York: Palgrave Macmillan, 2013). On ethnic
cleansing, see Gary Clayton Anderson, *The Conquest of Texas: Ethnic Cleansing in
the Promised Land, 1820–1875* (Norman: University of Oklahoma Press, 2005); and
Gary Clayton Anderson, *Ethnic Cleansing and the Indian: The Crime That Should
Haunt America* (Norman: University of Oklahoma Press, 2015).

29. United Nations, "Convention on the Prevention and Punishment of the Crime of
Genocide, Adopted by the General Assembly of the United Nations on 9 December 1948," in *Treaty Series*, vol. 78, no. 121, p. 280.

30. On Lemkin, see Douglas Irvin-Erickson, *Raphaël Lemkin and the Concept of Genocide* (Philadelphia: University of Pennsylvania Press, 2017). On Germany, see
Donald Bloxham, *The Final Solution: A Genocide* (Oxford: Oxford University
Press, 2009); and Peter Longerich, *Holocaust: The Nazi Persecution and Murder of
the Jews* (Oxford: Oxford University Press, 2010). On Rwanda, see Thierry Cruvellier, *Court of Remorse: Inside the International Criminal Tribunal for Rwanda*,
translated by Chari Voss (Madison: University of Wisconsin Press, 2010); Jens Meierhenrich, "How Many Victims Were There in the Rwandan Genocide? A Statistical Debate," *Journal of Genocide Research* 22:1 (2020): 72–82; and Omar
Shahabudin McDoom, "Contested Counting: Toward a Rigorous Estimate of the
Death Toll in the Rwandan Genocide," *Journal of Genocide Research* 22:1 (2020):
83–93.

31. Alan Houston, ed., *Franklin: The Autobiography and Other Writings on Politics,
Economics, and Virtue* (Cambridge: Cambridge University Press, 2004), 330.

32. Richard Drinnon, *Facing West: The Metaphysics of Indian-Hating and Empire-Building* (Norman: University of Oklahoma Press, 1997); William A. Pencak and
Daniel K. Richter, eds., *Friends and Enemies in Penn's Woods: Indians, Colonists,
and the Racial Construction of Pennsylvania* (University Park: Pennsylvania State
University Press, 2004); Rob Harper, "State Intervention and Extreme Violence in
the Revolutionary Ohio Valley," *Journal of Genocide Research* 10:2 (2008): 233–48.

33. Daniel K. Richter, *Facing East from Indian Country: A Native History of Early America* (Cambridge, MA: Harvard University Press, 2001), 2, emphasis in original. See
also Nancy Shoemaker, *A Strange Likeness: Becoming Red and White in Eighteenth-Century North America* (Oxford: Oxford University Press, 2004), 129–40.

34. Edward E. Baptist, *The Half Has Never Been Told: Slavery and the Making of American Capitalism* (New York: Basic Books, 2014); Calvin Schermerhorn, *The Business of Slavery and the Rise of American Capitalism, 1815–1860* (New Haven: Yale
University Press, 2015); Sven Beckert and Seth Rockman, eds., *Slavery's Capitalism:
A New History of American Economic Development* (Philadelphia: University of
Pennsylvania Press, 2016); Joshua D. Rothman, *The Ledger and the Chain: How
Domestic Slave Traders Shaped America* (New York: Basic Books, 2021).

35. Benjamin Madley, "Reexamining the American Genocide Debate: Meaning, Historiography and New Methods," *American Historical Review* 120:1 (2015): 98–139, quotation on 114. See Grenier, *First Way of War*.

36. Paul Conrad, *The Apache Diaspora: Four Centuries of Displacement and Survival* (Philadelphia: University of Pennsylvania Press, 2021), 10–11.

37. See, e.g., Brendan C. Lindsay, *Murder State: California's Native American Genocide, 1846–1873* (Lincoln: University of Nebraska Press, 2012); and Benjamin Madley, *An American Genocide: The United States and the California Indian Catastrophe, 1846–1873* (New Haven: Yale University Press, 2016).

38. Madley, "Reexamining the American Genocide Debate," 108–9. For recent work on Native American genocide, see Ben Kiernan, *Blood and Soil: A World History of Genocide and Extermination from Sparta to Darfur* (New Haven: Yale University Press, 2007), 213–48, 310–63; Brendan Rensink, "Genocide of Native Americans: Historical Facts and Historiographic Debates," in Samuel Totten and Robert K. Hitchcock, eds., *Genocide of Indigenous Peoples* (New Brunswick, NJ: Transaction, 2011), 15–36; Alfred A. Cave, *Lethal Encounters: Englishmen and Indians in Colonial Virginia* (Lincoln: University of Nebraska Press, 2013); Alex Alvarez, *Native America and the Question of Genocide* (Lanham, MD: Rowman and Littlefield, 2014); Andrew Woolford, Jeff Benvenuto, and Alexander Laban Hinton, eds., *Colonial Genocide in Indigenous North America* (Durham, NC: Duke University Press, 2014); Edward B. Westermann, *Hitler's Ostkrieg and the Indian Wars: Comparing Genocide and Conquest* (Norman: University of Oklahoma Press, 2016); and Ostler, *Surviving Genocide*. For Native American genocide in global perspective, see Alfred A. Cave, "Genocide in the Americas," in Dan Stone, ed., *The Historiography of Genocide* (New York: Palgrave Macmillan, 2008), 273–95.

39. Madley, "Reexamining the American Genocide Debate," 108; Ostler, *Surviving Genocide*, 383–84. Arguments for Native American genocide that rely on "lumping" include Russell Thornton, *American Indian Holocaust and Survival: A Population History since 1492* (Norman: University of Oklahoma Press, 1987); David E. Stannard, *American Holocaust: The Conquest of the New World* (New York: Oxford University Press, 1992); Ward Churchill, *A Little Matter of Genocide: Holocaust and Denial in the Americas, 1492 to the Present* (San Francisco: City Lights Books, 1997); Winona LaDuke, *All Our Relations: Native Struggles for Land and Life* (Cambridge, MA: South End Press, 1999); Elizabeth Cook-Lynn, *Anti-Indianism in Modern America: A Voice from Tatekeya's Earth* (Urbana: University of Illinois Press, 2001); Barbara Alice Mann, *The Tainted Gift: The Disease Method of Frontier Expansion* (Santa Barbara, CA: Praeger, 2009); and Roxanne Dunbar-Ortiz, *An Indigenous Peoples' History of the United States* (Boston: Beacon Press, 2014). For examples of "lumping" that argue against genocide, see James Axtell, *Beyond 1492: Encounters in Colonial North America* (New York: Oxford University Press, 1992), esp. 261–63; Guenter Lewy, "Were American Indians the Victims of Genocide?"

Commentary 118 (September 2004): 55–63; and Anderson, *Ethnic Cleansing and the Indian*, esp. 13.

40. Walter L. Hixson, "Policing the Past: Indian Removal and Genocide Studies," *Western Historical Quarterly* 47:4 (2016): 439–43, quotations on 441, 442. See also, from the same issue, Gary Clayton Anderson, "The Native Peoples of the American West: Genocide or Ethnic Cleansing?," 407–33; Boyd Cothran, "Melancholia and the Infinite Debate," 435–38; Margaret D. Jacobs, "Genocide or Ethnic Cleansing? Are These Our Only Choices?," 444–48; and Benjamin Madley, "Understanding Genocide in California under United States Rule, 1846–1873," 449–61.

41. Tai S. Edwards and Paul Kelton, "Germs, Genocides, and America's Indigenous Peoples," *Journal of American History* 107:1 (2020): 52–76, quotation on 76. On disease and Native Americans, see David S. Jones, *Rationalizing Epidemics: Meanings and Uses of American Indian Mortality since 1600* (Cambridge, MA: Harvard University Press, 2004); Paul Kelton, *Epidemics and Enslavement: Biological Catastrophe in the Native Southeast* (Lincoln: University of Nebraska Press, 2007); Tai S. Edwards, "Disruption and Disease: The Osage Struggle to Survive in the Nineteenth-Century Trans-Missouri West," *Kansas History* 36 (Winter 2013–14): 218–33; Elizabeth A. Fenn, *Encounters at the Heart of the World: A History of the Mandan People* (New York: Hill and Wang, 2014); and Catherine M. Cameron, Paul Kelton, and Alan C. Swedlund, eds., *Beyond Germs: Native Depopulation in North America* (Tucson: University of Arizona Press, 2015).

42. Edwards and Kelton, "Germs, Genocides, and America's Indigenous Peoples," 68.

43. See, e.g., Lee, *Cutting-Off Way*, 15–34.

44. The literature in this area is vast, and much of it comes from the fields of ethnohistory, anthropology, and archaeology. For overviews, see Georg Friederici, "Scalping in America," in *Annual Report of the Board of Regents of the Smithsonian Institution . . . for the Year Ending June 30, 1906* (Washington, DC: Government Printing Office, 1907), 423–38; Cornelius J. Jaenen, *Friend and Foe: Aspects of French-Amerindian Cultural Contact in the Sixteenth and Seventeenth Centuries* (New York: Columbia University Press, 1976), 122–27; James Axtell and William C. Sturtevant, "The Unkindest Cut, or Who Invented Scalping," *William and Mary Quarterly*, 3rd ser., 37:3 (1980): 451–72; Richard J. Chacon and David H. Dye, eds., *The Taking and Displaying of Human Body Parts as Trophies by Amerindians* (New York: Springer, 2007); Peotto, "Dark Mimesis"; and Mairin Odle, *Under the Skin: Tattoos, Scalps, and the Contested Language of Bodies in Early America* (Philadelphia: University of Pennsylvania Press, 2023), esp. 68–112.

45. Andrés Reséndez, *The Other Slavery: The Uncovered Story of Indian Enslavement in America* (New York, NY: Houghton Mifflin Harcourt, 2016), 5, 324. See also James F. Brooks, *Captives and Cousins: Slavery, Kinship, and Community in the Southwest Borderlands* (Chapel Hill: University of North Carolina Press, 2002);

Alan Gallay, *The Indian Slave Trade: The Rise of the English Empire in the American South, 1670–1717* (New Haven: Yale University Press, 2002); Christina Snyder, *Slavery in Indian Country: The Changing Face of Captivity in Early America* (Cambridge, MA: Harvard University Press, 2010); Brett Rushforth, *Bonds of Alliance: Indigenous and Atlantic Slaveries in New France* (Chapel Hill: The University of North Carolina Press, 2012); Catherine M. Cameron, *Captives: How Stolen People Changed the World* (Lincoln: University of Nebraska Press, 2016); and William S. Kiser, *Borderlands of Slavery: The Struggle over Captivity and Peonage in the American Southwest* (Philadelphia: University of Pennsylvania Press, 2017).

46. See Ari Kelman, *A Misplaced Massacre: Struggling over the Memory of Sand Creek* (Cambridge, MA: Harvard University Press, 2013).

47. On fraud in New France, see H. R. Casgrain, ed., *Voyage au Canada dans le nord de l'Amérique septentrionale fait depuis l'an 1751 à 1761 par J. C. B.* (Quebec: Impremerie Léger Brousseau, 1887), 115; Francis Parkman, *Count Frontenac and New France under Louis XIV* (New York: Charles Scribner's Sons, 1915), 313; and Jean-François Lozier, "Lever des chevelures en Nouvelle-France: La politique française du paiement des scalps," *Revue d'Histoire de l'Amérique Française* 56:4 (2003): 531. On fraud in New England, see Axtell, *Natives and Newcomers*, 267. On fraud in Mexico, see George Wilkins Kendall, *Narrative of the Texan-Santa Fé Expedition*, vol. 2 (New York: Harper and Brothers, 1844), 57–58; James Hobbs, *Wild Life in the Far West: Personal Adventures of a Border Mountain Man* (Waterford, CT: Wiley, Waterman and Eaton, 1875), 89–90; Samuel E. Chamberlain, *Recollections of a Rogue* (London: Museum Press, 1957), 270, 274; Francisco R. Almada, *Diccionarrio de historia, geografía, y biografía Chihuahuenses* (Juarez: Impresora de Juárez, 1968), 39; and William B. Griffen, *Apaches at War and Peace: The Janos Presidio, 1750–1858* (Albuquerque: University of New Mexico Press, 1988), 223–24.

48. The film, called *Bounty*, was produced by Adam Mazo, Tracy Rector, and Ben Pender-Cudlip. See https://upstanderproject.org/bounty.

49. On the effects of European colonialism on Native Americans, see Stannard, *American Holocaust*; Noble David Cook, *Born to Die: Disease and New World Conquest, 1492–1650* (Cambridge: Cambridge University Press, 1998); Elizabeth A. Fenn, *Pox Americana: The Great Smallpox Epidemic of 1775–82* (New York: Hill and Wang, 2001); and Alfred W. Crosby Jr., *The Columbian Exchange: Biological and Cultural Consequences of 1492* (Westport, CT: Praeger, 2003).

50. Nancy Scheper-Hughes and Philippe Bourgois, eds., *Violence in War and Peace* (Malden, MA: Blackwell, 2004), 1.

51. Macarena Gómez-Barris, *Where Memory Dwells: Culture and State Violence in Chile* (Berkeley: University of California Press, 2008); Kidada Williams, "Regarding the Aftermaths of Lynching," *Journal of American History* 101:3 (2014): 856–58, quotation on 856.

1 "Lifting Hair" in French Canada and Louisiana

1. Cyprien Tanguay, *A travers les registres* (Montreal: Cadieux and Derome, 1886), 91–95; Jean-François Lozier, "Lever des chevelures en Nouvelle-France: La politique française du paiement des scalps," *Revue d'Histoire de l'Amérique Française* 56:4 (2003): 525.

2. Georg Friederici, "Scalping in America," in *Annual Report of the Board of Regents of the Smithsonian Institution . . . for the Year Ending June 30, 1906* (Washington, DC: Government Printing Office, 1907), 423–38; James Axtell and William C. Sturtevant, "The Unkindest Cut, or Who Invented Scalping," *William and Mary Quarterly*, 3rd ser., 37:3 (1980): 455–72; Thomas S. Abler, "Scalping, Torture, Cannibalism and Rape: An Ethnohistorical Analysis of Conflicting Cultural Values in War," *Anthropologica* 34:1 (1992): 6–9; James Axtell, *Natives and Newcomers: The Cultural Origins of North America* (Oxford: Oxford University Press, 2001), 262–63; Cameron B. Strang, "Violence, Ethnicity, and Human Remains during the Second Seminole War," *Journal of American History* 100:4 (2014): 973–94; Colin G. Calloway, *New Worlds for All: Indians, Europeans, and the Remaking of Early America* (Baltimore: Johns Hopkins University Press, 2013), 106.

3. "Relation of Some Iroquois Prisoners, 1644–1645," in Reuben Gold Thwaites, ed., *The Jesuit Relations and Allied Documents: Travels and Explorations of the Jesuit Missionaries in New France, 1610–1791*, 73 vols. (Cleveland, OH: Burrows Brothers, 1896–1901), 27:229–37. On the origins of "savage" in French colonial discourse, see Olive Patricia Dickason, *The Myth of the Savage and the Beginnings of French Colonialism in the Americas* (Edmonton: University of Alberta Press, 1984), 63–84.

4. "Letter from Reverend Father Jacques Bruyas," January 21, 1668, in Thwaites, *Jesuit Relations and Allied Documents*, 51:119–23. On Iroquois ceremonies involving scalps, see Daniel K. Richter, *Trade, Land, Power: The Struggle for Eastern North America* (Philadelphia: University of Pennsylvania Press, 2013), 72–74.

5. Pierre Margry, ed., *Lettres de Cavelier de La Salle et correspondance relative á ses entreprises (1678–1685), découvertes et établissements des français dans l'ouest et dans le sud de l'Amérique septentrionale*, 6 vols. (Paris: Maisonneuve, 1879), 2:101–2.

6. David J. Weber, *Bárbaros: Spaniards and Their Savages in the Age of Enlightenment* (New Haven: Yale University Press, 2005), 99.

7. On "lifting hair," see Lozier, "Lever des chevelures en Nouvelle-France," 515.

8. "Ordinance of the Director and Council of New Netherland, Offering a Reward for the Heads of Raritan Indians," July 4, 1641, in Edmund B. O'Callaghan, ed., *Laws and Ordinances of New Netherland, 1638–1674* (Albany, NY: Weed, Parsons, 1868), 28–29.

9. Oliver A. Rink, *Holland on the Hudson: An Economic and Social History of Dutch New York* (Ithaca, NY: Cornell University Press, 1986), 216–21; Evan Haefali, "Kieft's War and the Cultures of Violence in Colonial America," in Michael A.

Bellesiles, ed., *Lethal Imagination: Violence and Brutality in American History* (New York: New York University Press, 1999), 19–21; Bernard Bailyn, *The Barbarous Years: The Conflict of Civilizations, 1600–1675* (New York: Alfred A. Knopf, 2012), 218–23; Andrew Lipman, *Saltwater Frontier: Indians and the Contest for the American Coast* (New Haven: Yale University Press, 2015), 142–64; Jeffrey Ostler, *Surviving Genocide: Native Nations and the United States from the American Revolution to Bleeding Kansas* (New Haven: Yale University Press, 2019), 19–20; Richard R. Johnson, "The Search for a Usable Indian: An Aspect of the Defense of Colonial New England," *Journal of American History* 64:3 (1977): 624, 641.

10. J. Franklin Jameson, ed., *Narratives of New Netherland, 1609–1664* (New York: Charles Scribner's Sons, 1909), 211, 213–14, quotation on 214.

11. Quoted in Bailyn, *Barbarous Years*, 220.

12. William Scranton Simmons, *Cautantowwit's House: An Indian Burial Ground on the Island of Conanicut in Narragansett Bay* (Providence, RI: Brown University Press, 1970), 52–55; Kathleen J. Bragdon, *Native People of Southern New England* (Norman: University of Oklahoma Press, 1996), 190–91; Ron Williamson, " 'Otinontsiskiaj Ondaon' ('The House of the Cut-Off Heads'): The History and Archaeology of Northern Iroquoian Trophy Taking," in Richard Chacon and David Dye, eds., *The Taking and Displaying of Human Body Parts as Trophies by Amerindians* (New York: Springer, 2007), 190–221.

13. Francis Parkman, *Count Frontenac and New France under Louis XIV* (New York: Charles Scribner's Sons, 1915), 352, 364–69. On King William's War, see W. J. Eccles, *The French in North America, 1500–1783* (East Lansing: Michigan State University Press, 1998), 105–12; John A. Lynn, *The Wars of Louis XIV: 1667–1714* (London: Routledge, 1999), 191–265; Guy Chet, *Conquering the American Wilderness: The Triumph of European Warfare in the Colonial Northeast* (Amherst: University of Massachusetts Press, 2003), 70–99; James S. Pritchard, *In Search of Empire: The French in the Americas, 1670–1730* (Cambridge: Cambridge University Press, 2004), 301–57; and Jenny Hale Pulsipher, *Subjects unto the Same King: Indians, English, and the Contest for Authority in Colonial New England* (Philadelphia: University of Pennsylvania Press, 2005), 253–62.

14. "Examination of Magsigpen, an Indian," September 15, 1688, "Examination of Derrick Wessels," September 25, 1688, "Information Communicated by the Magistrates of Schenectady," September 29, 1688, in John Romeyn Brodhead, ed., *Documents Relative to the Colonial History of the State of New-York*, 15 vols. (Albany, NY: Weed, Parsons, 1858), 3:561–62, 564, 565.

15. "Lettre du Gouverneur de Frontenac et de L'Intendant Bochart Champigny au Ministre," November 11, 1692, in *Rapport de l'archiviste de la province de Québec pour 1927–1928* (L.-Amable Proulx: Imprimeur de Sa Majesté le Roi, 1928), 123–28. See also Robert Le Blant, *Histoire de la Nouvelle France: Les sources narratives du début du XVIII siècle et le recueil de Gédéon de Catalogne* (Dax, France: P. Predeu,

1940), 213–14. On disputes between the two men, see W. J. Eccles, *Frontenac, the Courtier Governor* (Montreal: McGill-Queen's University Press, 1959), 250–51. For monetary exchange rates, see Margaret Haig Roosevelt Sewall Ball, "Grim Commerce: Scalps, Bounties, and the Transformation of Trophy-Taking in the Early American Northeast, 1450–1770" (MA thesis, University of Colorado at Boulder, 2013), 94.

16. "Lettre du Gouverneur de Frontenac et de L'Intendant Bochart Champigny au Ministre, November 4, 1693, "Memoire du Roi au Gouverneur de Frontenac et a l'Intendant Buchart Champigny," in *Rapport de l'archiviste . . . 1927–1928*, 174, 90, 139, 144; "Memoire du Roi au Comte de Frontenac et de Champigny," June 14, 1695, in Jean Gervais Protais Blanchet et al., eds., *Collection de manuscrits contenant lettres, mémoires, et autres documents historiques relatifs a la Nouevelle-France*, 4 vols. (Quebec: Côté, 1884–85), 2:183.

17. "Lettre du Gouverneur de Frontenac et de L'Intendant Bochart Champigny au Ministre," November 9, 1694, in *Rapport de l'archiviste . . . 1927–1928*, 202; Eccles, *Frontenac*, 251–52. On French administration, see Rémi Chénier, *Québec: A French Colonial Town in America, 1660 to 1690* (Ottawa: National Historic Sites Parks Service, 1991), 38.

18. Chénier, *Québec*, 45–46.

19. Parkman, *Count Frontenac and New France*, 308, 335–40.

20. Frontenac to Minister, October 20, 1691, quoted in Parkman, *Count Frontenac and New France*, 338.

21. Lozier, "Lever des chevelures en Nouvelle-France," 521, 526–27.

22. Richard White, *The Middle Ground: Indians, Empires, and Republics in the Great Lakes Region, 1650–1815* (New York: Cambridge University Press, 1991).

23. Kenneth M. Morrison, *The Embattled Northeast: The Elusive Ideal of Alliance in Abenaki-Euramerican Relations* (Berkeley: University of California Press, 1984), 133–64.

24. Colin G. Calloway, *The Western Abenakis of Vermont, 1600–1800: War, Migration, and the Survival of an Indian People* (Norman: University of Oklahoma Press, 1990), 6–10, 14–15, 18–22, quotation on 10. On the Eastern Abenakis, see André Sévigny, *Les Abénaquis: Habitat et migrations (17e et 18e siècles)* (Montreal: Bellarmin, 1976). On King Philip's War, see Lisa Brooks, *Our Beloved Kin: A New History of King Philip's War* (New Haven: Yale University Press, 2018).

25. Pritchard, *In Search of Empire*, 335, 337; Eccles, *French in North America*, 106. On Iroquois relations with New France, see Ned Blackhawk, *The Rediscovery of America: Native Peoples and the Unmaking of U.S. History* (New Haven: Yale University Press, 2023), 73–105. On alliances between the Iroquois Confederacy and English settlers, see Richard Aquila, *The Iroquois Restoration: Iroquois Diplomacy on the Colonial Frontier, 1701–1754* (Detroit, MI: Wayne State University Press, 1983), 125–27, 191–92, 233–45; and Richard L. Haan, "Covenant and Consensus: Iroquois and

English, 1676–1760," in Daniel K. Richter and James H. Merrell, eds., *Beyond the Covenant Chain: The Iroquois and Their Neighbors in Indian North America, 1600–1800* (Syracuse, NY: Syracuse University Press, 1987), 41–57.

26. On *petite guerre*, see John Grenier, *The First Way of War: American Warmaking on the Frontier* (New York: Cambridge University Press, 2005), 1–5, 10–11, 32–34. On Indigenous ways of war, see Wayne E. Lee, *The Cutting-Off Way: Indigenous Warfare in Eastern North America, 1500–1800* (Chapel Hill: University of North Carolina Press, 2023), 15–34.

27. Lozier, "Lever des chevelures en Nouvelle-France," 515, 519, 540.

28. Historian Thomas Peotto refers to this racialized dehumanization aspect as "the scalping paradigm." See Thomas Peotto, "Dark Mimesis: A Cultural History of the Scalping Paradigm" (PhD diss., University of British Columbia, 2018), esp. ii.

29. Parkman, *Count Frontenac and New France*, 309–10, 310nn2,3.

30. Chénier, *Québec*, 227.

31. Minister to Villebon, April 1692, quoted in Parkman, *Count Frontenac and New France*, 365.

32. Parkman, *Count Frontenac and New France*, 366–69.

33. Parkman, *Count Frontenac and New France*, 383–86; Pritchard, *In Search of Empire*, 344–45.

34. Villebon to Minister, September 19, 1694, quoted in Parkman, *Count Frontenac and New France*, 389.

35. Parkman, *Count Frontenac and New France*, 394–95.

36. Pritchard, *In Search of Empire*, 345–46.

37. Pritchard, *In Search of Empire*, 338.

38. On Queen Anne's War, see Pritchard, *In Search of Empire*, 358–401; Calloway, *Western Abenakis of Vermont*, 101–3; and John Grenier, *The Far Reaches of Empire: War in Nova Scotia, 1710–1760* (Norman: University of Oklahoma Press, 2008), 50–52.

39. Cornelius J. Jaenen, *Friend and Foe: Aspects of French-Amerindian Cultural Contact in the Sixteenth and Seventeenth Centuries* (New York: Columbia University Press, 1976), 126–27.

40. Monsieur de Vaudreuil to Governor Joseph Dudley, March 26, 1705, in Blanchet et al., *Collection de manuscrits*, 2:428–31.

41. Governor Dudley to the Council of Trade and Plantations, March 1, 1709, in Cecil Headlam, ed., *Calendar of State Papers, Colonial Series, America and West Indies*, 45 vols. (London: Her Majesty's Stationery Office, 1922), 24:230–53.

42. Abenaki Statement to Monsieur Marquis de Vaudreuil, September 14, 1706, in Blanchet et al., *Collection de manuscrits*, 2:456–57; *Bulletin des Recherches Historiques*, 38:569–72.

43. Monsieur Marquis de Vaudreuil response to Abenakis, September 14, 1706, in Blanchet et al., *Collection de manuscrits*, 2:458–59.

44. J. C. Sainty, *Office-Holders in Modern Britain*, vol. 3: *Officials of the Boards of Trade, 1660–1870* (London: University of London, 1974), 28–37.

45. William Goold, *Col. Arthur Noble, of Georgetown, Fort Halifax; Col. William Vaughan, of Matinicus and Damariscotta* (Portland, ME: Stephen Berry, 1881), 295.

46. George Vaughan to the Council of Trade and Plantations, July 6, 1708, in Headlam, *Calendar of State Papers*, 24:18–33.

47. Address of the Council and Assembly of the Massachusetts Bay to the Queen, October 20, 1708, in Headlam, *Calendar of State Papers*, 24:300–322.

48. Kathleen DuVal, *The Native Ground: Indians and Colonists in the Heart of the Continent* (Philadelphia: University of Pennsylvania Press, 2006), 4–12; Kathleen DuVal, "Interconnectedness and Diversity in 'French Louisiana,' " in Gregory A. Waselkov, Peter H. Wood, and Tom Hatley, eds., *Powhatan's Mantle: Indians in the Colonial Southeast* (Lincoln: University of Nebraska Press, 2006), 138–39; Patricia Galloway, " 'The Chief Who Is Your Father': Choctaw and French Views of the Diplomatic Relation," in Waselkov, Wood, and Hatley, *Powhatan's Mantle*, 349–64. On Indian slaving and trading with the English, see Alan Gallay, *The Indian Slave Trade: The Rise of the English Empire in the American South, 1670–1717* (New Haven: Yale University Press, 2002), 129–32, 296–99. For population figures, see James Pritchard, "Population in French America, 1670–1730: The Demographic Context of Colonial Louisiana," in Bradley G. Bond, ed., *French Colonial Louisiana and the Atlantic World* (Baton Rouge: Louisiana State University Press, 2005), 175–99.

49. Valerie Lambert, *Choctaw Nation: A Study of American Indian Resurgence* (Lincoln: University of Nebraska Press, 2007), 19–22; Patricia Galloway, *Choctaw Genesis, 1500–1700* (Lincoln: University of Nebraska Press, 1995), 27–74; Marcia Haag and Henry Willis, eds., *Choctaw Language and Culture: Chahta Anumpa* (Norman: University of Oklahoma Press, 2001), 241–44; James Taylor Carson, *Searching for the Bright Path: The Mississippi Choctaws from Prehistory to Removal* (Lincoln: University of Nebraska Press, 1999), 8–25; James R. Atkinson, *Splendid Land, Splendid People: The Chickasaw Indians to Removal* (Tuscaloosa: University of Alabama Press, 2003), 1; Galloway, " 'Chief Who Is Your Father,' " 352.

50. See, e.g., Richebourg Gaillard McWilliams, ed. and trans., *Fleur de Lys and Calumet: Being the Pénicaut Narrative of French Adventure in Louisiana* (Tuscaloosa: University of Alabama Press, 1953), 73–79.

51. On Indian slavery in the English colonies, see Gallay, *Indian Slave Trade*; Margaret Ellen Newell, *Brethren by Nature: New England Indians, Colonists, and the Origins of American Slavery* (Ithaca, NY: Cornell University Press, 2015); and Wendy Warren, *New England Bound: Slavery and Colonization in Early America* (New York: Liveright, 2016).

52. Lozier, "Lever des chevelures en Nouvelle-France," 524–28, 541–42; Calloway, *Western Abenakis of Vermont*, 18.

53. Shannon Lee Dawdy, *Building the Devil's Empire: French Colonial New Orleans* (Chicago: University of Chicago Press, 2008), 14–15, 63.

54. Margry, *Mémoires et documents*, 5:479–80, 483.

55. Jean-Baptiste Le Moyne de Bienville to Louis Phélypeaux, Comte de Pontchartrain, April 10, 1706, King Louis XIV to Sieur de Muy, June 30, 1707, in Dunbar Rowland and Albert Godfrey Sanders, eds., *Mississippi Provincial Archives: French Dominion*, 4 vols. (Jackson: Press of the Mississippi Department of Archives and History, 1932), 3:33–34, 52. On Bienville's Indian diplomacy, see Gallay, *Indian Slave Trade*, 128–29; Patricia Galloway, *Practicing Ethnohistory: Mining Archives, Hearing Testimony, Constructing Narrative* (Lincoln: University of Nebraska Press, 2006), 245–48; and Mathé Allain, *"Not Worth a Straw": French Colonial Policy and the Early Years of Louisiana* (Lafayette: University of Southwestern Louisiana, 1988), 75–76.

56. Bienville to the Regent, August 8, 1721, National Archives of Canada, Colonial Archives, C13A Series, General Correspondence, Louisiana (hereafter cited as Colonial Archives, Louisiana).

57. Arrell M. Gibson, *The Chickasaws* (Norman: University of Oklahoma Press, 1971), 4–12, quotations on 4, 12.

58. Daniel H. Usner Jr., *American Indians in the Lower Mississippi Valley: Social and Economic Histories* (Lincoln: University of Nebraska Press, 1998), 17–20.

59. Bienville to the Council, September 13, 1723, "Minutes of the Council of Commerce of Louisiana," February 8, 1721, in Rowland and Sanders, *Mississippi Provincial Archives*, 3:375–77, 303, quotation on 375. On the Natchez campaign, see "Journal des principaux événements de la guerre des Natchez et de la campagne de M. de Bienville contre cette nation," December 10, 1723, Colonial Archives, Louisiana.

60. Matthew Jennings, *New Worlds of Violence: Cultures and Conquests in the Early American Southeast* (Knoxville: University of Tennessee Press, 2011), 89; Carson, *Searching for the Bright Path*, 28–29. On excessive expenditures, see "Résumé de diverses piéces sur la traite avec les sauvages (1731/1732)," Colonial Archives, Louisiana.

61. "Letter from Father le Petit, Missionary, to Father d'Avaugour, Procurator of the Missions in North America," July 12, 1730, in Thwaites, *Jesuit Relations and Allied Documents*, 68:121. For firsthand accounts of French-Choctaw relations during these conflicts, see Régis du Roulet to Jouanes, February 27, March 16, 1731, Colonial Archives, Louisiana. For French perspectives on the Natchez uprising, see Winston De Ville, trans. and ed., *Massacre at Natchez in 1729: The Rheims Manuscript* (Ville Platte, LA: Provincial Press, 2003); Périer, "Relations du massacre des Natchez arrive le 28 novembre 1729," March 18, 1730, Colonial Archives, Louisiana; and Fr. Philibert, "État des personnes du poste des Natchez qui ont été massacrées le 28 novembre 1729 par les Sauvages voisins dont ledit poste porte le nom (237 personnes), June 9, 1730, Colonial Archives, Louisiana. On racial views in the

French colonies, see Guillaume Aubert, " 'The Blood of France': Race and Purity of Blood in the French Atlantic World," *William and Mary Quarterly*, 3rd ser., 61:3 (2004): 441–42; and Saliha Belmessous, "Assimilation and Racialism in Seventeenth and Eighteenth-Century French Colonial Policy," *American Historical Review* 110:2 (2005): 322–26. On the Natchez War, see Daniel H. Usner, *Indians, Settlers, and Slaves in a Frontier Exchange Economy: The Lower Mississippi Valley before 1783* (Chapel Hill: University of North Carolina Press, 1992), 65–76; James F. Barnett Jr., *The Natchez Indians: A History to 1735* (Jackson: University Press of Mississippi, 2007), 101–31; DuVal, *Native Ground*, 95–96; and DuVal, "Interconnectedness and Diversity in 'French Louisiana,' " 142–48.

62. "Letter from Father le Petit, Missionary, to Father d'Avaugour, Procurator of the Missions in North America," 195, 199.

63. Bienville to Minister, February 10, 1736, Colonial Archives, Louisiana; "Letter of Father Mathurin le Petit to the Reverend Father Franciscus Retz, General of the Society of Jesus, at Rome," June 25, 1738, in Thwaites, *Jesuit Relations and Allied Documents*, 69:29–32; "Relation de Claude Drouët de Richarville sur le désastre infligé par les Chicachas á d'Artaguiette," 1736, Colonial Archives, Louisiana; "Relation par Parisien, anspessade, de la défaite infligée par les Chicachas á une troupe aux ordres d'Artaguiette," March 25, 1736, Colonial Archives, Louisiana; Bienville to Jean-Fréderic Phélypeaux, Comte de Maurepas, June 28, 1736, in Rowland and Sanders, *Mississippi Provincial Archives*, 1:311–14. See also Atkinson, *Splendid Land, Splendid People*, 48.

64. Bienville to Minister of the Colonies, May 2, June 28 (two separate letters), 1736, Colonial Archives, Louisiana. See also Atkinson, *Splendid Land, Splendid People*, 42–60.

65. Bienville to Maurepas, February 28, 1737, in Rowland and Sanders, *Mississippi Provincial Archives*, 3:693.

66. Diron d'Artaguette to Maurepas, May 8, 1737, in Rowland and Sanders, *Mississippi Provincial Archives*, 1:338–40, quotation on 340. On Choctaw campaigns, see Bienville to Minister, June 17, 1737, Colonial Archives, Louisiana.

67. Bienville to Maurepas, December 20, 1737, in Rowland and Sanders, *Mississippi Provincial Archives*, 3:702–4.

68. On the Choctaw alliance, see Bienville to Minister, May 28, 1740, Colonial Archives, Louisiana. On logistical setbacks, see Bienville to Minister, May 9, 1740, Colonial Archives, Louisiana. On the peace, see Edme Gatien Salmon to Minister, May 4, 1740, Colonial Archives, Louisiana. See also Atkinson, *Splendid Land, Splendid People*, 62–73; DuVal, "Interconnectedness and Diversity in 'French Louisiana,' " 149–52; and DuVal, *The Native Ground*, 97.

69. "Journal de la Campagne des Tcicahas (Chicachas), 1740, in *Rapport de l'archiviste de la province de Québec pour 1922–1923* (Ls-A. Proulx, QU: Imprimeur de Sa Majesté le Roi, 1923), 178.

70. Statement by George Johnson, October 2, 1754, quoted in Jessica Yirush Stern, *Their Lives in Objects: Native Americans, British Colonists, and Cultures of Labor and Exchange in the Southeast* (Chapel Hill: University of North Carolina Press, 2017), 103–4.

71. DuVal, "Interconnectedness and Diversity in 'French Louisiana,' " 136; Atkinson, *Splendid Land, Splendid People*, 28–29; Galloway, *Choctaw Genesis*, 201–3. For statistics on the number of Indians enslaved in the southern English colonies, see Gallay, *Indian Slave Trade*, 299.

72. "Newspaper Extracts," 1748, in Blanchet et al., *Collection de manuscrits*, 3:414.

73. "Abstract of M. de La Galissonnière's Despatches," January 8, 1748, in Edmund B. O'Callaghan and Berthold Fernow, eds., *Documents Relative to the Colonial History of the State of New York*, 15 vols. (Albany, NY: Weed, Parsons, 1856–87), 10:132; Lozier, "Lever des chevelures en Nouvelle-France," 529–30.

74. H. R. Casgrain, ed., *Voyage au Canada dans le nord de L'Amerique septentrionale fait dupuis l'an 1751 à 1761* (Quebec: Impremerie Léger Brousseau, 1887), 112–15, quotations on 113.

75. Monsieur Duquesne to the Minister, October 10, 1754, in Blanchet et al., *Collection de manuscrits*, 3:515–16.

76. M. des Bourbes to M. de Surlaville, April 18, 1756, in Gaston du Boscq de Beaumont, ed., *Les derniers hours de l'Acadie (1748–1758): Correspondances et mémoires* (Paris: Emile Lechevalier, 1899), 185–88.

77. "Journal de l'expédition d'Amérique commencée en l'année 1756, le 15 mars," in *Rapport de l'archiviste de la province de Québec pour 1923–1924* (Ls-A. Proulx, QU: Imprimeur de Sa Majesté le Roi, 1924), 281.

78. Edward P. Hamilton, ed. and trans., *Adventure in the Wilderness: The American Journals of Louis Antoine de Bougainville, 1756–1760* (Norman: University of Oklahoma Press, 1964), 141–42, quotation on 142.

79. "Journal de la campagne de 1758 commencé le 23 juin," in *Rapport de l'archiviste . . . 1923–1924*, 343, 345–46; Robert Rogers, *Journals of Major Robert Rogers* (London: J. Millan, 1765), 22.

80. Charles Coste, ed., *Aventures militaires au XVIII siècle, d'aprés les mémoires de Jean-Baptiste d'Aleyrac* (Paris: Berger-Levrault, 1935), 35; Claude de Bonnault, "Les aventures de M. d'Aleyrac," *Bulletin de Recherches Historiques* 44 (1938): 52–58.

81. Lozier, "Lever des chevelures en Nouvelle-France," 513–42.

2 Hunting Scalps in the Atlantic Coast Colonies and Early American Republic

1. For early renditions of Duston's captivity and escape, see Cotton Mather, *Humiliations Follow'd with Deliverances* (Boston: B. Green and J. Allen, 1697), 41–49; A. H. Quint, ed., *Journal of the Rev. John Pike, of Dover, N.H.* (Cambridge, MA: John Wilson, 1876), 19; and George Wingate Chase, *The History of Haverhill, Massachusetts,*

from Its First Settlement, in 1640, to the Year 1860 (Haverhill, MA: Published by the Author, 1861), 186–94. For scholarly analyses, see Laurel Thatcher Ulrich, *Good Wives: Image and Reality in the Lives of Women in Northern New England, 1650–1750* (New York: Vintage Books, 1991), 167–72; Teresa A. Toulouse, "Hannah Duston's Bodies: Domestic Violence and Colonial Male Identity in Cotton Mather's Decennium Luctuosum," in Janet Moore Lindman and Michele Lise Tarter, eds., *A Centre of Wonders: The Body in Early America* (Ithaca, NY: Cornell University Press, 2001), 193–94; John Grenier, *The First Way of War: American Warmaking on the Frontier* (New York: Cambridge University Press, 2005), 40–41; and Barbara Cutter, "The Female Indian Killer Memorialized: Hannah Duston and the Nineteenth-Century Feminization of American Violence," *Journal of Women's History* 20:2 (2008): 13–14.

2. *The Acts and Resolves, Public and Private, of the Province of the Massachusetts Bay*, 21 vols. (Boston: Wright and Potter, 1869–1922), 7:153–54.

3. Mather, *Humiliations Follow'd with Deliverances*, 47, 49, emphasis in original. See also Laura M. Stevens, "The Christian Origins of the Vanishing Indian," in Nancy Isenberg and Andrew Burstein, eds., *Mortal Remains: Death in Early America* (Philadelphia: University of Pennsylvania Press, 2003), 23–24.

4. Edmund S. Morgan, *Visible Saints: The History of a Puritan Idea* (New York: New York University Press, 1963), 1–32; Edmund S. Morgan, *The Puritan Family: Religion and Domestic Relations in Seventeenth-Century New England*, new ed., rev. and enl. (New York: Harper and Row, 1966), 1–28. On Puritan religious beliefs and connections to Indian conflict, see Ann Kibbey, *The Interpretation of Material Shapes in Puritanism: A Study of Rhetoric, Prejudice, and Violence* (Cambridge: Cambridge University Press, 1986), 92–120.

5. Ulrich, *Good Wives*, 167.

6. Cutter, "Female Indian Killer Memorialized," 10–33; Erin L. Thompson, *Smashing Statues: The Rise and Fall of America's Public Monuments* (New York: W. W. Norton, 2022), 145–48.

7. Rob Harper, "Looking the Other Way: The Gnadenhutten Massacre and the Contextual Interpretation of Violence," *William and Mary Quarterly*, 3rd ser., 64:3 (2007): 622–24; Joyce E. Chaplin, "Natural Philosophy and an Early Racial Idiom in North America: Comparing English and Indian Bodies," *William and Mary Quarterly*, 3rd ser., 54:1 (1997): 229–31; Richard White, *The Middle Ground: Indians, Empires, and Republics in the Great Lakes Region, 1650–1815* (New York: Cambridge University Press, 1991), 387–96; Richard Drinnon, *Facing West: The Metaphysics of Indian-Hating and Empire-Building* (Norman: University of Oklahoma Press, 1997), 65–116.

8. Andrew Lipman, " 'A Meanes to Knitt Them Togeather' ": The Exchange of Body Parts in the Pequot War," *William and Mary Quarterly*, 3rd ser., 65:1 (2008): 3–28, esp. 17; Francis Jennings, *The Invasion of America: Indians, Colonialism, and the Cant of Conquest* (Chapel Hill: University of North Carolina Press, 1975), 146–70;

Jill Lepore, *The Name of War: King Philip's War and the Origins of American Identity* (New York: Alfred A. Knopf, 1998), 74–75, 92–93, 148, 173–80; Martha L. Finch, *Dissenting Bodies: Corporealities in Early New England* (New York: Columbia University Press, 2010), 56–60; Erik R. Seeman, *Death in the New World: Cross-Cultural Encounters, 1492–1800* (Philadelphia: University of Pennsylvania Press, 2010), 175; Bernard Bailyn, *The Barbarous Years: The Conflict of Civilizations, 1600–1675* (New York: Alfred A. Knopf, 2012), 502–3.

9. Benjamin Church, *Diary of King Philip's War, 1675–76*, edited by Alan and Mary Simpson (Chester, CT: Pequot Press, 1975), 106; Grenier, *First Way of War*, 1–5, 10–11, 32–34.

10. Grenier, *First Way of War*, 39; Margaret Haig Roosevelt Sewall Ball, "Grim Commerce: Scalps, Bounties, and the Transformation of Trophy-Taking in the Early American Northeast, 1450–1770" (MA thesis, University of Colorado at Boulder, 2013), 4.

11. See, e.g., James Axtell and William C. Sturtevant, "The Unkindest Cut, or Who Invented Scalping," *William and Mary Quarterly*, 3rd ser., 37:3 (1980): 455–72; Gregory T. Knouff, *The Soldiers' Revolution: Pennsylvanians in Arms and the Forging of Early American Identity* (University Park: Pennsylvania State University Press, 2004), 166–67; Lipman, " 'Meanes to Knitt Them Together,' " 3–28; and Cora Bender, " 'Transgressive Objects' in America: Mimesis and Violence in the Collection of Trophies during the Nineteenth Century Indian Wars," *Civil Wars* 11 (December 2009): 506–8.

12. Colin G. Calloway, *The Western Abenakis of Vermont, 1600–1800: War, Migration, and the Survival of an Indian People* (Norman: University of Oklahoma Press, 1990), 94–96; James S. Pritchard, *In Search of Empire: The French in the Americas, 1670–1730* (Cambridge: Cambridge University Press, 2004), 335–36; Jenny Hale Pulsipher, *Subjects unto the Same King: Indians, English, and the Contest for Authority in Colonial New England* (Philadelphia: University of Pennsylvania Press, 2005), 253–62.

13. *Acts and Resolves*, 7:562. In the 1690s, 50 pounds in colonial currency equated to about 38 British pounds sterling.

14. *Acts and Resolves*, 7:116.

15. *Acts and Resolves*, 8:31–32, 38–39, 44–45, 462; Samuel Penhallow, *The History of the Wars of New-England with the Eastern Indians; or, A Narrative of Their Continued Perfidy and Cruelty from the 10th of August, 1703 to the Peace Renewed 13th of July, 1713* (1726; reprint, Philadelphia: Oscar H. Harpel, 1859), 22.

16. *Acts and Resolves*, 8:66–67, 81, 399.

17. On the Abenaki population, see Calloway, *Western Abenakis of Vermont*, 6–10, 14–15, 18–22. For New England Indian populations, see Jeffrey Ostler, *Surviving Genocide: Native Nations and the United States from the American Revolution to Bleeding Kansas* (New Haven: Yale University Press, 2019), 398–99.

18. Nathaniel Bouton, ed., *Documents and Records Relating to the Province of New-Hampshire, from the Earliest Period of Its Settlement*, 7 vols. (Manchester, NH: John B. Clarke, 1868), 2:417–18, 3:348, 366.

19. Penhallow, *History of the Wars*, 48.

20. *Acts and Resolves*, 8:418.

21. *Acts and Resolves*, 8:99–100.

22. Penhallow, *History of the Wars*, 48, 93.

23. Governor Dudley to the Council of Trade and Plantations, March 1, 1709, in Cecil Headlam, ed., *Calendar of State Papers, Colonial Series, America and West Indies*, 45 vols. (London: Her Majesty's Stationery Office, 1922), 24:230–53.

24. *Acts and Resolves*, 9:174.

25. *Acts and Resolves*, 9:251.

26. For the Treaty of Utrecht's impact on Indians, see William C. Wicken, *Mi'kmaq Treaties on Trial: History, Land, and Donald Marshall Junior* (Toronto: University of Toronto Press, 2004), 99–117.

27. On Dummer's War (also called Grey Lock's War), see Calloway, *Western Abenakis of Vermont*, 113–31; Grenier, *First Way of War*, 47–52; and Wicken, *Mi'kmaq Treaties on Trial*, 76–83. On the Iroquois, see Richard R. Johnson, "The Search for a Usable Indian: An Aspect of the Defense of Colonial New England," *Journal of American History* 64:3 (1977): 642–44; and James Axtell, *Natives and Newcomers: The Cultural Origins of North America* (Oxford: Oxford University Press, 2001), 263–65.

28. Daniel K. Richter and James H. Merrell, eds., *Beyond the Covenant Chain: The Iroquois and Their Neighbors in Indian North America, 1600–1800* (Syracuse, NY: Syracuse University Press, 1987), 5–7; William N. Fenton, *The Great Law and the Longhouse: A Political History of the Iroquois Confederacy* (Norman: University of Oklahoma Press, 1998), 4–6, 21–22, 69; Timothy J. Shannon, *Iroquois Diplomacy on the Early American Frontier* (New York: Viking, 2008) 24–26. For population figures, see Ostler, *Surviving Genocide*, 393.

29. *Acts and Resolves*, 10:263, 269–71.

30. *Acts and Resolves*, 10:481, 484, 486. On Indian auxiliaries and British colonists, see Wayne E. Lee, *The Cutting-Off Way: Indigenous Warfare in Eastern North America, 1500–1800* (Chapel Hill: University of North Carolina Press, 2023), 158–81.

31. Frederic Kidder, *Capt. John Lovewell, and His Encounters with the Indians* (Boston: Bartlett and Halliday, 1865), 15–21, quotation on 18.

32. Grenier, *First Way of War*, 50–52. See also Alfred E. Kayworth and Raymond G. Potvin, *The Scalp Hunters: Abenaki Ambush at Lovewell Pond—1725* (Boston: Branden Books, 2002), 127–59.

33. Wicken, *Mi'kmaq Treaties on Trial*, 83.

34. Grenier, *First Way of War*, 66–67.

35. Calloway, *Western Abenakis of Vermont*, 143.

36. Bouton, *Documents and Records*, 5:231.

37. *Acts and Resolves*, 13:399; Bouton, *Documents and Records*, 5:374–75.

38. *Acts and Resolves*, 13:521–22; Bouton, *Documents and Records*, 5:410–11.

39. *Acts and Resolves*, 13:577–78.

40. *Acts and Resolves*, 13:712–13, 14:21–22; Calloway, *Western Abenakis of Vermont*, 152.

41. Monsieur de Beauharnois to William Shirley, July 26, 1747, in Jean Gervais Protais Blanchet et al., eds., *Collection de manuscrits contenant lettres, mémoires, et autres documents historiques relatifs a la Nouevelle-France*, 4 vols. (Quebec: Côté, 1884), 3:375.

42. Bouton, *Documents and Records*, 5:491–92.

43. *Acts and Resolves*, 14:38.

44. *Acts and Resolves*, 14:107, 15:308–9; Bouton, *Documents and Records*, 5:529, 532, 587.

45. Calloway, *Western Abenakis of Vermont*, 163–73. On Indian participation, see Fred Anderson, *Crucible of War: The Seven Years' War and the Fate of Empire in British North America, 1754–1766* (New York: Alfred A. Knopf, 2000), 117–21, 186–88.

46. Bouton, *Documents and Records*, 6:410–11. On militia operations, see Fred Anderson, *A People's Army: Massachusetts Soldiers and Society in the Seven Years' War* (Chapel Hill: University of North Carolina Press, 1984).

47. *Acts and Resolves*, 15:343–44, 356–57, 396. See also Colin Calloway, ed., *Dawnland Encounters: Indians and Europeans in Northern New England* (Hanover, NH: University Press of New England, 1991), 167–69.

48. William Waller Hening, ed., *The Statutes at Large; Being a Collection of all the Laws of Virginia, from the First Session of the Legislature in the Year 1619*, 13 vols. (Richmond, VA: Franklin Press, 1819), 6:465–66, 550–52; Robert Dinwiddie to Lord Loudon, April 6, May 2, 1757, Dinwiddie to William Pitt, May 14, 1757, and Dinwiddie to the Lords of Trade, May 16, 1757, all in R. A. Brock, ed., *The Official Records of Robert Dinwiddie, Lieutenant-Governor of the Colony of Virginia, 1751–1758*, 2 vols. (Richmond: Virginia Historical Society, 1884), 2:605–6, 616–17, 620–21, 623–24, quotation on 623. See also Colin G. Calloway, *The Indian World of George Washington: The First President, the First Americans, and the Birth of the Nation* (New York: Oxford University Press, 2018), 130–31, 163–64, 218.

49. Grenier, *First Way of War*, 62, 118, 125–30, 133.

50. Calloway, *Western Abenakis of Vermont*, 160, 174–82, quotation on 174. Rogers's count of six hundred scalps was likely exaggerated, as was his claim that the volunteers killed two hundred Abenakis in the ambush. The actual number of Abenaki dead has been estimated at thirty. Calloway, *Western Abenakis of Vermont*, 178.

51. Peter Silver, *Our Savage Neighbors: How Indian War Transformed Early America* (New York: W. W. Norton, 2008), 162; *Acts and Resolves*, 15:472–74, 552.

52. See, e.g., Bouton, *Documents and Records*, 5:789–90.

53. Charles Zebina Lincoln and William Johnson, eds., *The Colonial Laws of New York, from the Year 1664 to the Revolution*, 5 vols. (Albany, NY: James B. Lyon, 1894), 3:540–41.

54. Lincoln and Johnson, *Colonial Laws of New York*, 3:647, 719, 722.

55. James H. Merrell, *Into the American Woods: Negotiators on the Pennsylvania Frontier* (New York: W. W. Norton, 1999), 35–38; William A. Pencak and Daniel K. Richter, eds., *Friends and Enemies in Penn's Woods: Indians, Colonists, and the Racial Construction of Pennsylvania* (University Park: Pennsylvania State University Press, 2004), ix–xxi.

56. Henry J. Young, "A Note on Scalp Bounties in Pennsylvania," *Pennsylvania History* 24:3 (1957): 208–9; "Six Months on the Frontier of Northampton County, Penna., during the Indian War, October 1755–June 1756," *Pennsylvania Magazine of History and Biography* 39:3 (1915): 351–52. See also Paul A. W. Wallace, *Conrad Weiser, 1696–1760: Friend of Colonist and Mohawk* (Philadelphia: University of Pennsylvania Press, 1945), 414, 421.

57. "Minute of Comm'rs. Premiums for Scalps, 1756," in Samuel Hazard, ed., *Pennsylvania Archives: Selected and Arranged from the Original Documents in the Office of the Secretary of the Commonwealth, Conformably to the Acts of the of the General Assembly, February 15, 1851, and March 1, 1852*, ser. 1, 12 vols. (Philadelphia: Joseph Severns, 1852–56), 2:619.

58. Robert Hunter Morris to Charles Hardy, April 4, 18, 1756, in Hazard, *Pennsylvania Archives*, 2:606–7, 629–30.

59. Goldsbrow Banyar to William Johnson, July 26, 1755, in James Sullivan, ed., *The Papers of Sir William Johnson*, 14 vols. (Albany: University of the State of New York, 1921–65), 1:772.

60. Richard Peters to Johnson, February 2, 1756; and Johnson to William Shirley, April 24, 1756, in Sullivan, *Papers of Johnson*, 2:426, 447. See also Fintan O'Toole, *White Savage: William Johnson and the Invention of America* (Albany: State University of New York Press, 2005), 79–82.

61. Morris to Elisha Saltar, April 10, 1756, "Certificate of Indian Isaac, 1757," in Hazard, *Pennsylvania Archives*, 2:621–22, 3:315.

62. Silver, *Our Savage Neighbors*, 162.

63. Daniel Claus to William Johnson, April 5, 1756, in Sullivan, *Papers of Johnson*, 2:438–40, quotations on 439; Phyllis Vibbard Parsons, "The Early Life of Daniel Claus," *Pennsylvania History: A Journal of Mid-Atlantic Studies* 29:4 (1962): 361–65. On Quaker opposition, see Jane T. Merritt, *At the Crossroads: Indians and Empires on a Mid-Atlantic Frontier, 1700–1763* (Chapel Hill: University of North Carolina Press, 2003), 204.

64. Quoted in Silver, *Our Savage Neighbors*, 161.

65. Daniel K. Richter, *Facing East from Indian Country: A Native History of Early America* (Cambridge, MA: Harvard University Press, 2001), 185, 204–5. On Quaker views of Indians, see Daniel K. Richter, *Trade, Land, Power: The Struggle for Eastern North America* (Philadelphia: University of Pennsylvania Press, 2013), 227–50.

66. Young, "Note on Scalp Bounties in Pennsylvania," 209.

67. William Denny to Assembly, September 12, 1757, in Hazard, *Pennsylvania Archives*, 2:870–72, quotation on 871.

68. Grenier, *First Way of War*, 144. On Pontiac's War, see Gregory Evans Dowd, *War under Heaven: Pontiac, the Indian Nations, and the British Empire* (Baltimore: Johns Hopkins University Press, 2002); David Dixon, *Never Come to Peace Again: Pontiac's Uprising and the Fate of the British Empire in North America* (Norman: University of Oklahoma Press, 2005); and Richard Middleton, *Pontiac's War: Its Causes, Course and Consequences* (New York: Routledge, 2007).

69. Silver, *Our Savage Neighbors*, 163–68, quotation on 164; Dowd, *War under Heaven*, 81–82.

70. Silver, *Our Savage Neighbors*, 163–68, quotation on 167.

71. Silver, *Our Savage Neighbors*, 168.

72. See Susan Juster, *Sacred Violence in Early America* (Philadelphia: University of Pennsylvania Press, 2016).

73. Quoted in Young, "Note on Scalp Bounties in Pennsylvania," 212.

74. Alden T. Vaughan, "Frontier Banditti and the Indians: The Paxton Boys' Legacy, 1763–1775," *Pennsylvania History: A Journal of Mid-Atlantic Studies* 51:1 (1984): 3–4; Krista Camenzind, "Violence, Race, and the Paxton Boys," in Pencak and Richter, *Friends and Enemies in Penn's Woods*, 201–20.

75. *A Declaration and Remonstrance of the Distressed and Bleeding Frontier Inhabitants of the Province of Pennsylvania* (N.p.: n.p., 1764), 6–7.

76. *Declaration and Remonstrance*, 12–17, quotations on 12, 13. See also Dixon, *Never Come to Peace Again*, 223–24.

77. Young, "Note on Scalp Bounties in Pennsylvania," 210.

78. "A Narrative of the Captivity of John M'Cullough, Esq.," in Archibald Loudon, *A Selection, of Some of the Most Interesting Narratives, of Outrages, Committed by the Indians in their Wars, with the White People*, 2 vols. in 1 (Carlisle, PA: A. Loudon, 1808), 1:252–53, 283. See also Middleton, *Pontiac's War*, 171–72.

79. See, e.g., Rob Harper, "State Intervention and Extreme Violence in the Revolutionary Ohio Valley," *Journal of Genocide Research* 10:2 (2008): 233–48. For a seminal study, see Colin G. Calloway, *The American Revolution in Indian Country: Crisis and Diversity in Native American Communities* (Cambridge: Cambridge University Press, 1995).

80. Archibald Lochrey to Thomas Wharton, December 6, 1777, in Hazard, *Pennsylvania Archives*, 6:68–69; Young, "Note on Scalp Bounties in Pennsylvania," 213.

81. Lochrey to Joseph Reed, May 1, 1779, in Hazard, *Pennsylvania Archives*, 7:362–63.

82. Joseph Reed to George Washington, May 1, 1779, in William B. Reed, ed., *Life and Correspondence of Joseph Reed*, 2 vols. (Philadelphia: Lindsay and Blakiston, 1847), 2:96–99, quotations on 96, 99.

83. Harper, "State Intervention and Extreme Violence," 237–38. For the Indian alliance at Detroit, see Capt. Matthew Arbuckle to Col. William Fleming, July 26,

1777, and Gen. Edward Hand to Fleming, August 12, 1777, both in Reuben Gold Thwaites and Louise Phelps Kellogg, eds., *Frontier Defense on the Upper Ohio* (Madison: Wisconsin Historical Society, 1912), 25–27, 42–43. On British-Indian cooperation, see Jack M. Sosin, "The Use of Indians in the War of the American Revolution: A Reassessment of Responsibility," *Canadian Historical Review* 46 (June 1965): 101–21.

84. Bernard W. Sheehan, " 'The Famous Hair Buyer General': Henry Hamilton, George Rogers Clark, and the American Indian," *Indiana Magazine of History* 79:1 (1983): 13–14, quotation on 22. See also Paul A. W. Wallace, ed., *Thirty Thousand Miles with John Heckewelder* (Pittsburgh, PA: University of Pittsburgh Press, 1958), 158; Grenier, *First Way of War*, 16–17, 156–57; and Gregory Evans Dowd, *Groundless: Rumors, Legends, and Hoaxes on the Early American Frontier* (Baltimore: Johns Hopkins University Press, 2015), 183–85.

85. Thomas Jefferson to Governor of Detroit, July 22, 1779, in William Palmer, ed., *Calendar of Virginia State Papers and Other Manuscripts*, vol. 1: *1652–1781* (New York: Kraus, 1968), 321–24, quotation on 322.

86. Harper, "State Intervention and Extreme Violence," 237–38. For an example of neutral Delaware Indians, see Col. John Gibson to Hand, December 19, 1777, in Thwaites and Kellogg, *Frontier Defense on the Upper Ohio*, 178–79.

87. Calloway, *American Revolution in Indian Country*, 49, 218.

88. "Pres. Reed to Col. Brodhead, 1779," in Hazard, *Pennsylvania Archives*, 7:569–72, quotation on 569. On the moral issue, see Sheehan, " 'Famous Hair Buyer General,' " 2–4; and Axtell, *Natives and Newcomers*, 259–79. On Brodhead's activities, see Barbara Alice Mann, *George Washington's War on Native America* (Westport, CT: Praeger, 2005), 37–50; and Calloway, *Indian World of George Washington*, 274. On scalping during the American Revolution, see Wayne Lee, *Barbarians and Brothers: Anglo-American Warfare, 1500–1865* (New York: Oxford University Press, 2011), 212–13, 225, 227–28.

89. See Calloway, *American Revolution in Indian Country*, 26–64.

90. Harper, "State Intervention and Extreme Violence," 240–41; Gregory Evans Dowd, *A Spirited Resistance: The North American Indian Struggle for Unity, 1745–1815* (Baltimore: Johns Hopkins University Press, 1992), 75–78. For a firsthand account, see "The Murder of Cornstalk: Portion of the Narrative of Capt. John Stuart," in Thwaites and Kellogg, *Frontier Defense on the Upper Ohio*, 157–63.

91. Eugene F. Bliss, ed., *Diary of David Zeisberger, a Moravian Missionary among the Indians of Ohio*, 2 vols. (Cincinnati, OH: Robert Clarke, 1885), 1:36–37, quotation on 37.

92. On the role of race in frontier Indian wars, see Knouff, *Soldiers' Revolution*, 155–93; Camenzind, "Violence, Race, and the Paxton Boys," 201–20; and Eric Hinderaker, *Elusive Empires: Constructing Colonialism in the Ohio Valley, 1673–1800* (Cambridge: Cambridge University Press 1997), 185–87.

93. Samuel Hunter to Reed, April 2, 1780, Reed to Hunter, April 7, 1780, Reed to Brodhead, April 29, 1780, Brodhead to Reed, May 18, 1780, and Brodhead to Lochrey, May 20, 1780, all in Hazard, *Pennsylvania Archives*, 8:157, 166–68, 218, 249–50 (quotation), 12:239.

94. Reed to Joseph Montgomery, April 8, 1780, in Hazard, *Pennsylvania Archives*, 8:170.

95. Brodhead to the Delawares, May 27, 1780, in Louise Phelps Kellogg, ed., *Frontier Retreat on the Upper Ohio, 1779–1781* (Madison: Wisconsin Historical Society, 1917), 183–84.

96. *By His Excellency Joseph Reed, Esq. President, and the Supreme Executive Council, of the Commonwealth of Pennsylvania: A Proclamation* (Philadelphia: Francis Bailey, 1780).

97. On wartime inflation, see Robert E. Wright, *One Nation under Debt: Hamilton, Jefferson, and the History of What We Owe* (New York: McGraw Hill, 2008), 49–51, 54–56.

98. Alexander Fowler to Hand, July 22, 1780, in Kellogg, *Frontier Retreat on the Upper Ohio*, 224–25; Brodhead to Reed, 1780 (exact date unspecified), in Hazard, *Pennsylvania Archives*, 8:301; *Minutes of the Supreme Executive Council of Pennsylvania, from Its Organization to the Termination of the Revolution*, 16 vols. (Harrisburg, PA: Theo. Fenn, 1853), 12:632.

99. Silver, *Our Savage Neighbors*, 378n32; Young, "Note on Scalp Bounties in Pennsylvania," 217.

100. Young, "Note on Scalp Bounties in Pennsylvania," 211, 217; Axtell, *Natives and Newcomers*, 265, 273.

101. Emer de Vattel, *The Law of Nations; or, Principles of the Law of Nature, Applied to the Conduct and Affairs of Nations and Sovereigns*, 6th ed. (Philadelphia: T. and J. W. Johnson, 1844), 346–63, quotations on 346, 351; Francis Wharton, ed., *The Revolutionary Diplomatic Correspondence of the United States*, 2 vols. (Washington, DC: Government Printing Office, 1889), 1:604. On the "colonial military tradition," see Guy Chet, *Conquering the American Wilderness: The Triumph of European Warfare in the Colonial Northeast* (Amherst: University of Massachusetts Press, 2003), 1–3, 142–47.

102. On "communities of violence," see Lance R. Blyth, *Chiricahua and Janos: Communities of Violence in the Southwestern Borderlands, 1680–1880* (Lincoln: University of Nebraska Press, 2012), ix–x.

103. Benjamin Madley, "Reexamining the American Genocide Debate: Meaning, Historiography and New Methods," *American Historical Review* 120:1 (2015): 114. On atrocity and conquest as analytical frameworks, see Edward B. Westermann, *Hitler's Ostkrieg and the Indian Wars: Comparing Genocide and Conquest* (Norman: University of Oklahoma Press, 2016), 9–16, 159–61.

104. *Articles of Confederation and Perpetual Union between the States of New-Hampshire, Massachusetts-Bay, Rhode Island and Providence Plantations, Connecticut,*

New-York, New-Jersey, Pennsylvania, Delaware, Maryland, Virginia, North-Carolina, South-Carolina, and Georgia (Lancaster, PA: Francis Bailey, 1777), art. 6.

105. US Constitution, art. 1, sec. 8.

106. For populations, see Calloway, *Western Abenakis of Vermont,* 6–10, 14–15, 18–22; and Fenton, *Great Law and the Longhouse,* 4–6, 21–22.

107. Wiley Sword, *President Washington's Indian War: The Struggle for the Old Northwest, 1790–1795* (Norman: University of Oklahoma Press, 1985); Alan D. Gaff, *Bayonets in the Wilderness: Anthony Wayne's Legion in the Old Northwest* (Norman: University of Oklahoma Press, 2004); Grenier, *First Way of War,* 193–203; John Sugden, *Blue Jacket: Warrior of the Shawnees* (Lincoln: University of Nebraska Press, 2000); Colin Calloway, *The Victory with No Name: The Native American Defeat of the First American Army* (New York: Oxford University Press, 2015); Ostler, *Surviving Genocide,* 108–12, 120.

108. For an overview of the early US period, see Thomas Peotto, "Dark Mimesis: A Cultural History of the Scalping Paradigm" (PhD diss., University of British Columbia, 2018), 279–84.

109. Grenier, *First Way of War,* 205–14; Robert M. Owens, *Mr. Jefferson's Hammer: William Henry Harrison and the Origins of American Indian Policy* (Norman: University of Oklahoma Press, 2007); Adam Jortner, *Gods of Prophetstown: The Battle of Tippecanoe and the Holy War for the American Frontier* (New York: Oxford University Press, 2011); Ostler, *Surviving Genocide,* 141–64. On Tecumseh, see R. David Edmunds, *Tecumseh and the Quest for Indian Leadership* (New York: Pearson Longman, 2007).

110. Claudio Saunt, *A New Order of Things: Property, Power, and the Transformation of the Creek Indians, 1733–1816* (Cambridge: Cambridge University Press, 1999), 249–72; Grenier, *First Way of War,* 214–20; Gregory A. Waskelov, *A Conquering Spirit: Fort Mims and the Red Stick War of 1813–1814* (Tuscaloosa: University of Alabama Press, 2006); Ostler, *Surviving Genocide,* 164–78.

111. Rev. Thomas Lippincott, "The Wood River Massacre," *Journal of the Illinois State Historical Society* 4:4 (1912): 504–9; John Mack Faragher, *Sugar Creek: Life on the Illinois Prairie* (New Haven: Yale University Press, 1986), 32.

3 Bounty Massacres in the US-Mexico Borderlands

1. George F. Ruxton, *Adventures in Mexico and the Rocky Mountains* (New York: Harper and Brothers, 1848), 156–59; Richard King, "Obituary Notice of Lieutenant George Augustus Frederick Ruxton," *Journal of the Ethnological Society of London* 2 (1850): 150–58; Brian DeLay, *War of a Thousand Deserts: Indian Raids and the U.S.-Mexican War* (New Haven: Yale University Press, 2008), 274–77.

2. I use "Southern Apaches" rather than "Chiricahua Apaches" to collectively name the Chokonen, Chihene, Nednhi, and Bedonkohe subgroups whose homelands

straddled the U.S.-Mexico border. See Matthew Babcock, *Apache Adaptation to Hispanic Rule* (New York: Cambridge University Press, 2016), 261–63; and Paul Conrad, *The Apache Diaspora: Four Centuries of Displacement and Survival* (Philadelphia: University of Pennsylvania Press, 2021), 6–7.

3. Quotations are from Ruxton, *Adventures in Mexico*, 156–59. For reports on the massacre, see G. de Cuilty to José María Irigoyen, July 10, 1846, and Santiago Kirker to Irigoyen, July 13, 1846, both in *El Provisional*, July 14, 21, 1846 (*Periódico Oficial de Chihuahua*, University of Texas at El Paso, microfilm 472 [hereafter cited as *Periódico Oficial 472*], roll 2). On the Apaches' arrival at Galeana, see Cuilty to Irigoyen, June 3, 1846, in *El Provisional*, June 9, 1846 (*Periódico Oficial 472*, roll 2). One of Kirker's men recorded 139 Apaches killed and described the celebration in the capital. See James Hobbs, *Wild Life in the Far West: Personal Adventures of a Border Mountain Man* (Waterford, CT: Wiley, Waterman and Eaton, 1875), 86–88, 93–95. On the Galeana Massacre generally, see Edwin R. Sweeney, *Cochise: Chiricahua Apache Chief* (Norman: University of Oklahoma Press, 1991), 55–58; Edwin R. Sweeney, *Mangas Coloradas: Chief of the Chiricahua Apaches* (Norman: University of Oklahoma Press, 1998), 134–36; Ralph Adam Smith, *Borderlander: The Life of James Kirker, 1793–1852* (Norman: University of Oklahoma Press, 1999), 159–68; DeLay, *War of a Thousand Deserts*, 277; and Berndt Kühn, *Chronicles of War: Apache and Yavapai Resistance in the Southwestern United States and Northern Mexico, 1821–1937* (Tucson: Arizona Historical Society, 2014), 22.

4. See Yang Su, "Mass Killings in the Cultural Revolution: A Study of Three Provinces," in Joseph Esherick, Paul Pickowicz, and Andrew George Walder, eds., *The Chinese Cultural Revolution as History* (Stanford, CA: Stanford University Press, 2006), 96–123.

5. Jason Betzinez, *I Fought with Geronimo* (New York: Bonanza Books, 1959), 3–6. Betzinez misidentified the location of the massacre as Ramos and erroneously placed the date as 1850, but historian Edwin Sweeney has shown that it was indeed the event at Galeana that he described. Sweeney, *Cochise*, 412n64. See also Lance R. Blyth, *Chiricahua and Janos: Communities of Violence in the Southwestern Borderlands, 1680–1880* (Lincoln: University of Nebraska Press, 2012), 141–44.

6. Carlos Cásares to Cuilty, June 24, 1846, in *El Provisional*, July 14, 1846 (*Periódico Oficial 472*, roll 2).

7. Testimony of John Greiner, July 4, 1865, in *Condition of the Indian Tribes: Report of the Joint Special Committee, Appointed under Joint Resolution of March 3, 1865, with an Appendix*, 39th Cong., 2nd Sess., Senate Report No. 156, p. 328. On the Ácoma Treaty council, see William S. Kiser, *Dragoons in Apacheland: Conquest and Resistance in Southern New Mexico, 1846–1861* (Norman: University of Oklahoma Press, 2012), 132–38. For the use of alcohol as antecedent to massacre, see Hobbs, *Wild Life in the Far West*, 84, 86; Eve Ball, *In the Days of Victorio: Recollections of a Warm Springs Apache* (Tucson: The University of Arizona Press, 1970),

74; and Joseph C. Jastrzembski, "Treacherous Towns in Mexico: Chiricahua Apache Personal Narratives of Horrors," *Western Folklore* 54:3 (1995): 178–81.

8. John Russell Bartlett, *Personal Narrative of Explorations and Incidents in Texas, New Mexico, California, Sonora, and Chihuahua, 1850–1853*, 2 vols. (New York: D. Appleton, 1854), 1:322.

9. Keith Basso, ed., *Western Apache Raiding and Warfare: From the Notes of Grenville Goodwin* (Tucson: University of Arizona Press, 1971), 276–78; Keith H. Basso, *Wisdom Sits in Places: Landscape and Language among the Western Apache* (Albuquerque: University of New Mexico Press, 1996), 146.

10. Eve Ball, *Indeh: An Apache Odyssey* (Provo, UT: Brigham Young University Press, 1980), 11–12, 20–21, 56–65. See also Ball, *In the Days of Victorio*, 48.

11. Morris Edward Opler, *An Apache Life-Way: The Economic, Social, and Religious Institutions of the Chiricahua Indians* (New York: Cooper Square, 1965), quotation on 349.

12. Basso, *Western Apache Raiding and Warfare*, 276–78, quotation on 277. On Apache scalping, see Janne Lahti, *Wars for Empire: Apaches, the United States, and the Southwest Borderlands* (Norman: University of Oklahoma Press, 2017), 66–67. On medicine power, see Donald L. Fixico, *Call for Change: The Medicine Way of American Indian History, Ethos, and Reality* (Lincoln: University of Nebraska Press, 2013), 165–66. On Apache trauma, see Margery Hunt-Watkinson, "A Savage Land: Violence and Trauma in the Nineteenth-Century American Southwest" (PhD diss., Arizona State University, 2020), 272–316.

13. Conrad, *Apache Diaspora*, 4, 6, 9.

14. On the borderlands economy, see Samuel Truett, *Fugitive Landscapes: The Forgotten History of the U.S.-Mexico Borderlands* (New Haven: Yale University Press, 2006), 24–51. On scalp hunting in the Southwest Borderlands, see Thomas Peotto, "Dark Mimesis: A Cultural History of the Scalping Paradigm" (PhD diss., University of British Columbia, 2018), 320–35.

15. Conrad, *Apache Diaspora*, 10–11.

16. William S. Kiser, "The Business of Killing Indians: Contract Warfare and Genocide in the U.S.-Mexico Borderlands," *Journal of American History* 110:1 (2023): 15–39.

17. Smith, *Borderlander*, 270n20.

18. Andrés Reséndez, *The Other Slavery: The Uncovered Story of Indian Enslavement in America* (New York: Houghton Mifflin Harcourt, 2016).

19. See Conrad, *Apache Diaspora*.

20. Mark Santiago, *The Jar of Severed Hands: Spanish Deportation of Apache Prisoners of War, 1770–1810* (Norman: University of Oklahoma Press, 2011), 3–4.

21. Mark Santiago, *A Bad Peace and a Good War: Spain and the Mescalero Apache Uprising of 1795–1799* (Norman: University of Oklahoma Press, 2018), 8.

22. Ramón Eduardo Ruiz, *The People of Sonora and Yankee Capitalists* (Tucson: University of Arizona Press, 1988), 172–73.

23. David J. Weber, *The Mexican Frontier, 1821–1846: The American Southwest under Mexico* (Albuquerque: University of New Mexico Press, 1982), 86–87, 105; Babcock, *Apache Adaptation to Hispanic Rule*, 173, 202–5, 219. On localized Mexican Indian policy, see Francisco R. Almada, *Diccionario de historía, geografía y biografía sonorenses* (Chihuahua: Ruiz Sandoval, 1952), 74; William B. Griffen, *Utmost Good Faith: Patterns of Apache-Mexican Hostilities in Northern Chihuahua Border Warfare, 1821–1848* (Albuquerque: University of New Mexico Press, 1988), 43–111, 181–94; Victor Orozco Orozco, ed., *Las guerras indias en la historia de Chihuahua: Antología* (Juarez: Universidad Autónoma de Ciudad Juárez, Instituto Chihuahuense de la Cultura, 1992), 237–39; Pekka Hämäläinen, *The Comanche Empire* (New Haven: Yale University Press, 2008), 190–238; Jorge Chávez Chávez, "Los Apaches y la frontera norte de México, siglo XIX," in Jorge Chávez Chávez, ed., *Visiones históricas de la frontera* (Juarez: Universidad Autónoma de Ciudad Juárez, 2010), 25–51; and Blyth, *Chiricahua and Janos*, 123–54.

24. Griffen, *Utmost Good Faith*, 28–29.

25. Smith, *Borderlander*, 68–69.

26. DeLay, *War of a Thousand Deserts*, 159–60; Max L. Moorhead, *New Mexico's Royal Road: Trade and Travel on the Chihuahua Trail* (Norman: University of Oklahoma Press, 1958), 147–51; Ana Lilia Nieto Camacho, *Defensa y política en la frontera norte de México, 1848–1856* (Tijuana: Colegio de la Frontera Norte, 2012), 48–66.

27. Peter L. Rousseau, "Jacksonian Monetary Policy, Specie Flows, and the Panic of 1837," *Journal of Economic History* 62:2 (2002): 457–88; Alasdair Roberts, *America's First Great Depression: Economic Crisis and Political Disorder after the Panic of 1837* (Ithaca, NY: Cornell University Press, 2012).

28. José Fuentes Mares, *Y México se refugió en el desierto: Luis Terrazas, historia y destino* (Mexico City: Jus, 1954), 144. On the Mexican peso, see Markus A. Denzel, *Handbook of World Exchange Rates, 1590–1914* (Burlington, VT: Ashgate, 2010), 487–91.

29. William B. Griffen, "The Compás: A Chiricahua Family of the Late 18th and Early 19th Centuries," *American Indian Quarterly* 7:2 (1983): 37.

30. J. J. Johnson to Commandant General, April 24, 1837, *El Noticioso de Chihuahua*, May 5, 1837 (*Periódico Oficial* 472, roll 1); Rex W. Strickland, "The Birth and Death of a Legend: The Johnson 'Massacre' of 1837," *Arizona and the West* 18 (Autumn 1976): 257–86; Sweeney, *Mangas Coloradas*, 70–73; Kühn, *Chronicles of War*, 9; Babcock, *Apache Adaptation to Hispanic Rule*, 213–15, 220–23.

31. Robert Glass Cleland, *Pathfinders* (Los Angeles: Powell, 1929), 371–75.

32. Josiah Gregg, *Commerce of the Prairies*, edited by Max L. Moorhead (Norman: University of Oklahoma Press, 1954), 205–6, emphasis in original.

33. Ralph P. Bieber, ed., *Exploring Southwestern Trails, 1846–1854* (Glendale, CA: Arthur H. Clark, 1938), 114–15; John Russell Bartlett, *Personal Narrative of Explorations and Incidents in Texas, New Mexico, California, Sonora, and Chihuahua,*

1850–1853, 2 vols. (New York: D. Appleton, 1854), 1:322–23. John Cremony, a US Army officer who served in Arizona and New Mexico during the Civil War, offered one of the earliest exaggerations of the event when he claimed that four hundred Indians died. John C. Cremony, *Life among the Apaches* (San Francisco: A. Roman, 1868), 30–32.

34. Karl Jacoby, *Shadows at Dawn: A Borderlands Massacre and the Violence of History* (New York: Penguin Press, 2008), 162–63.

35. Conrad, *Apache Diaspora*, 180–81.

36. Testimony of John Greiner, July 4, 1865, in *Condition of the Indian Tribes*, 328. On the two wives, see Sweeney, *Mangas Coloradas*, 188.

37. Ball, *Indeh*, 22–23, 78, 81.

38. Ruth McDonald Boyer and Narcissus Duffy Gayton, *Apache Mothers and Daughters: Four Generations of a Family* (Norman: University of Oklahoma Press, 1992), 25–26; Basso, *Wisdom Sits in Places*, 146.

39. Sweeney, *Mangas Coloradas*, 74–75.

40. Pedro Olivares and Ángel Trías to Señor Governor, July 29, 1837, in *El Noticioso de Chihuahua*, August 6, 1837 (*Periódico Oficial* 472, roll 1).

41. "Gobierno General," in *El Noticioso de Chihuahua*, October 26, 1837 (*Periódico Oficial* 472, roll 1). For the Mexican abolition act, see "Ley queda abolida la esclavitud en la República, sin excepcion alguna," April 5, 1837, in Manuel Dublán y José Maria Lozano, eds., *Legislación mexicana; ó, Colección complete de las disposiciones legislativas expedidas desde la independencia de la republica*, vol. 3 (Mexico City: Dublán y Lozano, 1876), 352. For the British law, see "An Act for the Abolition of Slavery throughout the British Colonies," Acts of the Parliament of the United Kingdom, 3 & 4 Will. IV c.73, August 28, 1833.

42. Gregg, *Commerce of the Prairies*, 207–8.

43. Quotation from Hobbs, *Wild Life in the Far West*, 81; see also Smith, *Borderlander*, 5, 17, 25, 42, 47–48.

44. "Gobierno del estado," *El Fanal*, October 21, 1834 (*Periódico Oficial* 472, roll 1). On gun smuggling, see Weber, *Mexican Frontier*, 97–98.

45. "Gobierno del estado," *El Fanal*, November 11, 1834 (*Periódico Oficial* 472, roll 1).

46. José Agustín de Escudero, *Observaciones sobre el estado actual del departamento de Chihuahua* (Mexico City: Juan Ojeda, 1839), 18, 24.

47. Proclamation of Governor Simón Elías Gonzalez, May 18, 1838, in Orozco, *Guerras indias*, 253–55.

48. Circular of April 16, 1839, book 1, year 1839, Ciudad Juárez Municipal Archives, University of Texas at El Paso, microfilm 513, roll 29, frames 13–14 (hereafter cited as Juárez Archives); Circular of April 4, 1839, book 2, year 1839, Juárez Archives, microfilm 513, roll 30, frames 40–41.

49. "Gobierno del Departamento," *El Antenor*, December 31, 1839 (*Periódico Oficial* 472, roll 1); Ignacio Ronquillo to Pedro Trujillo, April 14, 1839, book 2, year 1839,

Juárez Archives, microfilm 513, roll 30, frames 264–65; Circular of January 15, 1840, book 2, year 1840, Juárez Archives, microfilm 513, roll 31, part 2, frame 491; Juan María Salazar to Alcalde de Paz, April 13, 1839, Archivo del Ayuntamiento de Chihuahua, University of Texas at El Paso, microfilm 491, roll 186, frames 91–92; Leslie E. Bliss and Arthur A. Woodward, eds., *Don Santiago Kirker* (Los Angeles: Muir Dawson, 1948), 7; Smith, *Borderlander*, 84–88, 101.

50. On California, see Benjamin Madley, *An American Genocide: The United States and the California Indian Catastrophe* (New Haven: Yale University Press, 2016), 250–53.

51. John E. Sunder, ed., *Matt Field on the Santa Fe Trail* (Norman: University of Oklahoma Press, 1960), 190–93, quotation on 192; Manuel Armijo to Diego Archuleta, September 11, 1839, New Mexico State Records Center and Archives, Mexican Archives of New Mexico, roll 26.

52. "Proyecto de Guerra Contra Apaches," *El Antenor*, December 10, 1839 (*Periódico Oficial* 472, roll 1).

53. Griffen, *Utmost Good Faith*, 172–75; Sweeney, *Mangas Coloradas*, 83; Weber, *Mexican Frontier*, 114–19.

54. Sweeney, *Mangas Coloradas*, 3, 27–28, 53–56.

55. "Ocurrencias de Apaches," *El Antenor*, January 21, 1840 (*Periódico Oficial* 472, roll 1); Simón Elías Gonzalez to Janos Commander, February 6, 1840, Janos Presidio Collection, University of Texas at El Paso, microfilm 498, roll 28.

56. Blyth, *Chiricahua and Janos*, 133–34; Griffen, *Utmost Good Faith*, 58–59, 200.

57. José María Elías González to Janos Military Commander, June 2, 1841, Nettie Lee Benson Latin American Collection, University of Texas at Austin, Presidio de San Felipe y Santiago de Janos Records, 1706–1858, part 7, folder 41, section 2 (hereafter cited as Presidio Records); "Ocurrencias de Apaches," *El Antenor*, January 21, 1840 (*Periódico Oficial* 472, roll 1).

58. "Ocurrencias de Apaches," *El Antenor*, April 14, 1840 (*Periódico Oficial* 472, roll 1).

59. Griffen, *Utmost Good Faith*, 171–72. On Spy Buck, see Bliss and Woodward, *Don Santiago Kirker*, 7; and Hobbs, *Wild Life in the Far West*, 81–100.

60. "Ocurrencias de Apaches," *El Antenor*, May 19, 1840 (*Periódico Oficial* 472, roll 1); Smith, *Borderlander*, 111–12; Griffen, *Utmost Good Faith*, 59, 171–72.

61. Francisco García Conde to Janos Military Commander, May 29, 1840, Presidio Records, part 7, folder 41, section 1.

62. George Wilkins Kendall, *Narrative of the Texan–Santa Fé Expedition*, 2 vols. (New York: Harper and Brothers, 1844), 2:57–58. See also Hobbs, *Wild Life in the Far West*, 89–90.

63. Quoted in Babcock, *Apache Adaptation to Hispanic Rule*, 218.

64. Sweeney, *Mangas Coloradas*, 9, 17, 85, 88–89, 92–95, 290.

65. Sweeney, *Mangas Coloradas*, 102–3, 107–36; Babcock, *Apache Adaptation to Hispanic Rule*, 238–39; Boyer and Gayton, *Apache Mothers and Daughters*, 25.

66. William B. Griffen, *Apaches at War and Peace: The Janos Presidio, 1750–1858* (Albuquerque: University of New Mexico Press, 1988), 215.

67. David J. Weber, ed. and trans., *Arms, Indians, and the Mismanagement of New Mexico: Donaciano Vigil, 1846* (El Paso: Texas Western Press, 1986), 1–7, quotation on 1.

68. Dr. A. Wislizenus, *Memoir of a Tour to Northern Mexico, Connected with Col. Doniphan's Expedition, in 1846 and 1847* (Washington, DC: Tippin and Streeper, 1848), 28.

69. José Barrios to Governor of Sonora, August 18, 1846, quoted in Sweeney, *Mangas Coloradas*, 140.

70. Hobbs, *Wild Life in the Far West*, 96–97.

71. Bliss and Woodward, *Don Santiago Kirker*, 10–11.

72. Ralph P. Bieber, ed., *Marching with the Army of the West, 1846–1848* (Glendale, CA: Arthur H. Clark, 1936), 237; Frank S. Edwards, *A Campaign in New Mexico with Colonel Doniphan* (Albuquerque: University of New Mexico Press, 1996), 62–63; William E. Connelley, *Doniphan's Expedition and the Conquest of New Mexico and California* (Kansas City, MO: Bryan and Douglas, 1907), 327, 388–89. On perpetration of atrocities by American volunteers, see Paul Foos, *A Short, Offhand, Killing Affair: Soldiers and Social Conflict during the Mexican-American War* (Chapel Hill: University of North Carolina Press, 2002), 113–16.

73. DeLay, *War of a Thousand Deserts*, 294–303.

74. Angel Trías to Emilio Langberg, October 10, 1849, Archives and Information Services Division, Texas State Library and Archives Commission, Texas Governor George T. Wood Records, box 301–18, folder 22 (hereafter cited as George T. Wood Records).

75. "Sketch of Colonel John C. Hays, Texas Ranger" (unpublished manuscript by John Caperton, 1922), 71–72, Dolph Briscoe Center for American History, The University of Texas at Austin, John Coffee Hays Collection, box 2R35.

76. On Leaton, see Jefferson Morgenthaler, *The River Has Never Divided Us: A Border History of La Junta de los Rios* (Austin: University of Texas Press, 2004), 50–53, 69–75, 78–80.

77. Langberg to Jefferson Van Horne, October 23, 1849, George T. Wood Records, box 301-18, folder 22.

78. Van Horne to George Deas, November 8, 1849, George T. Wood Records, box 301-18, folder 23.

79. "Gobierno del Estado," *El Faro*, May 29, 1849 (*Periódico Oficial* 472, roll 3); Ralph A. Smith, "Scalp Hunting: A Mexican Experiment in Warfare," *Great Plains Journal* 23 (January 1984): 72n7.

80. Blyth, *Chiricahua and Janos*, 146–51; Griffen, *Apaches at War and Peace*, 223–24; Almada, *Diccionarrio de historia, geografía, y biografía sonorenses*, 72–74; Francisco R. Almada, *Diccionarrio de historia, geografía, y biografía chihuahuenses* (Juarez: Impresora de Juárez, 1968), 39.

81. Benjamin Butler Harris, *The Gila Trail: The Texas Argonauts and the California Gold Rush*, edited by Richard H. Dillon (Norman: University of Oklahoma Press, 1960), 109.

82. Bliss and Woodward, *Don Santiago Kirker*, 11; Smith, *Borderlander*, 178, 224, 235–37.

83. José María Zuloaga to José B. Padilla, June 14, 1849, Presidio Records, part 7, folder 48, section 1; Griffen, *Apaches at War and Peace*, 227–29; Sweeney, *Mangas Coloradas*, 358–61.

84. Mabelle Eppard Martin, ed., "From Texas to California in 1849: Diary of C. C. Cox," *Southwestern Historical Quarterly* 29:2 (1925): 131.

85. "Gobierno del estado," *El Faro*, June 5, 1849 (*Periódico Oficial* 472, roll 3); "Contratas de sangre," *El Faro*, July 24, 1849 (*Periódico Oficial* 472, roll 3); "Chihuahua—Maj. Chevallie and the Indians," *Texas State Gazette* (Austin), October 20, 1849; Francisco R. Almada, "Gobernadores del estado: Gral. D. Angel Trías Sr.," *Boletín de la Sociedad Chihuahuense de Estudios Historicos* 3:12 (1942): 178; Francisco R. Almada, *Resumen de historia del estado de Chihuahua* (Mexico City: Librados Mexicanos, 1955), 235–36.

86. "Contratas de sangre."

87. Smith, "Scalp Hunting," 49–50.

88. Julius Froebel, *Seven Years' Travel in Central America, Northern Mexico, and the Far West of the United States* (London: Richard Bentley, 1859), 440–41. See also John G. Bourke, *On the Border with Crook* (New York: Charles Scribner's Sons, 1891), 117; and Grant Foreman, ed., *Marcy and the Gold Seekers: The Journal of Captain R. B. Marcy, with an Account of the Gold Rush over the Southern Route* (Norman: University of Oklahoma Press, 1939), 335–36.

89. George W. B. Evans, *Mexican Gold Trail: The Journal of a Forty-Niner*, edited by Glenn S. Dumke (San Marino, CA: Huntington Library, 2006), 133; "Apaches," *El Faro*, June 26, 1849 (*Periódico Oficial* 472, roll 3); "Indios barbaros," *El Faro*, July 7, 1849 (*Periódico Oficial* 472, roll 3).

90. "Extract from a Letter from Bvt. Maj. E. B. Babbitt," October 15, 1849, George T. Wood Records, box 301-18, folder 22.

91. George Crawford to John M. Clayton, November 8, 1849, and Crawford to George T. Wood, November 9, 1849, both in George T. Wood Records, box 301-18, folder 23.

92. Evans, *Mexican Gold Trail*, 133; "Apaches"; "Indios barbaros"; "Gobierno del estado," December 29, 1849; "Chihuahua—Maj. Chevallie and the Indians"; "Letter to Editor of State Gazette," *Texas State Gazette* (Austin), November 24, 1849; Horace Bell, *Reminiscences of a Ranger; or, Early Times in Southern California* (Santa Barbara, CA: Wallace Hebberd, 1927), 273–77.

93. "The Indian Troubles on the Colorado," *New-York Daily Tribune*, July 8, 1850; Foreman, *Marcy and the Gold Seekers*, 336n18; Samuel E. Chamberlain, *Recollections of a Rogue* (London: Museum Press, 1957), 258–90, quotations on 270, 273,

274, 290, emphasis in original; Harris, *Gila Trail*, 110–11. See also George Harwood Phillips, *Chiefs and Challengers: Indian Resistance and Cooperation in Southern California, 1769–1906* (Norman: University of Oklahoma Press, 2014), 98–100; Natale A. Zappia, *Traders and Raiders: The Indigenous World of the Colorado Basin, 1540– 1859* (Chapel Hill: University of North Carolina Press, 2014), 122–23; and Benjamin Madley, *An American Genocide: The United States and the California Indian Catastrophe, 1846–1873* (New Haven: Yale University Press, 2016), 180.

94. Peter H. Burnett to J. H. Bean, June 1, 1850, California Adjutant General's Office, Military Department, Adjutant General, Indian War Papers 1850–1880, microfilm F3753, roll 1, doc. 2. On the "Gila Expedition," see Wiliam B. Secrest, *When the Great Spirit Died: The Destruction of the California Indians, 1850–1860* (Sanger, CA: Word Dancer Press, 2003), 51–53; and Madley, *American Genocide*, 180–81, 191.

95. "Junta de guerra," *El Registro Oficial*, June 28, 1849, and "Secretaria del despacho del gobierno de Durango," *El Registro Oficial*, July 8, 1849, both in *Periódico Oficial de Durango*, University of Texas at El Paso, microfilm 493, roll 3.

96. Michael James Box, *Adventures and Explorations in New and Old Mexico* (New York: James Miller, 1869), 216–17.

97. Smith, "Scalp Hunting," 63–67.

98. Smith, "Scalp Hunting," 73nn11–13.

99. On the Seri tribe, see Edward Moser, "Seri Bands," *Kiva* 28:3 (1963): 14–27; and Conrad J. Bahre, "Historic Seri Residence, Range, and Sociopolitical Structure," *Kiva* 45:3 (1980): 197–209.

100. Smith, *Borderlander*, 231.

101. Griffen, *Apaches at War and Peace*, 232.

102. Edwin R. Sweeney, " 'I Had Lost All': Geronimo and the Carrasco Massacre of 1851," *Journal of Arizona History* 27 (Spring 1986): 35–52.

103. When interviewing Geronimo in the early 1900s, S. M. Barrett wrote, "It is impossible to get Geronimo to understand that [Mexican] troops served the general government instead of any particular town. He still thinks each town independent and each city a separate tribe." S. M. Barrett, ed., *Geronimo's Story of His Life* (New York: Duffield, 1906), 106n1.

104. Rachel St. John, *Line in the Sand: A History of the Western U.S.-Mexico Border* (Princeton, NJ: Princeton University Press, 2011), 12–38.

105. On "border lines," see Alice L. Baumgartner, "The Line of Positive Safety: Borders and Boundaries in the Rio Grande Valley, 1848–1880," *Journal of American History* 101:4 (2015): 1107.

106. Sylvester Mowry to James W. Denver, November 10, 1857, in *Report of the Commissioner of Indian Affairs, Accompanying the Annual Report of the Secretary of the Interior for the Year 1857* (Washington, DC: William H. Harris, 1858), 299, 303; Sylvester Mowry, *Arizona and Sonora: The Geography, History, and*

Resources of the Silver Region of North America (New York: Harper Brothers, 1864), 68.

107. Frederick A. Ober, *Travels in Mexico and Life among the Mexicans* (Denver, CO: Perry, 1883), 627, emphasis in original.

108. John Nicolson, ed., *The Arizona of Joseph Pratt Allyn: Letters from a Pioneer Judge, Observations and Travels, 1863–1866* (Tucson: University of Arizona Press, 1974), 68–70.

109. Daniel Ellis Conner, *Joseph Reddeford Walker and the Arizona Adventure* (Norman: University of Oklahoma Press, 1956), 188, 335.

110. On Goodwin, see Jacoby, *Shadows at Dawn*, 112–13. On the Camp Grant Massacre, see Chip Colwell-Chanthaphonh, *Massacre at Camp Grant: Forgetting and Remembering Apache History* (Tucson: University of Arizona Press, 2007); Ian W. Record, *Big Sycamore Stands Alone: The Western Apaches, Aravaipa, and the Struggle for Place* (Norman: University of Oklahoma Press, 2008), 230–45; and Jacoby, *Shadows at Dawn*.

111. Conner, *Joseph Reddeford Walker and the Arizona Adventure*, 227–28. See also Jacoby, *Shadows at Dawn*, 113–14.

112. Ball, *Indeh*, 20; Boyer and Gayton, *Apache Mothers and Daughters*, 52–53; Sweeney, *Mangas Coloradas*, 455–57; William S. Kiser, *Illusions of Empire: The Civil War and Reconstruction in the U.S.-Mexico Borderlands* (Philadelphia: University of Pennsylvania Press, 2022), 57–58.

113. Ball, *In the Days of Victorio*, 48.

114. Joseph Rodman West to William McCleave, June 21, 1863, in *The War of the Rebellion: A Compilation of the Official Records of the Union and Confederate Armies*, ser. 1 (Washington, DC: Government Printing Office, 1882), 50, pt. 2:490; Sweeney, *Cochise*, 213.

115. Albert J. Fountain to Dear Brother, October 24, 1863, in Maurice Garland Fulton Papers, University of Arizona, Tucson. I thank John P. Wilson for providing a transcript of this letter.

116. *Annual Report on the Commercial Relations between the United States and Foreign Nations, Made by the Secretary of State, for the Year Ending September 30, 1870* (Washington DC: Government Printing Office, 1871), 299.

117. *Memorial and Affidavits Showing Outrages Perpetrated by the Apache Indians, in the Territory of Arizona, during the Years 1869 and 1870* (San Francisco: Francis and Valentine, 1871); "The Indian Question," *Congressional Globe*, January 28, 1871, 307–12, quotation on 308.

118. Almada, *Diccionario de historia, geografía, y biografía sonorenses*, 76.

119. Dan L. Thrapp, *Victorio and the Mimbres Apaches* (Norman: University of Oklahoma Press, 1974), 3–10.

120. Ball, *Indeh*, 61. See also Basso, *Western Apache Raiding and Warfare*, 270–75.

121. On Lozen, see Thrapp, *Victorio and the Mimbres Apaches*, 306, 374n21. For firsthand accounts, see Ball, *In the Days of Victorio*, 11, 14–15, 128, quotation on 14; Ball, *Indeh*, 62; and Sherry Robinson, *Apache Voices: Their Stories of Survival as Told to Eve Ball* (Albuquerque: University of New Mexico Press, 2000), 3–15.

122. Robert N. Watt, *"I Will Not Surrender the Hair of a Horse's Tail": The Victorio Campaign, 1879* (Solihull, UK: Helion, 2017), 80–194.

123. Louis H. Scott to William Hunter, October 22, 1880, and Scott to Department of State, October 22, 1880, both in National Archives, RG59, US State Department, Despatches Received by the Department of State from U.S. Consuls in Chihuahua, 1826–1906, microcopy T-167, reel 3. On Tres Castillos, see D. Joaquín Terrazas, *Memorias* (Juarez: El Agricultor Mexicano, 1905), 74–82; Ball, *In the Days of Victorio*, 88–99; Robinson, *Apache Voices*, 17–26; Kühn, *Chronicles of War*, 240; and Robert N. Watt, *"Horses Worn to Mere Shadows": The Victorio Campaign, 1880* (Solihull, UK: Helion, 2019), 385–412.

124. Blyth, *Chiricahua and Janos*, 195–96.

125. "Greeting the Victors," *Santa Fe New Mexican*, November 2, 1880.

126. Terrazas, *Memorias*, 4.

127. Conrad, *Apache Diaspora*, 225–27.

128. "Money for Indian Scalps: Arizona and New-Mexico Settlers Propose to Destroy the Savages," *New York Times*, October 12, 1885.

129. Francisco R. Almada, *Juárez y terrazas: Aclaraciones históricas* (Chihuahua: Libros Mexicanos, 1958), 628.

130. Angie Debo, *Geronimo: The Man, His Time, His Place* (Norman: University of Oklahoma Press, 1976), 7.

131. I calculated the Chihuahua figures by combining the statistics in Griffen, *Utmost Good Faith*, 237–42, 254–307. For Comanche and Kiowa raiding, see DeLay, *War of a Thousand Deserts*, 313–40, casualty figure on 318.

132. Michael Steck to David Meriwether, July 30, 1855, University of New Mexico Center for Southwest Research, Inventory of the Michael Steck Papers, microcopy E93, series 2, roll 1. For the Apache population, see Sweeney, *Mangas Coloradas*, 7.

133. Bliss and Woodward, *Don Santiago Kirker*, 9; Smith, *Borderlander*, 170.

134. Escudero, *Observaciones sobre el estado actual del departamento de Chihuahua*, 12; Francisco R. Almada, "Los Apaches," *Boletín de la Sociedad Chihuahuense de Estudios Historicos* 2:1 (1939): 10–12.

135. On the effects of Apache raiding in northern Mexico, see Camacho, *Defensa y política en la frontera norte de México*, 48–66.

136. Barrett, ed., *Geronimo's Story of His Life*, 110; Sweeney, " 'I Had Lost All,' " 35–52.

137. Lindsay, *Murder State*, 4, 9–10, 26; Benjamin Madley, "California's Yuki Indians: Defining Genocide in Native American History," *Western Historical Quarterly* 39:3 (2008): 303–332.

138. Hobbs, *Wild Life in the Far West*, 81–100, 111–12, quotation on 409.

4 Scalping Atrocities on the Texas Frontier

1. Entry for "G. Baylor," 1860 US Census, Parker County, Texas, p. 25. I thank Jerry Thompson for alerting me to this source.

2. George Wythe Baylor, *Into the Far, Wild Country: True Tales of the Old Southwest*, edited by Jerry D. Thompson (El Paso: Texas Western Press, 1996), 149–71, quotations on 158, 159, 171; J. W. Wilbarger, *Indian Depredations in Texas: Reliable Accounts of Battles, Wars, Adventures, Forays, Murders, Massacres, etc.; Together with Biographical Sketches of Many of the Most Noted Indian Fighters and Frontiersmen of Texas* (Austin, TX: Hutchings, 1889), 519.

3. Baylor, *Into the Far, Wild Country*, 171; "Baylor's Scalps, Politics, Etc.," *Weekly Telegraph* (Houston), July 31, 1860. I thank my former student Ione Mathews for alerting me to this article.

4. For examples, see "Minutes of Indian Council at Tehuacana Creek," March 28, 1843, "Letter from R. H. Williams to Thomas G. Western," July 16, 1845, "The Comanche and Other Tribes of Texas; and the Policy to Be Pursued Respecting Them," David G. Burnet, September 29, 1847, "Letter from J. R. Baylor to R. S. Neighbors," October 7, 1855, "Letter from W. Jones to H. R. Runnels," October 17, 1858, "Letter from N. W. Battle, F. L. Denison, and J. M. Norris to Sam Houston," November 13, 1860, "Letter from W. W. O. Stanfield to Sam Houston," December 5, 1860, "Petition from Lampasas County to J. W. Throckmorton," July 15, 1866, and "Letter from S. F. Mains to J. A. Dumas," July 29, 1866, all in Dorman H. Winfrey and James M. Day, eds., *The Indian Papers of Texas and the Southwest, 1825–1916*, 5 vols. (Austin, TX: Pemberton Press, 1996), 1:156, 290–92, 3:84–99, esp. 87, 94, 251–53, 297, 4:42–44, 44–46, 95–96, 99–100.

5. W. B. DeWees, *Letters from an Early Settler of Texas* (Waco, TX: Texian Press, 1968), 37–40, quotations on 40; *Papers of James Hampton Kuykendall and William Kuykendall 1822–1897* (unpublished manuscript, 1940), 1:44–45, Dolph Briscoe Center for American History, University of Texas at Austin, Kuykendall Family Papers, box 3F82, folder 2.

6. Kelly F. Himmel, *The Conquest of the Karankawas and the Tonkawas, 1821–1859* (College Station: Texas A&M University Press, 1999), 48–49, 83–84.

7. See Andrew J. Torget, *Seeds of Empire: Cotton, Slavery, and the Transformation of the Texas Borderlands, 1800–1850* (Chapel Hill: University of North Carolina Press, 2015). For Anglo and Tejano population figures, see Torget, *Seeds of Empire*, 159–60.

8. George W. Bonnell to Secretary of War of the Republic of Texas, November 3, 1838, in *Communication from the Commissioner of Indian Affairs, and Other Documents, in Relation to the Texas Indians*, 30th Cong., 1st Sess., Senate Report No. 171, p. 38. See also Brian DeLay, *War of a Thousand Deserts: Indian Raids and the U.S.-Mexican War* (New Haven: Yale University Press, 2008), 76. On Houston's

Indian policy, see Anna Muckleroy, "The Indian Policy of the Republic of Texas, II," *Southwestern Historical Quarterly* 26:1 (1922): 8–11.

9. Sam Houston to the Texas Senate, November 8, 1836, in Ernest William Winkler, ed., *Secret Journals of the Senate of the Republic of Texas, 1836–1845* (Austin, TX: Austin Printing, 1911), 19.

10. Houston to "The Chiefs of Six Tribes," November 11, 1836, in Amelia W. Williams and Eugene C. Barker, eds., *The Writings of Sam Houston, 1813–1863*, 8 vols. (Austin, TX: Jenkins, 1970), 1:479–80.

11. "Annual Presidential Message to the Congress," November 21, 1837, in Williams and Barker, *Writings of Houston*, 2:158.

12. "Treaty with the Tonkaway Indians," November 22, 1837, in Winkler, *Secret Journals of the Senate of the Republic of Texas*, 103–4; Himmel, *Conquest of the Karankawas and the Tonkawas*, 64.

13. Joseph Baker to Mirabeau B. Lamar, January 2, 1839, in Charles Adams Gulick Jr. and Katherine Elliott, eds., *The Papers of Mirabeau Buonaparte Lamar*, 6 vols. (Austin, TX: A. C. Baldwin and Sons, 1922), 2:397–98.

14. Daniel Castro Romero, *Cuélcahen Ndé: The Castros of the Lipan Apache Band of Texas*, edited and translated by Santiago Castro Castro and Valentina Sambrano Rodriguez (San Antonio: Lipan Apache Band of Texas, 2004), 24–25; Nancy McGown Minor, *The Light Gray People: An Ethno-History of the Lipan Apaches of Texas and Northern Mexico* (Lanham, MD: University Press of America, 2009), 106; Jean Louis Berlandier, *The Indians of Texas in 1830*, edited by John C. Ewers (Washington, DC: Smithsonian Institution Press, 1969), 134; 1822 Lipan Apache Treaty, Eberstadt Collection, Dolph Briscoe Center for American History, University of Texas at Austin. See also Sherry Robinson, *I Fought a Good Fight: A History of the Lipan Apaches* (Denton: University of North Texas Press, 2013), 175–76.

15. Brian DeLay, "Independent Indians and the U.S.-Mexican War," *American Historical Review* 112:1 (2007): 35, 40; Thomas A. Britten, *The Lipan Apaches: People of Wind and Lightning* (Albuquerque: University of New Mexico Press, 2009), 184–94; Nancy McGown Minor, *Turning Adversity to Advantage: A History of the Lipan Apaches of Texas and Northern Mexico, 1700–1900* (Lanham, MD: University Press of America, 2009), 139–50; James David Nichols, *The Limits of Liberty: Mobility and the Making of the Eastern U.S.-Mexico Border* (Lincoln: University of Nebraska Press, 2018), 37–38.

16. Robinson, *I Fought a Good Fight*, 186, 220–21; Nichols, *Limits of Liberty*, 172. On tribal division, see Andrée F. Sjoberg, "Lipan Apache Culture in Historical Perspective," *Southwestern Journal of Anthropology* 9:1 (1953): 78–79, 93–94; and Minor, *Light Gray People*, 89–100, 106–8.

17. Minor, *Light Gray People*, 71–76, 109–16, 131–40, quotation on 71.

18. Robinson, *I Fought a Good Fight*, 3–8, 175, quotations on 4; Minor, *Light Gray People*, 6, 9–14, 81–83, 135–36; Morris Edward Opler, *Myths and Legends of the Lipan Apache Indians* (New York: American Folk-Lore Society, 1940), 36–37. For an indigenous history of the Cuélcahen Ndé, see Enrique Gilbert-Michael Maestas, "Culture and History of Native American Peoples of South Texas" (PhD diss., University of Texas at Austin, 2003).

19. Gary Clayton Anderson, *The Conquest of Texas: Ethnic Cleansing in the Promised Land, 1820–1875* (Norman: University of Oklahoma Press, 2005), 159–60.

20. Report of Edward Burleson, November 1, 1837, in *Journal of the House of Representatives, Republic of Texas, Called Session of September 25, 1837 and Regular Session Commencing November 6, 1837* (Houston, TX: Niles, 1838), 81–83.

21. I. W. Burton to Sam Houston, October 12, 1837, in Winkler, *Secret Journals of the Senate of the Republic of Texas*, 76.

22. Morris W. Foster, *Being Comanche: The Social History of an American Indian Community* (Tucson: University of Arizona Press, 1991), 36–38; Pekka Hämäläinen, *The Comanche Empire* (New Haven: Yale University Press, 2008), 25, 105, 151, 311. For an eyewitness account of Comanche marksmanship, see Josiah Gregg, *Commerce of the Prairies*, edited by Max L. Moorhead (Norman: University of Oklahoma Press, 1954), 245.

23. Thomas W. Kavanagh, *Comanche Political History: An Ethnohistorical Perspective, 1706–1875* (Lincoln: University of Nebraska Press, 1996), 2, 28–36, 57.

24. Ernest Wallace and E. Adamson Hoebel, *The Comanches: Lords of the South Plains* (Norman: University of Oklahoma Press, 1952), 155–84, 189, 245–84.

25. Wallace and Hoebel, *Comanches*, 245–84. On Comanche mourning, see Daniel J. Gelo and Christopher J. Wickham, *Comanches and Germans on the Texas Frontier: The Ethnology of Heinrich Berghaus* (College Station: Texas A&M University Press, 2018), 106; and Gregg, *Commerce of the Prairies*, 439. On the Comanche word for scalp, see Gregg, *Commerce of the Prairies*, 155.

26. Wallace and Hoebel, *Comanches*, 254–59, quotation on 256.

27. On medicine power, see Donald L. Fixico, *Call for Change: The Medicine Way of American Indian History, Ethos, and Reality* (Lincoln: University of Nebraska Press, 2013), 165–66. On Apaches, see Keith Basso, ed., *Western Apache Raiding and Warfare: From the Notes of Grenville Goodwin* (Tucson: University of Arizona Press, 1971), 276–78.

28. Houston to the Honorable House of Representatives, May 25, 1838, in *Journal of the House of Representatives, Republic of Texas, Second Congress, Adjourned Session* (Houston, TX: Telegraph Office, 1838), 171–73; "Highly Important," *Telegraph and Texas Register* (Houston), February 24, 1838 (first quotation); "The Commissioners Who Recently Left Bexar," *Telegraph and Texas Register* (Houston), March 17, 1838 (second quotation).

29. Paul D. Lack, "The Córdova Revolt," in Gerald E. Poyo, ed., *Tejano Journey, 1770–1850* (Austin: University of Texas Press, 1996), 89–109. See also Felipe A. Latorre and Dolores L. Latorre, *The Mexican Kickapoo Indians* (Austin: University of Texas Press, 1976), 10–11.

30. Hugh McLeod to Lamar, January 18, 1839, and Albert Sidney Johnston to Chief Bowles, April 10, 1839, both in Gulick and Elliott, *Papers of Lamar*, 2:423–24, 522–23.

31. Anderson, *Conquest of Texas*, 164–67. On Sam Houston's relations with the Cherokees, see Dianna Everett, *The Texas Cherokees: A People between Two Fires, 1819–1840* (Norman: University of Oklahoma Press, 1990), 70–71, 85–88.

32. "Fannin's First Campaign," in Wilbarger, *Indian Depredations in Texas*, 426–28.

33. Proceedings of November 24, 1838, in *Journal of the House of Representatives of the Republic of Texas, Regular Session of Third Congress, Nov. 5, 1838* (Houston, TX: S. Whiting, 1839), 84–86.

34. Stanley Siegel, *The Poet President of Texas: The Life of Mirabeau B. Lamar, President of the Republic of Texas* (Austin, TX: Pemberton Press, 1977), 7–13, 16, 19–20, 32, 37–38, 44.

35. First Annual Message of Mirabeau B. Lamar, December 19, 1838, in *Journal of the House of Representatives of the Republic of Texas, Regular Session of Third Congress, Nov. 5, 1838*, 167–95, quotations on 173–74, 176. See also "M. B. Lamar Speech in Defense of His Administration," May 28, 1840, in Gulick and Elliott, *Papers of Lamar*, 3:393–94. On Lamar's Indian policy, see Anna Muckleroy, "The Indian Policy of the Republic of Texas, III," *Southwestern Historical Quarterly* 26:2 (1922): 128–31.

36. Felix Huston to Lamar, December 31, 1838, in Gulick and Elliott, *Papers of Lamar*, 2:377.

37. See Anderson, *Conquest of Texas*.

38. "Republic of Texas in Account Current with John C. Hays," November 20, 1845, Archives and Information Services Division, Texas State Library and Archives Commission, Texas Adjutant General's Department Ranger Records, box 401-1242, folder 3 (hereafter cited as Texas Ranger Records); "Republic of Texas in Account Current with John C. Hays," October 27, 1845, Texas Ranger Records, box 401-1242, folder 3; "Pay Vouchers," Texas Ranger Records, box 401-1242, folder 15; "Pay Rolls and Extra-Duty Men," Texas Ranger Records, box 401-1242, folder 19; "Statement of Advances Made by the State of Texas for Frontier Defense, from February 28, 1855 to September 15, 1858," Texas Ranger Records, box 401-1153, folder 8. On Mexican peons, see Nichols, *The Limits of Liberty*, 80–102; and William S. Kiser, *Borderlands of Slavery: The Struggle over Captivity and Peonage in the American Southwest* (Philadelphia: University of Pennsylvania Press, 2017), 88–111.

39. Mark E. Nackman, "The Making of the Texan Citizen Soldier, 1835–1860," *Southwestern Historical Quarterly* 78:3 (1975): 231–53.

40. Anderson, *Conquest of Texas*, 8–9; Walter Prescott Webb, *The Texas Rangers: A Century of Frontier Defense* (Boston: Houghton Mifflin, 1935), 29–50.

41. R. H. Williams, *With the Border Ruffians: Memories of the Far West, 1852–1868*, edited by E. W. Williams (Lincoln: University of Nebraska Press, 1982), 168, 188–94, 221, 323.

42. Report of the Committee on Indian Affairs, January 9, 1839, in *Journal of the House of Representatives of the Republic of Texas*, 311–12, 318.

43. Joseph Milton Nance, *After San Jacinto: The Texas-Mexican Frontier, 1836–1841* (Austin: University of Texas Press, 1963), 85–88; H. P. N. Gammel, comp., *The Laws of Texas, 1822–1897*, vol. 2 (Austin, TX: Gammel, 1898), 84–85, 93. For the "militia act," see Gammel, *Laws of Texas*, 15–20, 29–30.

44. "The President's Address Calling for Volunteers for the Protection of the Frontiers," February 28, 1839, in Gulick and Elliott, *Papers of Lamar*, 2:474–75.

45. "Mexican Mode of Warfare against the Camanche [*sic*] and Apache Indians," *Niles' National Register* (Baltimore), September 7, 1839.

46. John J. Moore to Johnston, March 10, 1839, in Winfrey and Day, *Indian Papers of Texas and the Southwest*, 1:57–59; "Colonel Moore's Expedition," in Wilbarger, *Indian Depredations in Texas*, 144–46, quotation on 145. See also Anderson, *Conquest of Texas*, 175–76; DeLay, *War of a Thousand Deserts*, 76–77; and Robinson, *I Fought a Good Fight*, 192–96.

47. Noah Smithwick, *The Evolution of a State; or, Recollections of Old Texas Days*, edited by Alwyn Barr (Austin, TX: W. Thomas Taylor, 1995), vii–ix, 75, 125, 134–37, 153, 163, quotations on 136, 137. On Lipan Apache motivations in warfare, see Minor, *Light Gray People*, 131–32, 135–36. For Lipan accounts of the Comanche rivalry, see Opler, *Myths and Legends of the Lipan Apache Indians*, 236–59.

48. For firsthand reports, see Hugh McLeod to Lamar, March 20, 1840, Archives and Information Services Division, Texas State Library and Archives Commission, Andrew Jackson Houston Collection, box 2-22/172, folder 1958; Johnston to William S. Fisher, March 30, 1840, in Winfrey and Day, *Indian Papers of Texas and the Southwest*, 1:106–8. For the Nichols quotation, see Catherine W. McDowell, ed., *Now You Hear My Horn: The Journal of James Wilson Nichols, 1820–1887* (Austin: University of Texas Press, 1967), 40. On the Council House Massacre generally, see Kavanagh, *Comanche Political History*, 262–64; Anderson, *Conquest of Texas*, 181–83; DeLay, *War of a Thousand Deserts*, 77–78; and Hämäläinen, *Comanche Empire*, 216.

49. "Late and Important from Texas," *Texas Sentinel* (Austin), April 29, 1840.

50. On Potsanaquahip, see Hämäläinen, *Comanche Empire*, 216–18, 225, 310–11, 435n48.

51. J. H. Kerr to Moore, August 9, 1840, in Gulick and Elliott, *Papers of Lamar*, 3:428–29.

52. John J. Linn, *Reminiscences of Fifty Years in Texas* (New York: Sadlier, 1883), 338–44, quotation on 338.

53. William H. Watts to Editor of the Austin City Gazette, in *Telegraph and Texas Register* (Houston), September 2, 1840.

54. McDowell, *Now You Hear My Horn*, 55–74, quotations on 65–66; John Holmes Jenkins III, ed., *Recollections of Early Texas: The Memoirs of John Holland Jenkins* (Austin: University of Texas Press, 1958), 60–68. See also Joseph Milton Nance, *Attack and Counterattack: The Texas-Mexican Frontier, 1842* (Austin: University of Texas Press, 1964), 24n47.

55. On the raid, see Anderson, *Conquest of Texas*, 187–89; and Michael L. Collins, *Texas Devils: Rangers and Regulars on the Lower Rio Grande, 1846–1861* (Norman: University of Oklahoma Press, 2008), 21.

56. Huston to House of Representatives, September 20, 1840, in *Journals of the House of Representatives of the Republic of Texas, Fifth Congress First Session, 1840–1841* (Austin, TX: Cruger and Wing, 1841), 77.

57. Anderson, *Conquest of Texas*, 190–91.

58. "To Col. John H. Moore and his Volunteer Associates," *Texas Sentinel* (Austin), November 14, 1840; "The Citizens of Austin," *Telegraph and Texas Register* (Houston), November 18, 1840.

59. Eli Chandler to Branch T. Archer, May 26, 1841, in Harriet Smither, ed., *Journals of the Sixth Congress of the Republic of Texas, 1841–1842, to Which Are Added the Special Laws*, 3 vols. (Austin, TX: Capital Printing, 1945), 3:413–14; William W. Porter to Archer, June 5, 1841, and James Smith to Lamar, June 13, 1841, both in Archives and Information Services Division, Texas State Library and Archives Commission, Texas Adjutant General's Department Army Papers, box 401-1307, folder 15 (hereafter cited as Texas Army Papers).

60. Chandler to Archer, June 19, 1841, in Smither, *Journals of the Sixth Congress of the Republic of Texas*, 3:419–21; G. B. Erath to Archer, August 12, 1841, Texas Army Papers, box 401-1308, folder 3.

61. McDowell, *Now You Hear My Horn*, 76, 123–24; Mark B. Lewis to Archer, June 2, 1841, Texas Army Papers, box 401-1307, folder 14; "Andrew Nelson Erskine" (unpublished manuscript), 1–7, Dolph Briscoe Center for American History, University of Texas at Austin, Andrew Nelson Erskine Papers, box 2D107, folder 163.

62. John Coffee Hays, "Report of the Battle of Walker's Creek," June 16, 1844, in *Appendix to the Journals of the Ninth Congress of the Republic of Texas* (Washington, TX: Miller and Cushney, 1845), 32–33; Hays to Archer, July 1, 1841, Dolph Briscoe Center for American History, University of Texas at Austin, John Coffee Hays Collection, box 3F176, correspondence folder (hereafter cited as John Coffee Hays Collection); Hays to Archer, August 13, 1841, Texas Army Papers, box 401-1308, folder 3. See also Kavanagh, *Comanche Political History*, 268–69. On Hays generally, see "Sketch of Colonel John C. Hays, Texas Ranger" (unpublished manuscript by John Caperton, 1922), John Coffee Hays Collection, box 2R35.

63. Houston to L. B. Franks, January 5, 1842, in Smither, *Journals of the Sixth Congress*, 3:129.

64. Houston to Franks, February 1, 1842, in Smither, *Journals of the Sixth Congress*, 3:129–30.

65. Branch T. Archer to Lamar, September 30, 1841, and G. W. Hockley to Houston, June 23, 1842, both in Smither, *Journals of the Sixth Congress*, 3:362, 110–11.

66. "A Request in Behalf of Castro, the Lipan Chief," June 21, 1842, and "To the Texas Congress," June 27, 1842, both in Williams and Barker, *Writings of Sam Houston*, 3:73, 74–77.

67. "Seven Lipan Warriors," *Telegraph and Texas Register* (Houston), March 10, 1838; "A Report Has Reached Us," *Telegraph and Texas Register* (Houston), July 20, 1842. On Cuelgas de Castro, see Britten, *Lipan Apaches*, 184–94; Robinson, *I Fought a Good Fight*, 174–83; and Minor, *Light Gray People*, 106.

68. "The Lipans," *Telegraph and Texas Register* (Houston), November 23, 1842. On Flacco, see Robinson, *I Fought a Good Fight*, 191–92; and Minor, *Light Gray People*, 107.

69. Nichols, *Limits of Liberty*, 171–72, 174–78, 182–87; Minor, *Turning Adversity to Advantage*, 153–55.

70. For examples, see Edmund J. Davis to Elisha M. Pease, March 13, 1854, and Hamilton P. Bee to Pease, March 13, 1854, both in Winfrey and Day, *Indian Papers of Texas and the Southwest*, 5:159–63, 164–65.

71. On Narbonne, see "Commanche [*sic*] Ambassador," *Telegraph and Texas Register* (Houston), June 8, 1842.

72. Houston to Count Leontio de Narbonne, March 19, 1842, Houston to G. W. Adams, April 14, 1842, and Houston to H. E. Scott, July 5, 1842, all in Smither, *Journals of the Sixth Congress*, 3:131–32, 132–33, 135.

73. "Proceedings of the House of Representatives," in Smither, *Journals of the Sixth Congress*, 3:136–37.

74. Houston to Gentleman of the Senate and of the House of Representatives, December 1, 1842, in *Journals of the House of Representatives of the Seventh Congress of the Republic of Texas, Convened at Washington, on the 14th Nov., 1842* (Washington, TX: Thomas Johnson, 1843), 24–25.

75. Houston to Gentlemen of the Senate and of the House of Representatives, in *Journals of the House of Representatives of the Eighth Congress of the Republic of Texas* (Houston, TX: Cruger and Moore, 1844), 20.

76. *Correspondence with Texas, on the Subject of the Annexation*, 29th Cong., 1st Sess., House Exec. Doc. No. 2, pp. 31–136. See also Kavanagh, *Comanche Political History*, 264–78.

77. "Letter from J. P. Henderson to T. I. Fauntleroy," July 31, 1846, and "Letter from A. C. Horton to W. L. Marcy," August 8, 1846, both in Winfrey and Day, *Indian Papers of Texas and the Southwest*, 3:70–71, 71–73.

78. Robert S. Neighbors to William Medill, March 2, 1848, in *Communication from the Commissioner of Indian Affairs, and Other Documents, in Relation to the Texas Indians*, 30th Cong., 1st Sess., Senate Report No. 171, p. 24.

79. *Memorial of the Legislature of Texas, Praying the Reimbursement of Expenses Incurred by the State in Providing for the Military Defenses of Her Frontier in 1848*, 31st Cong., 1st Sess., Senate Misc. Doc. No. 97; *Claims for Spoliations Committed by Indians and Mexicans*, 36th Cong., 1st Sess., House Report No. 535; "Joint Resolution of Texas Legislature," November 23, 1857, Texas Ranger Records, box 401-1153, folder 7.

80. "The Army," *Congressional Globe*, May 23, 1850, p. 1049.

81. "Indian Appropriation Bill," *Congressional Globe*, September 27, 1850, p. 2035.

82. "House of Representatives," *Congressional Globe*, February 19, 1851, pp. 600–607, quotations on 602, 605, 606.

83. W. H. C. Whiting to George Deas, March 14, 1850, in *Report of the Secretary of War, Enclosing the Report of Lieutenant W. H. C. Whiting's Reconnaissance of the Western Frontier of Texas*, 31st Cong., 1st Sess., Senate Exec. Doc. No. 64, p. 248.

84. Randolph B. Marcy to Samuel Cooper, January 15, 1855, in *Message of the President of the United States Communicating in Compliance with a Resolution of the Senate of February 26, Calling for a Copy of the Report and Maps of Captain Marcy of His Explorations of the Big Witchita and Head Waters of the Brazos Rivers*, 34th Cong., 1st Sess., Senate Exec. Doc. No. 60, p. 40.

85. "The Indians—General Harney," *Texas State Gazette* (Austin), September 1, 1849.

86. General Orders No. 27, June 4, 1850, and George Brooks to Peter H. Bell, August 10, 1850, both in Archives and Information Services Division, Texas State Library and Archives Commission, Texas Governor Peter H. Bell Records, box 301-18, folder 2.

87. *Message of the President of the United States*, 24–25; "We Learn from the Austin Democrat," *Telegraph and Texas Register* (Houston), February 10, 1848.

88. George M. Brooke to Roger Jones, August 31, 1849, in *Documents Accompanying the Report of the Secretary of War to the President*, 31st Cong., 1st Sess., House Exec. Doc. No. 5, p. 143.

89. Report of Luke Lea, November 27, 1850, in *Annual Report of the Commissioner of Indian Affairs*, 31st Cong., 2nd Sess., Senate Exec. Doc. No. 1, p. 44. On the Indian Removal Act and Trail of Tears, see Francis Paul Prucha, *The Great Father: The United States Government and the American Indians*, abridged ed. (Lincoln: University of Nebraska Press, 1986), 64–93. On "alternative to extinction," see Prucha, *Great Father*, 110; and Robert A. Trennert Jr., *Alternative to Extinction: Federal Indian Policy and the Beginnings of the Reservation System* (Philadelphia: Temple University Press, 1975).

90. Ian Anson Lee, "The Mesilla Guard: Race and Violence in Nineteenth-Century New Mexico," *New Mexico Historical Review* 95:3 (2020): 323–53.

91. John C. Duval, *The Adventures of Big-Foot Wallace*, edited by Mabel Major and Rebecca Smith Lee (Lincoln: University of Nebraska Press, 1966), 112–13, 159–66, quotation on 159; Britten, *Lipan Apaches*, 207–8.

92. Duval, *The Adventures of Big-Foot Wallace*, 105–9, quotations on 106. See also "The San Antonio Ledger," *Texas State Gazette* (Austin), August 31, 1850.

93. Robinson, *I Fought a Good Fight*, 227; Nichols, *Limits of Liberty*, 172–73, 176; Minor, *From Adversity to Advantage*, 161–68.

94. "To the Editor of the State Gazette," *Texas State Gazette* (Austin), January 4, 1851.

95. Dr. A. Wislizenus, *Memoir of a Tour to Northern Mexico, Connected with Col. Doniphan's Expedition, in 1846 and 1847* (Washington, DC: Tippin and Streeper, 1848), 59.

96. DeLay, *War of a Thousand Deserts*, 306. On the US Army in antebellum Texas, see Robert M. Utley, *Frontiersmen in Blue: The United States Army and the Indian, 1848–1865* (Lincoln: University of Nebraska Press, 1967), 125–30; Durwood Ball, *Army Regulars on the Western Frontier, 1848–1861* (Norman: University of Oklahoma Press, 2001), 127–38; and Robert Wooster, *The American Military Frontiers: The United States Army in the West, 1783–1900* (Norman: University of Oklahoma Press, 2009), 125, 132.

97. Francis R. Lubbock, *Six Decades in Texas; or, Memoirs of Francis Richard Lubbock, Governor of Texas in War Time, 1861–1863* (Austin, TX: Ben C. Jones, 1900), 183.

98. Melinda Rankin, *Texas in 1850* (Boston: Damrell and Moore, 1850), 171–72. See also "Remarks of Col. V. E. Howard," *Texas State Gazette* (Austin), June 29, 1850.

99. Robert S. Neighbors to Peter H. Bell, March 23, 1850, in *Appendix to the House of Representatives Journals, of the Third Legislature, State of Texas, Second Session* (Austin, TX: Wm. H. Cushney, 1850), 4–5, quotation on 5. See also William S. Kiser, *Dragoons in Apacheland: Conquest and Resistance in Southern New Mexico, 1846–1861* (Norman: University of Oklahoma Press, 2012), 76.

100. William M. Williams to Charles G. Keenan, August 26, 1850, in *Journals of the House of Representatives of the State of Texas, Extra Session—Third Legislature* (Austin: Texas State Gazette Office, 1850), 64–68, 86. See also *Appendix to the House of Representatives Journals, of the Third Legislature, State of Texas, Second Session*, 102.

101. Report of Edward Burleson, August 30, 1850, in *Journals of the Senate of the State of Texas, Extra Session—Third Legislature* (Austin: Texas State Gazette Office, 1850), 75–77. See also "The Frontier—The Government," *Texas State Gazette* (Austin), May 11, 1850; "The State Gazette," *Texas State Gazette* (Austin), October 26, 1850; "The State Gazette," *Texas State Gazette* (Austin), November 16, 1850; and "Frontier Defense," *Texas State Gazette* (Austin), October 23, 1852.

102. Collins, *Texas Devils*, 51–53; Wilbarger, *Indian Depredations in Texas*, 616–19; John Salmon Ford, *Rip Ford's Texas*, edited by Stephen B. Oates (Austin: University of Texas Press, 1963), 177–79, 184–87.

103. Williams, *With the Border Ruffians*, 188–94, quotations on 192, 194.
104. Frederick Law Olmsted, *A Journey through Texas; or, A Saddle-Trip on the Southwestern Frontier* (Austin: University of Texas Press, 1978), 297–98, 300, 302.
105. "From the Austin Intelligencer," in *Report of the Secretary of War*, 35th Cong., 2nd Sess., Senate Exec. Doc. No. 1, pp. 253–54.
106. See, e.g., Hardin R. Runnels to James Bowland, October 4, 1858, Texas Ranger Records, box 401-1153, folder 8.
107. John S. Ford to Runnels, May 22, 1858, and A. Nelson to Ford, May 21, 1858, both in *Protection of the Frontier of Texas*, 35th Cong., 2nd Sess., House Exec. Doc. 27, 17–21, 21–22; J. E. Powell to Lieutenant [Robert] Offley, August 26, 1858, in *Report of the Secretary of War*, 35th Cong., 2nd Sess., Senate Exec. Doc. No. 1, pp. 421–23. See also Hämäläinen, *Comanche Empire*, 310; Himmel, *Conquest of the Karankawas and the Tonkawas*, 115–16; and Richard B. McCaslin, *Fighting Stock: John S. "Rip" Ford of Texas* (Fort Worth: Texas Christian University Press, 2011), 71–75.
108. Indian Depredation Claims, Archives and Information Services Division, Texas State Library and Archives Commission, Records Relating to Indian Affairs, box 2-9/32, folders 3, 4, 9, 10, box 2-9/33, folders 2, 6, 9, 11, 12; Lorenzo Castro to Sam Houston, February 20, 1861, Records Relating to Indian Affairs, box 2-9/33, folder 9.
109. W. J. Maltby, *Captain Jeff; or, Frontier Life in Texas with the Texas Rangers* (Colorado, TX: Whipkey, 1906), frontispiece.
110. On Texas military autonomy during the Civil War, see William S. Kiser, *Illusions of Empire: The Civil War and Reconstruction in the U.S.-Mexico Borderlands* (Philadelphia: University of Pennsylvania Press, 2022), 4–5, 76–77, 79, 142–43.
111. Jerry D. Thompson, *John Robert Baylor: Texas Indian Fighter and Confederate Soldier* (Hillsboro, TX: Hill Junior College Press, 1971), 3–11.
112. "Petition Concerning Indian Depredations [undated]," in Winfrey and Day, *Indian Papers of Texas and the Southwest*, 4:453–54, quotations on 453.
113. Thompson, *John Robert Baylor*, 13–22. For an example of Baylor's campaigning in Texas, see George H. Thomas to John Withers, May 26, 1859, in *Report of the Secretary of War*, 36th Cong., 1st Sess., Senate Exec. Doc. No. 2, p. 373.
114. For the muster rolls listing men attached to Baylor's command, see Martin Hardwick Hall, *Sibley's New Mexico Campaign* (Austin: University of Texas Press, 1960), 307–29. On the Confederate invasion of New Mexico, see Donald S. Frazier, *Blood and Treasure: Confederate Empire in the Southwest* (College Station: Texas A&M University Press, 1995); Jerry D. Thompson, *A Civil War History of the New Mexico Volunteers and Militia* (Albuquerque: University of New Mexico Press, 2015); Andrew E. Masich, *Civil War in the Southwest Borderlands, 1861–1867* (Norman: University of Oklahoma Press, 2017); and Megan Kate Nelson, *The Three-Cornered War: The Union, the Confederacy, and Native Peoples in the Fight for the West* (New York: Scribner, 2020).

115. On "border lines," see Alice L. Baumgartner, "The Line of Positive Safety: Borders and Boundaries in the Rio Grande Valley, 1848–1880," *Journal of American History* 101:4 (2015): 1107.

116. Nichols, *Limits of Liberty*, 37–38, 170–71, 173. For examples of Lipan raiding, see Michael L. Collins, *A Crooked River: Rustlers, Rangers, and Regulars on the Lower Rio Grande, 1861–1877* (Norman: University of Oklahoma Press, 2018), 105–11, 152–54.

117. John R. Baylor to Santiago Vidaurri, June 21, 1861, and Vidaurri to Baylor, June 29, 1861, both in "Important Diplomatic Correspondence: Letters on the Subject of the Texan Frontier between the Rebel Secretary of State, Gen. Vidaurri, Governor of Nueva Leon and Coahuila, and Col. Baylor, of the Texan Army," *New York Times*, October 31, 1861. On Vidaurri's Indian policies, see Isidro Vizcaya Canales, *Tierra de guerra viva: Invasión de los indios bárbaros al noreste de México, 1821–1885* (Monterrey: Academia de Investigaciones, 2001), 349–61.

118. William S. Kiser, *Turmoil on the Rio Grande: The Territorial History of the Mesilla Valley, 1846–1865* (College Station: Texas A&M University Press, 2011), 156–72.

119. Thompson, *John Robert Baylor*, 66–79.

120. "Attack on Pino Alto by the Indians," *Mesilla (NM) Times*, October 3, 1861.

121. Edward H. Jordan to Jose Agustín Quintero, March 18, 1862, Juan B. Méndez to Civil Political Chief of the District of Brazos, March 26, 1862, and Luis Terrazas to Henry Hopkins Sibley, March 17, 1862, all in John P. Wilson, ed., *When the Texans Came: Missing Records from the Civil War in the Southwest, 1861–1862* (Albuquerque: University of New Mexico Press, 2001), 233, 234–35, 231–32. On the Mexican and Confederate responses, see "Invasión al estado de Chihuahua," *El Veracruzano Libre*, May 9, 1862; Judah P. Benjamin to Terrazas, January 20, 1863, and Sibley to Terrazas, May 17, 1862, both in Wilson, *When the Texans Came*, 237–38 (quotation), 235; Terrazas to Benjamin, April 9, 1863, Library of Congress, Manuscript Division, Confederate States of America Records, Department of State, 1859–1868, MSS16550, reel 8. See also Kiser, *Illusions of Empire*, 47; and Wilson, *When the Texans Came*, 230–40.

122. For Poston's role, see Charles D. Poston to David Meriwether, July 10, 1856, New Mexico State Records Center and Archives, Territorial Archives of New Mexico, roll 98, frames 260–61. On the Arizona Guards, see Martin Hardwick Hall, "Thomas J. Mastin's 'Arizona Guards,'" *New Mexico Historical Review* 49:2 (1974): 143–51; and Edwin R. Sweeney, *Mangas Coloradas: Chief of the Chiricahua Apaches* (Norman: University of Oklahoma Press, 1998), 420–22. On the Mesilla Guard, see William S. Kiser, *Dragoons in Apacheland: Conquest and Resistance in Southern New Mexico, 1846–1861* (Norman: University of Oklahoma Press, 2012), 262–69.

123. Baylor to Thomas Helm, March 20, 1862, in *The War of the Rebellion: A Compilation of the Official Records of the Union and Confederate Armies*, ser. 1

(Washington, DC: Government Printing Office, 1882), 50, pt. 1:942 (hereafter cited as *Official Records*). See also Martin Hardwick Hall, "Planter vs. Frontiersman: Conflict in Confederate Indian Policy," in Frank E. Vandiver, Martin Hardwick Hall, and Homer L. Kerr, eds., *Essays on the American Civil War* (Austin: University of Texas Press, 1968), 55–72.

124. For Baylor's resignation, see Baylor to Alexander M. Jackson, March 17, 1862, in Wilson, *When the Texans Came*, 197. Baylor's order was first published under the title "Terrible Revelations," September 27, 1862, *Marshall (MO) Republican*. See also Hall, "Planter vs. Frontiersman," 58–60.

125. George Randolph to John B. Magruder, November 7, 1862, and Jefferson Davis to Secretary of War, March 29, 1863, both in *Official Records*, 15:857, 919.

126. Baylor to Magruder, December 29, 1862, *Official Records*, 15:918.

127. Baylor to "Mr. Editor," October 8, 1862, *Tri-Weekly Telegraph* (Houston, TX), October 17, 1862.

128. Hall, "Planter vs. Frontiersman," 71.

129. Williams, *With the Border Ruffians*, 322–42, quotations on 323–24.

130. For a seminal study, see Monica Muñoz Martinez, *The Injustice Never Leaves You: Anti-Mexican Violence in Texas* (Cambridge, MA: Harvard University Press, 2018). See also Américo Paredes, *"With His Pistol in His Hand": A Border Ballad and Its Hero* (Austin: University of Texas Press, 1958); David Montejano, *Anglos and Mexicans in the Making of Texas, 1836–1986* (Austin: University of Texas Press, 1987); Robert M. Utley, *Lone Star Justice: The First Century of the Texas Rangers* (New York: Berkley, 2002); Charles H. Harris III and Louis R. Sadler, *The Texas Rangers and the Mexican Revolution: The Bloodiest Decade, 1910–1920* (Albuquerque: University of New Mexico Press, 2004); Elliott Young, *Catarino Garza's Revolution on the Texas-Mexico Border* (Durham, NC: Duke University Press, 2004); Benjamin H. Johnson, *Revolution in Texas: How a Forgotten Rebellion and Its Bloody Suppression Turned Mexicans into Americans* (New Haven: Yale University Press, 2005); and Arnoldo De León, *War along the Border: The Mexican Revolution and Tejano Communities* (College Station: Texas A&M University Press, 2012). The "Refusing to Forget" project, cofounded in 2014 by John Morán González, Sonia Hernández, Benjamin Johnson, and Monica Muñoz Martinez, chronicles and preserves histories of this violence. See www.refusingtoforget.org.

5 Volunteer Campaigning on the Pacific Coast

1. Harry L. Wells, "The Ben Wright Massacre," *West Shore*, October 1, 1884, 314.

2. Report of Benjamin Wright, September 2, 1852, California Adjutant General's Office, Military Department, Adjutant General, Indian War Papers 1850–1880, microfilm F3753, roll 1, doc. 203 (hereafter cited as California Indian War Papers).

3. Quotations from "History of the Modocs," *New York Times,* July 17, 1873, and Statement of W. T. Kershaw, November 21, 1857, in *Protection Afforded by Volunteers of Oregon and Washington Territories to Overland Immigrants in 1854,* 35th Cong., 2nd Sess., House Misc. Doc. No. 47, pp. 42, 43. For firsthand accounts, see Charles McDermitt to John Bigler, December 19, 1852, in "Correspondence in Relation to the Claims of Wright and McDermitt's Command," in *Journal of the Fourth Session of the Legislature, Begun on the Third Day of January, 1853, and Ended on the Nineteenth Day of May, 1853, at the Cities of Vallejo and Benicia — Journal of the Senate, Fourth Session, Appendix* (San Francisco, CA: George Kerr, 1853), doc. 21, pp. 2–4; John E. Ross to George L. Curry, November 10, 1854, in *Protection Afforded by Volunteers of Oregon and Washington Territories to Overland Immigrants in 1854,* 14–16; and *Communication from C. S. Drew, Late Adjutant of the Second Regiment of Oregon Mounted Volunteers, Giving an Account of the Origin and Early Prosecution of the Indian War in Oregon,* 36th Cong., 1st Sess., Senate Misc. Doc. No. 59, p. 10. For secondary accounts, see Brendan C. Lindsay, *Murder State: California's Native American Genocide, 1846–1873* (Lincoln: University of Nebraska Press, 2012), 212–14, 337–38; Boyd Cothran, *Remembering the Modoc War: Redemptive Violence and the Making of American Innocence* (Chapel Hill: University of North Carolina Press, 2014), 42; Benjamin Madley, *An American Genocide: The United States and the California Indian Catastrophe, 1846–1873* (New Haven: Yale University Press, 2016), 201–2, 213–17; Jim Compton, *Spirit in the Rock: The Fierce Battle for Modoc Homelands* (Pullman: Washington State University Press, 2017), 22–23; and Robert Acquinas McNally, *The Modoc War: A Story of Genocide at the Dawn of America's Gilded Age* (Lincoln: University of Nebraska Press, 2017), 38–45. The eighteen men with Wright during the Lost River Massacre were: William T. Kershaw, J. G. Hallick, David "Old Tex" Helm, Isaac "Buckskin" Sandbanch, George Rodgers, Morris Rodgers, Jacob Rhodes, E. P. Jenner, J. C. Burgess, William Chance, William White, William Brown, "Coffin," "Rabbit," "Poland," "Nigger Bill," and two Indian guides named "Benice" and "Bob." See Henry L. Wells, *History of Siskiyou County, California, Illustrated with Views of Residences, Business Buildings and Natural Scenery, and Containing Portraits and Biographies of Its Leading Citizens and Pioneers* (Oakland, CA: D. J. Stewart, 1881), 133.

4. "Report of the Committee on Indian Affairs, on the Claims of Wright and McDermitt's Command," in *Journal of the Fourth Session of the Legislature — Journal of the Senate, Fourth Session, Appendix,* doc. 33, pp. 3–4; Madley, *American Genocide,* 216.

5. "Memorial from Citizens of Yreka in Relation to Indian Difficulties," September 7, 1852, California Indian War Papers, roll 1, doc. 204.

6. Wells, *History of Siskiyou County,* 129–33.

7. "Sacramento News," *Daily Alta California* (San Francisco), December 2, 1852.

8. Ben Wright to John Bigler, December 22, 1852, in "Correspondence in Relation to the Claims of Wright and McDermitt's Command," 4.

9. "Report of the Committee on Indian Affairs, on the Claims of Wright and McDermitt's Command," 3–4.

10. "An Act Authorizing the Treasurer of the State to Issue Bonds for the Payment of the Expenses of Volunteer Rangers under Captain B. Wright and Charles McDermitt, in Protecting the Overland Emigration on the Northeastern Frontier," April 16, 1853, in *The Statutes of California, Passed at the Fourth Session of the Legislature, Begun on the Third of January, 1853, and Ended on the Nineteenth Day of May, 1853, at the Cities of Vallejo and Benicia* (San Francisco, CA: George Kerr, 1853), 95–96. See also Statement of W. T. Kershaw, November 21, 1857, in *Protection Afforded by Volunteers of Oregon and Washington Territories to Overland Immigrants in 1854*, 41–43. Several men involved in Wright's campaign filed petitions with the California War Board and the State Comptroller's Office, seeking remuneration for personal expenses incurred. See William Rose to Winston S. Pierce, May 19, 1853, Elias Stone to Pierce, May 30, 1853, J. P. Goodall to H. H. McMeans, December 26, 1853, Affidavits of George G. Holmes, June 5, 1854, Goodall to Sam Bell, September 21, 1854, Power of Attorney from Waterman and Tolin, July 1, 1854, and Affidavit of David H. Lowry, October 28, 1854, all in California Indian War Papers, roll 1, docs. 212–18.

11. Statement of E. W. Conner, November 18, 1857, in *Protection Afforded by Volunteers of Oregon and Washington Territories to Overland Immigrants in 1854*, 39.

12. On Wright's death, see "Letter from Port Orford," *Daily Alta California* (San Francisco), March 20, 1856; Statement of W. T. Kershaw, November 21, 1857, in *Protection Afforded by Volunteers of Oregon and Washington Territories to Overland Immigrants in 1854*, 41; Cheewa James, *Modoc: The Tribe That Wouldn't Die* (Happy Camp, CA: Naturegraph, 2008), 26–28; Gray H. Whaley, *Oregon and the Collapse of Illahee: U.S. Empire and the Transformation of an Indigenous World, 1792–1859* (Chapel Hill: University of North Carolina Press, 2010), 196, 213, 269n92; Compton, *Spirit in the Rock*, 23; and McNally, *Modoc War*, 45.

13. Cothran, *Remembering the Modoc War*, 42.

14. Antonio Franco Coronel, *Tales of Mexican California: Cosas de California*, translated by Diane de Avalle-Arce and edited by Doyce B. Nunis Jr. (Santa Barbara CA: Bellerophon Books, 1994), 62.

15. Theodore T. Johnson, *Sights in the Gold Region, and Scenes by the Way* (New York: Baker and Scribner, 1850), 140, 157–58, 179–81, quotation on 181. For a similar incident, see William Shaw, *Golden Dreams and Waking Realities; Being the Adventures of a Gold-Seeker in California and the Pacific Islands* (London: Smith, Elder, 1851), 101–13.

16. Ramón Gil Navarro, *The Gold Rush Diary of Ramón Gil Navarro*, edited and translated by María del Carmen Ferreyra and David S. Reher (Lincoln: University of Nebraska Press, 2000), 54.

17. "A California Blood-Stain," *Hutchings' Illustrated California Magazine, July 1858 to June 1859*, vol. 3 (San Francisco: Hutchings and Rosenfield, 1859), 129–31. For

firsthand accounts of Paiutes, see Anna Paschall Hannum, ed., *A Quaker Forty-Niner: The Adventures of Charles Edward Pancoast on the American Frontier* (Philadelphia: University of Pennsylvania Press, 1930), 342–45; Francis P. Farquhar, ed., *Up and Down California in 1860–1864: The Journal of William H. Brewer, Professor of Agriculture in the Sheffield Scientific School from 1864 to 1903* (Berkeley: University of California Press, 1966), 300–302; and Robert F. Heizer, ed., *They Were Only Diggers: A Collection of Articles from California Newspapers, 1851–1866, on Indian and White Relations* (Ramona, CA: Ballena Press, 1974).

18. Dale L. Morgan, ed., *California as I Saw It: Pencillings by the Way of Its Gold and Gold Diggers! And Incidents of Travel by Land and Water by William M'Collum, M.D., a Returned Adventurer* (Los Gatos, CA: Talisman Press, 1960), 147–48.

19. W. Augustus Knapp, "An Old Californian's Pioneer Story—II," *Overland Monthly and Out West Magazine* 10:59 (1887): 507–8. See also Madley, *American Genocide,* 206–7.

20. "From the Shasta Region," *Daily Alta California* (San Francisco), May 1, 1853.

21. Dryden Laycock Deposition, February 25, 1860, California Indian War Papers, roll 2, doc. 441.

22. Madley, *American Genocide,* 222.

23. Michael F. Magliari, "The California Indian Scalp Bounty Myth: Evidence of Genocide or Just Faulty Scholarship?" *California History* 100:2 (2023): 4–30, esp. 5, 9.

24. See, e.g., Navarro, *Gold Rush Diary,* 51, 53, 54.

25. Jack Norton, *When Our Worlds Cried: Genocide in Northwestern California* (San Francisco, CA: Indian Historian Press, 1979), 38.

26. For firsthand accounts, see Joseph Warren Revere, *A Tour of Duty in California; Including a Description of the Gold Region* (New York: C. S. Francis, 1849), 155; and "Revolutionary Operations of the Early California Emigrants," *Daily Alta California* (San Francisco), July 24, 1852. See also Madley, *American Genocide,* 86, 97–99, 183, 197. On racism toward California Indians, see Clare V. McKanna Jr., *Race and Homicide in Nineteenth-Century California* (Reno: University of Nevada Press, 2002), 13–31; and Tomás Almaguer, *Racial Fault Lines: The Historical Origins of White Supremacy in California* (Berkeley: University of California Press, 2009), 107–52.

27. See Lindsay, *Murder State;* and Madley, *American Genocide.*

28. Madley, *American Genocide,* 3, 347, 480, 522; Lindsay, *Murder State,* 336. On population decline generally, see Sherburne F. Cook, *The Population of California Indians, 1769–1970* (Berkeley: University of California Press, 1976), xv, 58–60; Sherburne F. Cook, *The Conflict between the California Indian and White Civilization* (Berkeley: University of California Press, 1976), 3–12; and James J. Rawls, *Indians of California: The Changing Image* (Norman: University of Oklahoma Press, 1984), 171–76.

29. Lindsay, *Murder State,* 23.

30. Madley, *American Genocide*, 175, 530–33, 550.

31. Statement of Adjutant General Samuel Cooper, January 29, 1860, California Indian War Papers, roll 3, doc. 754. On the Mormon conflict, see David L. Bigler and Will Bagley, *The Mormon Rebellion: America's First Civil War, 1857–1858* (Norman: University of Oklahoma Press, 2011). On the Navajo and Apache conflicts, see William S. Kiser, *Coast-to-Coast Empire: Manifest Destiny and the New Mexico Borderlands* (Norman: University of Oklahoma Press, 2018). On US Army operations in California, see William F. Strobridge, *Regulars in the Redwoods: The U.S. Army in Northern California, 1852–1861* (Spokane, WA: Arthur H. Clarke, 1994).

32. David Pletcher, *The Diplomacy of Annexation: Texas, Oregon, and the Mexican War* (Columbia: University of Missouri Press, 1973).

33. 1850 and 1860 US Census. On the forms of slavery in California, see Michael Magliari, "Free State Slavery: Bound Indian Labor and Slave Trafficking in California's Sacramento Valley, 1850–1864," *Pacific Historical Review* 81:2 (2012): 155–92; and Stacey L. Smith, *Freedom's Frontier: California and the Struggle over Unfree Labor, Emancipation, and Reconstruction* (Chapel Hill: University of North Carolina Press, 2013).

34. Madley, *American Genocide*, 123–24.

35. J. M. Bondwrant and Richard H. Daly to Peter H. Burnett, January 13, 1850, California Indian War Papers, roll 1, doc. 49.

36. "An Act for the Government and Protection of Indians," April 22, 1850, in *The Statutes of California, Passed at the First Session of the Legislature, Begun the 15th Day of Dec. 1849, and ended the 22d day of April, 1850 at the City of Pueblo de San José* (San Jose, CA: J. Winchester, 1850), chap. 133, pp. 408–10. See also Kimberly Johnston-Dodds, *Early California Laws and Policies Related to California Indians* (Sacramento: California Research Bureau, 2002), 5–12. On the law's effects, see Smith, *Freedom's Frontier*, 18–24; Madley, *American Genocide*, 158–59; Andrés Reséndez, *The Other Slavery: The Uncovered Story of Indian Enslavement in America* (New York: Houghton Mifflin Harcourt, 2016), 264–65; and Kevin Waite, *West of Slavery: The Southern Dream of a Transcontinental Empire* (Chapel Hill: University of North Carolina Press, 2021), 103–4.

37. On Governor Burnett, see Smith, *Freedom's Frontier*, 61; Lindsey, *Murder State*, 140–43; Madley, *American Genocide*, 186–87.

38. "To the Democracy of San Francisco," *Daily Alta California* (San Francisco), April 1, 1850; "Sketch of Colonel John C. Hays, Texas Ranger" (unpublished manuscript by John Caperton, 1922), 77, Dolph Briscoe Center for American History, University of Texas at Austin, John Coffee Hays Collection, box 2R35.

39. "Political Rallies," *Daily Alta California* (San Francisco), April 1, 1850; John C. Hays, undated letter, "Pay Roll for Company H of California Volunteers Commanded by Capt. D. Aldrich," and McDougal to Committee on Military Affairs, February 15, 1854, all in California Indian War Papers, roll 1, docs. 160, 172.

40. "Act Concerning Volunteer or Independent Companies," and "Act Concerning the Organization of the Militia," in *The Statutes of California, Passed at the First Session of the Legislature* (1850), chap. 54, pp. 145–48, chap. 76, pp. 190–96. On California Indian policy, see Albert L. Hurtado, *Indian Survival on the California Frontier* (New Haven: Yale University Press, 1988), 125–48; Madley, *American Genocide*, 171–72.

41. John McDougal to James Birney, January 13, 1851, McDougal to David Broderick, January 18, 1851, McDougal to the Legislature of California, January 20, 1851, and McDougal to the Senate and House of Assembly, March 15, 1851, all in California Indian War Papers, roll 1, docs. 50, 51, 52 (first quotation), 60 (second quotation).

42. C. Gregory Crampton, ed., *The Mariposa Indian War, 1850–1851: Diaries of Robert Eccleston: The California Gold Rush, Yosemite, and the High Sierra* (Salt Lake City: University of Utah Press, 1957), 15–19, 25–33, quotations on 30, 33; "San Jose Intelligence," *Daily Alta California* (San Francisco), January 23, 1851; "San Joaquin Intelligence," *Daily Alta California* (San Francisco), February 7, 1851; "Indian Expedition," *Daily Alta California* (San Francisco), February 28, 1851. See also George Harwood Phillips, *"Bringing Them under Subjection": California's Tejón Indian Reservation and Beyond, 1852–1864* (Lincoln: University of Nebraska Press, 2004), 28–32; Lindsey, *Murder State*, 240–43; and Madley, *American Genocide*, 188–94.

43. McDougal to Millard Fillmore, March 1, 1851, California Indian War Papers, roll 1, doc. 187.

44. Madley, *American Genocide*, 199–200.

45. J. B. Reynolds to the State of California, March 22, 1851, Receipt from Quartermaster John G. Marvin, April 11, 1851, and Receipt from Quartermaster John G. Marvin, March 26, 1851, all in California Indian War Papers, roll 1, docs. 61, 64, 62.

46. McDougall to R. Roman, April 15, 1851, California Indian War Papers, roll 1, doc. 65. See also Madley, *American Genocide*, 207. For examples of war bonds, see California Indian War Papers, roll 3, docs. 953–58.

47. "An Act Concerning the Organization of the Militia," May 1, 1852, in *The Statutes of California, Passed at the Third Session of the Legislature, Begun on the Fifth of January, 1852, and Ended on the Fourth Day of May, 1852, at the Cities of Vallejo and Sacramento* (San Francisco: G. K. Fitch, 1852), 96–100; "Three Hours Later by the Antelope," *Daily Alta California* (San Francisco), March 25, 1852; "Frank Soule: Death of the Veteran Journalist and Pioneer," *Los Angeles Herald*, July 6, 1882.

48. On the war bonds, see Lindsay, *Murder State*, 237; and Madley, *American Genocide*, 207. For war bond statistics, see "Report of Commissioners: California War Debt," in *Appendix to Journals of the Senate, of the Eleventh Session of the Legislature of the State of California* (Sacramento, CA: C. T. Botts, 1860), doc. 12, pp. 8–12.

49. Roderick McKee to Luke Lea, April 5, 1852, in *Letter from the Secretary of the Interior, Communicating the Report of Edward F. Beale, Superintendent of Indian Affairs in California, Respecting the Condition of Indian Affairs in That State, March 3, 1853*, 32nd Cong., 2nd Sess., Senate Exec. Doc. No. 57, pp. 11–12, quotation on 12.

50. O. M. Wozencraft to Luke Lea, October 14, 1851, in *Report of the Secretary of the Interior, Communicating, in Compliance with a Resolution of the Senate, a Copy of the Correspondence between the Department of the Interior and the Indian Agents and Commissioners in California*, 33rd Cong., Special Session, Senate Exec. Doc. No. 4, p. 210; Undated extracts from letters of O. M. Wozencraft, in *Letter from the Secretary of the Interior*, 12–13.

51. "California Indians," *Daily Alta California* (San Francisco), September 24, 1851.

52. On Beale, see Rawls, *Indians of California*, 148–54.

53. Undated extracts from letters of Edw. F. Beale, in *Letter from the Secretary of the Interior*, 13–18.

54. E. A. Hitchcock to Redick McKee, March 23, 1852, in *Report of the Secretary of the Interior*, 302.

55. Norton, *When Our Worlds Cried*, 54–56; Russell Thornton, "Social Organization and the Demographic Survival of the Tolowa," *Ethnohistory* 31:3 (1984): 192–93; Madley, *American Genocide*, 222–24.

56. R. N. Woods to J. H. Jenkins, undated, and Jenkins to Edward F. Beale, January 30, 1853, in *Letter from the Secretary of the Interior*, 10, 10–11.

57. "Lo, the Poor Indian," *Daily Alta California* (San Francisco), April 7, 1855. For examples of California newspapers promoting Indian extermination, see Rawls, *Indians of California*, 176–86; and Madley, *American Genocide*, 220–22, 242–43, 307–9.

58. Farquhar, *Up and Down California*, 493–94, quotation on 493.

59. "Indian Slavery," *Daily Alta California* (San Francisco), April 14, 1862. For additional California newspaper accounts, see Robert F. Heizer, ed., *The Destruction of California Indians: A Collection of Documents from the Period 1847 to 1865 in Which Are Described Some of the Things That Happened to Some of the Indians of California* (Santa Barbara, CA: Peregrine Smith, 1974), 236–41; and Clifford E. Trafzer and Joel R. Hyer, eds., *Exterminate Them! Written Accounts of the Murder, Rape, and Enslavement of Native Americans during the California Gold Rush* (East Lansing: Michigan State University Press, 1999), 113–33. On Indian slavery during the Civil War, see Smith, *Freedom's Frontier*, 174–75, 182–92, 199–202.

60. George Hanson to William P. Dole, December 31, 1861, in *Report of the Commissioner of Indian Affairs, for the Year 1862* (Washington, DC: Government Printing Office, 1863), 315.

61. C. S. Drew to Jno. W. Davis, July 7, 1854, in *Protection Afforded by Volunteers of Oregon and Washington Territories to Overland Immigrants in 1854*, 3–5.

62. Davis to Drew, July 17, 1854, in *Protection Afforded by Volunteers of Oregon and Washington Territories to Overland Immigrants in 1854*, 5–6. On John Ross, see Whaley, *Oregon and the Collapse of Illahee*, 194–96.

63. Proclamation of John E. Ross, August 5, 1854, and Ross to Jesse Walker, August 8, 1854, both in *Protection Afforded by Volunteers of Oregon and Washington Territories to Overland Immigrants in 1854*, 7–8, 8; "Threatened Indian Difficulties on the Southern Emigrant Trail," *Daily Alta California* (San Francisco), August 3, 1854.

64. Walker to Ross, November 6, 1854, in *Protection Afforded by Volunteers of Oregon and Washington Territories to Overland Immigrants in 1854*, 12–14.

65. Drew to George L. Curry, December 30, 1854, in *Protection Afforded by Volunteers of Oregon and Washington Territories to Overland Immigrants in 1854*, 16–25, quotations on 21, 25. On racism and Indian affairs in California, see Robert F. Heizer and Alan F. Almquist, *The Other Californians: Prejudice and Discrimination under Spain, Mexico, and the United States to 1920* (Berkeley: University of California Press, 1971), 23–63.

66. George L. Curry to Joseph Lane, September 18, 20, 1854, and Curry to Franklin Pierce, September 25, 1854, all in *Protection Afforded by Volunteers of Oregon and Washington Territories to Overland Immigrants in 1854*, 8–9, 9–10, 10–12.

67. "From Crescent City," *Daily Alta California* (San Francisco), January 17, 1855; "A Battle with the Indians—Thirty Indians Killed," *Daily Alta California* (San Francisco), January 18, 1855 (quotation); Norton, *When Our Worlds Cried*, 56–57; Madley, *American Genocide*, 231–34. See also Austen D. Warburton and Joseph F. Endert, *Indian Lore of the North California Coast* (Santa Clara, CA: Pacific Pueblo Press, 1966), 167–68.

68. Thornton, "Social Organization and the Demographic Survival of the Tolowa," 189–91, quotation on 193.

69. Quotation from *Memorial Asking Congress to Assume the Expenses of the Existing Indian War*, January 31, 1856, in *Protection Afforded by Volunteers of Oregon and Washington Territories to Overland Immigrants in 1854*, 28. See also Oregon Territorial Assembly Resolutions, December 11, 1854, January 26, 1855, and February 3, 1858, "Memorial Asking Congress to Pay Certain Soldiers and Other Persons for Services Rendered and Supplies Furnished in the Rogue River War of 1854," January 31, 1856, and "Memorial to the Senate and House of Representatives of the United States in Congress assembled," January 13, 1857, all in *Protection Afforded by Volunteers of Oregon and Washington Territories to Overland Immigrants in 1854*, 25–26, 60, 29–30, 30–31.

70. Drew to Curry, December 14, 1857, with appended witness statements, in *Protection Afforded by Volunteers of Oregon and Washington Territories to Overland Immigrants in 1854*, 31–56, 60.

71. For congressional funding debates, see "Oregon War Debt," *Congressional Globe*, May 9, 1860, pp. 1989–91; "Oregon War Debt," *Congressional Globe*, May 16, 1860,

pp. 2117–20; "Oregon War Debt," *Congressional Globe*, May 30, 1860, pp. 2467–74; "Oregon War Debt," *Congressional Globe*, January 24, 1861, p. 547; and "Oregon and Washington War Debt," *Congressional Globe*, February 21, 1861, pp. 1100–1107.

72. For the treaty negotiations, see Kip Lawrence, *Indian Council in the Valley of the Walla-Walla* (San Francisco: Whitton, Towne, 1855); Darrell Scott, ed., *A True Copy of the Record of the Official Proceedings at the Council in the Walla Walla Valley, 1855* (Fairfield, WA: Ye Galleon Press, 1985); Jennifer Karson, ed., *Wiyaxayxt / Wiyaakaa'aw / As Days Go By: Our History, Our Land, Our People, the Cayuse, Umatilla, and Walla Walla* (Seattle: University of Washington Press, 2006), 77–80; and Elliott West, *The Last Indian War: The Nez Perce Story* (New York: Oxford University Press, 2009), 60–71. On Peo-Peo-Mox-Mox (alternatively spelled Piupiu-maksmaks), see Karson, *Wiyaxayxt / Wiyaakaa'aw / As Days Go By*, 82–83; and Whaley, *Oregon and the Collapse of Illahee*, 116–18.

73. "Late from Oregon," *California Farmer and Journal of Useful Sciences* (San Francisco), December 28, 1855 (quotation); "Later from Oregon Territory," *Daily Alta California* (San Francisco), December 5, 1855; "Oregon War News," *Marysville (CA) Daily Herald*, December 21, 1855.

74. "Highly Important News from Oregon," *Puget Sound Courier* (Steilacoom, Washington Territory), December 21, 1855.

75. Frances Fuller Victor, ed., *The Early Indian Wars of Oregon, Compiled from the Oregon Archives and Other Original Sources with Muster Rolls* (Salem, OR: Frank C. Baker, 1894), iii–iv, 445–46.

76. Karson, *Wiyaxayxt / Wiyaakaa'aw / As Days Go By*, 3, 224; Clifford E. Trafzer, ed., *Grandmother, Grandfather, and Old Wolf: Tamánwit Ku Sukát and Traditional Native American Narratives from the Columbia Plateau* (East Lansing: Michigan State University Press, 1998), 1–2.

77. Karson, *Wiyaxayxt / Wiyaakaa'aw / As Days Go By*, 78–79.

78. On the Lupton Massacre, see E. A. Schwartz, *The Rogue River Indian War and Its Aftermath, 1850–1980* (Norman: University of Oklahoma Press, 1997), 85–86; and Whaley, *Oregon and the Collapse of Illahee*, 204–5.

79. For the statistics, see Schwartz, *Rogue River Indian War and Its Aftermath*, 148–49. On the Rogue River War generally, see Schwartz, *Rogue River Indian War and Its Aftermath*, 91–147; Nathan Douthit, *Uncertain Encounters: Indians and Whites at Peace and War in Southern Oregon, 1820s–1860s* (Corvallis: Oregon State University Press, 2002), 133–62; and Whaley, *Oregon and the Collapse of Illahee*, 204–5, 217–19, 221–26.

80. Report of Board of Examiners of War Claims, December 31, 1855, California Indian War Papers, roll 3, doc. 740. On the California "war debt," see Madley, *American Genocide*, 218, 229–30, 238, 250–51, 253–54.

81. On Weller, see Madley, *American Genocide*, 250–53.

82. On Jarboe's campaign, see Lynwood Carranco and Estle Beard, *Genocide and Vendetta: The Round Valley Wars of Northern California* (Norman: University of

Oklahoma Press, 1981), 88–97; William B. Secrest, *When the Great Spirit Died: The Destruction of the California Indians, 1850–1860* (Sanger, CA: Word Dancer Press, 2003), 287–309; Benjamin Madley, "Patterns of Frontier Genocide, 1803–1910: The Aboriginal Tasmanians, the Yuki of California, and the Herero of Namibia," *Journal of Genocide Research* 6:2 (2004): 178–81; Frank H. Baumgardner III, *Killing for Land in Early California: Indian Blood at Round Valley, 1856–1863* (New York: Algora, 2006), 95–128; Benjamin Madley, "California's Yuki Indians: Defining Genocide in Native American History," *Western Historical Quarterly* 39:3 (2008): 317, 319; Lindsay, *Murder State*, 1–2, 195–209; and Madley, *American Genocide*, 276–80. The first recruits included David Blemis, William Daly, J. W. Graham, H. S. Hall, William Hedspeth, J. R. Martin, William Robertson, E. M. Wager, and James P. Watters. Walter S. Jarboe to John B. Weller, September 16, 1859, California Indian War Papers, roll 1, doc. 383. On Jarboe's background and death, see www.finda-grave.com/memorial/29000810/walter-s-jarboe.

83. Jarboe to Weller, September 16, 1859. On the Nome Cult reservation, see Baumgardner III, *Killing for Land in Early California*, 38–49.

84. Edward Johnson to W. W. Mackall, August 21, 1859, California Indian War Papers, roll 1, doc. 378.

85. John Adams to Mackall, September 3, 1859, California Indian War Papers, roll 1, doc. 380.

86. California Constitution (1850), art. 7, sec. 3.

87. Johnston-Dodds, *Early California Laws and Policies Related to California Indians*, 15–16. Dozens of these militias were urban social organizations and did not actively engage in field campaigns. See Madley, *American Genocide*, 174–75.

88. John W. Park to J. Neely Johnson, March 10, 1856, and Statement of Adjutant General Samuel Cooper, January 29, 1860, both in California Indian War Papers, roll 1, doc. 276, roll 3, doc. 754.

89. Weller to Jarboe, September 9, 1859, California Indian War Papers, roll 1, doc. 382. See also Madley, "California's Yuki Indians," 317, 319.

90. As of September 16, 1859, the Eel River Rangers included the following: J. Alexander, B. S. Birch, William H. Cole, S. S. Danney, Antonio Garsilla (Garcia), Johnathan W. Hackel, John D. Haskins, James B. Head, John J. Heaskene, William Hildreth, E. M. Hoard, William R. Pool, William O. Robertson, William Scott, F. S. Stout, William Wall, and James E. Wood. Jarboe to Weller, September 16, 1859.

91. Jarboe to Weller, October 1, 1859, California Indian War Papers, roll 1, doc. 388.

92. Jarboe to Weller, October 16, 1859, and Weller to Jarboe, October 23, 1859, both in California Indian War Papers, roll 1, docs. 398, 399.

93. Jarboe to Weller, October 28, 1859, California Indian War Papers, roll 1, doc. 400.

94. "Indian Troubles in Mendocino County," *Daily Alta California* (San Francisco), October 9, 1859.

95. "Indian Difficulties in Mendocino County," *Daily National Democrat* (Marysville, CA), October 11, 1859; "Affairs at Round Valley, Tehama County," *Daily National Democrat* (Marysville, CA), December 17, 1859; "Sixty Indians Killed in Mendocino County," *Daily Alta California* (San Francisco), January 1, 1860; "The Late Indian War in Mendocino County," *Daily Alta California* (San Francisco), January 22, 1860.

96. Edward Dillon to Mackall, January 27, 1860, California Indian War Papers, roll 2, doc. 423.

97. Jarboe to Weller, December 3, 1859, California Indian War Papers, roll 2, doc. 401.

98. Jarboe to Weller, December 20, 1859, California Indian War Papers, roll 2, doc. 404.

99. Officers of Mendocino County to Weller, undated, and Weller to Jarboe, January 3, 1860, both in California Indian War Papers, roll 2, docs. 407, 409.

100. "Governor's Annual Message," *Daily Alta California* (San Francisco), January 10, 1860.

101. Citizens of Mendocino County to John G. Downey, February 13, 1860, California Indian War Papers, roll 2, doc. 428.

102. Jarboe to Downey, February 18, 1860, California Indian War Papers, roll 2, doc. 432. Madley estimates that as many as four hundred Indians may have been killed during the campaign. Madley, *American Genocide*, 276–80, 532–33; Madley, "California's Yuki Indians," 319–22.

103. Jarboe to Downey, February 18, 1860.

104. Depositions of Residents, February 22–28, 1860, William Pollard Deposition, February 27, 1860, and Lawrence Battaile Deposition, February 28, 1860, all in California Indian War Papers, roll 2, docs. 436–72, 460, 462. Transcriptions of these depositions appear in *Appendix to Journals of the Senate, of the Eleventh Session of the Legislature of the State of California* (Sacramento, CA: C. T. Botts, 1860), doc. 11, pp. 15–75.

105. "Majority Report of the Special Joint Committee on the Mendocino War," and "Minority Report of the Special Joint Committee on the Mendocino War," both in *Appendix to Journals of the Senate, of the Eleventh Session of the Legislature of the State of California*, 3–7, 9–12.

106. Lindsay, *Murder State*, 212, 232; Madley, *American Genocide*, 276–80, 532–33; Madley, "California's Yuki Indians," 319–22.

107. H. H. Buckles Deposition, February 25, 1860, California Indian War Papers, roll 2, doc. 438.

108. Madley, "California's Yuki Indians," 304.

109. George M. Foster, "A Summary of Yuki Culture," *University of California Anthropological Records* 5:3 (1944): 161–63, 176–78, 186–88, 204–5, 208; Virginia P. Miller, "Yuki, Huchnom, and Coast Yuki," in Robert F. Heizer, ed., *Handbook of North American Indians*, vol. 8 (Washington, DC: Smithsonian Institution, 1978), 249–53.

110. *Communication from C. S. Drew.*
111. Madley, *American Genocide*, 271–76, 284.
112. "Report of the Expedition against the Indians in the Northern Part of This State, by Wm. C. Kibbe," January 18, 1860, in Robert F. Heizer, ed., *Reprints of Various Papers on California Archaeology, Ethnology and Indian History* (Berkeley: University of California Department of Anthropology, 1973), 54–60, quotations on 56, 57, 58.
113. "The Late Indian War," *Daily Alta California*, January 28, 1860.
114. Madley, *American Genocide*, 282–83.
115. "California War Debt," May 19, 1860, W. C. Kibbe to J. C. Burch, June 13, 1860, and Banking House of Sweeny, Rittenhouse, Fant & Co. to Kibbe, December 20, 1861, all in Indian War Papers, roll 3, docs. 792, 793, 847. See also "Report of Commissioners: California War Debt," in *Appendix to Journals of the Senate, of the Eleventh Session of the Legislature of the State of California*, doc. 12, pp. 3–12. For the "numberless scalps" quotation, see "Our Sacramento Correspondence," *Daily Alta California* (San Francisco), January 19, 1860.
116. Kibbe to Downey, December 1, 1860, Indian War Papers, roll 3, doc. 805.
117. "An Act for the Payment of Expenses incurred in the Suppression of Indian Hostilities in the State of California," March 2, 1861, in George P. Sanger, ed., *The Statutes at Large, Treaties, and Proclamations of the United States of America, from December 5, 1859 to March 3, 1863*, vol. 12 (Boston: Little, Brown, 1863), 199–200. For congressional debates on Kibbe's proposal, see "Indian Hostilities," *Congressional Globe*, January 19, 1861, pp. 477–79; "Indian Hostilities in California," *Congressional Globe*, February 22, 1861, pp. 1112–15; "California War Debt," *Congressional Globe*, February 28, 1861, p. 1278; and "Army Appropriation Bill—Again," *Congressional Globe*, June 14, 1861, pp. 2998–3005, esp. 3001.
118. Madley, *American Genocide*, 290–330, statistics on 299–300.
119. "A Bounty Offered for Indian Scalps," *Marysville (CA) Appeal*, May 12, 1861. See also Rawls, *Indians of California*, 185; and Madley, *American Genocide*, 197–98.
120. Magliari, "California Indian Scalp Bounty Myth," 9.
121. J. Manheim to Kibbe, August 26, 1862, California Indian War Papers, roll 3, doc. 589. On Lee's Civil War campaign, see James McPherson, *Battle Cry of Freedom: The Civil War Era* (New York: Oxford University Press, 1988), 524–45.
122. Harmon A. Good to Leland Stanford c/o William A. Kibbe, August 8, 1862, California Indian War Papers, roll 3, docs. 608–10; "Fight with the Indians," *Marysville (CA) Appeal*, August 9, 1862. For the nickname "Hi," see Robert A. Anderson, *Fighting the Mill Creeks: Being a Personal Account of Campaigns against Indians of the Northern Sierras* (Chico, CA: Chico Record Press, 1909), 4–85. Harmon Good met a brutal but symbolic death in May 1870, when an Indian shot him twelve times and smashed his head with rocks. Anderson, *Fighting the Mill Creeks*, 84–85; Madley, *American Genocide*, 334.

123. Eric Foner, *The Fiery Trial: Abraham Lincoln and American Slavery* (New York: W. W. Norton, 2010), 230–33.

124. For examples of claims, see California Indian War Papers, roll 3, docs. 708–736, 817. For an example of newspaper notices, see "Indian War Claims" in Walter Van Dyke to A. F. Phelan, July 13, 1857, California Indian War Papers, roll 3, doc. 781. On land bounties, see Madley, *American Genocide*, 237–38.

125. Hannum, *Quaker Forty-Niner*, 298–99.

126. Revere, *Tour of Duty in California*, 129.

127. "Indian Butcheries in California," *San Francisco Bulletin*, June 18, 1860. For additional newspaper accounts of massacres, see Heizer, *Destruction of California Indians*, 248–58, 260, 263–65.

128. J. Ross Browne, *Muleback to the Convention: Letters of J. Ross Browne, Reported to the Constitutional Convention, Monterey, September–October, 1849* (San Francisco: Book Club of California, 1950), i–xxii.

129. J. Ross Browne, "The Coast Rangers: A Chronicle of Events in California," in *Harper's New Monthly Magazine* 23 (June–November 1861): 306–16, quotations on 307, 312, 315. One of Browne's descriptions was drawn from the firsthand account in E. Gould Buffum, *Six Months in the Gold Mines: From a Journal of Three Years Residence in Upper and Lower California 1847–8–9* (Philadelphia: Lea and Blanchard, 1850), 100–101. On Browne generally, see Lindsay, *Murder State*, 282–85.

130. For firsthand accounts of the Sand Creek Massacre, see *Condition of the Indian Tribes: Report of the Joint Special Committee, Appointed under Joint Resolution of March 3, 1865, with an Appendix*, 39th Cong., 2nd Sess., Senate Report No. 156, pp. 26–98. For a scholarly analysis, see Ari Kelman, *A Misplaced Massacre: Struggling over the Memory of Sand Creek* (Cambridge, MA: Harvard University Press, 2013).

131. For Californian reactions, see "Justice for the Indians," *Daily Alta California* (San Francisco), January 13, 1865; "The Attack on the Telegraph," *Daily Alta California* (San Francisco), February 7, 1865; and "Conduct of the War," *Daily Alta California* (San Francisco), May 22, 1865.

132. For the quotation, see S. E. Brown affidavit in *Condition of the Indian Tribes*, 71. See also David Svaldi, *Sand Creek and the Rhetoric of Extermination* (Lanham, MD: University Press of America, 1989), 287–95.

133. *Condition of the Indian Tribes*, quotation on 5.

134. Statement of George L. Hoffman, July 14, 15, 1865, and Statement of Austin Wiley, both in *Condition of the Indian Tribes*, appendix, pp. 494, 498–99.

135. Madley, *American Genocide*, 330–33.

136. Madley, *American Genocide*, 334.

137. James, *Modoc*, 26.

138. Quotations from "Early Modoc History," *New York Times*, May 24, 1873, and "History of the Modocs," *New York Times*, July 17, 1873. See also "The Modoc

Troubles," *San Francisco Bulletin*, February 25, 1873; and "In the Modoc Camp," *New York Herald*, February 28, 1873. For a detailed account of the Modoc War based on newspaper reports, see Oliver Knight, *Following the Indian Wars: The Story of the Newspaper Correspondents among the Indian Campaigners* (Norman: University of Oklahoma Press, 1960), 104–58.

139. Cothran, *Remembering the Modoc War*, 8–10, 15; Madley, *American Genocide*, 336–45.

140. On the repatriation, see Cothran, *Remembering the Modoc War*, 11, 200n14. On the federal laws, see Jack F. Trope and Walter R. Echohawk, "The Native American Graves Protection and Repatriation Act: Background and Legislative History," in Jo Carrillo, ed., *Readings in American Indian Law: Recalling the Rhythm of Survival* (Philadelphia: Temple University Press, 1998), 178–87.

Conclusion

1. Joseph J. Blocker to Jeremiah Wilks, in Scott Cooper, dir., *Hostiles*, 133 mins. (Waypoint Entertainment), released December 22, 2017.

2. A. O. Scott, "Review: 'Hostiles' Grapples with the Contradictions of the Western," *New York Times*, December 21, 2017.

3. Cormac McCarthy, *Blood Meridian; or, The Evening Redness in the West* (New York: Random House, 1985).

4. Noah Gallagher Shannon, "Cormac McCarthy Cuts to the Bone," *Slate* (New York), October 5, 2012. See also John Sepich, *Notes on Blood Meridian* (Austin: University of Texas Press, 2008); and Michael Evans, "American Irregular: Frontier Conflict and the Philosophy of War in Cormac McCarthy's *Blood Meridian, or the Evening Redness in the West*," *Small Wars and Insurgencies* 22:4 (2011): 527–47. On McCarthy generally, see Barcley Owens, *Cormac McCarthy's Western Novels* (Tucson: University of Arizona Press, 2000).

5. Cormac McCarthy, *Blood Meridian; or, The Evening Redness in the West* (1985; reprint, New York: Modern Library, 2001), 98.

6. McCarthy, *Blood Meridian* (2001), 157.

7. McCarthy, *Blood Meridian* (2001), 54.

8. Caryn James, " 'Blood Meridian,' by Cormac McCarthy," *New York Times*, April 28, 1985.

9. Richard B. Woodward, "Cormac McCarthy's Venomous Fiction," *New York Times*, April 19, 1992.

10. See, e.g., Janne Lahti, "Silver Screen Savages: Images of Apaches in Motion Pictures," *Journal of Arizona History* 54:1 (2013): 51–84.

11. See, e.g., Benjamin Madley, *An American Genocide: The United States and the California Indian Catastrophe, 1846–1873* (New Haven: Yale University Press, 2016), 354–55.

12. Cassie Williams and Anjuli Patil, "Controversial Cornwallis Statue Removed from Halifax Park," January 31, 2018, *CBC News*, www.cbc.ca/news/canada/nova-scotia/cornwallis-statue-removal-1.4511858; Elizabeth McMillan, "Newly Renamed Peace and Friendship Park Celebrated in Halifax," June 21, 2021, *CBC News*, www.cbc.ca/news/canada/nova-scotia/peace-and-friendship-cornwallis-park-halifax-1.6073550; Anjuli Patil, "Cornwallis Name Gone from Lunenburg Street, but New Name Draws Criticism," December 4, 2023, *CBC News*, www.cbc.ca/news/canada/nova-scotia/lunenburg-cornwallis-street-replacement-misses-the-mark-1.7046549.

13. Judy Harrison, "FBI Is Investigating Suspected Native American Scalp Seized from Fairfield Auctioneer," November 10, 2022, *Bangor (ME) Daily News*, www.bangordailynews.com/2022/11/10/central-maine/fairfield-native-american-scalp/.

BIBLIOGRAPHY

Primary Sources

Manuscript Collections and Unpublished Documents

California State Archives, Sacramento

California Adjutant General's Office, Military Department, Adjutant General, Indian War Papers, 1850–1880

Library of Congress, Washington, DC

Manuscript Division, Confederate States of America Records, Department of State, 1859–1868, MSS16550

National Archives and Records Center, Washington, DC

Record Group 59 (RG59), US State Department, Despatches Received by the Department of State from US Consuls in Chihuahua, 1826–1906. Microcopy T-167

National Archives of Canada, Ottawa

Colonial Archives, C13A Series, General Correspondence, Louisiana

New Mexico State Records Center and Archives, Santa Fe

Mexican Archives of New Mexico, 1821–1846
Territorial Archives of New Mexico

Texas State Library and Archives Commission, Austin

Andrew Jackson Houston Collection
Records Relating to Indian Affairs
Texas Adjutant General's Department Army Papers
Texas Adjutant General's Department Departmental Correspondence
Texas Adjutant General's Department Ranger Records
Texas Governor George T. Wood Records
Texas Governor Peter H. Bell Records

University of Arizona, Tucson

Maurice Garland Fulton Papers

University of New Mexico, Albuquerque, Center for Southwest Research

Inventory of the Michael Steck Papers, Microcopy E93

University of Texas at Austin, Nettie Lee Benson Latin American Collection

Presidio de San Felipe y Santiago de Janos Records, 1706–1858

University of Texas at Austin, Dolph Briscoe Center for American History

Eberstadt Collection
Andrew Nelson Erskine Papers
John Coffee Hays Collection
Kuykendall Family Papers
Texas Rangers Papers

University of Texas at El Paso

Archivo del Ayuntamiento de Chihuahua, Microfilm 491
Ciudad Juárez Municipal Archives, Microfilm 513
Janos Presidio Collection, Microfilm 498
El Siglo XIX (Mexico City newspaper), Microfilm 488
Periódico Oficial de Chihuahua, Microfilm 472
Periódico Oficial de Durango, Microfilm 493

US Congress

House. *Claims for Spoliations Committed by Indians and Mexicans*. 36th Cong., 1st Sess.,
    House Report No. 535.
———. *Correspondence with Texas, on the Subject of the Annexation*. 29th Cong., 1st Sess.,
    House Exec. Doc. No. 2.

———. *Documents Accompanying the Report of the Secretary of War to the President.* 31st Cong., 1st Sess., House Exec. Doc. No. 5.

———. *Protection Afforded by Volunteers of Oregon and Washington Territories to Overland Immigrants in 1854.* 35th Cong., 2nd Sess., House Misc. Doc. No. 47.

———. *Protection of the Frontier of Texas.* 35th Cong., 2nd Sess., House Exec. Doc. 27.

Senate. *Annual Report of the Commissioner of Indian Affairs.* 31st Cong., 2nd Sess., Senate Exec. Doc. No. 1.

———. *Communication from the Commissioner of Indian Affairs, and Other Documents, in Relation to the Texas Indians.* 30th Cong., 1st Sess., Senate Report No. 171.

———. *Communication from C. S. Drew, Late Adjutant of the Second Regiment of Oregon Mounted Volunteers, Giving an Account of the Origin and Early Prosecution of the Indian War in Oregon.* 36th Cong., 1st Sess., Senate Misc. Doc. No. 59.

———. *Condition of the Indian Tribes: Report of the Joint Special Committee, Appointed under Joint Resolution of March 3, 1865, with an Appendix.* 39th Cong., 2nd Sess., Senate Report No. 156.

———. *Letter from the Secretary of the Interior, Communicating the Report of Edward F. Beale, Superintendent of Indian Affairs in California, Respecting the Condition of Indian Affairs in that State, March 3, 1853.* 32nd Cong., 2nd Sess., Senate Exec. Doc. No. 57.

———. *Memorial of the Legislature of Texas, Praying the Reimbursement of Expenses Incurred by the State in Providing for the Military Defenses of Her Frontier in 1848.* 31st Cong., 1st Sess., Senate Misc. Doc. No. 97.

———. *Message of the President of the United States Communicating in Compliance with a Resolution of the Senate of February 26, Calling for a Copy of the Report and Maps of Captain Marcy of His Explorations of the Big Witchita and Head Waters of the Brazos Rivers.* 34th Cong., 1st Sess., Senate Exec. Doc. No. 60.

———. *Report of the Secretary of the Interior, Communicating, in Compliance with a Resolution of the Senate, a Copy of the Correspondence between the Department of the Interior and the Indian Agents and Commissioners in California.* 33rd Cong., Special Session, Senate Exec. Doc. No. 4.

———. *Report of the Secretary of War, Enclosing the Report of Lieutenant W. H. C. Whiting's Reconnaissance of the Western Frontier of Texas.* 31st Cong., 1st Sess., Senate Exec. Doc. No. 64.

———. *Report of the Secretary of War.* 35th Cong., 2nd Sess., Senate Exec. Doc. No. 1.

———. *Report of the Secretary of War.* 36th Cong., 1st Sess., Senate Exec. Doc. No. 2.

Government Documents and Publications

Annual Report on the Commercial Relations between the United States and Foreign Nations, Made by the Secretary of State, for the Year Ending September 30, 1870. Washington, DC: Government Printing Office, 1871.

California Constitution. 1850.

Legislative Assembly of Nova Scotia. Assembly 58, Session 1. Transcripts, March 28, 2000.

Population of the United States in 1860; Compiled from the Original Returns of the Eighth Census. . . . Washington, DC: Government Printing Office, 1864.

Report of the Commissioner of Indian Affairs, Accompanying the Annual Report of the Secretary of the Interior for the Year 1857. Washington, DC: William H. Harris, 1858.

Report of the Commissioner of Indian Affairs for the Year 1862. Washington, DC: Government Printing Office, 1863.

The Seventh Census of the United States: 1850. Washington, DC: Robert Armstrong, 1853.

United States Constitution. 1788.

The War of the Rebellion: A Compilation of the Official Records of the Union and Confederate Armies. Series 1. 53 vols. Washington, DC: Government Printing Office, 1882–98.

Published Sources

"An Act for the Abolition of Slavery throughout the British Colonies." Acts of the Parliament of the United Kingdom, 3 & 4 Will. IV c.73, August 28, 1833.

The Acts and Resolves, Public and Private, of the Province of the Massachusetts Bay. 21 vols. Boston: Wright and Potter, 1869–1922.

Anderson, Robert A. *Fighting the Mill Creeks: Being a Personal Account of Campaigns against Indians of the Northern Sierras.* Chico, CA: Chico Record Press, 1909.

Appendix to Journals of the Senate of the Eleventh Session of the Legislature of the State of California. Sacramento: C. T. Botts, 1860.

Appendix to the House of Representatives Journals, of the Third Legislature, State of Texas, Second Session. Austin: Wm. H. Cushney, 1850.

Appendix to the Journals of the Ninth Congress of the Republic of Texas. Washington, TX: Miller and Cushney, 1845.

Articles of Confederation and Perpetual Union between the States of New-Hampshire, Massachusetts-Bay, Rhode Island and Providence Plantations, Connecticut, New-York, New-Jersey, Pennsylvania, Delaware, Maryland, Virginia, North-Carolina, South-Carolina, and Georgia. Lancaster, PA: Francis Bailey, 1777.

Ball, Eve. *Indeh: An Apache Odyssey.* Provo, UT: Brigham Young University Press, 1980.

———. *In the Days of Victorio: Recollections of a Warm Springs Apache.* Tucson: University of Arizona Press, 1970.

Barrett, S. M., ed. *Geronimo's Story of His Life.* New York: Duffield, 1906.

Bartlett, John Russell. *Personal Narrative of Explorations and Incidents in Texas, New Mexico, California, Sonora, and Chihuahua, 1850–1853.* 2 vols. New York: D. Appleton, 1854.

Basso, Keith, ed. *Western Apache Raiding and Warfare: From the Notes of Grenville Goodwin.* Tucson: University of Arizona Press, 1971.

Baylor, George Wythe. *Into the Far, Wild Country: True Tales of the Old Southwest.* Edited by Jerry D. Thompson. El Paso: Texas Western Press, 1996.

Beaumont, Gaston du Boscq de, ed. *Les derniers jours de l'Acadie (1748–1758): Correspondances et mémoires.* Paris: Emile Lechevalier, 1899.

Berlandier, Jean Louis. *The Indians of Texas in 1830.* Edited by John C. Ewers. Washington, DC: Smithsonian Institution Press, 1969.

Betzinez, Jason. *I Fought with Geronimo.* New York: Bonanza Books, 1959.

Bieber, Ralph P., ed. *Exploring Southwestern Trails, 1846–1854.* Glendale, CA: Arthur H. Clark, 1938.

——. *Marching with the Army of the West, 1846–1848.* Glendale, CA: Arthur H. Clark, 1936.

Blanchet, Jean Gervais Protais et al., eds. *Collection de manuscrits contenant lettres, mémoires, et autres documents historiques relatifs a la Nouevelle-France.* 4 vols. Quebec: Côté, 1884–85.

Bliss, Eugene F., ed. *Diary of David Zeisberger, a Moravian Missionary among the Indians of Ohio.* 2 vols. Cincinnati, OH: Robert Clarke, 1885.

Bliss, Leslie E., and Arthur A. Woodward, eds. *Don Santiago Kirker.* Los Angeles: Muir Dawson, 1948.

Bourke, John G. *On the Border with Crook.* New York: Charles Scribner's Sons, 1891.

Bouton, Nathaniel, ed. *Documents and Records Relating to the Province of New-Hampshire, from the Earliest Period of Its Settlement.* 7 vols. Manchester, NH: John B. Clarke, 1867–73.

Boyer, Ruth McDonald, and Narcissus Duffy Gayton. *Apache Mothers and Daughters: Four Generations of a Family.* Norman: University of Oklahoma Press, 1992.

Box, Michael James. *Adventures and Explorations in New and Old Mexico.* New York: James Miller, 1869.

Brock, R. A., ed. *The Official Records of Robert Dinwiddie, Lieutenant-Governor of the Colony of Virginia, 1751–1758.* 2 vols. Richmond: Virginia Historical Society, 1883–84.

Brodhead, John Romeyn, ed. *Documents Relative to the Colonial History of the State of New-York.* 15 vols. Albany, NY: Weed, Parsons, 1858.

Browne, J. Ross. *Adventures in the Apache Country: A Tour through Arizona and Sonora, with Notes on the Silver Regions of Nevada.* New York: Harper and Brothers, 1871.

——. *Muleback to the Convention: Letters of J. Ross Browne, Reported to the Constitutional Convention, Monterey, September–October, 1849.* San Francisco: Book Club of California, 1950.

Buffum, E. Gould. *Six Months in the Gold Mines: From a Journal of Three Years Residence in Upper and Lower California 1847–8–9.* Philadelphia: Lea and Blanchard, 1850.

Bulletin des Recherches Historiques. 68 vols. Levis, QU: George Roy et Antoine Roy, 1895–1968.

By His Excellency Joseph Reed, Esq. President, and the Supreme Executive Council, of the Commonwealth of Pennsylvania: A Proclamation. Philadelphia: Francis Bailey, 1780.

Calloway, Colin, ed. *Dawnland Encounters: Indians and Europeans in Northern New England.* Hanover, NH: University Press of New England, 1991.

Calvin, Ross, ed. *Lieutenant Emory Reports: Notes of a Military Reconnaissance.* Albuquerque: University of New Mexico Press, 1951.

Casgrain, H. R., ed. *Voyage au Canada dans le nord de l'Amerique septentrionale fait dupuis l'an 1751 à 1761 par J. C. B.* Quebec: Impremerie Léger Brousseau, 1887.

Chamberlain, Samuel E. *Recollections of a Rogue.* London: Museum Press, 1957.

Church, Benjamin. *Diary of King Philip's War, 1675–76.* Edited by Alan and Mary Simpson. Chester, CT: Pequot Press, 1975.

Cleland, Robert Glass. *Pathfinders.* Los Angeles: Powell, 1929.

Collections of the Nova Scotia Historical Society. Vol. 16. Halifax, NS: Wm. MacNab and Son, 1912.

Connelley, William E. *Doniphan's Expedition and the Conquest of New Mexico and California.* Kansas City, MO: Bryan and Douglas, 1907.

Coronel, Antonio Franco. *Tales of Mexican California: Cosas de California.* Translated by Diane de Avalle-Arce and edited by Doyce B. Nunis Jr. Santa Barbara, CA: Bellerophon Books, 1994.

Coste, Charles, ed. *Aventures militaires au XVIII siécle, d'aprés les mémoires de Jean-Baptiste d'Aleyrac.* Paris: Berger-Levrault, 1935.

Crampton, C. Gregory, ed. *The Mariposa Indian War, 1850–1851: Diaries of Robert Eccleston: The California Gold Rush, Yosemite, and the High Sierra.* Salt Lake City: University of Utah Press, 1957.

Cremony, John C. *Life among the Apaches.* San Francisco: A. Roman, 1868.

A Declaration and Remonstrance of the Distressed and Bleeding Frontier Inhabitants of the Province of Pennsylvania. N.p., 1764.

De Ville, Winston, trans. and ed. *Massacre at Natchez in 1729: The Rheims Manuscript.* Ville Platte, LA: Provincial Press, 2003.

DeWees, W. B. *Letters from an Early Settler of Texas.* Waco, TX: Texian Press, 1968.

Dublán, Manuel, and José Maria Lozano, eds. *Legislación mexicana; ó, Colección completa de las disposiciones legislativas expedidas desde la independencia de la republica.* Vol. 3. Mexico City: Dublán y Lozano, 1876.

Duval, John C. *The Adventures of Big-Foot Wallace.* Edited by Mabel Major and Rebecca Smith Lee. Lincoln: University of Nebraska Press, 1966.

Edwards, Frank S. *A Campaign in New Mexico with Colonel Doniphan.* 1847; reprint, Albuquerque: University of New Mexico Press, 1996.

Escudero, José Agustín de. *Observaciones sobre el estado actual del Departamento de Chihuahua.* Mexico City: Juan Ojeda, 1839.

Evans, George W. B. *Mexican Gold Trail: The Journal of a Forty-Niner*. Edited by Glenn S. Dumke. San Marino, CA: Huntington Library, 2006.

Farquhar, Francis P., ed. *Up and Down California in 1860–1864: The Journal of William H. Brewer, Professor of Agriculture in the Sheffield Scientific School from 1864 to 1903*. Berkeley: University of California Press, 1966.

Ford, John Salmon. *Rip Ford's Texas*. Edited by Stephen B. Oates. Austin: University of Texas Press, 1963.

Foreman, Grant, ed. *Marcy and the Gold Seekers: The Journal of Captain R. B. Marcy, with an Account of the Gold Rush over the Southern Route*. Norman: University of Oklahoma Press, 1939.

Froebel, Julius. *Seven Years' Travel in Central America, Northern Mexico, and the Far West of the United States*. London: Richard Bentley, 1859.

Gammel, H. P. N., comp. *The Laws of Texas, 1822–1897*. Vol. 2. Austin, TX: Gammel, 1898.

Gregg, Josiah. *Commerce of the Prairies*. Edited by Max L. Moorhead. Norman: University of Oklahoma Press, 1954.

Gulick, Charles Adams, Jr., and Katherine Elliott, eds. *The Papers of Mirabeau Buonaparte Lamar*. 6 vols. Austin, TX: A. C. Baldwin and Sons, 1922.

Hamilton, Edward P., ed. and trans. *Adventure in the Wilderness: The American Journals of Louis Antoine de Bougainville, 1756–1760*. Norman: University of Oklahoma Press, 1964.

Hammond, George P., and Edward H. Howes, eds. *Overland to California on the Southwestern Trail, 1849: Diary of Robert Eccleston*. Berkeley: University of California Press, 1950.

Hannum, Anna Paschall, ed. *A Quaker Forty-Niner: The Adventures of Charles Edward Pancoast on the American Frontier*. Philadelphia: University of Pennsylvania Press, 1930.

Harris, Benjamin Butler. *The Gila Trail: The Texas Argonauts and the California Gold Rush*. Edited and annotated by Richard H. Dillon. Norman: University of Oklahoma Press, 1960.

Hazard, Samuel, ed. *Pennsylvania Archives: Selected and Arranged from the Original Documents in the Office of the Secretary of the Commonwealth, Conformably to the Acts of the General Assembly, February 15, 1851, and March 1, 1852*. Series 1. 12 vols. Philadelphia: Joseph Severns, 1852–56.

Headlam, Cecil, ed. *Calendar of State Papers, Colonial Series, America and West Indies*. 45 vols. London: Her Majesty's Stationery Office, 1922.

Heizer, Robert F., ed. *The Destruction of California Indians: A Collection of Documents from the Period 1847 to 1865 in Which Are Described Some of the Things That Happened to Some of the Indians of California*. Santa Barbara, CA: Peregrine Smith, 1974.

———. *Reprints of Various Papers on California Archaeology, Ethnology and Indian History*. Berkeley: University of California Department of Anthropology, 1973.

———. *They Were Only Diggers: A Collection of Articles from California Newspapers, 1851–1866, on Indian and White Relations.* Ramona, CA: Ballena Press, 1974.

Henckaerts, Jean-Marie, and Louise Doswald-Beck, eds. *Customary International Humanitarian Law.* Vol. 1: *Rules.* Cambridge: Cambridge University Press, 2005.

Hening, William Waller, ed. *The Statutes at Large; Being a Collection of All the Laws of Virginia, from the First Session of the Legislature in the Year 1619.* 13 vols. Richmond, VA: Franklin Press, 1819.

Hobbs, James. *Wild Life in the Far West: Personal Adventures of a Border Mountain Man.* Waterford, CT: Wiley, Waterman and Eaton, 1875.

Houston, Alan, ed. *Franklin: The Autobiography and Other Writings on Politics, Economics, and Virtue.* Cambridge: Cambridge University Press, 2004.

Jameson, J. Franklin, ed. *Narratives of New Netherland, 1609–1664.* New York: Charles Scribner's Sons, 1909.

Jenkins, John Holmes, III, ed. *Recollections of Early Texas: The Memoirs of John Holland Jenkins.* Austin: University of Texas Press, 1958.

Johnson, Theodore T. *Sights in the Gold Region, and Scenes by the Way.* New York: Baker and Scribner, 1850.

Journal of the Fourth Session of the Legislature, Begun on the Third Day of January, 1853, and Ended on the Nineteenth Day of May, 1853, at the Cities of Vallejo and Benicia—Journal of the Senate, Fourth Session, Appendix. San Francisco: George Kerr, 1853.

Journal of the House of Representatives, Republic of Texas, Called Session of September 25, 1837 and Regular Session Commencing November 6, 1837. Houston, TX: Niles, 1838.

Journal of the House of Representatives, Republic of Texas, Second Congress, Adjourned Session. Houston, TX: Telegraph Office, 1838.

Journal of the House of Representatives of the Republic of Texas, Regular Session of Third Congress, Nov. 5, 1838. Houston, TX: S. Whiting, 1839.

Journals of the House of Representatives of the Republic of Texas, Fifth Congress First Session, 1840–1841. Austin, TX: Cruger and Wing, 1841.

Journals of the House of Representatives of the Seventh Congress of the Republic of Texas, Convened at Washington, on the 14th Nov., 1842. Washington, TX: Thomas Johnson, 1843.

Journals of the House of Representatives of the Eighth Congress of the Republic of Texas. Houston, TX: Cruger and Moore, 1844.

Journals of the House of Representatives of the State of Texas, Extra Session—Third Legislature. Austin: Texas State Gazette Office, 1850.

Journals of the Senate of the State of Texas, Extra Session—Third Legislature. Austin: Texas State Gazette Office, 1850.

Kellogg, Louise Phelps, ed. *Frontier Retreat on the Upper Ohio, 1779–1781.* Madison: Wisconsin Historical Society, 1917.

Kendall, George Wilkins. *Narrative of the Texan–Santa Fé Expedition.* 2 vols. New York: Harper and Brothers, 1844.

Kidder, Frederic. *Capt. John Lovewell, and His Encounters with the Indians.* Boston: Bartlett and Halliday, 1865.

Lawrence, Kip. *Indian Council in the Valley of the Walla-Walla.* San Francisco: Whitton, Towne, 1855.

Le Blant, Robert. *Histoire de la Nouvelle France: Les sources narratives du début du XVIII siècle et le recueil de Gédéon de Catalogne.* Dax, France: P. Predeu, 1940.

Lehnert, Pierre-Frédéric. *Album pintoresco de la República Mexicana.* Mexico City: Julio Michaud y Thomas, 1850.

Lincoln, Charles Zebina, and William Johnson, eds. *The Colonial Laws of New York, from the Year 1664 to the Revolution.* 5 vols. Albany, NY: James B. Lyon, 1894.

Linn, John J. *Reminiscences of Fifty Years in Texas.* New York: Sadlier, 1883.

Loudon, Archibald. *A Selection, of Some of the Most Interesting Narratives, of Outrages, Committed by the Indians in their Wars, with the White People.* 2 vols. in 1. Carlisle, PA: A. Loudon, 1808.

Lubbock, Francis R. *Six Decades in Texas; or, Memoirs of Francis Richard Lubbock, Governor of Texas in War Time, 1861–1863.* Austin, TX: Ben C. Jones, 1900.

Maltby, W. J. *Captain Jeff; or, Frontier Life in Texas with the Texas Rangers.* Colorado, TX: Whipkey, 1906.

Margry, Pierre, ed. *Découvertes et établissements des français dans l'ouest et dans le sud de l'Amérique septentrionale.* 6 vols. Paris: Maisonneuve, 1879–88.

Mather, Cotton. *Humiliations Follow'd with Deliverances.* Boston: B. Green and J. Allen, 1697.

McDowell, Catherine W., ed. *Now You Hear My Horn: The Journal of James Wilson Nichols, 1820–1887.* Austin: University of Texas Press, 1967.

McWilliams, Richebourg Gaillard, ed. and trans. *Fleur de Lys and Calumet: Being the Pénicaut Narrative of French Adventure in Louisiana.* Tuscaloosa: University of Alabama Press, 1953.

Memorial and Affidavits Showing Outrages Perpetrated by the Apache Indians, in the Territory of Arizona, during the Years 1869 and 1870. San Francisco: Francis and Valentine, 1871.

Minutes of the Supreme Executive Council of Pennsylvania, from Its Organization to the Termination of the Revolution. 16 vols. Harrisburg, PA: Theo. Fenn, 1831–53.

Morgan, Dale L., ed. *California as I Saw It: Pencillings by the Way of Its Gold and Gold Diggers! And Incidents of Travel by Land and Water by William M'Collum, M.D., a Returned Adventurer.* Los Gatos, CA: Talisman Press, 1960.

Mowry, Sylvester. *Arizona and Sonora: The Geography, History, and Resources of the Silver Region of North America.* New York: Harper Brothers, 1864.

Navarro, Ramón Gil. *The Gold Rush Diary of Ramón Gil Navarro*. Edited and translated by María del Carmen Ferreyra and David S. Reher. Lincoln: University of Nebraska Press, 2000.

Nicolson, John, ed. *The Arizona of Joseph Pratt Allyn: Letters from a Pioneer Judge, Observations and Travels, 1863–1866*. Tucson: University of Arizona Press, 1974.

O'Callaghan, Edmund B., ed. *Laws and Ordinances of New Netherland, 1638–1674*. Albany, NY: Weed, Parsons, 1868.

O'Callaghan, Edmund B., and Berthold Fernow, eds. *Documents Relative to the Colonial History of the State of New York*. 15 vols. Albany, NY: Weed, Parsons, 1856–87.

Ober, Frederick A. *Travels in Mexico and Life among the Mexicans*. Denver, CO: Perry, 1883.

Olmsted, Frederick Law. *A Journey through Texas; or, a Saddle-Trip on the Southwestern Frontier*. Austin: University of Texas Press, 1978.

Palmer, William, ed. *Calendar of Virginia State Papers and Other Manuscripts*. Vol. 1: *1652–1781*. New York: Kraus, 1968.

Penhallow, Samuel. *The History of the Wars of New-England with the Eastern Indians; or, A Narrative of Their Continued Perfidy and Cruelty from the 10th of August, 1703 to the Peace Renewed 13th of July, 1713*. 1726; reprint, Philadelphia: Oscar H. Harpel, 1859.

Quint, A. H., ed. *Journal of the Rev. John Pike, of Dover, N.H.* Cambridge, MA: John Wilson, 1876.

Rankin, Melinda. *Texas in 1850*. Boston: Damrell and Moore, 1850.

Rapport de l'archiviste de la province de Québec pour 1922–1923. Ls-A. Proulx, QU: Imprimeur de Sa Majesté le Roi, 1923.

Rapport de l'archiviste de la province de Québec pour 1923–1924. Ls-A. Proulx, QU: Imprimeur de Sa Majesté le Roi, 1924.

Rapport de l'archiviste de la province de Québec pour 1927–1928. L.-Amable Proulx, QU: Imprimeur de Sa Majesté le Roi, 1928.

Reed, William B., ed. *Life and Correspondence of Joseph Reed*. 2 vols. Philadelphia: Lindsay and Blakiston, 1847.

Revere, Joseph Warren. *A Tour of Duty in California; including a Description of the Gold Region*. New York: C. S. Francis, 1849.

Robinson, Sherry. *Apache Voices: Their Stories of Survival as Told to Eve Ball*. Albuquerque: University of New Mexico Press, 2000.

———. *I Fought a Good Fight: A History of the Lipan Apaches*. Denton: University of North Texas Press, 2013.

Rogers, Robert. *Journals of Major Robert Rogers*. London: J. Millan, 1765.

Romero, Daniel Castro. *Cuélcahen Ndé: The Castros of the Lipan Apache Band of Texas*. Edited and translated by Santiago Castro Castro and Valentina Sambrano Rodriguez. San Antonio: Lipan Apache Band of Texas, 2004.

Rowland, Dunbar, and Albert Godfrey Sanders, eds. *Mississippi Provincial Archives: French Dominion.* 4 vols. Jackson: Press of the Mississippi Department of Archives and History, 1927–32.

Ruxton, George F. *Adventures in Mexico and the Rocky Mountains.* New York: Harper and Brothers, 1848.

Sanger, George P., ed. *The Statutes at Large, Treaties, and Proclamations of the United States America, from December 5, 1859 to March 3, 1863.* Vol. 12. Boston: Little, Brown, 1863.

Scott, Darrell, ed. *A True Copy of the Record of the Official Proceedings at the Council in the Walla Walla Valley, 1855.* Fairfield, WA: Ye Galleon Press, 1985.

Shaw, William. *Golden Dreams and Waking Realities; Being the Adventures of a Gold-Seeker in California and the Pacific Islands.* London: Smith, Elder, 1851.

Smither, Harriet, ed. *Journals of the Sixth Congress of the Republic of Texas, 1841–1842, to Which Are Added the Special Laws.* 3 vols. Austin, TX: Capital Printing, 1945.

Smithwick, Noah. *The Evolution of a State; or, Recollections of Old Texas Days.* Edited by Alwyn Barr. Austin, TX: W. Thomas Taylor, 1995.

The Statutes of California, Passed at the First Session of the Legislature, Begun the 15th Day of Dec. 1849, and Ended the 22d Day of April, 1850 at the City of Pueblo de San José. San Jose, CA: J. Winchester, 1850.

The Statutes of California, Passed at the Third Session of the Legislature, Begun on the Fifth of January, 1852, and Ended on the Fourth Day of May, 1852, at the Cities of Vallejo and Sacramento. San Francisco, CA: G. K. Fitch, 1852.

The Statutes of California, Passed at the Fourth Session of the Legislature, Begun on the Third of January, 1853, and Ended on the Nineteenth Day of May, 1853, at the Cities of Vallejo and Benicia. San Francisco, CA: George Kerr, 1853.

Sullivan, James, ed. *The Papers of Sir William Johnson.* 14 vols. Albany: University of the State of New York, 1921–65.

Sunder, John E., ed. *Matt Field on the Santa Fe Trail.* Norman: University of Oklahoma Press, 1960.

Tanguay, Cyprien. *A travers les registres.* Montreal: Cadieux and Derome, 1886.

Terrazas, D. Joaquín. *Memorias.* Juarez: El Agricultor Mexicano, 1905.

Thwaites, Reuben Gold, ed. *The Jesuit Relations and Allied Documents: Travels and Explorations of the Jesuit Missionaries in New France, 1610–1791.* 73 vols. Cleveland, OH: Burrows Brothers, 1896–1901.

Thwaites, Reuben Gold, and Louise Phelps Kellogg, eds. *Frontier Defense on the Upper Ohio.* Madison: Wisconsin Historical Society, 1912.

United Nations. "Convention on the Prevention and Punishment of the Crime of Genocide, Adopted by the General Assembly of the United Nations on 9 December 1948." In *Treaty Series*, vol. 78, no. 121.

Vattel, Emer de. *The Law of Nations; or, Principles of the Law of Nature, Applied to the Conduct and Affairs of Nations and Sovereigns.* 6th ed. Philadelphia: T. and J. W. Johnson, 1844.

Wallace, Paul A. W., ed. *Thirty Thousand Miles with John Heckewelder.* Pittsburgh, PA: University of Pittsburgh Press, 1958.

Wharton, Francis, ed. *The Revolutionary Diplomatic Correspondence of the United States.* 2 vols. Washington, DC: Government Printing Office, 1889.

Weber, David J., ed. and trans. *Arms, Indians, and the Mismanagement of New Mexico: Donaciano Vigil, 1846.* El Paso: Texas Western Press, 1986.

Williams, Amelia W., and Eugene C. Barker, eds. *The Writings of Sam Houston, 1813–1863.* 8 vols. Austin, TX: Jenkins, 1970.

Williams, R. H. *With the Border Ruffians: Memories of the Far West, 1852–1868.* Edited by E. W. Williams. Lincoln: University of Nebraska Press, 1982.

Wilson, John P., ed. *When the Texans Came: Missing Records from the Civil War in the Southwest, 1861–1862.* Albuquerque: University of New Mexico Press, 2001.

Winfrey, Dorman H., and James M. Day, eds. *The Indian Papers of Texas and the Southwest, 1825–1916.* 5 vols. Austin, TX: Pemberton Press, 1996.

Winkler, Ernest William, ed. *Secret Journals of the Senate of the Republic of Texas, 1836–1845.* Austin, TX: Austin Printing, 1911.

Wislizenus, Dr. A. *Memoir of a Tour to Northern Mexico, Connected with Col. Doniphan's Expedition, in 1846 and 1847.* Washington, DC: Tippin and Streeper, 1848.

Secondary Sources

Books

Acuña, Rodolfo F. *Sonoran Strongman: Ignacio Pesqueira and His Times.* Tucson: University of Arizona Press, 1974.

Allain, Mathé. *"Not Worth a Straw": French Colonial Policy and the Early Years of Louisiana.* Lafayette: Center for Louisiana Studies, University of Southwestern Louisiana, 1988.

Almada, Francisco R. *Diccionarrio de historia, geografía, y biografía chihuahuenses.* Juarez: Impresora de Juárez, 1968.

———. *Diccionarrio de historia, geografía, y biografía sonorenses.* Chihuahua: Impresora Ruiz Sandoval, 1952.

———. *Juárez y terrazas: Aclaraciones históricas.* Chihuahua: Libros Mexicanos, 1958.

———. *Resumen de historia del estado de Chihuahua.* Mexico City: Librados Mexicanos, 1955.

Almaguer, Tomás. *Racial Fault Lines: The Historical Origins of White Supremacy in California.* Berkeley: University of California Press, 2009.

Alvarez, Alex. *Native America and the Question of Genocide*. Lanham, MD: Rowman and Littlefield, 2014.

Anderson, Fred. *Crucible of War: The Seven Years' War and the Fate of Empire in British North America, 1754–1766*. New York: Alfred A. Knopf, 2000.

———. *A People's Army: Massachusetts Soldiers and Society in the Seven Years' War*. Chapel Hill: University of North Carolina Press, 1984.

Anderson, Gary Clayton. *The Conquest of Texas: Ethnic Cleansing in the Promised Land, 1820–1875*. Norman: University of Oklahoma Press, 2005.

———. *Ethnic Cleansing and the Indian: The Crime That Should Haunt America*. Norman: University of Oklahoma Press, 2015.

Aquila, Richard. *The Iroquois Restoration: Iroquois Diplomacy on the Colonial Frontier, 1701–1754*. Detroit, MI: Wayne State University Press, 1983.

Atkinson, James R. *Splendid Land, Splendid People: The Chickasaw Indians to Removal*. Tuscaloosa: University of Alabama Press, 2003.

Axtell, James. *Beyond 1492: Encounters in Colonial North America*. New York: Oxford University Press, 1992.

———. *Natives and Newcomers: The Cultural Origins of North America*. New York: Oxford University Press, 2001.

Babcock, Matthew. *Apache Adaptation to Hispanic Rule*. New York: Cambridge University Press, 2016.

Baptist, Edward E. *The Half Has Never Been Told: Slavery and the Making of American Capitalism*. New York: Basic Books, 2014.

Bailyn, Bernard. *The Barbarous Years: The Conflict of Civilizations, 1600–1675*. New York: Alfred A. Knopf, 2012.

Ball, Durwood. *Army Regulars on the Western Frontier, 1848–1861*. Norman: University of Oklahoma Press, 2001.

Barnett, James F., Jr. *The Natchez Indians: A History to 1735*. Jackson: University Press of Mississippi, 2007.

Basso, Keith H. *Wisdom Sits in Places: Landscape and Language among the Western Apache*. Albuquerque: University of New Mexico Press, 1996.

Baumgardner, Frank H., III. *Killing for Land in Early California: Indian Blood at Round Valley, 1856–1863*. New York: Algora, 2006.

Belich, James. *Replenishing the Earth: The Settler Revolution and the Rise of the Anglo-World, 1783–1939*. Oxford: Oxford University Press, 2009.

Bell, Horace. *Reminiscences of a Ranger; or, Early Times in Southern California*. Santa Barbara, CA: Wallace Hebberd, 1927.

Beckert, Sven, and Seth Rockman, eds. *Slavery's Capitalism: A New History of American Economic Development*. Philadelphia: University of Pennsylvania Press, 2016.

Best, Geoffrey. *Humanity in Warfare: The Modern History of the International Law of Armed Conflicts*. New York: Columbia University Press, 1980.

Bigler, David L., and Will Bagley. *The Mormon Rebellion: America's First Civil War, 1857–1858*. Norman: University of Oklahoma Press, 2011.

Blackhawk, Ned. *The Rediscovery of America: Native Peoples and the Unmaking of U.S. History*. New Haven: Yale University Press, 2023.

———. *Violence over the Land: Indians and Empires in the Early American West*. Cambridge, MA: Harvard University Press, 2006.

Blyth, Lance R. *Chiricahua and Janos: Communities of Violence in the Southwestern Borderlands, 1680–1880*. Lincoln: University of Nebraska Press, 2012.

Bloxham, Donald. *The Final Solution: A Genocide*. Oxford: Oxford University Press, 2009.

Bragdon, Kathleen J. *Native People of Southern New England*. Norman: University of Oklahoma Press, 1996.

Britten, Thomas A. *The Lipan Apaches: People of Wind and Lightning*. Albuquerque: University of New Mexico Press, 2009.

Brooks, James F. *Captives and Cousins: Slavery, Kinship, and Community in the Southwest Borderlands*. Chapel Hill: University of North Carolina Press, 2002.

Brooks, Lisa. *Our Beloved Kin: A New History of King Philip's War*. New Haven: Yale University Press, 2018.

Calloway, Colin. *The American Revolution in Indian Country: Crisis and Diversity in Native American Communities*. Cambridge: Cambridge University Press, 1995.

———. *The Indian World of George Washington: The First President, the First Americans, and the Birth of the Nation*. New York: Oxford University Press, 2018.

———. *New Worlds for All: Indians, Europeans, and the Remaking of Early America*. Baltimore: Johns Hopkins University Press, 2013.

———. *The Victory with No Name: The Native American Defeat of the First American Army*. New York: Oxford University Press, 2015.

———. *The Western Abenakis of Vermont, 1600–1800: War, Migration, and the Survival of an Indian People*. Norman: University of Oklahoma Press, 1990.

Camacho, Ana Lilia Nieto. *Defensa y política en la frontera norte de México, 1848–1856*. Tijuana: Colegio de la Frontera Norte, 2012.

Cameron, Catherine M. *Captives: How Stolen People Changed the World*. Lincoln: University of Nebraska Press, 2016.

Cameron, Catherine M., Paul Kelton, and Alan C. Swedlund, eds. *Beyond Germs: Native Depopulation in North America*. Tucson: University of Arizona Press, 2015.

Carranco, Lynwood, and Estle Beard. *Genocide and Vendetta: The Round Valley Wars of Northern California*. Norman: University of Oklahoma Press, 1981.

Carson, James Taylor. *Searching for the Bright Path: The Mississippi Choctaws from Prehistory to Removal*. Lincoln: University of Nebraska Press, 1999.

Cave, Alfred A. *Lethal Encounters: Englishmen and Indians in Colonial Virginia*. Lincoln: University of Nebraska Press, 2013.

Chacon, Richard J., and David H. Dye, eds. *The Taking and Displaying of Human Body Parts as Trophies by Amerindians*. New York: Springer, 2007.

Chase, George Wingate. *The History of Haverhill, Massachusetts, from Its First Settlement, in 1640, to the Year 1860.* Haverhill, MA: Published by the Author, 1861.

Chénier, Rémi. *Québec: A French Colonial Town in America, 1660 to 1690.* Ottawa: National Historic Sites Parks Service, 1991.

Chet, Guy. *Conquering the American Wilderness: The Triumph of European Warfare in the Colonial Northeast.* Amherst: University of Massachusetts Press, 2003.

Churchill, Ward. *A Little Matter of Genocide: Holocaust and Denial in the Americas, 1492 to the Present.* San Francisco: City Lights Books, 1997.

Collins, Michael L. *A Crooked River: Rustlers, Rangers, and Regulars on the Lower Rio Grande, 1861–1877.* Norman: University of Oklahoma Press, 2018.

——. *Texas Devils: Rangers and Regulars on the Lower Rio Grande, 1846–1861.* Norman: University of Oklahoma Press, 2008.

Colwell-Chanthaphonh, Chip. *Massacre at Camp Grant: Forgetting and Remembering Apache History.* Tucson: University of Arizona Press, 2007.

Compton, Jim. *Spirit in the Rock: The Fierce Battle for Modoc Homelands.* Pullman: Washington State University Press, 2017.

Conner, Daniel Ellis. *Joseph Reddeford Walker and the Arizona Adventure.* Norman: University of Oklahoma Press, 1956.

Conrad, Paul. *The Apache Diaspora: Four Centuries of Displacement and Survival.* Philadelphia: University of Pennsylvania Press, 2021.

Cook, Noble David. *Born to Die: Disease and New World Conquest, 1492–1650.* Cambridge: Cambridge University Press, 1998.

Cook, Sherburne F. *The Conflict between the California Indian and White Civilization.* Berkeley: University of California Press, 1976.

——. *The Population of California Indians, 1769–1970.* Berkeley: University of California Press, 1976.

Cook-Lynn, Elizabeth. *Anti-Indianism in Modern America: A Voice from Tatekeya's Earth.* Urbana: University of Illinois Press, 2001.

Cothran, Boyd. *Remembering the Modoc War: Redemptive Violence and the Making of American Innocence.* Chapel Hill: University of North Carolina Press, 2014.

Courtwright, David T. *Violent Land: Single Men and Social Disorder from the Frontier to the Inner City.* Cambridge, MA: Harvard University Press, 1996.

Cress, Lawrence Delbert. *Citizens in Arms: The Army and Militia in American Society to the War of 1812.* Chapel Hill: University of North Carolina Press, 1982.

Crosby, Alfred W., Jr. *The Columbian Exchange: Biological and Cultural Consequences of 1492.* Westport, CT: Praeger, 2003.

Cruvellier, Thierry. *Court of Remorse: Inside the International Criminal Tribunal for Rwanda.* Translated by Chari Voss. Madison: University of Wisconsin Press, 2010.

Cunliffe, Marcus. *Soldiers and Civilians: The Martial Spirit in America, 1775–1865.* Boston: Little, Brown, 1968.

Dawdy, Shannon Lee. *Building the Devil's Empire: French Colonial New Orleans.* Chicago: University of Chicago Press, 2008.

Debo, Angie. *Geronimo: The Man, His Time, His Place.* Norman: University of Oklahoma Press, 1976.

DeLay, Brian. *War of a Thousand Deserts: Indian Raids and the U.S.-Mexican War.* New Haven: Yale University Press, 2008.

De León, Arnoldo. *War along the Border: The Mexican Revolution and Tejano Communities.* College Station: Texas A&M University Press, 2012.

DeLucia, Christine M. *Memory Lands: King Philip's War and the Place of Violence in the Northeast.* New Haven: Yale University Press, 2018.

Denzel, Markus A. *Handbook of World Exchange Rates, 1590–1914.* Burlington, VT: Ashgate, 2010.

Dickason, Olive. *Louisbourg and the Indians: A Study in Imperial Race Relations, 1713–1760.* Ottawa: University of Ottawa Press, 1971.

———. *The Myth of the Savage and the Beginnings of French Colonialism in the Americas.* Edmonton: University of Alberta Press, 1984.

Dixon, David. *Never Come to Peace Again: Pontiac's Uprising and the Fate of the British Empire in North America.* Norman: University of Oklahoma Press, 2005.

Douthit, Nathan. *Uncertain Encounters: Indians and Whites at Peace and War in Southern Oregon, 1820s–1860s.* Corvallis: Oregon State University Press, 2002.

Dowd, Gregory Evans. *Groundless: Rumors, Legends, and Hoaxes on the Early American Frontier.* Baltimore: Johns Hopkins University Press, 2015.

———. *A Spirited Resistance: The North American Indian Struggle for Unity, 1745–1815.* Baltimore: Johns Hopkins University Press, 1992.

———. *War under Heaven: Pontiac, the Indian Nations, and the British Empire.* Baltimore: Johns Hopkins University Press, 2002.

Drinnon, Richard. *Facing West: The Metaphysics of Indian-Hating and Empire-Building.* Norman: University of Oklahoma Press, 1997.

Dunbar-Ortiz, Roxanne. *An Indigenous Peoples' History of the United States.* Boston: Beacon Press, 2014.

DuVal, Kathleen. *The Native Ground: Indians and Colonists in the Heart of the Continent.* Philadelphia: University of Pennsylvania Press, 2006.

Eccles, W. J. *The French in North America, 1500–1783.* East Lansing: Michigan State University Press, 1998.

———. *Frontenac, the Courtier Governor.* Montreal: McGill-Queen's University Press, 1959.

Edmunds, R. David. *Tecumseh and the Quest for Indian Leadership.* New York: Pearson Longman, 2007.

Everett, Dianna. *The Texas Cherokees: A People between Two Fires, 1819–1840.* Norman: University of Oklahoma Press, 1990.

Faragher, John Mack. *Sugar Creek: Life on the Illinois Prairie.* New Haven: Yale University Press, 1986.

Fenn, Elizabeth A. *Encounters at the Heart of the World: A History of the Mandan People*. New York: Hill and Wang, 2014

———. *Pox Americana: The Great Smallpox Epidemic of 1775–82*. New York: Hill and Wang, 2001.

Fenton, William N. *The Great Law and the Longhouse: A Political History of the Iroquois Confederacy*. Norman: University of Oklahoma Press, 1998.

Finch, Martha L. *Dissenting Bodies: Corporealities in Early New England*. New York: Columbia University Press, 2010.

Fixico, Donald L. *Call for Change: The Medicine Way of American Indian History, Ethos, and Reality*. Lincoln: University of Nebraska Press, 2013.

Foner, Eric. *The Fiery Trial: Abraham Lincoln and American Slavery*. New York: W. W. Norton, 2010.

Foos, Paul. *A Short, Offhand, Killing Affair: Soldiers and Social Conflict during the Mexican-American War*. Chapel Hill: University of North Carolina Press, 2002.

Foster, Morris W. *Being Comanche: The Social History of an American Indian Community*. Tucson: University of Arizona Press, 1991.

Frazier, Donald S. *Blood and Treasure: Confederate Empire in the Southwest*. College Station: Texas A&M University Press, 1995.

Fuentes Mares, José. *Y México se refugió en el desierto: Luis Terrazas, historia y destino*. Mexico City: Jus, 1954.

Fujii, Lee Ann. *Show Time: The Logic and Power of Violent Display*. Ithaca, NY: Cornell University Press, 2021.

Gaff, Alan D. *Bayonets in the Wilderness: Anthony Wayne's Legion in the Old Northwest*. Norman: University of Oklahoma Press, 2004.

Gallay, Alan. *The Indian Slave Trade: The Rise of the English Empire in the American South, 1670–1717*. New Haven: Yale University Press, 2002.

Galloway, Patricia. *Choctaw Genesis, 1500–1700*. Lincoln: University of Nebraska Press, 1995.

———. *Practicing Ethnohistory: Mining Archives, Hearing Testimony, Constructing Narrative*. Lincoln: University of Nebraska Press, 2006.

Gelo, Daniel J., and Christopher J. Wickham. *Comanches and Germans on the Texas Frontier: The Ethnology of Heinrich Berghaus*. College Station: Texas A&M University Press, 2018.

Gibson, Arrell M. *The Chickasaws*. Norman: University of Oklahoma Press, 1971.

Gómez-Barris, Macarena. *Where Memory Dwells: Culture and State Violence in Chile*. Berkeley: University of California Press, 2008.

Goold, William. *Col. Arthur Noble, of Georgetown, Fort Halifax; Col. William Vaughan, of Matinicus and Damariscotta*. Portland, ME: Stephen Berry, 1881.

Grenier, John. *The Far Reaches of Empire: War in Nova Scotia, 1710–1760*. Norman: University of Oklahoma Press, 2008.

——. *The First Way of War: American Warmaking on the Frontier*. New York: Cambridge University Press, 2005.

Griffen, William B. *Apaches at War and Peace: The Janos Presidio, 1750–1858*. Albuquerque: University of New Mexico Press, 1988.

——. *Utmost Good Faith: Patterns of Apache-Mexican Hostilities in Northern Chihuahua Border Warfare, 1821–1848*. Albuquerque: University of New Mexico Press, 1988.

Haag, Marcia, and Henry Willis, eds. *Choctaw Language and Culture: Chahta Anumpa*. Norman: University of Oklahoma Press, 2001.

Hall, Martin Hardwick. *Sibley's New Mexico Campaign*. Austin: University of Texas Press, 1960.

Hämäläinen, Pekka. *The Comanche Empire*. New Haven: Yale University Press, 2008.

——. *Indigenous Continent: The Epic Contest for North America*. New York: Liveright, 2022.

Harper, Rob. *Unsettling the West: Violence and State Building in the Ohio Valley*. Philadelphia: University of Pennsylvania Press, 2018.

Harris, Charles H., III, and Louis R. Sadler. *The Texas Rangers and the Mexican Revolution: The Bloodiest Decade, 1910–1920*. Albuquerque: University of New Mexico Press, 2004.

Harrison, Simon. *Dark Trophies: Hunting and the Enemy Body in Modern War*. New York: Berghahn, 2012.

Hatfield, Shelley Bowen. *Chasing Shadows: Indians along the United States-Mexico Border, 1876–1911*. Albuquerque: University of New Mexico Press, 1998.

Heizer, Robert F., and Alan F. Almquist. *The Other Californians: Prejudice and Discrimination under Spain, Mexico, and the United States to 1920*. Berkeley: University of California Press, 1971.

Himmel, Kelly F. *The Conquest of the Karankawas and the Tonkawas, 1821–1859*. College Station: Texas A&M University Press, 1999.

Hinderaker, Eric. *Elusive Empires: Constructing Colonialism in the Ohio Valley, 1673–1800*. Cambridge: Cambridge University Press 1997.

Hixson, Walter L. *American Settler Colonialism: A History*. New York: Palgrave Macmillan, 2013.

Hurtado, Albert L. *Indian Survival on the California Frontier*. New Haven: Yale University Press, 1988.

Irvin-Erickson, Douglas. *Raphaël Lemkin and the Concept of Genocide*. Philadelphia: University of Pennsylvania Press, 2017.

Jacoby, Karl. *Shadows at Dawn: A Borderlands Massacre and the Violence of History*. New York: Penguin, 2008.

Jaenen, Cornelius J. *Friend and Foe: Aspects of French-Amerindian Cultural Contact in the Sixteenth and Seventeenth Centuries*. New York: Columbia University Press, 1976.

James, Cheewa. *Modoc: The Tribe That Wouldn't Die.* Happy Camp, CA: Naturegraph, 2008.

Jennings, Francis. *The Invasion of America: Indians, Colonialism, and the Cant of Conquest.* Chapel Hill: University of North Carolina Press, 1975.

Jennings, Matthew. *New Worlds of Violence: Cultures and Conquests in the Early American Southeast.* Knoxville: University of Tennessee Press, 2011.

Johnson, Benjamin H. *Revolution in Texas: How a Forgotten Rebellion and Its Bloody Suppression Turned Mexicans into Americans.* New Haven: Yale University Press, 2005.

Johnston-Dodds, Kimberly. *Early California Laws and Policies Related to California Indians.* Sacramento: California Research Bureau, 2002.

Jones, David S. *Rationalizing Epidemics: Meanings and Uses of American Indian Mortality since 1600.* Cambridge, MA: Harvard University Press, 2004.

Jortner, Adam. *Gods of Prophetstown: The Battle of Tippecanoe and the Holy War for the American Frontier.* New York: Oxford University Press, 2011.

Juster, Susan. *Sacred Violence in Early America.* Philadelphia: University of Pennsylvania Press, 2016.

Karson, Jennifer, ed. *Wiyaxayxt / Wiyaakaa'aw / As Days Go By: Our History, Our Land, Our People, the Cayuse, Umatilla, and Walla Walla.* Seattle: University of Washington Press, 2006.

Kavanagh, Thomas W. *Comanche Political History: An Ethnohistorical Perspective, 1706–1875.* Lincoln: University of Nebraska Press, 1996.

Kayworth, Alfred E., and Raymond G. Potvin. *The Scalp Hunters: Abenaki Ambush at Lovewell Pond—1725.* Boston: Branden Books, 2002.

Kelman, Ari. *A Misplaced Massacre: Struggling over the Memory of Sand Creek.* Cambridge, MA: Harvard University Press, 2013.

Kelton, Paul. *Epidemics and Enslavement: Biological Catastrophe in the Native Southeast.* Lincoln: University of Nebraska Press, 2007.

Kenny, Kevin. *Peaceable Kingdom Lost: The Paxton Boys and the Destruction of William Penn's Holy Experiment.* New York: Oxford University Press, 2009.

Kibbey, Ann. *The Interpretation of Material Shapes in Puritanism: A Study of Rhetoric, Prejudice, and Violence.* Cambridge: Cambridge University Press, 1986.

Kiernan, Ben. *Blood and Soil: A World History of Genocide and Extermination from Sparta to Darfur.* New Haven: Yale University Press, 2007.

Kiser, William S. *Borderlands of Slavery: The Struggle over Captivity and Peonage in the American Southwest.* Philadelphia: University of Pennsylvania Press, 2017.

———. *Coast-to-Coast Empire: Manifest Destiny and the New Mexico Borderlands.* Norman: University of Oklahoma Press, 2018.

———. *Dragoons in Apacheland: Conquest and Resistance in Southern New Mexico, 1846–1861.* Norman: University of Oklahoma Press, 2012.

———. *Illusions of Empire: The Civil War and Reconstruction in the U.S.-Mexico Borderlands.* Philadelphia: University of Pennsylvania Press, 2022.

——. *Turmoil on the Rio Grande: The Territorial History of the Mesilla Valley, 1846–1865.* College Station: Texas A&M University Press, 2011.

Knight, Oliver. *Following the Indian Wars: The Story of the Newspaper Correspondents among the Indian Campaigners.* Norman: University of Oklahoma Press, 1960.

Knouff, Gregory T. *The Soldiers' Revolution: Pennsylvanians in Arms and the Forging of Early American Identity.* University Park: Pennsylvania State University Press, 2004.

Kühn, Berndt. *Chronicles of War: Apache and Yavapai Resistance in the Southwestern United States and Northern Mexico, 1821–1937.* Tucson: Arizona Historical Society, 2014.

LaDuke, Winona. *All Our Relations: Native Struggles for Land and Life.* Cambridge, MA: South End Press, 1999.

Lahti, Janne. *Wars for Empire: Apaches, the United States, and the Southwest Borderlands.* Norman: University of Oklahoma Press, 2017.

Lambert, Valerie. *Choctaw Nation: A Study of American Indian Resurgence.* Lincoln: University of Nebraska Press, 2007.

Latorre, Felipe A., and Dolores L. Latorre. *The Mexican Kickapoo Indians.* Austin: University of Texas Press, 1976.

Lee, Wayne E. *Barbarians and Brothers: Anglo-American Warfare, 1500–1865.* New York: Oxford University Press, 2011.

——. *The Cutting-Off Way: Indigenous Warfare in Eastern North America, 1500–1800.* Chapel Hill: University of North Carolina Press, 2023.

Lepore, Jill. *The Name of War: King Philip's War and the Origins of American Identity.* New York: Alfred A. Knopf, 1998.

Lindsay, Brendan C. *Murder State: California's Native American Genocide, 1846–1873.* Lincoln: University of Nebraska Press, 2012.

Lipman, Andrew. *Saltwater Frontier: Indians and the Contest for the American Coast.* New Haven: Yale University Press, 2015.

Longerich, Peter. *Holocaust: The Nazi Persecution and Murder of the Jews.* Oxford: Oxford University Press, 2010.

Lynn, John A. *The Wars of Louis XIV: 1667–1714.* London: Routledge, 1999.

Madley, Benjamin. *An American Genocide: The United States and the California Indian Catastrophe, 1846–1873.* New Haven: Yale University Press, 2016.

Mann, Barbara Alice. *George Washington's War on Native America.* Westport, CT: Praeger, 2005.

——. *The Tainted Gift: The Disease Method of Frontier Expansion.* Santa Barbara, CA: Praeger, 2009.

Martin, James Kirby, and Mark Edward Lender. *A Respectable Army: The Military Origins of the Republic, 1763–1789.* Hoboken, NJ: Wiley Blackwell, 2015.

Martinez, Monica Muñoz. *The Injustice Never Leaves You: Anti-Mexican Violence in Texas.* Cambridge, MA: Harvard University Press, 2018.

Masich, Andrew E. *Civil War in the Southwest Borderlands, 1861–1867.* Norman: University of Oklahoma Press, 2017.

McCarthy, Cormac. *Blood Meridian; or, The Evening Redness in the West*. New York: Modern Library, 2001.

McCaslin, Richard B. *Fighting Stock: John S. "Rip" Ford of Texas*. Fort Worth: Texas Christian University Press, 2011.

McGaw, William Cochran. *Savage Scene: The Life and Times of James Kirker, Frontier King*. New York: Hastings House, 1972.

McKanna, Clare V., Jr. *Race and Homicide in Nineteenth-Century California*. Reno: University of Nevada Press, 2002.

McNally, Robert Acquinas. *The Modoc War: A Story of Genocide at the Dawn of America's Gilded Age*. Lincoln: University of Nebraska Press, 2017.

McPherson, James. *Battle Cry of Freedom: The Civil War Era*. New York: Oxford University Press, 1988.

Merrell, James H. *Into the American Woods: Negotiators on the Pennsylvania Frontier*. New York: W. W. Norton, 1999.

Merritt, Jane T. *At the Crossroads: Indians and Empires on a Mid-Atlantic Frontier, 1700–1763*. Chapel Hill: University of North Carolina Press, 2003.

Middleton, Richard. *Pontiac's War: Its Causes, Course and Consequences*. New York: Routledge, 2007.

Minor, Nancy McGown. *The Light Gray People: An Ethno-History of the Lipan Apaches of Texas and Northern Mexico*. Lanham, MD: University Press of America, 2009.

———. *Turning Adversity to Advantage: A History of the Lipan Apaches of Texas and Northern Mexico, 1700–1900*. Lanham, MD: University Press of America, 2009.

Montejano, David. *Anglos and Mexicans in the Making of Texas, 1836–1986*. Austin: University of Texas Press, 1987.

Moorhead, Max L. *New Mexico's Royal Road: Trade and Travel on the Chihuahua Trail*. Norman: University of Oklahoma Press, 1958.

Morgan, Edmund S. *The Puritan Family: Religion and Domestic Relations in Seventeenth-Century New England*. New ed., rev. and enl. New York: Harper and Row, 1966.

———. *Visible Saints: The History of a Puritan Idea*. New York: New York University Press, 1963.

Morgenthaler, Jefferson. *The River Has Never Divided Us: A Border History of La Junta de los Rios*. Austin: University of Texas Press, 2004.

Morrison, Kenneth M. *The Embattled Northeast: The Elusive Ideal of Alliance in Abenaki-Euramerican Relations*. Berkeley: University of California Press, 1984.

Moses, A. Dirk, ed. *Genocide and Settler Society: Frontier Violence and Stolen Indigenous Children in Australian History*. New York: Berghahn Books, 2004.

Nance, Joseph Milton. *After San Jacinto: The Texas-Mexican Frontier, 1836–1841*. Austin: University of Texas Press, 1963.

———. *Attack and Counterattack: The Texas-Mexican Frontier, 1842*. Austin: University of Texas Press, 1964.

Nelson, Megan Kate. *The Three-Cornered War: The Union, the Confederacy, and Native Peoples in the Fight for the West*. New York: Scribner, 2020.

Newell, Margaret Ellen. *Brethren by Nature: New England Indians, Colonists, and the Origins of American Slavery*. Ithaca, NY: Cornell University Press, 2015.

Nichols, James David. *The Limits of Liberty: Mobility and the Making of the Eastern U.S.-Mexico Border*. Lincoln: University of Nebraska Press, 2018.

Norton, Jack. *When Our Worlds Cried: Genocide in Northwestern California*. San Francisco: Indian Historian Press, 1979.

Odle, Mairin. *Under the Skin: Tattoos, Scalps, and the Contested Language of Bodies in Early America*. Philadelphia: University of Pennsylvania Press, 2023.

Opler, Morris Edward. *An Apache Life-Way: The Economic, Social, and Religious Institutions of the Chiricahua Indians*. New York: Cooper Square, 1965.

——. *Myths and Legends of the Lipan Apache Indians*. New York: American Folk-Lore Society, 1940.

Orozco, Victor Orozco, ed. *Las guerras indias en la historia de Chihuahua: Antología*. Juarez: Universidad Autónoma de Ciudad Juárez, Instituto Chihuahuense de la Cultura, 1992.

Ostler, Jeffrey. *Surviving Genocide: Native Nations and the United States from the American Revolution to Bleeding Kansas*. New Haven: Yale University Press, 2019.

O'Toole, Fintan. *White Savage: William Johnson and the Invention of America*. Albany: State University of New York Press, 2005.

Owens, Barcley. *Cormac McCarthy's Western Novels*. Tucson: University of Arizona Press, 2000.

Owens, Robert M. *Mr. Jefferson's Hammer: William Henry Harrison and the Origins of American Indian Policy*. Norman: University of Oklahoma Press, 2007.

Paredes, Américo. *"With His Pistol in His Hand": A Border Ballad and Its Hero*. Austin: University of Texas Press, 1958.

Paul, Daniel N. *We Were Not the Savages: A Micmac Perspective on the Collision of European and Aboriginal Civilizations*. Halifax, NS: Nimbus, 1993.

Parkman, Francis. *Count Frontenac and New France under Louis XIV*. New York: Charles Scribner's Sons, 1915.

Pencak, William A., and Daniel K. Richter, eds. *Friends and Enemies in Penn's Woods: Indians, Colonists, and the Racial Construction of Pennsylvania*. University Park: Pennsylvania State University Press, 2004.

Phillips, George Harwood. *"Bringing Them under Subjection": California's Tejón Indian Reservation and Beyond, 1852–1864*. Lincoln: University of Nebraska Press, 2004.

——. *Chiefs and Challengers: Indian Resistance and Cooperation in Southern California, 1769–1906*. Norman: University of Oklahoma Press, 2014.

Pitts, Jennifer. *Boundaries of the International: Law and Empire*. Cambridge, MA: Harvard University Press, 2018.

Pletcher, David. *The Diplomacy of Annexation: Texas, Oregon, and the Mexican War.* Columbia: University of Missouri Press, 1973.

Pritchard, James S. *In Search of Empire: The French in the Americas, 1670–1730.* Cambridge: Cambridge University Press, 2004.

Prucha, Francis Paul. *The Great Father: The United States Government and the American Indians.* Abridged ed. Lincoln: University of Nebraska Press, 1986.

Pulsipher, Jenny Hale. *Subjects unto the Same King: Indians, English, and the Contest for Authority in Colonial New England.* Philadelphia: University of Pennsylvania Press, 2005.

Radding, Cynthia. *Wandering Peoples: Colonialism, Ethnic Spaces, and Ecological Frontiers in Northwestern Mexico, 1700–1850.* Durham, NC: Duke University Press, 1997.

Rawls, James J. *Indians of California: The Changing Image.* Norman: University of Oklahoma Press, 1984.

Record, Ian W. *Big Sycamore Stands Alone: The Western Apaches, Aravaipa, and the Struggle for Place.* Norman: University of Oklahoma Press, 2008.

Reilly, Hugh J. *Bound to Have Blood: Frontier Newspapers and the Plains Indian Wars.* Lincoln: University of Nebraska Press, 2010.

Reséndez, Andrés. *The Other Slavery: The Uncovered Story of Indian Enslavement in America.* New York: Houghton Mifflin Harcourt, 2016.

Riches, David, ed. *The Anthropology of Violence.* Oxford: Basil Blackwell, 1986.

Richter, Daniel K. *Facing East from Indian Country: A Native History of Early America.* Cambridge, MA: Harvard University Press, 2001.

———. *Trade, Land, Power: The Struggle for Eastern North America.* Philadelphia: University of Pennsylvania Press, 2013.

Richter, Daniel K., and James H. Merrell, eds. *Beyond the Covenant Chain: The Iroquois and Their Neighbors in Indian North America, 1600–1800.* Syracuse, NY: Syracuse University Press, 1987.

Rink, Oliver A. *Holland on the Hudson: An Economic and Social History of Dutch New York.* Ithaca, NY: Cornell University Press, 1986.

Roberts, Alasdair. *America's First Great Depression: Economic Crisis and Political Disorder after the Panic of 1837.* Ithaca, NY: Cornell University Press, 2012.

Rothman, Joshua D. *The Ledger and the Chain: How Domestic Slave Traders Shaped America.* New York: Basic Books, 2021.

Ruiz, Ramón Eduardo. *The People of Sonora and Yankee Capitalists.* Tucson: University of Arizona Press, 1988.

Rushforth, Brett. *Bonds of Alliance: Indigenous and Atlantic Slaveries in New France.* Chapel Hill: University of North Carolina Press, 2012.

Sainty, J. C. *Office-Holders in Modern Britain.* Vol. 3: *Officials of the Boards of Trade, 1660–1870.* London: University of London, 1974.

Salas, Miguel Tinker. *In the Shadow of the Eagles: Sonora and the Transformation of the Border during the Porfiriato*. Berkeley: University of California Press, 1997.

Santiago, Mark. *A Bad Peace and a Good War: Spain and the Mescalero Apache Uprising of 1795–1799*. Norman: University of Oklahoma Press, 2018.

———. *The Jar of Severed Hands: Spanish Deportation of Apache Prisoners of War, 1770–1810*. Norman: University of Oklahoma Press, 2011.

Saunt, Claudio. *A New Order of Things: Property, Power, and the Transformation of the Creek Indians, 1733–1816*. Cambridge: Cambridge University Press, 1999.

Scheper-Hughes, Nancy, and Philippe Bourgois, eds. *Violence in War and Peace*. Malden, MA: Blackwell, 2004.

Schermerhorn, Calvin. *The Business of Slavery and the Rise of American Capitalism, 1815–1860*. New Haven: Yale University Press, 2015.

Schwartz, E. A. *The Rogue River Indian War and Its Aftermath, 1850–1980*. Norman: University of Oklahoma Press, 1997.

Secrest, William B. *When the Great Spirit Died: The Destruction of the California Indians, 1850–1860*. Sanger, CA: Word Dancer Press, 2003.

Seeman, Erik R. *Death in the New World: Cross-Cultural Encounters, 1492–1800*. Philadelphia: University of Pennsylvania Press, 2010.

Sepich, John. *Notes on Blood Meridian*. Austin: University of Texas Press, 2008.

Sévigny, André. *Les Abénaquis: Habitat et migrations (17e et 18e siècles)*. Montreal: Bellarmin, 1976.

Shannon, Timothy J. *Iroquois Diplomacy on the Early American Frontier*. New York: Viking, 2008.

Shaw, Malcolm N. *International Law*. 5th ed. Cambridge: Cambridge University Press, 2003.

Shoemaker, Nancy. *A Strange Likeness: Becoming Red and White in Eighteenth-Century North America*. Oxford: Oxford University Press, 2004.

Shy, John. *A People Numerous and Armed: Reflections on the Military Struggle for American Independence*. Ann Arbor: University of Michigan Press, 1990.

Siegel, Stanley. *The Poet President of Texas: The Life of Mirabeau B. Lamar, President of the Republic of Texas*. Austin, TX: Pemberton, 1977.

Silver, Peter. *Our Savage Neighbors: How Indian War Transformed Early America*. New York: W. W. Norton, 2008.

Simmons, William Scranton. *Cautantowwit's House: An Indian Burial Ground on the Island of Conanicut in Narragansett Bay*. Providence, RI: Brown University Press, 1970.

Smith, Ralph Adam. *Borderlander: The Life of James Kirker, 1793–1852*. Norman: University of Oklahoma Press, 1999.

Smith, Stacey L. *Freedom's Frontier: California and the Struggle over Unfree Labor, Emancipation, and Reconstruction*. Chapel Hill: University of North Carolina Press, 2013.

Snyder, Christina. *Slavery in Indian Country: The Changing Face of Captivity in Early America*. Cambridge, MA: Harvard University Press, 2010.

Splawn, A. J. *Ka-mi-akin, the Last Hero of the Yakimas*. Portland, OR: Kilham Stationery, 1917.

St. John, Rachel. *Line in the Sand: A History of the Western U.S.-Mexico Border*. Princeton, NJ: Princeton University Press, 2011.

Stannard, David E. *American Holocaust: The Conquest of the New World*. Oxford: Oxford University Press, 1992.

Stern, Jessica Yirush. *Their Lives in Objects: Native Americans, British Colonists, and Cultures of Labor and Exchange in the Southeast*. Chapel Hill: University of North Carolina Press, 2017.

Storms, C. Gilbert. *Reconnaissance in Sonora: Charles D. Poston's 1854 Exploration of Mexico and the Gadsden Purchase*. Tucson: University of Arizona Press, 2015.

Strobridge, William F. *Regulars in the Redwoods: The U.S. Army in Northern California, 1852–1861*. Spokane, WA: Arthur H. Clarke, 1994.

Sugden, John. *Blue Jacket: Warrior of the Shawnees*. Lincoln: University of Nebraska Press, 2000.

Svaldi, David. *Sand Creek and the Rhetoric of Extermination*. Lanham, MD: University Press of America, 1989.

Sweeney, Edwin R. *Cochise: Chiricahua Apache Chief*. Norman: University of Oklahoma Press, 1991.

——. *Mangas Coloradas: Chief of the Chiricahua Apaches*. Norman: University of Oklahoma Press, 1998.

Sword, Wiley. *President Washington's Indian War: The Struggle for the Old Northwest, 1790–1795*. Norman: University of Oklahoma Press, 1985.

Tattrie, Jon. *Daniel Paul: Mi'kmaw Elder*. Lawrencetown Beach, NS: Pottersfield Press, 2017.

Thompson, Erin L. *Smashing Statues: The Rise and Fall of America's Public Monuments*. New York: W. W. Norton, 2022.

Thompson, Jerry D. *A Civil War History of the New Mexico Volunteers and Militia*. Albuquerque: University of New Mexico Press, 2015.

——. *John Robert Baylor: Texas Indian Fighter and Confederate Soldier*. Hillsboro, TX: Hill Junior College Press, 1971.

Thornton, Russell. *American Indian Holocaust and Survival: A Population History since 1492*. Norman: University of Oklahoma Press, 1987.

Thrapp, Dan L. *The Conquest of Apacheria*. Norman: University of Oklahoma Press, 1967.

——. *Victorio and the Mimbres Apaches*. Norman: University of Oklahoma Press, 1974.

Tilly, Charles. *The Politics of Collective Violence*. Cambridge: Cambridge University Press, 2003.

Torget, Andrew J. *Seeds of Empire: Cotton, Slavery, and the Transformation of the Texas Borderlands, 1800–1850*. Chapel Hill: University of North Carolina Press, 2015.

Trafzer, Clifford E., ed. *Grandmother, Grandfather, and Old Wolf: Tamánwit Ku Sukát and Traditional Native American Narratives from the Columbia Plateau*. East Lansing: Michigan State University Press, 1998.

Trafzer, Clifford E., and Joel R. Hyer, eds. *Exterminate Them! Written Accounts of the Murder, Rape, and Enslavement of Native Americans during the California Gold Rush*. East Lansing: Michigan State University Press, 1999.

Trennert, Robert A., Jr. *Alternative to Extinction: Federal Indian Policy and the Beginnings of the Reservation System*. Philadelphia: Temple University Press, 1975.

Ulrich, Laurel Thatcher. *Good Wives: Image and Reality in the Lives of Women in Northern New England, 1650–1750*. New York: Vintage Books, 1991.

Usner, Daniel H. *American Indians in the Lower Mississippi Valley: Social and Economic Histories*. Lincoln: University of Nebraska Press, 1998.

——. *Indians, Settlers, and Slaves in a Frontier Exchange Economy: The Lower Mississippi Valley before 1783*. Chapel Hill: University of North Carolina Press, 1992.

Utley, Robert M. *Frontiersmen in Blue: The United States Army and the Indian, 1848–1865*. Lincoln: University of Nebraska Press, 1967.

——. *Lone Star Justice: The First Century of the Texas Rangers*. New York: Berkley, 2002.

Victor, Frances Fuller, ed. *The Early Indian Wars of Oregon, Compiled from the Oregon Archives and Other Original Sources with Muster Rolls*. Salem, OR: Frank C. Baker, 1894.

Vizcaya Canales, Isidro. *Tierra de guerra viva: Invasión de los Indios bárbaros al noreste de México, 1821–1885*. Monterrey: Academia de Investigaciones, 2001.

Waite, Kevin. *West of Slavery: The Southern Dream of a Transcontinental Empire*. Chapel Hill: University of North Carolina Press, 2021.

Wallace, Ernest, and E. Adamson Hoebel. *The Comanches: Lords of the South Plains*. Norman: University of Oklahoma Press, 1952.

Wallace, Paul A. W. *Conrad Weiser, 1696–1760: Friend of Colonist and Mohawk*. Philadelphia: University of Pennsylvania Press, 1945.

Warburton, Austen D., and Joseph F. Endert. *Indian Lore of the North California Coast*. Santa Clara, CA: Pacific Pueblo Press, 1966.

Warren, Wendy. *New England Bound: Slavery and Colonization in Early America*. New York: Liveright, 2016.

Waskelov, Gregory A. *A Conquering Spirit: Fort Mims and the Red Stick War of 1813–1814*. Tuscaloosa: University of Alabama Press, 2006.

Watt, Robert N. *"Horses Worn to Mere Shadows": The Victorio Campaign, 1880*. Solihull, UK: Helion, 2019.

——. *"I Will Not Surrender the Hair of a Horse's Tail": The Victorio Campaign, 1879*. Solihull, UK: Helion, 2017.

Webb, Walter Prescott. *The Texas Rangers: A Century of Frontier Defense*. Boston: Houghton Mifflin, 1935.

Weber, David J. *Bárbaros: Spaniards and Their Savages in the Age of Enlightenment*. New Haven: Yale University Press, 2005.

———. *The Mexican Frontier, 1821–1846: The American Southwest under Mexico*. Albuquerque: University of New Mexico Press, 1982.

Wells, Henry L. *History of Siskiyou County, California, Illustrated with Views of Residences, Business Buildings and Natural Scenery, and Containing Portraits and Biographies of its Leading Citizens and Pioneers*. Oakland, CA: D. J. Stewart, 1881.

West, Elliott. *The Last Indian War: The Nez Perce Story*. New York: Oxford University Press, 2009.

Westermann, Edward B. *Hitler's Ostkrieg and the Indian Wars: Comparing Genocide and Conquest*. Norman: University of Oklahoma Press, 2016.

Whaley, Gray H. *Oregon and the Collapse of Illahee: U.S. Empire and the Transformation of an Indigenous World, 1792–1859*. Chapel Hill: University of North Carolina Press, 2010.

White, Richard. *The Middle Ground: Indians, Empires, and Republics in the Great Lakes Region, 1650–1815*. New York: Cambridge University Press, 1991.

Wicken, William C. *Mi'kmaq Treaties on Trial: History, Land, and Donald Marshall Junior*. Toronto: University of Toronto Press, 2004.

Wilbarger, J. W. *Indian Depredations in Texas: Reliable Accounts of Battles, Wars, Adventures, Forays, Murders, Massacres, etc.; Together with Biographical Sketches of Many of the Most Noted Indian Fighters and Frontiersmen of Texas*. Austin, TX: Hutchings, 1889.

Witgen, Michael. *An Infinity of Nations: How the Native New World Shaped Early North America*. Philadelphia: University of Pennsylvania Press, 2012.

Woolford, Andrew, Jeff Benvenuto, and Alexander Laban Hinton, eds. *Colonial Genocide in Indigenous North America*. Durham, NC: Duke University Press, 2014.

Wooster, Robert. *The American Military Frontiers: The United States Army in the West, 1783–1900*. Norman: University of Oklahoma Press, 2009.

Wright, Robert E. *One Nation under Debt: Hamilton, Jefferson, and the History of What We Owe*. New York: McGraw Hill, 2008.

Young, Elliott. *Catarino Garza's Revolution on the Texas-Mexico Border*. Durham, NC: Duke University Press, 2004.

Journal Articles and Book Chapters

Abler, Thomas S. "Scalping, Torture, Cannibalism and Rape: An Ethnohistorical Analysis of Conflicting Cultural Values in War." *Anthropologica* 34:1 (1992): 3–20.

Almada, Francisco R. "Gobernadores del Estado: Gral. D. Angel Trías Sr." *Boletín de la Sociedad Chihuahuense de Estudios Historicos* 3:12 (1942): 172–88.

———. "Los Apaches." *Boletín de la Sociedad Chihuahuense de Estudios Historicos* 2:1 (1939): 5–15.

Anderson, Gary Clayton. "The Native Peoples of the American West: Genocide or Ethnic Cleansing?" *Western Historical Quarterly* 47:4 (2016): 407–33.

Aubert, Guillaume. " 'The Blood of France': Race and Purity of Blood in the French Atlantic World." *William and Mary Quarterly*, 3rd ser., 61:3 (2004): 439–78.

Axtell, James, and William C. Sturtevant. "The Unkindest Cut, or Who Invented Scalping." *William and Mary Quarterly*, 3rd ser., 37:3 (1980): 451–72.

Bahre, Conrad J. "Historic Seri Residence, Range, and Sociopolitical Structure." *Kiva* 45:3 (1980): 197–209.

Baumgartner, Alice L. "The Line of Positive Safety: Borders and Boundaries in the Rio Grande Valley, 1848–1880." *Journal of American History* 101:4 (2015): 1106–22.

Belmessous, Saliha. "Assimilation and Racialism in Seventeenth- and Eighteenth-Century French Colonial Policy." *American Historical Review* 110:2 (2005): 322–49.

Bender, Cora. " 'Transgressive Objects' in America: Mimesis and Violence in the Collection of Trophies during the Nineteenth Century Indian Wars." *Civil Wars* 11 (December 2009): 502–13.

Bonnault, Claude de. "Les aventures de M. d'Aleyrac." *Bulletin de Recherches Historiques* 44 (1938): 52–58.

Browne, J. Ross. "The Coast Rangers: A Chronicle of Events in California." *Harper's New Monthly Magazine* 23 (June–November 1861): 306–16.

"A California Blood-Stain." *Hutchings' Illustrated California Magazine, July 1858 to June 1859*, 3:129–31. San Francisco: Hutchings and Rosenfield, 1859.

Camenzind, Krista. "Violence, Race, and the Paxton Boys." In William A. Pencak and Daniel K. Richter, eds., *Friends and Enemies in Penn's Woods: Indians, Colonists, and the Racial Construction of Pennsylvania*, 201–20. University Park: Pennsylvania State University Press, 2004.

Cave, Alfred A. "Genocide in the Americas." In Dan Stone, ed., *The Historiography of Genocide*, 273–95. New York: Palgrave Macmillan, 2008.

Chaplin, Joyce E. "Natural Philosophy and an Early Racial Idiom in North America: Comparing English and Indian Bodies." *William and Mary Quarterly*, 3rd ser., 54:1 (1997): 229–52.

Chávez, Jorge Chávez. "Los Apaches y la frontera norte de México, siglo XIX." In Jorge Chávez Chávez, ed., *Visiones históricas de la frontera*, 17–51. Juarez: Universidad Autónoma de Ciudad Juárez, 2010.

Cothran, Boyd. "Melancholia and the Infinite Debate." *Western Historical Quarterly* 47:4 (2016): 435–38.

Cutter, Barbara. "The Female Indian Killer Memorialized: Hannah Duston and the Nineteenth-Century Feminization of American Violence." *Journal of Women's History* 20:2 (2008): 10–33.

DeLay, Brian. "Independent Indians and the U.S.-Mexican War." *American Historical Review* 112:1 (2007): 35–68.

DuVal, Kathleen. "Interconnectedness and Diversity in 'French Louisiana.' " In Gregory A. Waselkov, Peter H. Wood, and Tom Hatley, eds., *Powhatan's Mantle: Indians in the Colonial Southeast*, 133–62. Lincoln: University of Nebraska Press, 2006.

Edwards, Tai S., and Paul Kelton. "Germs, Genocides, and America's Indigenous Peoples." *Journal of American History* 107:1 (2020): 52–76.

Edwards, Tai S. "Disruption and Disease: The Osage Struggle to Survive in the Nineteenth-Century Trans-Missouri West." *Kansas History* 36 (Winter 2013–14): 218–33.

Evans, Michael. "American Irregular: Frontier Conflict and the Philosophy of War in Cormac McCarthy's *Blood Meridian, or the Evening Redness in the West*." *Small Wars and Insurgencies* 22:4 (2011): 527–47.

Foster, George M. "A Summary of Yuki Culture." *University of California Anthropological Records* 5:3 (1944): 155–244.

Friederici, Georg. "Scalping in America." In *Annual Report of the Board of Regents of the Smithsonian Institution . . . for the Year Ending June 30, 1906*, 423–38. Washington, DC: Government Printing Office, 1907.

Fujii, Lee Ann. "The Puzzle of Extra-Lethal Violence." *Perspectives on Politics* 11:2 (2013): 410–26.

Galloway, Patricia. " 'The Chief Who Is Your Father': Choctaw and French Views of the Diplomatic Relation." In Gregory A. Waselkov, Peter H. Wood, and Tom Hatley, eds., *Powhatan's Mantle: Indians in the Colonial Southeast*, 345–70. Lincoln: University of Nebraska Press, 2006.

Griffen, William B. "The Compás: A Chiricahua Family of the Late 18th and Early 19th Centuries." *American Indian Quarterly* 7:2 (1983): 21–49.

Haan, Richard L. "Covenant and Consensus: Iroquois and English, 1676–1760." In Daniel K. Richter and James H. Merrell, eds., *Beyond the Covenant Chain: The Iroquois and Their Neighbors in Indian North America, 1600–1800*, 41–57. Syracuse, NY: Syracuse University Press, 1987.

Haefali, Evan. "Kieft's War and the Cultures of Violence in Colonial America." In Michael A. Bellesiles, ed., *Lethal Imagination: Violence and Brutality in American History*, 17–40. New York: New York University Press, 1999.

Hall, Martin Hardwick. "Planter vs. Frontiersman: Conflict in Confederate Indian Policy." In Frank E. Vandiver, Martin Hardwick Hall, and Homer L. Kerr, eds., *Essays on the American Civil War*, 55–72. Austin: University of Texas Press, 1968.

——. "Thomas J. Mastin's 'Arizona Guards.' " *New Mexico Historical Review* 49:2 (1974): 143–51.

Harper, Rob. "Looking the Other Way: The Gnadenhutten Massacre and the Contextual Interpretation of Violence." *William and Mary Quarterly*, 3rd ser., 64:3 (2007): 621–44.

———. "State Intervention and Extreme Violence in the Revolutionary Ohio Valley." *Journal of Genocide Research* 10:2 (2008): 233–48.

Hixson, Walter L. "Policing the Past: Indian Removal and Genocide Studies." *Western Historical Quarterly* 47:4 (2016): 439–43.

Jacobs, Margaret D. "Genocide or Ethnic Cleansing? Are These Our Only Choices?" *Western Historical Quarterly* 47:4 (2016): 444–48.

Jastrzembski, Joseph C. "Treacherous Towns in Mexico: Chiricahua Apache Personal Narratives of Horrors." *Western Folklore* 54:3 (1995): 169–96.

Johnson, Richard R. "The Search for a Usable Indian: An Aspect of the Defense of Colonial New England." *Journal of American History* 64:3 (1977): 623–51.

King, Richard. "Obituary Notice of Lieutenant George Augustus Frederick Ruxton." *Journal of the Ethnological Society of London* 2 (1850): 150–58.

Kiser, William S. "The Business of Killing Indians: Contract Warfare and Genocide in the U.S.-Mexico Borderlands." *Journal of American History* 110:1 (2023): 15–39.

Knapp, W. Augustus. "An Old Californian's Pioneer Story—II." *Overland Monthly and Out West Magazine* 10:59 (1887): 499–509.

Lack, Paul D. "The Córdova Revolt." In Gerald E. Poyo, ed., *Tejano Journey, 1770–1850*, 89–109. Austin: University of Texas Press, 1996.

Lahti, Janne. "Silver Screen Savages: Images of Apaches in Motion Pictures." *Journal of Arizona History* 54:1 (2013): 51–84.

Lee, Ian Anson. "The Mesilla Guard: Race and Violence in Nineteenth-Century New Mexico." *New Mexico Historical Review* 95:3 (2020): 323–53.

Lewy, Guenter. "Were American Indians the Victims of Genocide?" *Commentary*, September 2004, 55–63.

Lipman, Andrew. " 'A Meanes to Knitt Them Togeather': The Exchange of Body Parts in the Pequot War." *William and Mary Quarterly*, 3rd ser., 65:1 (2008): 3–28.

Lippincott, Rev. Thomas. "The Wood River Massacre." *Journal of the Illinois State Historical Society* 4:4 (1912): 504–9.

Lozier, Jean-François. "Lever des chevelures en Nouvelle-France: La politique française du paiement des scalps." *Revue d'Histoire de l'Amérique Française* 56:4 (2003): 513–42.

Madley, Benjamin. "Understanding Genocide in California under United States Rule, 1846–1873." *Western Historical Quarterly* 47:4 (2016): 449–61.

———. "Reexamining the American Genocide Debate: Meaning, Historiography and New Methods." *American Historical Review* 120:1 (2015): 99–139.

———. "California's Yuki Indians: Defining Genocide in Native American History." *Western Historical Quarterly* 39:3 (2008): 303–332.

———. "Patterns of Frontier Genocide 1803–1910: The Aboriginal Tasmanians, the Yuki of California, and the Herero of Namibia." *Journal of Genocide Research* 6:2 (2004): 167–92.

Magliari, Michael F. "The California Indian Scalp Bounty Myth: Evidence of Genocide or Just Faulty Scholarship?" *California History* 100:2 (2023): 4–30.

——. "Free State Slavery: Bound Indian Labor and Slave Trafficking in California's Sacramento Valley, 1850–1864." *Pacific Historical Review* 81:2 (2012): 155–92.

Martin, Mabelle Eppard, ed. "From Texas to California in 1849: Diary of C. C. Cox." *Southwestern Historical Quarterly* 29:2 (1925): 128–46.

McDoom, Omar Shahabudin. "Contested Counting: Toward a Rigorous Estimate of the Death Toll in the Rwandan Genocide." *Journal of Genocide Research* 22:1 (2020): 83–93.

Meierhenrich, Jens. "How Many Victims Were There in the Rwandan Genocide? A Statistical Debate." *Journal of Genocide Research* 22:1 (2020): 72–82.

Miller, Virginia P. "Yuki, Huchnom, and Coast Yuki." In Robert F. Heizer, ed., *Handbook of North American Indians*, 8:249–55. Washington, DC: Smithsonian Institution Press, 1978.

Moser, Edward. "Seri Bands." *Kiva* 28:3 (1963): 14–27.

Muckleroy, Anna. "The Indian Policy of the Republic of Texas, II." *Southwestern Historical Quarterly* 26:1 (1922): 1–29.

——. "The Indian Policy of the Republic of Texas, III." *Southwestern Historical Quarterly* 26:2 (1922): 128–48.

Nackman, Mark E. "The Making of the Texan Citizen Soldier, 1835–1860." *Southwestern Historical Quarterly* 78:3 (1975): 231–53.

Ostler, Jeffrey. " 'To Extirpate the Indians': An Indigenous Consciousness of Genocide in the Ohio Valley and Lower Great Lakes, 1750s–1810." *William and Mary Quarterly*, 3rd ser., 72:4 (2015): 587–622.

——. " 'Just and Lawful War' as Genocidal War in the (United States) Northwest Ordinance and Northwest Territory, 1787–1832." *Journal of Genocide Research* 18:1 (2016): 1–20.

Parsons, Phyllis Vibbard. "The Early Life of Daniel Claus." *Pennsylvania History: A Journal of Mid-Atlantic Studies* 29:4 (1962): 357–72.

Pritchard, James. "Population in French America, 1670–1730: The Demographic Context of Colonial Louisiana." In Bradley G. Bond, ed., *French Colonial Louisiana and the Atlantic World*, 175–203. Baton Rouge: Louisiana State University Press, 2005.

Rensink, Brendan. "Genocide of Native Americans: Historical Facts and Historiographic Debates." In Samuel Totten and Robert K. Hitchcock, eds., *Genocide of Indigenous Peoples*, 15–36. New Brunswick, NJ: Transaction, 2011.

Rousseau, Peter L. "Jacksonian Monetary Policy, Specie Flows, and the Panic of 1837." *Journal of Economic History* 62:2 (2002): 457–88.

Sheehan, Bernard W. " 'The Famous Hair Buyer General': Henry Hamilton, George Rogers Clark, and the American Indian." *Indiana Magazine of History* 79:1 (1983): 1–28.

"Six Months on the Frontier of Northampton County, Penna., during the Indian War, October 1755–June 1756." *Pennsylvania Magazine of History and Biography* 39:3 (1915): 345–52.

Sjoberg, Andrée F. "Lipan Apache Culture in Historical Perspective." *Southwestern Journal of Anthropology* 9:1 (1953): 76–98.

Smith, Ralph A. "Scalp Hunting: A Mexican Experiment in Warfare." *Great Plains Journal* 23 (January 1984): 41–81.

Sosin, Jack M. "The Use of Indians in the War of the American Revolution: A Reassessment of Responsibility." *Canadian Historical Review* 46 (June 1965): 101–21.

Stevens, Laura M. "The Christian Origins of the Vanishing Indian." In Nancy Isenberg and Andrew Burstein, eds. *Mortal Remains: Death in Early America*, 17–30. Philadelphia: University of Pennsylvania Press, 2003.

Strang, Cameron B. "Violence, Ethnicity, and Human Remains During the Second Seminole War." *Journal of American History* 100:4 (2014): 973–94.

Strickland, Rex W. "The Birth and Death of a Legend: The Johnson 'Massacre' of 1837." *Arizona and the West* 18 (Autumn 1976): 257–86.

Su, Yang. "Mass Killings in the Cultural Revolution: A Study of Three Provinces." In Joseph Esherick, Paul Pickowicz, and Andrew George Walder, eds., *The Chinese Cultural Revolution as History*, 96–123. Stanford, CA: Stanford University Press, 2006.

Sweeney, Edwin R. " 'I Had Lost All': Geronimo and the Carrasco Massacre of 1851." *Journal of Arizona History* 27 (Spring 1986): 35–52.

Thornton, Russell. "Social Organization and the Demographic Survival of the Tolowa." *Ethnohistory* 31:3 (1984): 187–96.

Toulouse, Teresa A. "Hannah Duston's Bodies: Domestic Violence and Colonial Male Identity in Cotton Mather's Decennium Luctuosum." In Janet Moore Lindman and Michele Lise Tarter, eds., *A Centre of Wonders: The Body in Early America*, 193–210. Ithaca, NY: Cornell University Press, 2001.

Trope, Jack F., and Walter R. Echohawk. "The Native American Graves Protection and Repatriation Act: Background and Legislative History." In Jo Carrillo, ed., *Readings in American Indian Law: Recalling the Rhythm of Survival*, 178–87. Philadelphia: Temple University Press, 1998.

Vaughan, Alden T. "Frontier Banditti and the Indians: The Paxton Boys' Legacy, 1763–1775." *Pennsylvania History: A Journal of Mid-Atlantic Studies* 51:1 (1984): 1–29.

Wells, Harry L. "The Ben Wright Massacre." *West Shore*, October 1, 1884, 314–20.

Williams, Kidada. "Regarding the Aftermaths of Lynching." *Journal of American History* 101:3 (2014): 856–58.

Williamson, Ron. " 'Otinontsiskiaj Ondaon' ('The House of the Cut-Off Heads'): The History and Archaeology of Northern Iroquoian Trophy Taking." In Richard Chacon and David Dye, eds., *The Taking and Displaying of Human Body Parts as Trophies by Amerindians*, 190–221. New York: Springer, 2007.

Wolfe, Patrick. "Settler Colonialism and the Elimination of the Native." *Journal of Genocide Research* 8:4 (2006): 387–409.

Young, Henry J. "A Note on Scalp Bounties in Pennsylvania." *Pennsylvania History* 24:3 (1957): 207–18.

Newspapers and Periodicals

APTN National News (Winnipeg, MB)

Roache, Trina. " 'It's Not Forgotten': Mi'kmaq Bounty Never Rescinded." February 21, 2018.

Bangor (ME) Daily News

Harrison, Judy. "FBI Is Investigating Suspected Native American Scalp Seized from Fairfield Auctioneer." November 10, 2022.

CBC News (Canada)

McMillan, Elizabeth. "Newly Renamed Peace and Friendship Park Celebrated in Halifax." June 21, 2021.

Meloney, Nic. " 'The Scalp of Edward Cornwallis' to Be Sold Online by Mi'kmaq Group." December 2, 2017.

Patil, Anjuli. "Cornwallis Name Gone from Lunenburg Street, but New Name Draws Criticism." December 4, 2023.

"Two Hundred Year-Old Scalp Law Still on Books in Nova Scotia." January 4, 2000.

Williams, Cassie, and Anjuli Patil. "Controversial Cornwallis Statue Removed from Halifax Park." January 31, 2018.

California Farmer and Journal of Useful Sciences (San Francisco)

"Late from Oregon." December 28, 1855.

Chronicle Herald (Halifax, NS)

Paul, Daniel N. "Scalp Proclamations Weren't Just Aimed at Mi'kmaw Warriors." March 29, 2019.

Coast (Halifax, NS)

Boon, Jacob. "It's 2015 and a Scalping Law Is Still on the Books." January 7, 2015.

Congressional Globe (Washington, DC)

"The Army." May 23, 1850.

"Army Appropriation Bill—Again." June 14, 1860.

"California War Debt." February 28, 1861.

"House of Representatives." February 19, 1851.

"Indian Appropriation Bill." September 27, 1850.

"Indian Hostilities." January 19, 1861.

"Indian Hostilities in California." February 22, 1861.

"The Indian Question." January 28, 1871.

"Oregon and Washington War Debt." February 21, 1861.

"Oregon War Debt." May 9, 1860.

"Oregon War Debt." May 16, 1860.

"Oregon War Debt." May 30, 1860.

"Oregon War Debt." January 24, 1861.

Daily Alta California (San Francisco)

"The Attack on the Telegraph." February 7, 1865.

"A Battle with the Indians—Thirty Indians Killed." January 18, 1855.

"California Indians." September 24, 1851.

"Conduct of the War." May 22, 1865.

"From Crescent City." January 17, 1855.

"From the Shasta Region." May 1, 1853.

"Governor's Annual Message." January 10, 1860.

"Indian Expedition." February 28, 1851.

"Indian Slavery." April 14, 1862.

"Indian Troubles in Mendocino County." October 9, 1859.

"Justice for the Indians." January 13, 1865.

"The Late Indian War." January 28, 1860.

"The Late Indian War in Mendocino County." January 22, 1860.

"Later from Oregon Territory." December 5, 1855.

"Letter from Port Orford." March 20, 1856.

"Lo, the Poor Indian." April 7, 1855.

"Our Sacramento Correspondence." January 19, 1860.

"Political Rallies." April 1, 1850.

"Revolutionary Operations of the Early California Emigrants." July 24, 1852.

"Sacramento News." December 2, 1852.

"San Joaquin Intelligence." February 7, 1851.

"San Jose Intelligence." January 23, 1851.

"Sixty Indians Killed in Mendocino County." January 1, 1860.

"Threatened Indian Difficulties on the Southern Emigrant Trail." August 3, 1854.

"Three Hours Later by the Antelope." March 25, 1852.

"To the Democracy of San Francisco." April 1, 1850.

Daily National Democrat (Marysville, CA)

"Affairs at Round Valley, Tehama County." December 17, 1859.

"Indian Difficulties in Mendocino County." October 11, 1859.

El Antenor (Chihuahua)

"Gobierno del departamento." December 31, 1839.
"Ocurrencias de Apaches." January 21, 1840.
"Ocurrencias de Apaches." April 14, 1840.
"Ocurrencias de Apaches." May 19, 1840.
"Proyecto de guerra contra Apaches." December 10, 1839.

El Fanal (Chihuahua)

"Gobierno del estado." October 21, 1834.
"Gobierno del estado." November 11, 1834.

El Faro (Chihuahua)

"Apaches." June 26, 1849.
"Contratas de sangre." July 24, 1849.
"Gobierno del estado." May 29, 1849.
"Gobierno del estado." June 5, 1849.
"Gobierno del estado." December 29, 1849.
"Indios barbaros." July 7, 1849.

El Noticioso de Chihuahua

"Gobierno general." October 26, 1837.
J. J. Johnson to Commandant General, April 24, 1837. In May 5, 1837, issue.
Pedro Olivares and Ángel Trías to Señor Governor, July 29, 1837. In August 6, 1837, issue.

El Provisional (Chihuahua)

Carlos Cásares to G. de Cuilty, June 24, 1846. In July 14, 1846, issue.
G. de Cuilty to José María Irigoyen, June 3, 1846. In June 9, 1846, issue.
G. de Cuilty to José María Irigoyen, July 10, 1846. In July 14, 1846, issue.
Santiago Kirker to José María Irigoyen, July 13, 1846. In July 21, 1846, issue.

El Registro Oficial (Durango)

"Junta de guerra." June 28, 1849.
"Secretaria del despacho del gobierno de Durango." July 8, 1849.

El Veracruzano Libre

"Invasión al Estado de Chihuahua." May 9, 1862.

Halifax (NS) Herald

Paul, Daniel N. "All Doubletalk, No Action on Repealing Proclamation." December 8, 2000.
Tattrie, Jon. "Hair Ad Raised Ire of Mi'kmaq." April 25, 2010.

Los Angeles Herald

"Frank Soule: Death of the Veteran Journalist and Pioneer." July 6, 1882.

Marshall (MO) Republican

"Terrible Revelations." September 27, 1862.

Marysville (CA) Appeal

"A Bounty Offered for Indian Scalps." May 12, 1861.
"Fight with the Indians." August 9, 1862.

Marysville (CA) Daily Herald

"Oregon War News." December 21, 1855.

Mesilla (NM) Times

"Attack on Pino Alto by the Indians." October 3, 1861.

New-York Daily Tribune

"The Indian Troubles on the Colorado." July 8, 1850.

New York Herald

"In the Modoc Camp." February 28, 1873.

New York Times

"Early Modoc History." May 24, 1873.
"History of the Modocs." July 17, 1873.
"Important Diplomatic Correspondence: Letters on the Subject of the Texan Frontier between the Rebel Secretary of State, Gen. Vidaurri, Governor of Nueva Leon and Coahuila, and Col. Baylor, of the Texan Army." October 31, 1861.
James, Caryn. " 'Blood Meridian,' by Cormac McCarthy." April 28, 1985.
"Money for Indian Scalps: Arizona and New-Mexico Settlers Propose to Destroy the Savages." October 12, 1885.

Scott, A. O. "Review: 'Hostiles' Grapples with the Contradictions of the Western." December 21, 2017.
Woodward, Richard B. "Cormac McCarthy's Venomous Fiction." April 19, 1992.

Niles National Register (Baltimore)

"Mexican Mode of Warfare against the Camanche [sic] and Apache Indians." September 7, 1839.

Puget Sound Courier (Steilacoom, Washington Territory)

"Highly Important News from Oregon." December 21, 1855.

San Francisco Bulletin

"Indian Butcheries in California." June 18, 1860.
"The Modoc Troubles." February 25, 1873.

Santa Fe New Mexican

"Greeting the Victors." November 2, 1880.

Slate (New York)

Shannon, Noah Gallagher. "Cormac McCarthy Cuts to the Bone." October 5, 2012.

Telegraph and Texas Register (Houston)

"The Citizens of Austin." November 18, 1840.
"Commanche [sic] Ambassador." June 8, 1842.
"The Commissioners Who Recently Left Bexar." March 17, 1838.
"Highly Important." February 24, 1838.
"The Lipans." November 23, 1842.
"A Report Has Reached Us." July 20, 1842.
"Seven Lipan Warriors." March 10, 1838.
William H. Watts to Editor of the Austin City Gazette. September 2, 1840.
"We Learn from the Austin Democrat." February 10, 1848.

Texas Sentinel (Austin)

"Late and Important from Texas." April 29, 1840.
"To Col. John H. Moore and his Volunteer Associates." November 14, 1840.

Texas State Gazette (Austin)

"Chihuahua—Maj. Chevallie and the Indians." October 20, 1849.
"The Frontier—The Government." May 11, 1850.
"Frontier Defense." October 23, 1852.
"The Indians—General Harney." September 1, 1849.
"Letter to Editor of State Gazette." November 24, 1849.
"Remarks of Col. V. E. Howard." June 29, 1850.
"The San Antonio Ledger." August 31, 1850.
"The State Gazette." October 26, 1850.
"The State Gazette." November 16, 1850.
"To the Editor of the State Gazette." January 4, 1851.

Tri-Weekly Telegraph (Houston, TX)

John R. Baylor to "Mr. Editor." October 17, 1862.

Weekly Telegraph (Houston, TX)

"Baylor's Scalps, Politics, Etc." July 31, 1860.

Films

Mazo, Adam, Tracy Rector, and Ben Pender-Cudlip, producers. *Bounty*. 9 mins. Upstander Project. https://upstanderproject.org/bounty.
Cooper, Scott, director. *Hostiles*. 133 mins. Waypoint Entertainment. Released December 22, 2017.

Websites

www.findagrave.com/memorial/29000810/walter-s-jarboe
www.refusingtoforget.org

Dissertations and Theses

Ball, Margaret Haig Roosevelt Sewall. "Grim Commerce: Scalps, Bounties, and the Transformation of Trophy-Taking in the Early American Northeast, 1450–1770." MA thesis. University of Colorado at Boulder, 2013.
Hunt-Watkinson, Margery. "A Savage Land: Violence and Trauma in the Nineteenth-Century American Southwest." PhD diss. Arizona State University, 2020.
Maestas, Enrique Gilbert-Michael. "Culture and History of Native American Peoples of South Texas." PhD diss. University of Texas at Austin, 2003.
Peotto, Thomas. "Dark Mimesis: A Cultural History of the Scalping Paradigm." PhD diss. University of British Columbia, 2018.

ACKNOWLEDGMENTS

O ver the course of several years of working on this project, I benefited
from the guidance of many colleagues and friends, as well as the support
of multiple institutions. As is true with all books, this one would not have
been possible without the generosity and contributions of other scholars and
professionals.

The research, ideas, and interpretations found throughout this book developed with many conversations, presentations, and informal peer reviews. I
thank two longtime friends and professional colleagues, Jerry Thompson and
John P. Wilson—both of whom are walking encyclopedias on primary sources
related to the Southwest—for sharing copies of archival material and personal
notes, as well as their ideas for shaping the narrative itself. Paul Conrad gra-
ciously shared research material from his work on the Southern Apaches, which
helped immensely during pandemic closures. Joaquín Rivaya-Martínez lis-
tened to my ideas about scalp hunting in northern Mexico and offered thoughts
based on his exhaustive research in that area. During my time at Arizona State
University, Grace Hunt-Watkinson's research and writing on Apache trauma
provided me with an early opportunity to discuss the topic. And some of my earliest conversations on scalp hunting involved the late historian Ed Sweeney, a
close friend whose books inspired me at an early age to become a historian. I offer my sincere thanks to Jerry, Jack, Paul, Joaquín, Grace, and Ed for their direct
contributions to this book.

At Texas A&M University–San Antonio, I am fortunate to be part of a fantastic
History Program. Philis Barragán-Goetz, DB Briscoe, Bill Bush, Ally Castillo,

Francis Galan, Beth Hasseler, Sandra Lara, Mike O'Brien, Amy Porter, and Zhaojin Zeng are an incredible group of colleagues to work with. I owe a special and profound debt of gratitude to Ed Westermann, who read multiple drafts of some chapters and provided me with a firm grounding in the theoretical field of genocide studies based on his own professional expertise. I also thank the dean of the College of Arts & Sciences, Debra Feakes, for her support of faculty research. Outside of Texas A&M–San Antonio, my scholarship has benefited from many professional friendships with people whose work I admire and whose ideas have helped me to develop my own analytical frameworks for borderlands history: Matt Babcock, Alice Baumgartner, Kent Blansett, Lance Blyth, James Brooks, Walter Buenger, Catherine Clinton, Brian DeLay, Jim Downs, Andy Graybill, Charles Harris, Anne Hyde, Peter Iverson, Susan Johnson, Pat Kelly, Farina King, Bob Lockhart, Kyle Longley, David Montejano, Elaine Nelson, Katherine Osburn, Chuck Rankin, Andrés Reséndez, Ray Sadler, Calvin Schermerhorn, Brooks Simpson, Omar Valerio-Jimenez, Kevin Waite, Bob Watt, Elliott West, and Robert Wooster. A special word of thanks to Adina Popescu Berk, my editor at Yale University Press, for her encouragement and support of this project from the beginning.

An abbreviated version of chapter 3 was published as an article in the June 2023 issue of *Journal of American History*. Working with the *JAH* provided an important opportunity to revise and rethink some of the central concepts presented in this book, and I am particularly grateful to *JAH* editors Benjamin Irvin and Stephen Andrews for believing in my project from the outset and for ensuring a rigorous peer review process that not only improved that article but also affected the larger book manuscript. I also thank the six anonymous reviewers for that *JAH* article for their close attention to detail and thoughtful advice on key frameworks involving genocide. Last, I appreciate the work of Erin Greb, who produced customized cartography for both the *JAH* article and this book.

Every historian depends heavily on libraries and archives. First and foremost, I want to thank Juana Rivas and Kathy Poorman at UTEP. In the summer of 2020, at the height of Covid lockdowns, they allowed me special access to their library's microfilm holdings containing the majority of the primary-source Mexican archival material used to write chapter 3 of this book. Without this truly incredible act on their part, it would have been impossible for me to complete the aforementioned *JAH* article, as well as chapter 3, and my entire project would have been delayed for nearly two years. Additional research took place at libraries and archives in Arizona, New Mexico, and Texas. In particular, I appreciate the assistance of Marisa Jefferson and Rachel Poppen at the Dolph Briscoe Center for American History at the University of Texas at Austin, Caroline Jones and Saima Kadir at the Texas State Library and Archives Commission in Austin, Linda Gill and Adrian Johnson at the Benson Latin American Center at UT–Austin, Christina Jensen at Southern Methodist University's De-Golyer Library, and several assistants at the University of Texas at San Antonio's special collections. At Texas A&M University–San Antonio, Sarah Timm, Emily Bliss-Zaks, and Tim Gritten provided generous research support, especially in 2020–21 when Interlibrary Loan (ILL) services were temporarily discontinued due to the pandemic. Because ILL could not provide most of the books I needed for research, Sarah, Emily, and Tim purchased those books for our library's collection, and they had them all mailed directly to my home in San Antonio to use at a time when the physical library was closed. Over the past couple of years, several people have asked me how I managed to write a book during Covid, when so many libraries and archives were closed. The answer lies in large part with the people named above, who went above and beyond their professional responsibilities to provide me with the resources I needed, and also with thousands of unnamed archivists around the world who have spent the past two decades digitizing millions (if not billions) of documents. The pandemic opened my eyes to the unbelievable research materials that are now available and easily accessible online, and for that we should all thank our librarian and archivist friends.

Last, as always, I am appreciative of my loving and supporting family: my parents, Dan and Jerine; my sister, Christine; and my wife, Nicole. My beautiful daughters, Cassidy (age six) and Allyson (age three), still prefer Bluey, Blippi, and the Berenstain Bears for bedtime stories, but soon enough perhaps they will take interest in the books their dad wrote.

INDEX

First Nations. *See* specific tribe names
Fish, Hamilton, 126
Fisher, William S., 150
Five Nations. *See* Iroquois Confederacy
Flacco (Lipan Apache), 155–56
Flacco the Younger (Lipan Apache), 156, 219
Fopp, Bill, 178
Ford, John S. "Rip," 164–65
Fort Augusta, PA, 78
Fort Bliss, TX, 123
Fort Boise, OR, 190
Fort Clark, TX, 167
Fort Crook, CA, 199
Fort Dalles, OR, 190
Fort Duquesne, PA, 50
Fort Edward, NY, 52
Fort Ewell, TX, 164
Fort Fillmore, NM, 123, 168
Fort Inge, TX, 164
Fort Jones, OR, 189
Fort Klamath, OR, 211
Fort Lancaster, TX, 172
Fort Lane, OR, 189, 197
Fort Lydius, NY, 51
Fort Lyon, CO, 209
Fort Massachusetts, MA, 69
Fort McLane, NM, 125
Fort McRae, NM, 126
Fort Merrill, TX, 159
Fort Mims Massacre, 91
Fort Orange, NY, 37
Fort Pitt, PA, 84, 86
Fort Randolph, VA, 83
Fort Richelieu, Canada, 22
Fort St. George, ME, 49
Fort Thorn, NM, 169
Fort Webster, NM, 123
Fort William Henry, NY, 35
Fountain, Albert J., 126
Franklin, Benjamin, 12, 87
Franks, L. B., 155, 157
French and Indian War (Seven Years' War), 1, 50–52, 70–72, 75, 84, 88
French Intervention, 125, 126
Frenchtown, CA, 188, 196

Frontenac, Louis de Buade, comte de, 27–33, *29*, 34, 38, 43, 46, 52
Fronteras, Mexico, *101*, 120
fur trade, 23, 30–31, 51, 105, 181

Galeana Massacre, 93–96, 113–14, 123, 151, 216
García Conde, Francisco, 111, 112
García Conde, Pedro, 123
Gayton, Narcissus Duffy (Apache), 104
genocide, 21, 43, 50, 60–61, 96, 98, 104, 119, 172–73, 216–19; and Canadian First Nations, 3, 5, 30; in California, 177, 180–81; defined, 10–11; in Mexico, 130–32; and reparations, 3; and scalp warfare, 12–14; scholarly debates on, 12–14; splitting approach to, 53–54, 57; statistics on, 11, 57, 180. *See also* Rwanda; United Nations
Georgia, 91
Geronimo (Apache), 95, 123, 128–30, 252n103
Giddings, Joshua R., 158
Gila Expedition, 121
Gila River, 103
Gilman, John, 61
Glanton, John Joel, 97, 119–21, 129, 131, 133, 162, 170, 214
Godfrey and Teller, 185
Gold Rush, 108, 117, 119, 147, 174, 178–79, 182–83, *191*, 208
Gomez (Apache), 119
González, José María Elías, 110, 113, 123
González, Simón Elías, 107
Good, Harmon, 207, 210, 277n122
Goodwin, John Noble, 124, 125
Goose Lake, CA, 190
Grande Ronde, OR, 197
Grant, Ulysses S., 210–11
Great Lakes, 22, 30, 64, 77, 82
Great Sun (Natchez), 44
Gregg, Josiah, 103, 105
Greiner, John, 95, 104
Grey Lock (Wabanaki), 65
Groton, MA, 60
Guadalupe River, TX, 143, 155, 161